Research Methods
for Social Work

David E. Cournoyer
University of Connecticut

Waldo C. Klein
University of Connecticut

Allyn and Bacon

Boston ■ London ■ Toronto ■ Sydney ■ Tokyo ■ Singapore

Series Editor, Social Work and Family Therapy: *Judy Fifer*
Editor in Chief, Social Sciences: *Karen Hanson*
Editorial Assistant: *Julianna Cancio*
Marketing Manager: *Jackie Aaron*
Production Administrator: *Annette Joseph*
Production Coordinator: *Holly Crawford*
Editorial-Production Service and Electronic Composition: *Omegatype Typography, Inc.*
Composition Buyer: *Linda Cox*
Manufacturing Buyer: *Julie McNeill*
Cover Administrator: *Jenny Hart*

Library of Congress Cataloging-in-Publication Data

Cournoyer, David E.
    Research methods for social work / David E. Cournoyer, Waldo C.
Klein.
        p.   cm.
    Includes bibliographical references and index.
    ISBN 0-205-28741-7
    1. Social service—Research—Methodology.   I. Klein, Waldo C.
II. Title.
HV11.C788   2000
361.3'2'072—dc21   99-18625
                                                                       CIP

Printed in the United States of America

    10   9   8   7   6   5   4   3   2   1   04   03   02   01   00   99

To mentors and teachers who are not turned off by a quirky but inquisitive mind, especially: Edwin Nebelkopf, Jack Werboff, Ronald Rohner, Robert Green, and Elizabeth Pinner, and to the social work graduate students who encouraged us to write this book.   DEC

To Martin, who has consistently pointed to a way, and to Lin and Erin, who have steadfastly shared that path.   WCK

CONTENTS

PREFACE

Throughout the decade of the 1990s, social workers have continued to call for an increase in practice-relevant social work research. Our professional code of ethics requires social workers to be competent both as consumers of empirically based knowledge and in the generation of new knowledge. The curriculum policy statement of the Council on Social Work Education mandates the teaching of research skills in all undergraduate and graduate programs.

As we enter the new millennium, the need for empirically oriented social workers remains acute. Social work professionals continue to intervene in a myriad of severe and chronic social problems that by some accounts are worsening. The current emphasis on efficiency and effectiveness throughout the helping professions means that social workers must choose interventions that have a high probability of producing measurable improvement in target problems or risk loss of public support. The ability to demonstrate effectiveness at the level of individuals and small systems as well as at the community and larger societal levels remains a daily challenge to the profession.

Our overarching purpose in writing this book is to help social work students progress down the path of competence in the use of fundamental research tools in all facets of social work practice and thereby improve the quality of their practice. More than providing a list of techniques and exhortation to use them, we have attempted to communicate a sense of what are scientific perspectives on social work practice, the principles that underlie modern views of science, and how to combine a myriad of small scientific acts into activities that support various aspects of practice.

Very few of us in the profession of social work made our career selections with the intention of becoming "researchers." Indeed, only a relative handful of social workers identify themselves foremost as researchers. Rather, professional social workers constantly use the tools of research to answer the practical questions that they confront in practice. Is the intervention that I am using with this client working? Would it be cost-effective for us to adopt this new treatment program for use with clients in our agency? Are there behaviors or other "signs" that can alert me to the likelihood of recognized problems occurring in the lives of my clients? These are all basic practice questions; credible answers to them depend on the application of research skills in practice. Furthermore, it is these questions and countless others like them that flow from social work practice with client systems of all sizes that make the practice of social research important to us. We think that the process of research, like any puzzle, can be interesting in its own right. However, it is the applied value of social work research that makes it worthy of our professional interest.

The role of research in social work is best illustrated by drawing an analogy to a set of tools or equipment. Over our lives, we have accumulated different sets of tools for different hobbies and activities—traditional tools for building and fixing things, tools for a wide range of household tasks from cleaning to baking, and tools for playing games and participating in sporting activities. Three important points are to be made with this analogy. First, in order to participate in many activities, you need equipment. You cannot easily bake without an oven of some sort; you cannot easily turn a screw without a screwdriver; you cannot play volleyball without some sort of ball and net. Second, better equipment facilitates improved performance. This is not to say that the quality of the tools makes or breaks the performance. Experts with inferior tools are still often capable of impressive results. (One of us recalls the experience in young adolescence of buying an inexpensive guitar. The skilled musician working as a salesperson demonstrated capacities of the instrument that your author was never quite able to emulate!) The skill of the salesperson introduces our third and final point of the analogy. Practice with the appropriate tools or equipment enhances the quality of the performance. Very few of us have the "natural talent" to perform any task at a level that is truly noteworthy without dedicated practice and skill building—and we suspect that even those with "natural talent" are most often products of social environments that nurtured or supported the development of those talents.

This book is about these three points. As practicing social workers, each of us needs a basic repertoire of equipment. This includes a range of intervention techniques as well as a range of research techniques to be using simultaneously. Second, we need to practice with all of these tools—both interventive and research skills—to become maximally proficient. Finally, we should never become too comfortable with our level of professional expertise unless we are using the finest equipment available. In a largely intellectual exercise like social work practice, this means that we should always be working to acquire the knowledge that will best equip us for professional practice. In these chapters, we provide you with a fundamental set of research skills, familiarize you with their application in practice, and provide suggestions on how you can continue your professional development with the acquisition of more advanced skills.

In this process, we have moved away from some of the traditional approaches to presenting social research content. Many of the traditional approaches to research have tried to "cut the pie" into slices representing qualitative or quantitative research, and inductive or deductive logic. In our view, all approaches to research are coequal parts of the larger scientific process. Each contributes essential, albeit different, slices to make up the whole. Stemming from our holistic view of science, we see the various approaches to doing research as being different arrangements of the fundamental research tools.

For example, the process of sampling has been traditionally thought of as a mechanism through which a representative collection of subjects is identified for use in some kind of group-based research. And yet the very same sampling logic can be applied to gathering a collection of behaviors from across the spectrum of time or physical places. Instead of relegating this second application of the logic to the discussion of "qualitative" research as distinct from "quantitative" research, we think it makes more sense to understand the basic tool—

sampling, for example—with an understanding of its appropriate application in various research approaches.

Even the distinction between qualitative and quantitative research to which we have alluded is unnecessarily artificial. In the course of doing "quantitative" research, social work researchers routinely gather "qualitative" data and vice versa. Because this is true, it seems that the distinction between the two may approach meaninglessness. We prefer to understand the unique differences in numeric and nonnumeric data and the various ways they are most effectively collected and analyzed—regardless of the specific research approach that is being used.

In this same vein, inductive and deductive logical processes have often been paired with "qualitative" and "quantitative" research, respectively. Yet, we are well aware of heavily inductive epidemiological studies that rely on quantitative data and of deductive studies in which a single qualitative observation provides strong evidence in support of an important conclusion. (Consider the confirmatory power of a celestial observation of a single black hole with regard to the theory that predicted its presence.) Induction and deduction are not competitors; they are colleagues in the advancement of our understanding of the world around us.

In short, the important questions that face social work researchers are best answered when we are prepared to match the demands posed by the practice question to the research approach that can most effectively answer it. Consider the breadth of professional social work practice. We work with individuals, their families, small groups, formal organizations, communities, and even whole societies. The breadth of our research interests parallels our collective practice. The appropriate approach to research in a given area of practice may call for the use of induction or deduction, numeric or nonnumeric data, investigation of a single-client system or multiple-client systems, and so forth. The only gauge for success is that meaningful questions are effectively answered with ethical means.

We came to the task of writing this book after years of individually teaching research methods to social work students, assisting agencies in conducting research activities to evaluate the quality of their own programs, and doing our own research within the university. Along the way, we found that our own ideas were challenged and clarified in lively informal discussions between ourselves. These discussions initially concerned how we were conducting different research activities, but moved increasingly to how we were seeking to communicate research skills (and the importance of those skills) to social workers. Several years ago, our discussions led us to the next step of an innovative coteaching process. We've had a lot of fun. We agreed to accept in-class challenges from one another as we also accept challenges from our students. We've had the opportunity for one of us to observe students while the other sought to present a difficult concept. We've had the opportunity to jump in with an alternative explanation that has sometimes worked to clarify the content. With this book, we've had the opportunity to struggle with committing that exciting teaching and learning process to paper.

This book provides the fundamental research skills to practice social work across the range of practice. Chapter 1 provides a basis for the entire enterprise by discussing the nature of scientific reasoning and critical thinking. We take the position that, although there are many ways of knowing things about the world around us, the methods of science that include the use of clear theory, observation, and logic are the best for producing the kind of knowledge on which professional social work must be based. Even with the protections against the common errors in human perception that are provided by scientific reasoning and critical thinking, we must be aware of the sociocultural influences that operate to shape and influence our social work practice, including research.

Chapter 2 offers a grounding in the ethics of research. The profession of social work has described itself as being value-driven throughout its history. The NASW *Code of Ethics* identifies six core values—service, social justice, dignity and worth of the person, importance of human relationships, integrity, and competence—that serve as the foundation of social work's purpose. Each of these values is present in the professional ethics that guide social work research. Far from being isolated in research seclusion, social work research is vibrant and engaged in the lives of real people—and must adhere to the same ethical standards as any other form of social work practice.

Chapter 3 investigates the way that social work questions are drawn out of this sociocultural environment. Questions that are professionally useful in social work have several distinct characteristics. They are conceptualized in meaningful terms and make reference to things that are observable in the world. These questions are testable in principle and always have multiple potential answers. Finally, social work research questions must be meaningful to practice. As we have already suggested, however, the origins of all research questions are sociocultural. Because this is true, we must be conscious of the influence that intellectual "fashion" can have on the selection of research questions. Similarly, we must recognize the sway that our preference for this or that research paradigm or the values that we hold can have on question selection. With all this in mind, Chapter 3 provides guidance to formulating research questions that are pertinent to the relevant stakeholders.

Chapter 4 introduces measurement as a core research tool. Research measurement boils down to the process of recording an observation in ways that increase the likelihood that other independent observers of the phenomenon will report the same observation and attach the same meaning to that observation. These two qualities are embodied in the terms *reliability* and *validity*. Whether we are using numeric or nonnumeric data, our measurements are meaningful only as long as they may be replicated and understood as meaningful by others.

Measurements are rarely (if ever) made for the sake of measurement alone, however. We make measurements in order to draw some further inference related to the phenomena being measured. Some of these inferences rely on inductive logic, whereas others depend on deduction. Chapter 5 describes three kinds of inference—explanatory, predictive, and descriptive—and the ways that a small set of research design tools can be organized to strengthen the inferences that we seek to make.

Whenever we incorporate our measurements into research designs in order to make scientific inference, we wish for our inferences to apply to some larger class of the phenomena of interest. This requires appropriate sampling, the subject of Chapter 6. Whenever we seek to extend the findings of our research activity beyond the individual or individuals who are actually involved in our investigation, we need to employ a sampling strategy that will best support our generalization. By the same token, when we take a set of selected behaviors from an individual client as representative of that client's behavior more regularly, we must be conscious of the important role that sampling can play in our judgment.

Chapter 7 explores data collection techniques as social settings in which measurements are made. These social settings include dialogues between the researcher and subjects, the use of written questions or other instruments, and direct observation. Each of these social settings may be used for data collection along a continuum that ranges from settings that are quite fixed to those that are very flexible. Rather than being an arbitrary choice made by the researcher, the selection of a particular data collection strategy reflects the nuances of the research question being posed.

The analysis of collected data is discussed in Chapters 8 and 9. Data analysis is a set of activities designed to accomplish three general tasks: (1) reducing information overload (data reduction), (2) discovering patterns among variables, and (3) estimating the generalizability of findings. Although the specific activities employed in analyzing numerical and nonnumerical data differ, these tasks apply to all forms of data. Because social work research often involves the analysis of both numerical and nonnumerical data, the development of skills for use with data of both types is imperative.

Chapter 10 pulls all of the research adventure together in its application to practice evaluation. As social workers intervene with client systems, they are ethically bound to evaluate the outcomes of those interventions. These applications may be with small systems like individual clients or families, or large complex systems like formal organizations or whole communities. Regardless, the required evaluation calls forth the very research skills that have been discussed as parts of the scientific process. In that sense, the book concludes as it began: with a clear commitment to the continuous improvement of all aspects of social work practice through the application of fundamental research tools.

Our primary acknowledgment of support in writing this book is of the many students who have helped us formulate our approach to this material. It is easy to recall the enthusiastic students who posed the stimulating questions and engaged us in lively and enlightening discussions about the application of research techniques to this or that practice application. However, a bigger debt of thanks is owed to those students who diligently struggled with concepts they found foreign and difficult to comprehend. If this book is successful in presenting social work research from a perspective that future students find meaningful, it is due in no small part to the challenges presented to us by students who found the more traditional approach unsatisfactory. We hope that we will be able to continue to hear your voices in the semesters to come.

We also offer our thanks to colleagues who suggested to us that we had a unique perspective on teaching social work research. It is heartening to know that colleagues we hold in high regard value our efforts to teach these fundamentals. We hope that this book advances the interest expressed by many of those colleagues, that research skills should be taught as a routine part of practice, rather than a unique form of social work.

We also thank the following reviewers for their comments on the manuscript: Jude M. Antonyappan, East Carolina University; Fred Childers, California State University, Fresno; and Sophia F. Dziegielewski, University of Central Florida.

Finally, our deepest appreciation is offered to our families. These are the people who tolerated us when our frustrations spilled over, tried to appear interested when we recited portions of the book during dinner, who put up with our (more than occasional) omission of household tasks, and who cheered the milestones along the way.

1 Scientific Reasoning and Critical Thinking

Ways of Knowing

Relationship of This Chapter to the Goals of the Book

This book is about using science in the practice of social work. The techniques and procedures discussed in this book are designed to address the needs of professionals for knowledge that transcends the limitations of casual, everyday thinking. This chapter looks broadly at the question of the nature of knowledge and how our species, with our unique ways of knowing, can develop knowledge about ourselves and our environment that generates true and useful statements about the empirical world. In this chapter, we describe different ways of knowing, assumptions of science as one method, common human errors of reason that produce the need for a rigorous method, and some macro trends in scientific thinking.

In addition to the preceding, we discuss critical thinking, a topic that we find closely tied to the idea of the scientific process. **Critical thinking** refers to the process of generating and applying knowledge while seeking to avoid the pitfalls and fallacies of human reasoning. By exercising strong critical thinking skills in all phases of research, our skills as social workers and as plain everyday human information processors will be improved.

This chapter presents a broad overview of many topics that are discussed in depth in subsequent chapters. As research instructors, we have sometimes shared the frustration that superficial introduction of concepts can produce. Indeed, the research process follows a circular path in that decisions made at one stage may well need to be modified in light of subsequent decisions. Decisions about **sampling,** a data collection method, and a research design may be simultaneously affecting one another. And yet, we are constrained to teaching this content in a somewhat linear form—the learning of the second week can only be preceded by the first week and never by the third week. To facilitate learning, this chapter presents not only some very basic principles and ideas, but also a "big picture" view of science as an activity onto which all of the rest of this course might be logically attached.

Application of This Chapter to the Roles of Social Workers

The contents of this chapter are relevant across the multiple roles that social workers might take in relationship to science and the research process. As a student, these skills work to make you better consumers and integrators of the information with which you are presented. An understanding of the logic of science and of the nature of critical thinking is valuable in analyzing and understanding one's own approach to acquiring knowledge in the classroom, in reading, in discussions, and in the field. When people have a better understanding of the assumptions that necessarily underlie their philosophy of science, they are better able to understand how and why some things seem to "ring" more or less true. We would strongly encourage the use of critical thinking in reading assignments and classroom lectures. It is the stuff of which good learning debates are made!

As practitioners, our need for these skills is no less acute. Although we still need to be critical consumers of current practice research information, we also must be responsive to the professional demands placed on us by our client systems. When we listen to clients or gather information by which we must assess communities or other social environments, we are engaged in various phases of the scientific process. We want to believe that our client systems are improving as we ply our professional skills. Critical thinking and the scientific process help us ensure that they are—or move us toward remedies when they are not. And as our practice wisdom develops, we have a responsibility to assess each development against the standards of critical thinking—and to invite the critical scrutiny of colleagues when we believe that we may have developed some new insight that benefits practice.

The image of a social scientist tends to be that of one who labors to produce new knowledge. However, we do not wish to narrowly limit the term social scientist to those who are employed in academic settings or "think tanks" of one ilk or another. Instead, we see social scientists as all who seek a more complete understanding of social life through the application of the principles of science and critical thinking. Social workers tend to participate in science in all its knowledge-generating phases, and also in the task of using the knowledge of science to achieve goals of the profession such as social justice.

Learning Objectives

After reading this chapter, you should be able to:

1. describe the nature of science
2. identify common logical errors and fallacies of human reason
3. identify solutions to the logical errors provided by scientific methods
4. define the concept of "paradigm shift"
5. define and recognize the terms *theory* and *hypothesis*

Key Terms and Concepts

Epistemology

Definition of Epistemology and Discussion of Logical Positivism.   **Epistemology** is the study of the basis of knowing or the nature of knowledge. An epistemology, or philosophy of science, that has been common in Western science is **logical positivism.** The guiding principle of logical positivism is that there is a reality that exists outside of people, and knowledge about this reality can be verified empirically, that is, through direct sensory experience. In its extreme form, logical positivism largely ignores the degree of filtering and interpretation of experience that goes into an observation, grossly underestimating the role of values, beliefs, culture, and experience in generating knowledge.

Powerful debates have raged over the existence of an empirical world and the possibility of knowledge that transcends culture. These debates are a good and useful practice. Our own take on the debates is that there probably is an objective reality that exists independent of us, but the only kind of knowledge we can generate about it is that informed by culture. However, we also believe that the use of systematic methods and procedures for developing knowledge can reduce the extent to which our knowledge simply reflects the limitations of human reason. Although we acknowledge that the scientific method is only one way of knowing, it is a powerful way of knowing that has evolved to avoid most of the common fallacies of human reasoning to which most of the other ways of understanding reality succumb.

Alternative Ways of Knowing.   If you were asked the simple question, "How do you know?" you would probably respond that you had read the information, or heard it shared in a conversation, or even presented in a more formal setting by an "expert." It may be that you had had an earlier experience that caused you to be familiar with the issue you were now reporting. Sometimes a person becomes stubborn (well, maybe not you, but perhaps someone you know!) and says, "I just *know* that it's true." There are still other possible ways we might "know."

Do all of these different ways of knowing produce equivalent knowledge? We think not. Some ways of knowing produce knowledge that is perfectly appropriate for some purposes but not for others. For instance, if a person wishes to consider the relative positioning of the stars and planets for guidance in making a financial investment, some of us might think that is odd or even imprudent behavior, but it is a personal decision that we would allow the person to make. On the other hand, if we were aware that our own stockbroker had decided to give up reading the *Wall Street Journal* in favor of astrology, we would likely seek the services of a new financial advisor! What's the difference? Clearly, it is in the manner through which one comes to "know" given information.

Jensen (1989) has offered an orderly approach to recognizing four common "ways of knowing" or understanding reality. He proposes that the basic tools we might choose to use or not use in understanding reality are data, or empirical experience, and logic. By constructing a 2 × 2 table of using or not using data, and using or not using logic, these four "ways of knowing" can be compared.

As illustrated in Table 1.1, **mysticism** is a way of understanding reality that relies on neither logic nor data. Hmmmm, what is there then? That's the point. This kind of understanding is mystical. It is believed without any reference to logic or data. We would like to say that it is common among primitive people—as if it were not also common among "moderns." That, however, is not the case. Many people, probably most people, believe some things without the benefit of either empirical data or logic. We don't have a problem with such thinking—as long as the belief holder does not confuse such mystical thinking with science.

Perhaps you will be more comfortable with an example and a slight language change. Many persons express belief in a supreme being who exists outside of the material universe in which we live. What data can be offered in support of such a claim? Certainly not empirical data since the definition proposed places this being beyond empirical data. What about logic? How many people could

TABLE 1.1   Use of Data and Logic and Four Ways of Knowing

	Logic Not Used	Logic Used
Data Used	Empiricism	Science
Data Not Used	Mysticism	Rationalism

Source: Donald D. Jensen, 1989, Pathologies of science, precognition, and modern psychophysics, *The Skeptical Inquirer, 13,* 147. Used by permission of the Skeptical Inquirer.

mount a logical defense for the necessity of a supreme being? Some, notably Aristotle, have, but many people continue to express such a belief without a logical defense. In reality, beliefs in supreme beings are generally held without reference to data or logic, as a sort of self-evident truth. Mysticism is the cover term for knowing based on self-evident truths, matters of "faith."

Rationalism is a way of knowing based on a compelling logical argument, without recourse to an empirical test. Following the laws for creating logically true propositions, it is possible to reason what must exist. Unfortunately, our powers of rationalism have sometimes fallen short of the task. It is not too difficult to imagine wonderful contraptions that exist only in the mind. When it comes time to test these inventions in some "real-world" application, their flaws become apparent. This is the shortcoming of rationalism without empiricism.

Empiricism is a way of generating knowledge that assumes that knowledge is located in the empirical world and can be derived directly from experience without deductive processes. This approach ignores the fact that knowledge exists in the minds of people, not in the empirical world, and thus is constructed from meaning systems. In Jensen's (1989) typology, this kind of thinking would be called empiricism. The problem with this form of naive empiricism is that it overlooks the role of the person in shaping experiences. History is filled with mistaken conclusions based on repeated empirical observation. Even some of our more current social science offers evidence of the flaws of simple empiricism. For example, the repeated observation that people in lower economic strata do not typically save money "for a rainy day" has been taken as empirical evidence of their "present orientation" and inability to anticipate "deferred gratification." Case after case of observing poor people is likely to confirm the lack of such activity. However, none of these untempered empirical observations directly lead the observer to appreciate that saving for the future is difficult when resources are all required to meet daily needs. Can you believe it when you *have* seen it with your own eyes?—not necessarily. This is the shortcoming of empiricism without rational thinking to make sense of the observations.

Curiously, some of the same people who suggested "trusting your eyes" probably also counseled, "Don't believe everything you hear." One view encourages us to trust our empirical sense of the world around us, whereas the other advises restraint. Is there any way to reconcile these two folk sayings? It seems to us that the folk wisdom here is guiding us to build our sense of reality on at least two bases. First, we are to use our senses to experience the world about us. But rather than stopping there and simply believing our eyes (or ears, or tongue, or nose, or sense of touch), we are to use our brain and THINK. We must raise the question of how these empirical pieces can rationally and logically fit together to make a meaningful whole.

By now it should almost be anticlimatic to turn to Jensen's final quadrant, that of science. Science represents the way of knowing that relies on both empirical data and the application of logic. This is the seeing, hearing, tasting, smelling, or touching of the world and thinking about that experience in a way that allows us to make sense of the empirical experience. Beyond the use of empirical data and logic, science builds on what is already known or believed to be true about the world about us. This preexisting knowledge is represented in **theory.** Science pursues logical relationships that are predicted by theory and demonstrated with empirical data. Finally, the scientific method requires that both the results of scientific investigation and the methods by which findings are made be held up for the scrutiny of others. This allows findings to be confirmed and added to a growing body of theory, or to be rejected as unfounded.

Consistent with our view that there are many ways of knowing the world, we hold that the method of science is only one of these. But for the purposes of professional social work (and many other areas of life as well), we believe that the method of science represents the best way of knowing and understanding the world about us.

Relative Merits of Various Ways of Knowing.   In order to make a judgment that the knowledge of science is superior, we need to be explicit about our standards of assessment. What makes one way of knowing better than others? In asking this question, we remind the reader (and ourselves) that we are concerned with knowing and understanding the world about us *for the purpose* of doing professional social work. So, as social workers, how do we assess knowledge? We believe there are four key attributes.

A good way of knowing things in professional social work should be measurable. Obviously, we do not suggest **measurement** in a rigid or narrow sense, like pounds and ounces, or gallons and cups, although this is one way of measuring. And, quite clearly, not everything can be measured in terms of pounds or gallons. Hudson (1985) identified four ways of measuring things: magnitude, duration, frequency, and switch. Recognizing different ways of measuring things can be very useful in setting intervention goals while working with clients. *Magnitude* comes closest to the idea of measuring something in gallons or pounds or some other standardized unit. We might say that a client has a serious problem with depression because he or she has a very high score on a recognized depression inventory. A second way of measuring things is *duration.* Duration is usually measured in units of time, indicating how long the phenomenon is present, such as the length of time a temper tantrum lasts. Third, we can measure the *frequency* of something happening. Frequent arguing in a domestic partnership may be taken to indicate a "big" problem even though the duration of those arguments may be relatively low. Finally, Hudson called the fourth way of measuring *switch*—the simple presence or absence of the thing being measured. (A simple way of remembering this last one is to think of an electric switch—it is either on or off.)

Along with being measurable, a good way of knowing the world should be objective. In this context, **objectivity** means that different observers using the same methods will all report the same experience of "reality." That's a fine definition in a technical sense, but we run into problems when we have individual judges with their individual biases experiencing the world. This problem raises the essential point. When each of us is experiencing a different reality because of the unique individual perspective that we bring to the task, we do not have an objective sense of that reality. We only have objectivity when a substantial portion of us experiences the same reality. If we turn to a basic college dictionary, we are more likely to find a definition such as **intersubjective.** Intersubjective experiences take place when all of us (or that substantial portion of the collective) share individual subjective experiences that are the same. Voilà! We have an objective experience—the same experience being reported by different judges using different methods.

If this discussion of what is and what isn't real is distressing to you, relax. The long and short is that the things that really have meaning to us as social workers (and for that matter, as people more generally) are socially constructed (Berger & Luckmann, 1966). When these social constructions are defined clearly enough or shared widely enough among people so as to be routinely recognized, we are comfortable saying that they have "objective reality"; until then, they are relegated to subjective experience.

The third quality that a way of knowing reality should have is that it should allow the experience to be repeated. The process of repeating the circumstances that lead to the observation is called **replication.** When we find that the same circumstances result in the same consequences repeatedly, we are given assurance that the first observation was not simply a fluke or a failure of our testing apparatus—be it mechanical or mental. Replication is really the answer to the question, "Are you sure?" Replication says, "Yes, watch. I'll show you again."

Finally, these three qualities of our way of knowing what is real—measurable, objective, and replicable—must be combined with our powers of **reason.** A part of understanding new things about reality is struggling to fit them into what is already known. This is the rational aspect and the application of logic. When "each way of knowing" is evaluated against these standards, we believe that science stands alone in producing the best information about what is real. Science is not flawless. Mistakes have been made and whole new ways of understanding the world have emerged. (We will discuss paradigm shifts later in the chapter.) Still and all, it has been the most productive approach to fruitfully exploring our world to date.

The Nature of Science

Definition of Science.   Let's explore just exactly what we mean by **science.** Science refers to a particular way of gaining knowledge about the world. Science has two aspects, one logical and one cultural and historical. The logic of science consists of a collection of rules and principles that describe how to conduct observations and test theories. As a cultural and historical process, science consists of the efforts of people to generate culturally relevant knowledge through the application of these rules and principles. Much of this book is dedicated to the explanation of the logic of the **scientific method,** that is, the formal methods used to guide observations and test theories. However, we will also remind the reader that actually conducting observation and testing theory involve sociocultural processes, and, therefore, the knowledge we actually generate reflects the values, preoccupations, and social structure in which scientists work.

The scientific method rests on five fundamental requirements. Science is an approach to generation of knowledge that is based on (1) empirical observations, (2) logic, (3) theories, (4) theory testing by applying logic and observation, and

(5) public evaluation of theories through peer review and replication. The scientific method is an open-ended process. That is, the cycle of making observations, organizing these logically into theories, testing the theories, publishing the findings to allow review and replication, and either fine-tuning theories or generating new ones is potentially endless. We don't mean to suggest that once you start, it is impossible to stop. Rather, think of the whole process as a spiral that keeps rolling along, sometimes more quickly, sometimes more slowly, but never ending up in quite the same place. Whether that spiral is taking us closer to some ultimate "truth" is still the subject of debate, but the implicit goal of the scientific method is developing ever closer approximations of truth through observation and theory generation and testing.

Wallace (1971) developed a circular image of the scientific process that is very helpful in understanding how all the pieces are intended to fit together. The model is an excellent description of the logic behind science as a process (Figure 1.1).

Empirical Observation.   We'll start examining the process of science at the bottom of Wallace's diagram at the word "observation," not because it is the beginning (a circle doesn't have a beginning—or an end), but because it seems to represent the smallest conceptual unit on the figure. An **empirical observation** is a specific, unique piece of information originating in a sensory experience. Although the word *observation* might suggest something that you saw with your eyes, it could be an auditory observation or information gathered by any of your five senses. Observations are a bit more than sensation in that a lot of filtering and defining—of which we are often not consciously aware—goes on. Despite the fact that observations are really meanings assigned to sensations, and thus cultural, most of us have the probably correct impression that there is something going on out there and we can learn about it through our senses. This certainly is one of the basic assumptions of science.

Observation done in the context of science, like all observation, is not all-inclusive but selective. Within science, the kinds of observations that are made, and how they are made, reflect in part the interests of scientists. As we work around the process of science, we will arrive back at this point, primed by some theory to look for specific kinds of experience. Scholars interested in the history of science often study the cultural and social forces that influence this process. We will return to this point when we discuss paradigm shifts. First, let us proceed with the logical order of the process of science.

Empirical Generalization.   **Empirical generalizations** are abstractions drawn from collections of observations. Over time, each of us has the experience of beginning to see regularities in the world about us. As youngsters in grade school, we notice the ranges of behaviors that are typical. Awareness of what is typical allows us to notice that some children tend to get into trouble more frequently than others. We may also notice that children who are more frequently in trouble often perform poorly on the various academic exercises compared to their peers as well. We

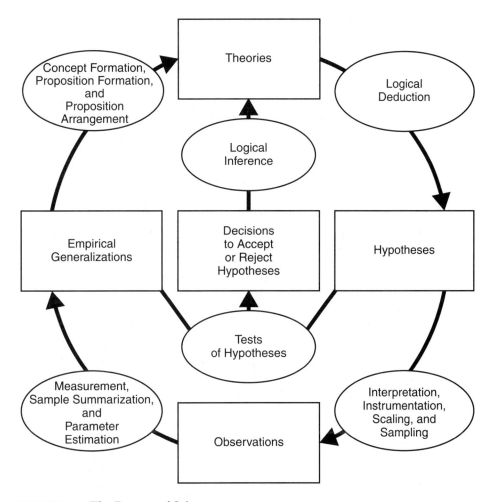

FIGURE 1.1   The Process of Science

Source: Reprinted with permission from Wallace, Walter L. *The Logic of Science in Sociology* (New York: Aldine de Gruyter). Copyright © 1971 by Walter L. Wallace.

may even generalize and find ourselves thinking that children who are often in trouble tend to become children who don't do as well academically. The farther down this chain of thinking we go, the more we risk making an untrue generalization. The methods we will discuss in this book are intended in part to minimize (but not eliminate) the chances of making empirical generalizations that are not reflective of the observations from which they were supposed to originate.

Glaser and Strauss (1964) conducted a major study of the dying experience in which they spent time talking to and watching people with terminal illnesses. They were making empirical observations. They then considered the whole collection of empirical observations and made some generalizations about them. They were about the business of understanding their social world through the scientific method. The scientific process of making empirical generalizations concerns finding the commonalities among empirical observations. These generalizations are just interpretations of things that have been observed.

Turning observations into empirical generalizations usually involves manipulation of symbolic representations of the observations. Data analysis is one name given to this process. **Data analysis** consists of systematic procedures for extracting generalizations from observations. Chapters 8 ("Numerical Data Analysis") and 9 ("Nonnumerical Data Analysis") will discuss this process and describe some techniques used to extract generalizations from observations while keeping the generalizations grounded in the observations.

Theory Development.   A theory is a network of propositions that seeks to explain the relationships among a related set of variables. Theories are both the result of observational processes and reasoning, and also the source of testable hypotheses that lead to more observation. A **hypothesis** is a statement about the predicted relationship between two or more variables according to a theory. It is common for a hypothesis to describe the expected impact of an **independent variable**—that is, a variable taken as a cause—on a **dependent variable,** a variable taken as an effect or outcome. If the empirical generalizations can be thought of as the "what," theories are the "why and how." Humans seem discontent to simply know that something happened; we are strongly disposed to speculate about why things are happening. We want to offer tentative explanations for our generalizations. We want to suggest the conditions under which we might expect more of the empirical observations about which we are generalizing to occur. We want a good theory.

Theories are used to describe, predict, and explain empirical events. A good theory aids in description by providing an interrelated system of concepts used to help people communicate about experience. These concepts also inform the process of observation by specifying ways of measuring empirical events. Chapter 4 ("Measurement") describes techniques for moving from personal conceptualizations through public, shared nominal and operational definitions of concepts. These concepts and measurement procedures associated with them allow the generation of ideas about how the empirical world is organized. Ideas about organization provide the basis for predicting empirical events. Finally, by identifying general causal/functional relationships, theories provide explanations concerning how certain forces produce the predicted events.

Good scientific theory has other desirable qualities. Good theories are grounded in real-world observations. A good theory is *parsimonious,* or efficient. All else being equal, the simpler a theory is, the better it is. Finally, a good theory needs to be open to the possibility of being refuted. This sounds paradoxical; but if you think about it, we think you'll agree that a theory that has no possibility of being wrong would represent a closed system. There would be no room for further clarification; there could be no room for testing.

Hypothesis Testing.   One of the ways a theory is tested is to see if logical propositions derived from the theory generate true statements about empirical events.

Statements used to test a theory are often called hypotheses. A h
is a statement drawn from theory that indicates a relationship
more variables. So, going back to an earlier example, we migl
theory that predicts a relationship between behavior problems
children and subsequent academic achievement. Our hypothesis statement might
read something like this: Grade school children who experience a higher number
of disciplinary actions for inappropriate behavior will demonstrate lower levels of
academic performance. Fine, so how do we put this hypothesis to the test? As suggested by the cycle of science, we return to making empirical observations. We collect data (empirical observations) and use the data to determine if empirical
events unfold as the theory predicts. If we find that our hypothesized relationship
holds true, we have generated support for our theory. If we are unable to say with
some reasonably strong certainty that our hypothesized relationship holds, it is
"back to the drawing board." That means we (or more likely others in the scientific community concerned with problems and issues like ours) make more empirical observations, generalizations, and seek to refine our theory so that better
predictions might be made and supported with subsequent hypothesis testing.

Inductive and Deductive Reasoning.   So now we've talked our way around the
cycle of science. Perhaps you've noticed something different about moving up the
left side of the wheel in contrast to moving down the right side. On the left side,
we moved from thinking about specific observations to thinking about general
classes of observations and the connections between them—from empirical observations to explanatory theories. On the right side, we start with those relationships among general classes of variables contained in theory and move to testing
predictions against the behavior of specific individuals. These two processes,
starting with observations and ending up with generalization, and starting with
generalizations and ending up with specific observations, constitute two different
types of thinking. The type of thinking that characterizes science seems to be
dependent on if one is working on the right or left side of the cycle. The left side of
the cycle of science consists of the processes of **induction** (moving from the specific to the general) and the right side is characterized by **deduction** (moving from
the general to the specific).

Induction and deduction are both essential for science to proceed. Unfortunately, much of Western science, perhaps especially in the human sciences, has
placed an emphasis on the deductive side of the process. Let's take a closer look at
some of the issues involved. Induction is a process that starts by looking at specific
cases and asks how they might be logically tied together so as to be more meaningful. If we look carefully, it should be clear that good inductive research does not
proceed from an a priori theoretical stance. That would be the antithesis of induction. Rather, inductive research proceeds with as open a mind as is possible and
asks: "What's going on here?" "What do these observations mean?" and so forth.
In his excellent book, *Theoretical Sensitivity,* Glaser (1978) urges readers to be sensitive to the emergent theory in the inductive process. As inductive researchers, we
must be listening for that new voice, that new idea, and, at all costs, we must avoid
stomping it out with our previously established and familiar theoretical structures.

So what of deduction? Is it nothing more than an old battle-ax waiting to fell another budding emergent theory? No, not at all. Deduction is the process that starts from an established theory and draws from it related hypotheses. If the theory is correct and true, it should be possible to use the principles of the theory to predict something about the empirical world. In posing and then testing such a hypothesis, we are employing the deductive process of moving from the general case (the theory) to the specific (the empirical observations against which the hypothesis is tested).

In the process of moving round and round the cycle of science, portions of the theory that are found by hypothesis testing to produce consistently accurate prediction are used with more confidence, and those hypotheses that do not produce predictions that are consistent with observations are reconsidered, clarified by further grounding in empirical observation, or perhaps abandoned. This new information may lead to more observation and induction as we look for inspiration through observation or a reexamination of the basis on which hypotheses were deduced.

Both inductive and deductive processes are important to social work researchers. On the inductive side, we ground our ideas in observables. This helps us to operate from conceptual systems that match the realities of our constituents. On the deductive side, we seek to expedite our work with clients by extrapolating from general knowledge to particular situations and individuals. Practice theories make us better helpers by specifying general principles that can be used to design interventions that have a high probability of working.

In part, the differences between inductive and deductive reasoning lie at the heart of the ongoing debate about the best approach to research in social work practice. For some, the thrill of the field and grounded exploration of the sensory world dominate their view of science. For others, carefully reasoning about the world and forcing out secrets through logic and hypothesis testing dominate their view. For science (including the science of social work practice) to move forward, both are necessary, and each should be practiced with the kind of methodological rigor that will best advance our understanding of people in their complex social environments.

Theorizing and Doing Science.   Splitting the cycle of science vertically gave us the inductive and deductive halves of the process. If we split the cycle horizontally, we discover another dimension that separates the top of the cycle from the bottom. Basically, the dominant activity at the top of the cycle, whether we are in the inductive or deductive mode, is working with logic and theories. Whether we are putting together the products of induction (upper left side of the cycle) to better understand some phenomenon through theory development, or using the implications of a theory to reason about what will probably happen if we take certain actions on behalf of our clients (upper right side of the cycle), we are primarily working with ideas, theories, and logic at the top of the cycle. Contrast this with the lower half of the circle, where we are applying the ideas of science to various tasks. In the lower right quadrant, we might apply standardized tests or observation protocols, or look for risk factors operating in specific contexts. In the lower left, we would conduct activities such as attempting to describe large populations based on observations with samples. Again, the emphasis here is on gathering new information. The bottom of the cycle of science is a very active place.

Quantitative and Qualitative Measurement.   By training and perhaps temperament, people who do science often develop preferences for various positions on the cycle of science. Given the competitiveness of most Western cultures (where a lot of scientific thought originated), it is not surprising that debates have erupted over the years concerning the best form of science. **Quantitative methods** is a label that has been attached to scientific activity that combines use of numbers, deduction, and hypothesis testing. Historically, quantitative methods have been contrasted with qualitative methods. **Qualitative methods** are characterized by the use of nonnumeric data, induction, and exploratory methods. Although it is probably possible to locate general areas on the cycle of science where these lie, it seems a fruitless exercise to attempt to determine which is better for social work. Clearly, quantitative and qualitative methods are two sides of the same process. The tendency to train social scientists who are skilled in only a few methods seems to be at the root of the problem and is an unproductive strategy for producing scientifically oriented social workers. In our own practice evaluation work, we often start with methods that are inductive and exploratory, and end up testing hypotheses. However, we are equally likely to start with a hypothesis and finish up with an exploratory study to clarify the context. Rarely do we have an activity that can be characterized as wholly quantitative or wholly qualitative. It seems foolish to get stuck on one part of the cycle and limit our understanding of either the context or the accuracy of our theories.

The part of the qualitative versus quantitative debate that pitches number crunchers against linguists and others who prefer words seems particularly misguided. In fact, finding something generally antagonistic about numbers or words misses an important characteristic of human meaning systems. The choice to use words rather than numbers to represent experience does not usually reflect the nature of some empirical event, but rather the state of our thinking about it. Anything that is well enough understood to be recognized consistently can be quantified. Recall the discussion of the ways of measuring things—magnitude, duration, frequency, and switch. These are all quantifications of the object being measured. If nothing else, we should always be able to identify the presence or absence of the construct we are trying to measure (switch). What then is the role of research methods that do not use numbers? Sometimes our thinking about some experience has not reached the point where we can identify quantitative aspects. This is especially true when we are involved in exploratory study of areas of experience where meaning systems are not well worked out. In these contexts, the richer, if less precise, symbols of speech are of greater value in moving toward conceptual clarity. Also, when an observation can be adequately represented in words or pictures, it is easier to communicate and contributes to the accessibility of knowledge.

Social workers don't have the luxury of being stuck in one part of the cycle of science for long. Many social work tasks with individuals and communities require understanding the clients' point of view, a task best addressed through the nonnumeric, open inquiry of qualitative methods. At the other end of the cycle, increasing emphasis on accountability and effectiveness has resulted in the development of sophisticated quantitative methods of program evaluation at the level of both groups and individuals. Some of these will be discussed more fully in Chapter 10 ("Practice Evaluation in Single and Multiple Systems").

Critical Thinking

Definition of Critical Thinking.   Critical thinking refers to careful reflection on the validity of statements. The subject of critical thinking can be our own statements as well as the statements and claims made by others. Critical thinking is at once disciplined and creative. It seeks the evidence for propositions rather than accepting ideas without both logical and empirical support. Critical thinking requires self-knowledge, particularly our susceptibility toward what Jensen (1989) called frauds, finagles, propaganda, or prejudice. In addition to awareness of our limitations, critical thinking also requires the will to confront those limitations and the courage to live with uncertainty. The latter is especially important to the person who would like to transcend, even a little, the programming of enculturation and socialization. How can we learn new truths if we are unable to accept that our truth is not certain?

Critical thinking is necessary to avoid taking erroneous actions based on false logic. All of us can think of occasions on which people (and probably each one of us as well) were wrong in their judgment about some situation. Sometimes we were "taken in" by someone who was intentionally misrepresenting a situation. (P. T. Barnum suggested that a sucker was born every minute!) Other times, we were just plain wrong in our assessment. Critical thinking helps to reduce the number of times that we will be wrong. More important than the fact that most of us would prefer to be right than wrong is the belief that our clients deserve the best. All of our clients are better served when we strive to exercise our best critical thinking.

Common Logical Errors and Fallacies.   It is often said that one of the things that separates human beings from most other animals (some of the higher-order mammals may be the exception) is our capacity for abstract reasoning. There is no question that the human cognitive processes are able to make accurate higher-order conclusions based on lower-order information. We don't know all of how these amazing processes work. We do know, however, that as remarkable as human reasoning seems to be, it is prone to making some systematic errors in the way information is processed. It is likely that these errors stem from cultural influences as well as the basic cognitive apparatus. Whatever the source of human logical errors or fallacies of reasoning, they are pervasive. In part, the methods of science that have arisen over the years are in direct response to these systematic mistakes that humans tend to make when they reason carelessly about their experience.

The **fallacies of reason** in which we are interested are regularized ways of mishandling information that we use in decision making. In addition to the four general fallacies described by Jensen (1989; frauds, finagles, propaganda, and prejudice), many mental habits that produce errors have been noted. Gilovich (1991) provides a very long list of bad mental habits through which fallacies appear to work. For example, some cognitive determinants of questionable beliefs include misinterpretation of random data, misinterpretation of incomplete or unrepresentative data, and biased interpretation of ambiguous or inconsistent data. Repeated demonstration has shown that people are generally not capable of determining if a set of observations is random or if a meaningful pattern exists. People tend to err in the direction of finding patterns where there are none. Likewise, no matter how potentially biased and atypical a sample may be, people are prone to treat the characteristics of that sample as representative of a whole population. When faced with ambiguous or incomplete data, people consistently interpret the observations in the direction of expectations, prejudices, or that proscribed by authority. The direction of these errors is determined in part by social forces and motivation, including seeing what we want to see, believing what we are told without considering the quality of the information, and believing what we believe others believe (Gilovich, 1991).

Levy (1997) also lists a series of mental errors that are particularly important to persons in helping professions. He includes biasing of conclusions by the language used to describe an event, treating abstract ideas as if they were real, treating names as explanations, confusing experiences that occur on a continuum with all-or-nothing states, blurring the distinction between "is" and "should" and correlation and causation, and ignoring the possibility that the same effect may arise from different causes (multiple causation). These are particularly important in the context of helping professions because these tend to lead to erroneous sources of intervention with subsequent reduced probability of success.

Knowledge about these sources of errors in judgment is an important part of professional self-awareness. This knowledge is important to allow us to recognize and avoid them in our thinking and in the claims that others might make. Many of the techniques of science that are discussed here arose in part as ways to reduce the likelihood that the forces listed here will produce errors in our thinking. This is the source of the feeling described by novice scientists, that of formality, artificiality, and skepticism. It is one of the paradoxes of education that the more one learns, the less certain one is about anything. A big part of this is understanding just how limited our powers of reasoning are when we are not operating in a critical mode. Listed in what follows are a few more sources of error in casual thinking.

Anecdotal Information.   **Anecdotal information** is information content that is transmitted through the recounting of the relevant events. In its least rigorous form, anecdotal information amounts to little more than casual storytelling. We each share more or less factual accounts of events that we have experienced daily (directly or indirectly) with our friends and family. In a more rigorous and professional form, these stories may be called "case histories" and follow a fairly structured format. Yet another kind of anecdotal information involves the use of testimonials. In this case, the anecdote is given a special power through its strong first-person presentation.

Although strong case histories can be powerful tools in teaching and learning professional practice, there are two related potential problems with using anecdotal information. The first concerns the degree to which the anecdote is based on accurate and factual information itself. The human mind seems to revel in finding what it was looking for. Believers in the Loch Ness monster are much more likely to find convincing evidence of its existence than skeptics. When we are presented with anecdotal information, we must exercise caution that it is based on an accurate (remember "replicable" and "intersubjective") assessment. The second caution concerns the degree to which the anecdote illustrates something that might be taken as typical. Critical thinking can equip us to investigate the forms of measurement that were used in developing the anecdote and to ask just how representative this case might be of a general population.

Overgeneralization.   Another of the common fallacies in our thinking is **overgeneralization.** An obvious illustration might start with the statement, "Yes, that's true. I knew a person once who…." In this case, it would appear that two errors are about to be made. In addition to the overgeneralization being made by extrapolating from "the person" once known, this overgeneralization is based on anecdotal information as well! Especially when we *want* to believe in something, it is easy to elevate the known cases that support our stance to the position of proof positive. However, such is not the stuff of critical thinking. It is often tempting to draw strong generalizations when dealing with the complexities of human behavior. However, before we draw such conclusions, we must put our tentative assumptions about how people will behave "generally" to some critical tests.

Authority.   Even authority can play into our uncritical thinking. We are often prone to accepting information as true because it is presented by an **authority.** To a degree, such acceptance is valuable and important because it saves us from the need to rediscover all kinds of well-established information. For example, we'd like to think that your reading of this book will help you to be better social workers because you will accept at least some of what it says based on authority: We wrote the book; the publisher was willing to publish it; your instructor selected it—all sources of some authority. We'd also like to think that you will be thinking critically in coming to your own conclusions about the importance of these matters in social work practice. In that regard, even authorities must be held to standards of evidence in making their claims. And authorities, perhaps especially, should be willing to make the basis of their claims available for public scrutiny.

On the other hand, we seem all too willing to accept information from authorities who do not make the basis of their claims clear and whose credentials do not justify our belief. The strongest image may be that of the frontier medicine wagons that traveled from town to town selling the elixir "proven" to cure all manner of maladies—based on the authority of the "doctor" who drove the wagon. Although the level of sophistication has increased considerably, the same false faith in claimed authority exists today in the selling of modern "elixirs." These include cures for AIDS, many cancers, depression, overweight, underenergy, and a whole range of other ailments.

I Read It Somewhere.   This common fallacy is a variation of the authority fallacy. Be warned, it takes little more to write a simple book than the time to put the words on paper and a publisher willing to shoulder the risk of printing and binding the volume. And in these days of personal computers and desktop publishing, it is likely even easier to go to press! Being commercially printed does not make something fact. Indeed, the same standards of evidence must exist for printed matter as for persons of authority more generally. One protection for the quality of much scientific publication (including the social sciences along with the physical sciences) is the peer review process utilized by most quality journals. However, sometimes work of questionable quality slips by these reviewers. In the final analysis, there is no substitute for one's own critical thinking.

The Power of Popularity.   When we talk about the popularity of an idea, we mean more than a period of high fashion that might be associated with a favored idea or perspective, although this sort of popularity must certainly be included. We are also including ideas that may be held to be common sense or that everybody knows. Notions that are considered common sense or known by everybody may well be correct. You've heard it said, "That many people can't be wrong." Yes, they can; history is filled with such ideas that have been shown to be wrong. By exercising critical thinking skills whenever we are presented with new (or sometimes old) ideas, we are exercising personal responsibility to reduce the likelihood that we are being beguiled by popular but erroneous ideas.

Protections from Logical Errors Provided by Scientific Methods.   Scientific methods provide a number of safeguards against logical errors, thus providing a clear path to critical thinking. In a sense, they do this by making the process of coming to know something a series of steps or subdecisions. To start with, we must always ask ourselves, "What is the nature of this claim to 'truth'?" "What is the evidence that supports this claim?"

When we apply the scientific method to questions like these, we quickly see that all claims of scientific knowledge must first be supported by data and meet the demands of basic logic. But beyond these basics, the scientific method requires that our data be of a quality that justifies our conclusions. This raises the matters of measurement reliability and measurement validity. If we seek to apply our findings to individuals or groups beyond those from whom we initially collected the empirical data, the scientific method requires that we use methods that provide adequate external validity to justify such generalization. If we wish to make claims of causal relationships, the scientific method guides us to explore our subject with experimental designs that allow variables to be observed in ways that reduce or eliminate the possibility that the changes we observe could have resulted from any other forces than the causal factor that we are investigating. Finally, the scientific method tests the hypothesized findings against the possibility that they just occurred by chance.

Wow! If the last paragraph seemed like a big process condensed into a single paragraph, you are right. The rest of this book is little more than an amplification of the preceding paragraph—it is about the scientific method. We will explore the issues of measurement, sampling, experiments, and other structured approaches to investigation, and various forms of analysis. Although we know that most of our readers will never be employed as social science researchers in a narrow sense, we believe that every practicing social worker will be able to function more effectively to produce desired change in client systems by utilizing scientific thinking in practice. By doing so, we reduce the likelihood of making logical errors that impede our own clear understanding and our client systems' progress.

Sociocultural Forces at Work: Paradigm Shifts

Definition of Paradigms.   A **paradigm** is a system of beliefs about reality. So, we might ask, "What is reality?" and the answer might come back, "It depends on what you believe." That's all well and good, but when you go home after a hard day and want to plunk down in your favorite chair, it had better be there. And, indeed, it likely will be. That's because the chair is part of the physical system of atoms and molecules that all hang together in predictable ways so that we are able to construct chairs (and other things) and sit in them without too many surprises. So reality is more than a set of beliefs; it is a set of beliefs that is consistent with empirical data. A paradigm is the shorthand way of discussing a set of such beliefs.

Understanding the general nature of paradigms is important in social research because a paradigm substantially defines what is an appropriate area in which to seek answers to the questions that we have about reality. It is also important to recognize that we have big paradigms that shape the basic nature of scientific investigation (e.g., the positivist paradigm that has guided most Western thought for the past hundred years or so), and paradigms that are more narrow and limited to specialty areas of investigation. Let's look at a quick example of one of these smaller paradigms related to the abuse of alcohol.

Not too many years ago in this country (say, the middle of the last century), alcohol abuse was seen very largely as a moral problem. The whole belief system around behaviors that were not socially acceptable suggested that perpetrators of these behaviors suffered a moral flaw. Their behaviors were the work of Satan. The paradigm in which these beliefs were held was one that relied heavily on the ultimate powers of good and evil to explain all manner of observable behavior (as well as other happenings in the physical world such as weather, public health, and the economy). Given the paradigm, it is completely reasonable that the treatment for alcohol abuse involved going to church, following the moral example of others, and rejecting the devil whiskey. Since then, we can see at least two distinct changes in the paradigm that helps us to understand human behavior. First, the paradigm changed to put less emphasis on spiritual forces and more on individual initiative and responsibility. U.S. President Teddy Roosevelt, who counseled pulling oneself up by the bootstraps, illustrates an example of this change. With respect to alcohol abuse, 12-step programs put additional emphasis on owning one's *problem* (while still including involvement of a Higher Power). More recently, we have seen even more change in this paradigm as we have become aware of the role of genetics, nutrition, and a host of other potentially related variables. Can all of these views be "correct"? This is not clear. But it is important to understand that they were all correct within the context of the prevailing paradigm.

Definition of a Paradigm Shift.   The term **paradigm shift** is used to describe the transition from one system of beliefs about reality to another. As in the preceding example from social science, the physical sciences have gone through their paradigm shifts as well. The classic examples concern the shift from viewing Earth as the center of the solar system to the current understanding of the planets all orbiting around the Sun. Likewise, a major paradigm shift occurred when a flat worldview was replaced with a sphere. Less quickly recognized were the paradigm shifts that were ushered in with Newtonian physics and Einstein's theory of relativity.

As stated earlier, paradigms largely define those areas that are appropriate for investigation and confine the range of answers that one might find. This makes our investigation more efficient in the short run but limits the extremes of our search in the long haul. Paradigm shifts occur when these limitations no longer allow investigators to account for all of their empirical observations within the confines of the prevailing paradigm. In what is no doubt the most influential book on paradigms and their shifts, Thomas Kuhn (1970) referred to the observations that do not fit within the prevailing paradigm as **anomalies.** Simply put, as things are observed that cannot be explained within the paradigm, they are set off to the side and essentially ignored. However, as the accumulation of these things, these anomalies, grows, it becomes more and more difficult for them to be ignored. Perhaps because of regularities that become apparent among the anomalies, perhaps as a fresh new insight, the system of beliefs about reality is amended or replaced so as to account for the old anomalies. It is this fundamental change in the worldview that is called a paradigm shift.

Contemporary Debates That May Signal Paradigm Shifts.   Over the past two or three decades, a growing number of social workers have raised questions about issues that, quite simply, haven't fit well within the prevailing positivist paradigm, and have offered challenges to the traditional positivist model of science (Heineman, 1981; Tyson, 1995; Witkin, 1991). With growing clarity, these writers have called for a shift in the paradigm that guides the development of social work knowledge. Although this new perspective has involved discussion of qualitative versus quantitative methods, and deduction versus induction, it involves more than these simple contrasts. Katherine Tyson (1995) has offered the most complete exposition of these ideas in her book titled *New Foundations for Scientific Social and Behavioral Research: The Heuristic Paradigm.* Although it may be early to declare that a paradigm shift is indeed underway, it is important to acknowledge that new perspectives are emerging to better account for the anomalies that have occurred under the old. Whether the present paradigm is able to transform itself to accommodate the heuristic that Tyson proposes or whether it falls away to be replaced by a wholly new emergent paradigm can be known only as the future unfolds. What is certain is that these are exciting times for social work research and knowledge building.

2 Ethics in Social Work Research

Ethics in Social Work

Relationship of This Chapter to the Whole

Virtually every choice made in conducting social work research is imbued with values. By values, we mean the ideals we hold for personal conduct, be those values personal, organizational, professional, or societal in origin. The principles of conduct that arise from those values are called **ethics.** Ethics are used to help us choose the right conduct. In keeping with the principle of intersubjectivity, we see the development and application of ethics as a social event, requiring open and frank discussion to be truly useful. Ethicists such as social worker Fredric Reamer have proposed an **ethical analysis** as a process by which social workers can "iden-tify and reason about ethical dilemmas encountered in practice" (1990, p. 22).

The application of ethical considerations to the conduct of social work research is more than an exercise in the identification of gross misdeeds of others. Many books on research ethics (or ethics chapters in research foundations texts) begin by presenting the "classic" cases of unethical behavior. Nazi cooptation of the medical profession during the Holocaust is the most horrendous example. However, the practices of presumably well-intentioned scholars like Stanley Mil-gram (1963) (authority experiments) and Laud Humphreys (1979) ("tea room" behavior) are also questioned with respect to specific practices employed in the conduct of their respective research. These are, indeed, classic illustrations of **eth-ical dilemmas** facing social work researchers. Yet, our concern is not so much that our students or the readers of this book might commit such major ethical blunders as these, but rather that "lesser" ethical quagmires are experienced in the more routine practice of social work research. It is on such everyday research ethics that we focus.

This chapter is placed near the beginning of this book because ethical con-cerns should be part of every decision you make concerning social work research. Ethics are involved in the ways we go about formulating our research questions, structuring our designs, determining our measurement systems, sampling for our data collection, managing our data, and reporting our results. In this chapter, we provide the basis for struggling with these issues as competent social work researchers. Understanding ethical principles does not offer any guarantee of clear answers to the sometimes difficult situations experienced in social work research. Rather, such understanding provides a basis from which to more fully struggle with practice and research dilemmas in order to most fully realize ethical goals and standards. By the end of the chapter, you will have sources of guidance that you can bring to bear in seeking resolutions to the ethical challenges that are imbedded in the research process.

Ethics in the Larger Society

Ethics represent a set of guidelines for behavior that reflects the values operating within the context of a relationship. This relationship may operate at quite high levels of social organization (society at large) or at more personal levels. Likewise, ethics range from a reflection of desired states in relationships (e.g., being "nice" to your neighbor) to imperatives that are mandated by law, regulation, or formal association. The range of values that is reflected in any ethical position may be quite broad—from value preferences that are so individualized as to be embodied in what might be called "personal ethics" to those values regarded by some to constitute immutable and eternal ethical principles applicable to all people in all places over all time.

Over the years, ethicists have tended to identify two broad classes of ethical principles—deontological and teleological ethics. **Deontological ethics** are those that assume the existence of those immutable principles suggested earlier. The idea that the taking of any human life is wrong, regardless of the circumstances, is an illustration of a deontological ethic. The "right" or "wrong" of any action is in the "doing," not in the consequence of the action. Thus, from a position of deontological ethics, all failure to tell the truth is unethical, even though untoward consequences may result from truth telling. In this regard, deontological ethics might be considered "ethics of means." In contrast, **teleological ethics** hold that "right" and "wrong" are judged in the outcome or consequences of some action. Nothing is ethical or unethical in and of itself; only by an analysis of its costs and benefits can an action be judged. For this reason, teleological ethics might be considered "ethics of ends." Of course, the kind of ethical cost-benefit analysis that is assumed in determining teleological ethics presupposes certain values associated with each cost and with each benefit.

In practice, the application of either deontological or teleological ethics can produce ethical dilemmas. An ethical dilemma results when two different ethical principles can be applied to the same situation to produce conflicting results. The fact is that ethical principles can only give guidance to action. Any final evaluation of ethical standing comes only after the evaluation of competing standards, and even then disagreement can persist.

Even with these limitations, every society operates with various systems of ethics in place. One system of ethical principles within a society is represented by the ethical standards that are codified into laws. Beyond the obvious (at least within our cultural experience) prohibitions against behaviors like murder and incest, our society has codified a wide range of other ethical principles concerning the use of corporal discipline in families, and other behaviors that some might consider "personal." Even in business, contract law has codified the ethical principles that guide commercial relationships.

At the personal level, most individuals hold to an individualized system of ethics that guides personal relationships. Clearly, one's personal ethics are likely to involve significant overlap with societal ethics as expressed in laws. Beyond that, however, personal ethics address the everyday issues of personal relationships such as truthfulness (but what if the truth is likely to do more harm than a "little fib"?) and interpersonal respect.

In between the societal and personal levels, many people are guided by systems of ethics that derive from their formal associations with one another. Such affiliations as religious membership, club/society membership, or membership in one's professional organizations may carry the responsibility for additional specific ethical obligations. It is these latter professional ethics to which we now turn our attention.

Ethics in Professional Social Work

All professionals have a fundamental ethical responsibility to perform in a competent manner, that is, to be accountable for their professional commitments and the means by which they achieve those commitments. From its earliest roots, professional social work has seen itself imbued with strong ethical principles. The notion of moral philanthropy clearly communicates an ethical sense on the part of early case workers. Although the specific nature of professional ethics has evolved over the past century, social workers have had an unambiguous understanding that they were a part of a *value-driven* profession. Since World War II, discussions of social work "morality" have been organized around two themes: values central to the profession (e.g., self-worth, dignity, acceptance of others, etc.) and principles to guide practice (e.g., confidentiality, workers' responsibility to oppose discrimination, etc.) (Reamer, 1990). In their most current form, these values and the practice principles that flow from them are explicitly represented in the NASW *Code of Ethics* (National Association of Social Workers, 1997).

Every social work student and practitioner should have and be familiar with the current *Code of Ethics* as the fundamental document for guidance in making ethical professional decisions. The *Code* is readily available from the national office of NASW and state chapters or can be downloaded from the World Wide Web at *www.naswdc.org*. If you do not have a copy readily available, perhaps this chapter can serve as the impetus for securing one and becoming familiar with it.

The section of the *Code* addressing its purpose begins with the statement, "Professional ethics are at the core of social work" (NASW, 1997), and proceeds to explicate the ethics of our profession by specifying six professional values. These values include service, social justice, dignity and worth of the person, importance of human relationships, integrity, and competence. The main body of the NASW *Code of Ethics* then provides the particular ethical standards that serve as guides to practice. These standards are organized around ethical responsibilities to clients, to colleagues, in practice settings, as professionals, to the profession, and to the broader society. The NASW *Code of Ethics* was crafted to inform all aspects of professional practice behaviors, including research activities.

Ethics in Social Work Research

We will raise issues for consideration in this chapter that may seem best resolved by simply *avoiding* the practice of research. But that is not possible under the NASW *Code of Ethics*. Although the *Code* speaks specifically to how research should be conducted in a number of standards, Sections 5.02(a) and (b) leave no doubt that professional social workers have clear ethical responsibilities with respect to research activities. Those sections read: "(a) Social workers should monitor and evaluate policies, the implementation of programs, and practice interventions. (b) Social workers should promote and facilitate evaluation and research to contribute to the development of knowledge" (NASW, 1997). Understand that there are ethical issues involved in failing to do social work research as much as there are ethical issues involved in doing social work research.

Moving beyond the basic mandate to "monitor and evaluate" practice and to "promote and facilitate evaluation and research," our professional ethics provide guidance at virtually every step involved in competent social work research. Social work research is ethically driven in both the "doing" of the research process at each of these steps, as well as in the interpretation and application of research findings. Note here that ethical standards shape the research process and not vice versa. Scientific study can provide essential information about what is; however, empirical research can never say what ought to be. We can study the frequency with which some ethical position is held within a sample or the consequences of particular behaviors, but we can never prove the right or wrong of any ethical position with only the tools of science.

Levy (1993) has identified four premises of ethics that need to be considered in social work practice. These premises are especially relevant to social work research given the commitment of social workers to advocating on behalf of vulnerable people. The premises concern the relative positions of actors, the relative vulnerabilities of actors, the relative risks for actors, and the relative opportunities for actors. In most social work settings, including research, the professional social worker occupies a position of higher power and less vulnerability/risk, and is the person who stands to gain more directly through the completion of a research endeavor. These differences along with social workers' ethical responsibilities require that we redouble our vigilance in seeking out and understanding the ethical guideposts that are available to us. In this chapter, we identify the ethical principles that guide social work research and demonstrate their unequivocal association with the activities that make up the research enterprise.

Learning Objectives

After reading this chapter, you should be able to identify key ethical principles related to:

1. selecting and informing persons who will participate in research
2. preventing and detecting potential harm to participants
3. reporting research
4. exploring ethical conflicts
5. listing sources of ethical guidance

Key Terms and Concepts

Equitable Selection of Subjects

The issue of selecting subjects for research, or sampling, is very important if we are to make any generalizations about our research and apply those generalizations to other people who were not actually studied. The logical requirements behind sampling strategies and the actual methods of sampling are the subject of Chapter 6. In this section, we discuss the ethical requirements that must also be considered.

The ethical principle of **equitable selection of subjects** requires that all relevant subjects (at least in theory) have an equal chance of being included in our research. You may think about this requirement from either of two perspectives—unfair inclusion or unfair exclusion. The basic principle here is that all groups should share equally in the benefits of research knowledge and also share equally in any risk posed by the process of obtaining that knowledge. In discussing the professional commitment to social justice, the NASW *Code of Ethics* calls on social workers to ensure equality of opportunity. It would be inconsistent with the idea of social justice to limit research knowledge to a particular group at the expense of less favored groups. This is particularly true of research that seeks to evaluate social programs or social policy in which the impact is likely to be different on members of nondominant groups. Likewise, in needs assessment, the exclusion of members of some groups reduces the likelihood that service needs of the excluded groups will be correctly addressed. On the other hand, it would be unethical to selectively recruit research subjects from some socially vulnerable group in cases in which the research posed substantial risks. The Tuskeegee experiment in which African American men were selected for a study of the effects of untreated syphilis violated several ethical principles, one of which was equitable selection, in that all the risk was borne by African Americans (Jones, 1981). Moreover, when the ethical mandate for equitable selection of subjects is violated, we are likely to be producing research that is of inferior quality as well as unethical. Over the years, many pharmaceutical products have been tested on samples of relatively young adult men. The principle of equitable selection of subjects would guide researchers to draw subjects of both sexes as well as across a wider age range (assuming the product being tested is ultimately intended for a market that includes men and women of varying ages). This may appear to be making a tempest in a teapot; however, failure to attend to this ethical standard can result in findings that fail to identify significant side effects for members of the population who were excluded from the study. To claim that some intervention is effective for the population when it has not been tested for subgroups in the population or to ignore the possibility of significant side effects for subgroups in the population is unethical.

We understand that the situation we have just described is common in practice. Social work interventions, like many pharmaceuticals, have not received the kind of broad population assessment that is required to make blanket statements concerning effectiveness or side effects. So, what are we to do when we are practicing at the limits of what is known? The NASW *Code of Ethics* provides some guidance. Section 1.04(c) allows that in such areas, "social workers should exercise careful judgment and take responsible steps...[including research] to ensure the competence of their work and to protect clients from harm." Such an approach is consistent with what Klein and Bloom (1994) have called using the *best available information*. Using the best available information is an ethical approach that includes drawing information from observable results; basing interventions on a conceptual framework to provide a context of meaning for results; using appropriate technology or instrumentation in measurement; acknowledging values regarding goals and actions related to the intervention; and being open to the critical response of the professional community, which permits corrective modification. Through the use of the best available information and disciplined professional experience that accumulates with practice, social workers can bring to bear a more completely developed "practice wisdom" (Klein & Bloom, 1995) to provide ethical guidance in areas where a fully formed knowledge base does not exist.

Gender.   Aside from intentional behaviors directed at selecting research subjects in other than equitable ways, bias can present itself in unintentional ways. Nelson (1994) reports that students are more likely to request female clients to participate in single-system evaluations than male clients. Without any additional information, we are not able to say that such inclusion operates to the benefit or detriment of female clients; however, the exclusion of men (or the overreliance on women) demonstrates an unintentional but nonetheless inequitable selection of subjects. Furthermore, Nelson points out that the selection of target behaviors for monitoring and the way that such behaviors are operationalized need to account for gender differences that exist.

Underrepresentation of women and women's perspectives in research has led to serious concerns about research practices (Gilligan, 1982). What we study, how we study it, and the conclusions we derive are the result of social consensus, and the exclusion of women from the process is likely to produce research of less value. To the degree that social work research is intended to improve the quality of interventions, many of which are with women, we face the likelihood of less effective practice and ethical insensitivity, if not outright unethical behavior, when we fail to consider the implications of inequitable selection of subjects.

Race and Culture.   Social work researchers can behave so as to unfairly exclude (or include) subjects by racial or cultural backgrounds. Nelson (1994) again has noted the tendency among practitioners to avoid asking clients of different ethnic backgrounds to participate in single-system designs or other practice evaluations. Although such behaviors may be grounded in the practitioner's sensitivity to concerns that some minority clients may have about research, these behaviors operate to preclude some groups from the benefits (or risks) of participation. Rather than excluding some groups from participation for any reason, it would be better to more fully explore the willingness of potential subjects to equitably participate, to fully disclose the levels of participation, and to make corrective adjustments as are available in the analysis.

Informed Consent

A first step after equitably identifying subjects for potential participation in a research project is to seek their **informed consent.** Informed consent involves securing a research subject's consent to participate in the research, after he or she has been informed with respect to the nature of the participation. The level of detail in this exposition of the project may vary from one study to another. However, in general, the following components are required: that participation is voluntary and that the subject may withdraw at any time without penalty; that information provided by the subject will be held in confidence; and that the risks and benefits of participation will be completely disclosed.

The requirement for informed consent is not unique to social work research; it is mandated by the NASW *Code of Ethics* as a part of all client relationships. Sections 1.03(a) through (f) spell out the requirements of ethical informed consent for social work practice generally, and Section 5.02(e) addresses the special requirements of informed consent in evaluation and research. According to the *Code,* informed consent should include the "nature, extent and duration of the participation requested and disclosure of the risks and benefits of participation" (NASW, 1997). Participation in research must take place without undue inducements or any penalty, implied or real, for the decision to withdraw or not participate in research at all. The *Code* also stipulates that clients have the right to ask questions. Further, it is the social worker's responsibility to ensure the client's understanding in the event that language comprehension or a lack of other capacities limits the client's ability to provide *informed* consent.

These cases of "limited capacity" to understand the nature of participation in research when providing informed consent are more common than might initially seem to be the case. Research in which subjects may suffer from developmental disabilities or cognitive impairment from any cause would involve the potentiality for limited capacity. The incidence of Alzheimer's disease among people of advanced age creates the need for special attention in securing informed consent from advanced-age seniors, especially in nursing home populations. In all research with children, the capacity to provide informed consent should be addressed by obtaining the informed consent of responsible adults. Where third parties are used to provide proxy consent for clients, it remains the social worker's responsibility to ensure that this third party is acting in a manner that is consistent with the client's best interests.

Some research methods, such as naturalistic observation or participant observation, are really not amenable to the use of informed consent. In using these methods, the social work researcher is often acting the role of a member of the group that is being studied. To secure informed consent from the members of the studied group would be to expose the true role of the researcher and potentially change the behaviors that were the subject of investigation. When the decision is made to use this kind of *blind* participant observation, the NASW *Code of Ethics* requires that "rigorous and responsible review" has found the procedures to be justified because of the study's prospective value and the lack of alternative effective methods not requiring this **deception.** Although the *Code* refers to clients in much of its discussion of informed consent, we believe that it is within the spirit of the *Code* that these prescriptions apply equally to subjects in social work research. It is very often the case that research subjects are, in fact, agency clients. When we seek to involve these people in research projects to provide generalizable knowledge, we must adhere to the requirement of informed consent consistent with our *Code of Ethics* and other regulatory requirements to be discussed in what follows.

Voluntary Participation

Voluntary participation is a principle of ethical research practice that flows directly from the requirements of informed consent. The principle of voluntary participation prohibits securing consent to participate in research through coercion. By coercion, we mean forcing participation by exercise of the social dominance of the researcher. On its face, this seems simple enough. However, avoidance of coercion requires consideration of several issues.

The first of these relates to the previously discussed standard of informed consent. It is impossible for an individual to voluntarily participate in any activity about which he or she has not been fully informed—informed consent is a necessary precondition to voluntary participation. Beyond being free to voluntarily choose to participate in a research activity about which one has been informed, this principle implies continuing rights to the subject. If a person is free to initially volunteer to participate in a project, logically one must remain free to discontinue participation, that is, to withdraw from the study.

Our second point of special concern about voluntary participation involves the use of incentives for participation. **Incentives** are items used to encourage participation in a research activity. Incentives that are symbolic and of low cost are rarely a threat to voluntary participation. However, incentives that are valuable enough to cause individuals to participate against their best interest are coercive. A good practical rule for the ethical use of incentives is to use them to provoke interest, acknowledge appreciation, or compensate for minor inconvenience. Incentives or payments should be limited to a reasonable value that can serve as a motivation or acknowledgment for participation without unduly swaying an individual to participate in an activity in which he or she would not otherwise participate.

Finally, the possibility of "coercion" should be considered whenever research involves subjects who are members of **vulnerable populations.** Vulnerable populations include mental health clients, prisoners, children, people with AIDS or other stigmatized physical illness, individuals receiving economic security benefits, people of color, women, and others. This is a broad net and we do not wish to create a uniformity that is not present. However, whenever research subjects are selected from a group that could be considered to be a vulnerable population, the researcher is responsible for ensuring that potential subjects do not feel "pressured" to participate. The nature of such pressure will vary with the nature of the vulnerability of a group. Prisoners may feel that they will be "overlooked" for benefits within the prison if they do not demonstrate their "cooperation" through research participation. Women employees in a traditional male-dominated organization may feel the need to demonstrate that they are "team players" by participating in research. In the final analysis, it is the social work researcher who must bear the responsibility that these coercive influences do not result in an ethical violation.

Privacy and Confidentiality

The standards for protecting the *privacy and confidentiality* of clients contained in the NASW *Code of Ethics* (Secs. 1.07[a] through [r]) and included in virtually all beginning practice classes are equally applicable in the practice setting defined by the relationship between a social worker and research participants. In research practice, there are additional aspects of **confidentiality** that require our attention.

An initial concern with *privacy* is raised in research when we gather data about subjects. Depending on the research methods that we employ in investigating our research question, we may or may not be explicit about the precise information that we seek from research subjects. Some methods that are intended to develop theory or an understanding of meaning systems rely more heavily on open-ended questions and an unstructured format to draw out information and seek connections among these bits of data. Other methods seek more definitive answers to predetermined questions in order to test hypothesized relationships. In these cases, the information sought may be well specified in advance. In either case, it is the ethical responsibility of the social work researcher to seek only that information that is relevant to the investigation. Admittedly, this may be a more fuzzy line of separation with some methods than with others. However, the principle is clear: Our capacity to do research with an individual is a privilege extended to us by the research subject, and within the bounds of the privilege granted to us, we have an ethical responsibility to respect that person's privacy.

Next, because the purpose of research is to identify and *make known* some aspect of human behavior, we are not going to keep research information "in the file" in the same way that we might in other practice venues. In social work research, our obligations to confidentiality are met by protecting the identity of our research subjects. In some cases, we are able to do this by maintaining subject **anonymity,** that is, collecting data in such a way that identifying information is never recorded. For example, this can be accomplished by using a mail survey that includes no identifying information in the return packet. Other times, subject confidentiality is protected by reporting information in its aggregated form only, even though raw data may contain identifying information. Data collected in this form are not anonymous, but with proper safeguards to privacy, they may be labeled *confidential.* When aggregated information is presented in findings, care must still be taken that no category is so small as to allow the identification of a research participant. As always, it is the responsibility of the social work researcher to ensure that the subjects' identities cannot be deduced.

A final special circumstance of **respect for privacy** and confidentiality in the research relationship involves the maintenance of subject records. As indicated, we are sometimes able to ensure confidentiality by using anonymously provided information. When this is not possible, we can use an array of social work practice procedures for protecting confidentiality (e.g., not discussing individual subjects, keeping records locked or otherwise secured, etc.). One major difference (and advantage with respect to maintaining confidentiality) in research records is that in many cases the connection (i.e., identifier) between an individual and his or her research information can be severed, thus ensuring permanent confidentiality. For example, imagine conducting a research project involving a comparison between clients' status on some outcome variable before they receive a new agency-sponsored intervention and after the intervention has been provided. The need to connect these pretest scores with posttest scores would likely preclude the possibility that the research would be done anonymously. Typically, in such circumstances, individuals are given identifying numbers and a master list is maintained to associate those numbers with the people they represent. However, after all of the data have been collected, entered into a format appropriate for analysis, screened for correctness, and analyzed, there would be no reason for maintaining the master list. The destruction of that list eliminates most reasonable possibilities of ever identifying an individual with any particular research response. Some researchers believe that it is better to continue to maintain confidential control over these master lists. However, once you are certain that you will no longer need to associate particular responses with particular persons, the continued existence of a master list creates both an unnecessary responsibility for the researcher and an unnecessary risk to the privacy of the research subjects.

Reasonable Risk/Harm to Subjects

Those who voluntarily accept participation in research activities should be free from unreasonable **risk of harm** as a result of that participation. Many research studies have at least some level of risk of harm, although the nature of the harm and the extent of the risk vary widely. What if someone agrees to participate in a study of injection drug use and those research records are subpoenaed into a court proceeding? What if by voluntarily agreeing to participate in a randomized clinical trial comparing two interventions, an individual fails to receive an intervention that is ultimately shown to be superior? These are only two of many very real situations in which research subjects do face the risk of real harm. How are these circumstances reconciled with our ethical requirement to avoid harming subjects?

What Constitutes Risk and Harm?   In the extreme, we are surrounded by risk all of the time. Any time we choose to take some action, we experience opportunity costs: the loss of benefits associated with other actions that we might have taken. With every behavior, we risk the results of the action taken as well as those potential benefits associated with actions that we have foregone. When research subjects experience such risks are we violating our ethical standards? We do not believe so. However, if we were aware that an individual would *actually miss a known and certain benefit* as a result of participation in our research *and we failed to inform the participant* of that eventuality, we believe that we would have violated our ethical obligation. The ethical issue here is that full disclosure to the potential research subject is necessary so that he or she can assess the reasonableness of the risk.

In light of the wide range of potential risk, is it possible to actually provide full disclosure of *all* risks to research subjects—even those that are likely to be completely inconsequential? The *level of risk* associated with some actions would be generally agreed on by virtually all potential research participants, whereas other risks might be differentially evaluated by individuals. By identifying all *reasonable* risks to potential subjects, we are empowering them to make the determination of acceptable risk. A part of this personal evaluation involves the benefits that may result from the research. Generally, these benefits are considered in the larger social sense—for instance, what might be learned may benefit *others*—although the direct benefits to individuals participating are sometimes also considered. Thus, because you may have had personal experiences with a particular disease or disorder, you may be willing to accept a higher risk of harm than some other person. As long as the level of risk does not rise so high as to represent a virtual certainty of harm, there is nothing unethical about your fully informed decision to take the risk.

The Paradox of Payment.   Ruth Macklin (1989) has identified a curious paradox in evaluating the risks and benefits to research subjects. If payment is considered as a benefit resulting from participation in research, then it follows that higher payments result in higher benefits, and higher benefits are likely to balance higher risk. At the same time, as the level of payment to a research subject increases, the likelihood that the payment acts as a coercive influence also increases. Participants may "agree" to assume higher risks than would otherwise have been the case. This means high payments result in research that is less acceptable—and therein lies the paradox.

Although some, including Macklin, are concerned that any payment to "patients" or clients for participation in research that might serve some therapeutic purpose with respect to their own condition is unethical, we believe that the larger question involves the use of "payment" at all. As we discussed earlier, this is one of those gray areas in which some arbitrary standard for the "appropriate" level of payments does not exist. For us, the resolution of the payment issue is twofold. First, in general, payments to research participants should be valued at a level that expresses a "token" appreciation for participation. Research on survey methods suggests that the value of incentive payments is not so important as the social statement that the offer of an incentive makes (Erdos, 1983). Beyond this, if the payment is actually intended as a "payment" rather than as a token "incentive" to participate, it should reflect a reasonably low wage scale. One or two times the federal minimum wage (say, $10) does not seem coercive to us as a "payment" for participation in a lengthy (45–60-minute) face-to-face interview. When in doubt, however, our strongest counsel is to consult with respected colleagues about the value that any incentive offered might take.

Withholding Treatment

Later in this book, we will make the case that some kinds of research questions are best tested through experimental or quasi-experimental designs. One feature of these designs is to withhold treatment from participants under certain conditions. Although strengthening the test of the research question, this practice may also create an ethical dilemma. There are two conditions under which withholding interventions from research subjects is a preferred form of research. The first of these involves the creation of a **control group**—a group of research subjects from whom the intervention being tested is withheld in order to draw comparisons to another group of subjects who receive the intervention. The other condition in which an intervention might be withheld or even withdrawn is in the use of **single-system designs**—again for the purpose of drawing comparisons between the subjects' conditions. Such a practice may be ethical or not. Let's look at each.

Control Groups.   As you will learn in Chapter 5, control groups are a necessary part of a family of research designs called true experiments. **True experiments** are powerful tools that allow strong inferences to be made about the potential causes of behaviors under study. Although these designs may provide the strongest evidence regarding the effectiveness of interventions, they require exercise of considerable power over participants, including withholding treatment from one group of participants. In some cases, this practice seems justified; in others, it is not.

The ethical question that some people raise is, "How can we ethically decide to give the new intervention being tested to some subjects but refuse to provide it to others?" Resolution of this concern involves three important issues. These are the presumed efficacy of the intervention being tested, the nature of the disclosure and the assignment of subjects to the control group, and the provisions for follow-up services with the control group members.

First, let's consider the presumed efficacy of intervention. Remember that the intervention is being tested with a true experimental design involving a control group *because* we want to know *whether* it is effective. Too often, people are prone to believing that the *new approach* is the best approach. If we were certain of this, there would be no point in subjecting the intervention to clinical trials. However, it is precisely because we do not know whether the intervention is effective that we are testing it. Thus, although we are withholding the intervention from the control group, we are withholding an intervention of uncertain effect. The members of the control group may actually avoid being subjected to an ineffective treatment. In that case, we might better question the ethics of applying the intervention to the members of the experimental group who received the new treatment.

The second ethical issue involved in the use of control groups concerns the degree to which subjects are told of the intervention and the manner in which subjects are assigned to either the treatment or control group. Consistent with the ethical standards that have already been discussed in this chapter, informed consent and voluntary participation require us to disclose the nature of the research as well as the risks and benefits that are associated with participation in the study. The fact that control groups will be used is certainly a part of what we have called the "nature of the research." In addition, the means by which subjects are determined to either receive or not receive the intervention is a part of that nature. For reasons that will be developed more fully in subsequent chapters, we recommend that a random assignment procedure be used. In this way, each subject has an equal (fair) chance of receiving or not receiving the intervention being tested. Being provided with this information as a part of the informed consent procedure empowers individuals to determine for themselves whether they wish to participate in the study.

Finally, the follow-up provisions that are made for research subjects in the control group are an important part of a full ethical use of control groups. At a minimum, members of the control group should have the option of becoming first-priority consumers of the intervention should it be shown to be efficacious. In this way, any harm that they may have suffered as a result of their control group participation might be minimized or eliminated through the provision of the (now known to be) effective intervention.

The recognition and application of these three safeguards in concert provide an ethical basis for the use of control groups. With a recognition that an intervention may or may not be effective, fully informed individuals can agree to be randomly assigned to either treatment or control groups. If the intervention is found to be effective, control group members who wish to receive the treatment may elect to do so.

Single-System Designs.   Single-system designs (SSDs) are a family of research designs that are extremely important in evaluating social work practice. These designs were developed to look at *single systems*—quite often individuals—to determine if targeted behaviors are changing in intended directions. In contrast to research using control groups in which comparisons are made between the different groups, in SSDs, the comparisons are made between the different patterns of an individual's (or single system's) own behavior at different points in time. The ethical question arises when a treatment might be delayed in order to facilitate these comparisons.

A part of every ethical social work intervention involves assessment. The purpose of the assessment is to understand the nature of the client's problem as well as the level or degree to which the problem exists. Appropriate assessment information may be acquired by interviewing the client about current and past states of the problem, asking the client to complete standardized assessment scales, using behavioral checklists with the client, or from still other sources. Depending on the nature of the client's presenting problems, the assessment may span more than one session, and any intervention may be appropriately delayed until after the assessment is completed. During this period prior to the initiation of the formal intervention, continued assessment of the client's problems can take place.

In the language of SSDs, this period of assessment, which occurs before the intervention is initiated, is a part of a **baseline period.** It is used as the standard of comparison against which the client's progress (or lack thereof) under the condition of the intervention can be evaluated. As such, it presents no challenge to any ethical expectation. However, delaying an intervention that is *clearly required* constitutes an ethical violation. If a new client presented even modestly unambiguous indications of harming himself, herself, or others, the ethical response would be to intervene immediately (although that intervention may still take various theoretically appropriate courses). However, by far, the majority of cases with which social workers are involved allow for a more unhurried approach to assessment. In these cases, delaying a treatment in order to establish a baseline in an SSD presents no ethical difficulty. Later in this chapter, we return to this as well as several other ethical issues that have been raised in the use of SSDs.

Deception and Debriefing

Social workers should avoid using research methods that involve deception. Use of deception in research is inconsistent with the ethical requirement to inform research subjects about the study in which they are participating. However, in situations in which disclosure of some aspects of the research is likely to bias the responses of an individual (but not jeopardize his or her participation), it may be ethically defensible to withhold disclosure of those aspects, at least for a time.

If a research proposal involves deception, it is imperative that the opinions of colleagues be sought. More formally, such a research proposal must be presented to the appropriate **institutional review board** for its approval. Either colleagues or the institutional review board can potentially provide suggestions for alternative research designs that do not require deception. In the final analysis, colleagues and institutional review boards can also help us "put on the brakes" before we commit ethical violations.

If, after a full and thorough review, a research design involving deception is approved and implemented, the informed consent procedure needs to be crafted in such a way that subjects are made aware that deception may exist even though they aren't told the specific form that it might take. Further, the researcher has an ethical responsibility to fully **debrief** research subjects. This involves a complete explanation of the research including the deception. If after debriefing, the subjects are still not comfortable with some aspect of their participation, it is the researcher's responsibility to provide such services as may be necessary to restore the client to the preresearch state. If this sounds like a major responsibility, we have made our point. When researchers assume the responsibility for deception, they must also assume the responsibility for the consequences of that deception. It is not a matter to be taken lightly.

Data Monitoring

In practice-oriented research, the researcher has an ethical responsibility to monitor research results throughout the process and modify or terminate the study if clear evidence of either unanticipated harm or clear benefits emerges. As research is proceeding, the researcher has an ethical responsibility for maintaining the integrity of the data and for monitoring the data for preliminary findings. These findings may reflect unanticipated negative consequences as well as those that are strongly supportive of the research hypothesis. In each case, the researcher may have an ethical responsibility for prematurely terminating the investigation, albeit for different reasons. If **data monitoring** demonstrates that the research is producing unanticipated negative consequences for some or all of the subjects, the ethical response is likely to terminate the study. Because these negative consequences were unanticipated, it would have been impossible for subjects to have been informed of them in advance. Because these newly recognized consequences presumably involve some significant risk of harm to the subjects, the ethical standards already discussed require their disclosure. The biasing effect of such disclosure may potentially invalidate the results of the study, thus justifying its termination.

Data monitoring that clearly indicates strongly positive results may also justify premature termination. In this case, the concern is positive regard for subjects who may be in a control group. If the measured effect of the intervention is so large as to eliminate the likelihood of chance fluctuation, only limited additional information may be gained by continuing the study. If this is the case, termination of the study allows that the now-confirmed effective intervention can be offered to control group members consistent with professional ethics.

Reporting Research

One might think that when only the final write-up of a research endeavor remains, all of the ethical challenges would be past. Not so! Even in report writing, the requirements of ethical behavior prevail. In this section, we discuss ethical considerations related to several major considerations in writing research reports.

Objectivity in Judgment.   Interpretation of research findings is also subject to ethical standards. All science involves some degree of interpretation and filtering of experience. The nature of that filtering determines the degree of objectivity (intersubjectivity) of conclusions drawn from research. An important ethical responsibility of social work researchers is to document the process by which generalizations are drawn from observations. Because analysis of numeric data involves application of simple, well-defined manipulations of data, intersubjectivity is potentially high for these kinds of data. However, exploratory studies, and in particular those that employ open-response-format questions and nonnumeric data, may proceed from data collection to interpretation through methods that are not always well specified. In all types of research, but particularly in the exploratory, nonnumeric types, it is ethically required that the connection between observations on one hand, and interpretation and conclusion on the other be clearly specified. This is partly a question of competent data analysis (Chapters 8 and 9) and also extends to writing conclusions and recommendations. The important distinction is in documentation of how *observations are represented and meanings extracted.* By its nature, quantitative measurement requires that the coding schema of measurement be established a priori—in advance of measurements being taken. In the process of such measurement systems being established, they are (or at least should be as a matter of both good practice and ethics) exposed to thorough validation procedures that evaluate the adequacy of the measurement system. Thus, by the time the measurement system is used, it should have passed muster with respect to its fundamental conceptualization and the way that meaning is to be attached to specific observations. (These processes do not offer any guarantees with respect to the ethical *use* of the measurement system, only the safeguard provided by intentional professional scrutiny of the measurement system that the conceptualizations behind the system are reasonable.)

Nonnumeric measurement also requires that meaning be attached to the observations made. However, in the case of exploratory studies using nonnumeric data, much of the "meaning attachment" process comes *after* the observation is made. This is an appropriate and even essential approach in some research areas. However, the ethical challenge arises when individual researchers conduct their meaning attachment activities without documentation or regard for alternative interpretations. As we will discuss throughout this book, the human mind is adept at finding that for which it is looking. Ethical researchers must be conscious of the imposition of meaning on data and report fully the meaning attachment and interpretation procedures in the final report.

Proper Credit.   Research activities are frequently the result of contributions of many individuals. Some of these have directly contributed to the implementation of a study; others have provided the intellectual foundation on which the study stands. The general ethical principle is that it is improper to take credit for another's work or fail to acknowledge substantial contributions of others. People who contribute in important ways to a particular study are acknowledged as coauthors or in footnotes. Persons on whose work a study is based are generally referenced within the report. The most basic of these failures concerns the full citation of others' work. It might be argued that much of what each of us knows we learned by reading the work of others. Although this may be true, what is of concern here is the direct use of others' work as a kind of "building block" on which our own work rests. When we cross that invisible and somewhat arbitrary line between what informed people are generally likely to know and the stepping-stone pieces of knowledge that have been provided by our intellectual predecessors in the area, and on which our argument is based, we need to give **proper credit.** Although the specific form that proper citation is expected to take may vary by the context, it is expected to contain all of the necessary information to allow a reader to locate the original information source.

Section 4.08 of the NASW *Code of Ethics* requires that "(a) Social workers should take responsibility and credit, including authorship credit, only for work they have actually performed and to which they have contributed. (b) Social workers should honestly acknowledge the work of and the contributions made by others" (NASW, 1997). Depending on the degree of participation, this may take the form of shared authorship on a final report or other publication that evolves from the project. In other cases, due credit may be given with an acknowledgment provided in a preface or even a footnote. The operating principle that we offer in acknowledging colleagues in research is that those who make *creative or intellectual contributions* over and above what is involved in the physical conduct of research should be formally acknowledged in some way, and others may be acknowledged as well.

Looking "Beyond the Moment."   The researcher's ethical responsibilities continue even beyond reporting the basic research findings. How are unexpected results to be handled? There are explicit analytical requirements for reporting findings that just "popped up" in post hoc analysis. We believe that such findings must be appropriately explained so that they might be given proper interpretation.

Similarly, are there ethical requirements for reporting unpopular results? Is there an ethical responsibility for reporting all findings or can those that might incur some "political fallout" be sidestepped? Although it may not be comfortable, we believe that all substantive findings should be reported. That said, we also believe that there are contexts in which certain questions cannot be explored with sufficient objectivity or in which the results have a high probability of being used as tools of exploitation or oppression. As we discussed earlier, the methods of science provide useful tools for minimizing errors and distortions, but highly charged social contexts and poorly conceptualized questions may overwhelm even the most careful researcher. When the damage produced by a study will more than offset any value that is likely to be derived from the actual research findings, it may be wise and ethical to terminate the effort.

Failure to communicate negative results—that is, those studies in which the evidence did not support the research hypothesis—constitutes an important problem in social work research. Thomas Edison indicated that he learned more from his mistakes than from his successes. Yet, Western scholarship is organized around a system that generally offers publication forums to findings that achieve **statistical significance** or some other indication of support for the research hypothesis. Although this may save us all from reading countless studies that failed to produce statistically significant findings, it also leaves the door wide open for those unsuccessful studies to be unknowingly replicated again and again. If the failure to confirm the hypothesis is likely to be due to limitations in the design and implementation of the study, an ethical violation may be suggested, that is, incompetent research is no more acceptable than incompetent practice in that it wastes resources and exposes clients needlessly to risk. If, however, failure to confirm the research hypothesis reflects an ineffective intervention, our ethical commitment to knowledge building would be better served with a forum for sharing our negative results as well as those that are positive.

Oftentimes, new research uncovers conflicts with previous research. These conflicts need to be exposed and a reconciliation between them sought. It is hardly enough to say to the readers of our research report, even implicitly, "There; I've shown that a conflict exists between my findings and those previously shown. Somebody is clearly wrong—go figure it out." At a minimum, researchers have an ethical responsibility to suggest future directions for research and theory development. Jones (1990) writes: "The researcher does not discharge his [sic] full responsibility to science by simply reporting research findings. There is also a responsibility to offer more general conclusions and explanations which will lend insight into and understanding of occurrences" (p. 689).

Sources of Ethical Guidance

NASW *Code of Ethics*

Much has been said in this chapter about the National Association of Social Workers *Code of Ethics*. It is a superb document that acknowledges in its preamble that ethical practice is not a matter of clearly defined "wrongs" and "rights." Instead, "core values, and the [ethical] principles that flow from them, must be balanced within the context and complexity of human experience" (NASW, 1997). In this regard, we view the *Code* as a kind of a road map to ethical practice in which the major intersections or ethical guideposts are marked. We are left to discover the ethical routings among these guideposts representing the core values of the profession.

We have earlier said that all social workers should be familiar with their *Code of Ethics*. But beyond some general familiarity, we strongly encourage social workers, especially those involved in social work research, to return to the *Code* whenever they are confronted with ethical challenges. As suggested in the preamble of the *Code* quoted earlier, the purpose of such reference will not be to provide definitive answers for these challenges, but to provide assistance in struggling through to their ethical resolution.

The applicability of the NASW *Code of Ethics* to the research process should have been made clear in the preceding sections. We hope that each of our readers values its relevance and incorporates its guidance into their own social work practice.

Code of Federal Regulations

A professional code of ethics, like the NASW *Code of Ethics,* applies only to the members of the professional association that promulgates the code. In order to ensure compliance with general ethical standards across all disciplines, the federal government incorporated a set of standards into the *Code of Federal Regulations* (1997). These regulations are applicable to any biomedical or behavioral research that involves human subjects. Thus, as a practical matter, all of the research likely to be of interest to social workers falls under the purview of these federal guidelines. However, no social work researcher should feel overly burdened by compliance with **45 CFR 46,** for the principles that it puts forth are generally included in the NASW *Code of Ethics* with which compliance is already required.

Paralleling the NASW *Code,* 45 CFR 46 sets forth the principles of minimal risk to subjects, equitable selection of subjects, requirements of privacy and confidentiality, informed consent by subjects, and data monitoring. In order to ensure compliance with these standards, 45 CFR 46 also requires organizations to establish *institutional review boards.* Although the NASW *Code of Ethics* does not require agencies to establish these review panels, it does require that social work researchers consult with appropriate institutional review boards as a part of ensuring subjects' rights and protections (NASW, 1997, Sec. 5.02[d]).

Institutional Review Boards.   Institutional review boards (IRBs) are required in all organizations that receive federal funding and participate in biomedical or behavioral research. The federal funding does not need to be targeted in support of the research. Thus, most human service agencies through whom research subjects might be identified should have an IRB in place. As a practical matter, agencies in which *generalizable* research (intended for purposes other than internal quality assurance or client evaluation) is rarely done are probably quite safe with a written policy identifying a review procedure to be used should research be proposed. On the other hand, universities, colleges, hospitals, and community mental health agencies should have functioning IRBs.

Grigsby and Roof (1993) have suggested that social work researchers may be uninformed or inexperienced in dealing with IRBs. We expect that this may be true as well. Much of the research that social work practitioners do is evaluative in nature (internal quality assurance or single-system designs) and not intended to be generalized beyond the agency or organization in which it is performed. This is an important distinction, because the federal regulations define research requiring the review of an IRB as involving those scientific activities that contribute to a *generalizable knowledge.* The intention to publish research findings for a wider audience would be an indication of the attempt to produce generalizable knowledge and consequently require IRB approval. As a result, many social workers have not needed to become familiar with IRB procedures.

In our experience, it seems that IRBs are often thought of as one more "bureaucratic layer" at best and the "ethics police" at worst. We encourage a more tempered view. The role of IRBs is to review and approve research proposals that do not pose unacceptable ethical risks. In those cases that have potential ethical problems, a good IRB should make suggestions for how the proposal might be modified to meet ethical standards. Because ethical judgments are not always clear and because it is sometimes true that researchers fail to see all of the ethical implications that might be present in a particular case, IRBs should be thought of as allies in our commitment to maintain ethical practice.

There are a number of common research situations in which a research project might be exempt from IRB review. In general, studies that are exempt from review are those that pose *absolutely no risk* to research participants because participants are able to remain *anonymous* or because the behaviors and issues being studied have *no potential* for causing the research participants embarrassment or any other kind of harm. These standards are likely to be more narrowly imposed if the research involves vulnerable populations, like children, nursing home residents, prisoners, and others who may not be fully able to advocate on their own behalf.

In addition to seeking to advance a more collaborative view of IRBs among new researchers, we hope that we are also contributing to a future where all IRBs might more fully assume their responsibilities for providing ethical guidance and suggestion, rather than limiting their role to more basic review and rejection of proposals that raise ethical challenges. We fully expect that in the next few years, some of you who are reading about IRBs today will be asked to serve your organizations through membership on an IRB. When that happens, we wish you well as you wrestle with these complex and engaging ideas, and we hope that the discussions in this chapter might provide you with an initial foundation.

Consultation

IRBs represent a unique kind of professional consultation and we believe they should be fully utilized to ensure high ethical standards. However, informal consultation with colleagues provides a source of ethical litmus testing that is also extremely valuable. We have found value in posing friendly ethical "debates" with colleagues who are familiar with our research question and methods, as well as with colleagues for whom the context of the debate is new. Each can be very valuable in providing unique ethical perspectives that may not have been considered.

Let us share a fun example. Over the years, one of the authors has mentally toyed with the idea of using ultraviolet code numbers on surveys for the purpose of reducing follow-up mailings to nonrespondents. These numbers would be invisible except when viewed under a special light. Numbers using visible ink are often used in survey research in order to save money on follow-up mailings and to avoid troubling respondents with second and third mailings after they have shown the courtesy of responding to the survey. In this mental experiment, the ultraviolet code numbers would be used *only* for the purpose of eliminating participants from follow-up mailings. Confidentiality rather than anonymity would be indicated in the informed consent statement, and the ultraviolet identifier would be physically removed immediately on deleting the respondent's name from the follow-up mailing lists. Is this an ethical violation? One of us says, "Yes, absolutely," and the other thinks, "Probably not." More important, because the debate has been posed with a number of colleagues and the resolution to the question is not at all clear, the procedure has not been employed. Moreover, periodic debates of this nature pave the way for more substantive ethical discussions when those issues arise.

Special Guidelines in Single-System Designs

The use of single-system designs (SSDs) has raised a special set of ethical questions in research. Because SSDs are so well suited for use in social work practice, it is appropriate to address the ethical concerns in the use of SSDs in a dedicated section. We first review the concern already noted regarding the delay of treatment that may be involved in establishing a baseline in a SSD. Then, we will turn to ethical concerns involving the withdrawal of an intervention and informed consent.

You will recall that SSDs typically involve the comparison of a client's level on some variable (the **change target** for the social work intervention) before the treatment is implemented with the client's level on that variable after the treatment has been initiated. A stable pretreatment level of the change variable should be established so that accurate comparisons can be made with the posttreatment levels. This way, both the social worker and the client will be able to see that change has taken place. Ideally, this stable baseline measurement is able to be established during the assessment phase of the social work process. However, it is sometimes necessary and appropriate that the actual treatment phase of the intervention be postponed until a relatively stable baseline is established. Herein lies the ethical challenge. As indicated before, unless the client's problem presents an immediate threat of harm to himself, herself, or others, we believe that more is to be gained (a teleological ethical value) by obtaining the stable baseline measurement against which to measure the desired change. If, after a reasonable period of time, a stable baseline does not emerge, it is possible that the treatment goal is to establish that kind of stability at a level that is acceptable to the client. However, in the absence of baseline measurement, the social worker and client will be unable to distinguish session-to-session "change" from the chance fluctuation that was observed during the unstable baseline period.

A related ethical concern involves an SSD called a "withdrawal design." **Withdrawal designs** follow the same basic pattern of SSDs by beginning with a baseline phase followed by the treatment phase. However, after the target change has been achieved, the treatment is withdrawn in order to observe changes in the target variable. For example, consider the use of a behavioral technique or a psychotropic medication for the management of some client problem. If the problem behavior has dropped off to acceptable levels during the treatment phase and it increases concurrently with the withdrawal of the treatment, both the social worker and the client have strong reason to believe that the amelioration of the problem was related to the application of the treatment. Reinitiation of the treatment and a subsequent diminution of the problem variable strengthens this inference even further.

When such withdrawal designs are intentionally considered and employed with full knowledge and consent of the client, we see no ethical violation. They serve important evaluative purposes and are in the best interest of the client as well as the social worker with an interest in continuous quality improvement. Of course, if there are reasons to suspect that the withdrawal of the treatment variable would have strong or irreversible negative effects on the client, the use of withdrawal designs would not be ethically justified. As always, the goals of practice must dictate the methods of evaluation.

A unique issue concerns the need to submit SSDs to an IRB for review and approval, as well as the need to follow the kind of informed consent procedures outlined before. These issues hinge on the legitimate question as to whether SSDs constitute "research" as interpreted by federal guidelines and others or whether they are more appropriately considered to be evaluative tools that fall outside the parameters of "research." Federal guidelines have generally been interpreted to define research as composed of those scientific activities aimed at producing *generalizable* knowledge. We have alluded to this distinction in some of our previous comments. Federal guidelines for the involvement of human subjects in research were more generally conceptualized with an experimental model of research in mind. In this model, a research question is explicitly formulated, an appropriate research design developed, and subjects recruited for participation. In contrast, **practice evaluation** involves a process that incorporates many of the tools of research but is applied to research "subjects" whose *primary involvement* in the process is the amelioration of some presenting problem in their interaction with the social environment in which they live. The "research" involvement is secondary to the therapeutic relationship. The former model of research is intended to answer specific questions and provide the newly acquired insights to others in the scientific community and beyond. In the latter model—practice evaluation—the goal is to ensure that the goals of practice with a particular client system have been met. New knowledge or insights are a valuable potential outcome, but are secondary to the goal of evaluating effective practice. This distinction has important ramifications with respect to the requirements for IRB review and for informed consent procedures.

In short, if SSDs are employed as a model of practice evaluation and *do not have wider generalization as a purpose,* the consensus is that they are not covered by the definition of "research" in federal regulations (Grigsby and Roof, 1993). In that case, SSDs used for practice evaluation do not require approval by an IRB for use. Moreover, it is similarly not necessary for other kinds of agency-based quality assurance or program evaluation *that do not have wider generalization as a purpose* to seek IRB approval. If, however, an organization would wish to have the additional assurance of ethical compliance in the use of these designs, Nelson (1994) has suggested the use of internal committees capable of providing prompt review for these evaluative designs.

One might argue then that if 45 CFR 46 does not consider SSDs as "research," the requirement for informed consent of client/subjects is also unnecessary. With respect to the federal regulations, this may indeed be true. However, all social work practice, including research, is subject to the NASW *Code of Ethics.* The *Code* makes clear that informed consent procedures are a requirement of ethical practice whether a participant in an SSD is defined as a client (Secs. 1.03[a] through [f]) or a research subject (Sec. 5.02[e]). Furthermore, Millstein, Dare-Winters, and Sullivan (1994) note that silence about our evaluative efforts can offer significant negative impacts on the practice relationship.

Martin Bloom and John Orme (1993) have provided 10 ethical principles that serve to guide single-system evaluation. These draw heavily from traditional ethical thought, but are applied to the specific context of social work practice. We share their 10 principles to further advance the ethical use of these powerful tools in the evaluation of social work practice.

1. Provide demonstrable help.
2. Demonstrate that no harm is done.
3. Because evaluation is intrinsic to good practice, the practitioner should involve the client in the consideration of evaluation of his or her situation while coming to agreement on the overall practice relationship.
4. Involve the client in the identification of the specific problem and/or objective, and in the data collection process, as far as possible.
5. Evaluation should enhance practice, not impede it. Evaluation should intrude as little as possible on the intervention process, while still being capable of collecting useful and usable information.
6. Stop evaluation whenever it is painful or harmful to the client physically, psychologically, or socially, without prejudice to the services offered.
7. Maintain confidentiality with regard to the data resulting from evaluation of the client/situation.
8. Balance the benefits of evaluating practice against the costs of not evaluating practice.
9. Provide a client bill of rights as an intrinsic part of a code of ethics for evaluating practice.
10. Include evaluation as part of any formal or informal theory of practice. Recognize that any evaluation process reflects the values of the researcher.

By understanding these 10 principles and employing them in practice, we believe that the likelihood of ethically applying SSDs will be ensured.

Sources of Ethical Conflict

The chapter has been about recognizing and resolving the kinds of ethical conflicts that occur in social work research. There is the well-known adage that the best defense is often a strong offense. In that regard, we are well served by a brief exploration of some of the common circumstances from which ethical conflicts arise. When situations that are ripe with ethical challenges arise, we are well served by early recognition of them. These include differences among agency, worker, and client values or desires; the interest that researchers or their employers often have in "confirming" a desired outcome; and the impact that funding sources may have on research decisions.

Agency-Worker-Client Differences

It is not unusual for agencies, the social workers employed by them, and the clients served to have different interests, or at least different approaches to the achievement of those interests. The very first ethical standard in the NASW *Code of Ethics* states: "Social workers' primary responsibility is to promote the well-being of clients" (1997, Sec. 1.01). This commitment may be superseded only in cases of conflict with larger societal goals or specific legal obligations. At the same time, the *Code* calls social workers to "take reasonable steps to ensure that their employing organizations' practices are consistent with the NASW *Code of Ethics*" (Sec. 3.09[d]).

We believe that these two statements provide the basis on which ethical differences among these parties might be successfully resolved. We recognize that this is more easily said than done. However, if social workers in all facets of human service organizations operate under the guidance of the NASW *Code*, a productive foundation is in place. If one finds that ethical conflicts are a common feature of practice within an agency, it might be advisable to form an ethics committee. We would suggest that this group should not function as some kind of arbitrating tribunal, but rather as a forum where ethical issues—presently operating or as anticipated scenarios—might be considered and discussed in order to identify a range of potential solutions. This is consistent with the ethical practice that we have promoted throughout this chapter. Practice contexts in which ethical challenges do not arise are not realistic; practice contexts in which forums do not exist for the successful resolution of ethical challenges do not represent good practice.

Desire for "Confirmation" (Preordained Outcomes)

There are times when new approaches to service delivery or problem intervention appear so attractive that strong forces emerge to "prove" that the new approach "works." This is dangerous thinking. We often see a milder version in our students when they propose research that will "prove that intervention X works better than the traditional approach to services." Whenever research is undertaken to prove a point, special caution must be exercised to maintain the kind of objective standards that would allow the same findings to be replicated by other researchers.

In the extreme, "research" is sometimes proposed in which there can be only one acceptable answer. Such activities are not research. Rather, they are a set of scientific-looking activities that are contrived to perpetrate or maintain a myth. This is strong language, but we feel strongly. If any research project is not open equally to the possibility of its being "wrong" as well as its being "right," it is an unethical hoax that cannot be called research at all. Preordained conclusions have no place in ethical research.

Funding (Whose Priorities? What Pressures?)

It is an unfortunate reality that much quality research tends to be resource-intensive. Generally, the demand for resources is met by seeking and securing outside funding for research projects. It is also true that resources in support of research sometimes come with funders' expectations attached. The best way to avoid ethical conflicts with funders, real or potential, is to be explicit about the goals and methods of the proposed research. When differences exist with respect to priorities, we believe that all interests are best served when those differences are placed on the table for open discussion. If mutually acceptable compromises cannot be determined concerning research methods and standards, the collaboration should not be pursued. It is far easier to terminate a planning process than a research project that is in full implementation.

Summary

The discussion of ethical behavior is rich for fruitful debate. In this chapter, we have reviewed the role of ethics in society, in a profession, and, most especially, in social work research. We have considered a number of specific research areas that require special ethical attention, the sources to which one can turn for ethical guidance, and some common circumstances from which ethical challenges arise. Throughout all of this, we have been consistent in our view that the final resolution of any ethical challenge comes as a result of reflection and debate involving sometimes competing ethical principles.

Charles Levy has offered six brief questions to guide social workers through this complex maze of factors. We believe that his questions provide a fitting summary to this chapter.

1. What principles of ethics are applicable in the practice situation, and to whom (or to what) are they applicable?
2. In relation to the social worker's primary responsibilities, how may priorities be justifiably ordered when ranking both the applicable principles of ethics and those (persons and interests) to whom they are applicable?

3. What are the risks and probable consequences to be taken into account by the social worker when making ethical judgments in a practice situation?
4. What considerations and values are sufficiently compelling to supersede the principles of ethics that might otherwise be suited to the practice situation?
5. What provisions and precautions will be required of the social worker in order to cope with the consequences of the social worker's ethical judgments and actions?
6. How can the contemplated decisions and actions be evaluated in the context of ethical and professional responsibility? (Levy, 1993, p. 53)

3 Formulation of Research Questions

Asking Questions

Relationship of This Chapter to the Whole

Science is as much about asking questions as it is about finding answers. Good questions are important because a good question is likely to point to the path containing its answer. In this chapter, we discuss how cultural knowledge, logic, and knowledge of empirical methods are used to phrase useful questions. It is important to note that not all important questions are researchable. By this, we mean that only some questions are expressed in ways that allow empirical investigation—what we call researchable questions—and other questions are expressed in ways that are not subject to such exploration. Examples of researchable questions include anything from uncovering the personal meaning systems of individuals to confirmation of certain causal/functional relationships. Questions not subject to empirical exploration include matters of faith, taste, or preference when these are expressed in terms of value or worth. Also poorly worded or vague questions are potentially unresearchable. Professionally useful research questions are likely to be those that are conceptualized clearly, make reference to observables, allow multiple answers, and are testable in principle. In addition to these criteria, professionally useful research questions should also be about something that is important, at least in proportion to the resources required to obtain an answer.

It is important to note that research questions are sociocultural in origin, that is, research questions emerge from cultural contexts and reflect the value base and knowledge of the questioner. We propose that questions social scientists choose to study, or choose not to study, are the consequences of sociopolitical forces, past and present, and do not result exclusively from a rational process of taking existing theory to the next step. Sociopolitical forces may do much to maintain the positive relevance of research or they may result in potentially important, but "unfashionable" questions receiving little attention.

Likewise, the research training of the questioner and personal preferences for styles of research will also influence the choice of a research question and the form of its expression. An old Americanism states that "When all you have is a hammer, everything looks like a nail." This applies equally to incompletely trained persons who persistently attempt to apply the methods of experimentation, field research, or some other favorite method in inappropriate contexts. As will be discussed, having enough tools in your kit to select one appropriate to the question, rather than rephrasing the question to match your tools, is one mark of a well-trained empirical social worker. In this context, we suggest that the values and knowledge of stakeholders—persons likely to be affected by the results of an empirical investigation of a question—be included in question formulation.

Relevance to the Roles of Social Workers

A prominent experimental social scientist visiting a small college campus asked a gathering of students what they found the most difficult about their research methods courses. One surprising answer was "Finding a question to study!" This is a common complaint among students in social work research classes. Many instructors require students to design and/or conduct a research study as part of their training. Students frequently report spending an inordinate amount of time in the selection of a topic. Over many years of working with social work students, we have become convinced that, aside from the usual cases of procrastination, this difficulty arises from two related problems. One problem is that many students arrive in social work classes without a clear idea of what is scientific thinking, and lack the skills to formulate a researchable social work question. The second problem is that the tendency to emphasize the rational aspects of science misleads students concerning the origins of research questions. Although this whole book is about scientific thinking, this chapter provides special emphasis on the identification of researchable questions for social work students.

Understanding the nature and origins of researchable ideas is important in your role as a social work practitioner as well as your role as a student. Evaluation of practice is an ethical requirement for social workers, as is the ability to use and contribute to the empirical base of the profession. This chapter will help you get off to a good start by describing the characteristics of researchable questions and explaining how to translate everyday practice interests into researchable questions. Learning to ask researchable questions will also add value to the hours you spend studying the empirical basis of interventions in your social work classes, because researchable questions are excellent devices for anchoring ideas more firmly in the mind.

Finally, this chapter will help you to understand some of the sociocultural hurdles you need to leap in order to obtain the resources you need in the pursuit of new knowledge. For those of you who become active scholars, the ability to ask researchable questions will become so automatic that you will find a world with many more researchable questions than time and resources allow you to answer. Understanding the sociopolitical side of social science research is a great help in the quest for expanded research resources to answer emerging questions.

Learning Objectives

After reading this chapter, you should be able to:

1. describe the characteristics of researchable, empirical questions
2. list examples of questions that are amenable to empirical inquiry
3. describe the ways that direct experience, beliefs, social forces, and theory influence questions that are asked by researchers
4. identify the value bases of questions

Key Terms and Concepts

Researchable (Empirical) and Nonempirical Questions

Much of science can be reduced to the design and testing of mental models (theories) that are expected to account for regularities in the empirical world. Although that world is knowable to us only in an indirect and human way, the methods of science help us untangle some of the logical fallacies associated with human thought and perception and come to consensus about states and relationships in the empirical world. It must seem logical, therefore, that the kinds of questions of interest to people when using their scientific reasoning are questions that reference people, things, and events in the empirical world. Questions that ask about the state of the empirical world, the pattern of forces that may account for current states in the world, or how consistent a set of observations is with a theory designed to explain, predict, or control empirical events are all researchable questions. In Chapter 1, we discussed Jensen's (1989) description of four ways of knowing (mysticism, rationalism, empiricism, and science) based on the use of logic (reason) and data (observation). This distinction applies to scientifically useful questions also, that is, the use of both logic and references to observables are two characteristics that make scientific propositions and questions different from other types of questions. Researchable questions are usually logical propositions about observable things, events, or people.

It seems possible that the definition of researchable questions proposed earlier is so broad that very little would seem not to qualify. Can you imagine questions that do not test ideas about the empirical world or do not involve logical propositions? Yes, in fact it is quite easy. Many kinds of questions tend to be argued on purely philosophical, religious, political, or mystical grounds. Ideas about right and wrong, good and evil, the ultimate meaning of life all have researchable aspects, such as determining what the beliefs of a group of individuals are, but many questions in these areas are formed in ways that do not reference empirical events. Individuals who believe as a matter of faith in the Book of Genesis as a literal accounting of the origins of the universe are little affected either by the logical difficulties this account contains or the strong observational data inconsistent with the biblical account. Likewise, anything that comes under the rubric of taste or preference is likely to be unresolvable through empirical observation. What is the best clothing style, the best society, the best religious organization? What criteria are optimal for making judgments of "best" in any of these contexts? These are not researchable questions as stated.

Having said that questions of value, belief, or taste are not researchable, we can state that science may have something to contribute to these areas also, but only if we start from a place other than determining what is "good," "right," or "moral." To the extent that discussions of values and beliefs include assumptions about empirical events, science can enter into the process to test those assumptions. We can conduct surveys to determine the proportion of people who hold certain beliefs. Exploratory methods can be used to identify the meaning systems in which values are embedded. We can even look at the behavior consequences of holding certain beliefs. However, science is not likely to resolve questions about the ultimate "right or wrong" of a value or belief.

Many questions include both empirical and nonempirical aspects. Consider the question concerning corporal punishment. Is it good to use physical punishment to discipline children? Western social scientists have long been suspicious that corporal punishment does more harm to children and families than good. Family sociologist Murray A. Straus is one of the strongest opponents of corporal punishment. Straus titled his book on the subject *Beating the Devil out of Them: Corporal Punishment in American Families* (1991). The main thesis of the book is that corporal punishment is not an effective form of discipline and, in fact, is hurtful and likely to be the precursor of more child misbehavior, family violence, and violence outside of the family. Straus provides evidence from his own studies of thousands of families and the results of hundreds of other studies that clearly document negative consequences of corporal punishment. The paradox here is that the assumed beneficial or at least benign effects of corporal punishment are not the sole criteria for making decisions about behaviors such as corporal punishment. The Bible contains language that has been interpreted as requiring parents to provide physical punishment as a matter of moral necessity. What is a person to do when moral teachings command behaviors that scientists suggest may lead to negative consequences for families? How should scientific findings and belief systems enter into public policy decisions and definitions of concepts such as child abuse? The answers are not clear.

Straus was successful in describing and explaining the antecedents and consequences of corporal punishment in the United States. However, persons who regard corporal punishment as a biblically sanctioned, essential form of parenting are not likely to be influenced by his treatment of the subject. All the evidence of the harmful effects does not mitigate the moral imperative to "beat the devil out of them." These are examples of questions that are important, but not satisfactorily resolved exclusively within the context of scientific study.

Although scientific study is not designed to answer moral questions in absolute terms, that does not mean that scientific study is not relevant to moral debates. For instance, science is unlikely to ever rule on the moral rightness of taking retribution on some criminals through capital punishment. However, science is well equipped to determine whether capital punishment is an effective deterrent to crime (in persons other than the executed). Likewise, if one can define "holy" or "moral" in terms of actions of people in the real world, it is possible to ask whether corporal punishment results in people who are more "holy" or "moral." Often, rules for human conduct are based on beliefs about the consequences of that conduct. Because those beliefs are expressed in terms of observables, they are amenable to test. See the point? "Is TV violence bad?" is a moral question not amenable to scientific study. However, when translated into "Does TV violence produce increased violence in children?" it is a researchable question. Table 3.1 offers some researchable questions that span many social work interests. Although finding answers to these questions would involve many different research techniques, they are all amenable to scientific exploration.

Some of the questions listed in Table 3.1 are paraphrased from studies in scholarly journals. Others reflect questions that social workers have asked us. Some of these questions are general and exploratory, whereas some are very precise predictions about empirical events called hypotheses. The questions cover very different topics. However, there is a pattern—do you see it? All the questions ask about aspects of the empirical world; that is, things that we could all experience. The

TABLE 3.1   Examples of Researchable Questions

Do patients with major depression who receive a standardized therapeutic intervention show decreased depression after treatment?

Do youth who are teamed up with mentors demonstrate fewer problem behaviors when compared to youth who do not have mentors?

Do frail elders who receive in-home support services report higher quality of life than frail elders who do not receive such services?

Are rates of alcoholism higher among Japanese Americans than other ethnic groups in the United States?

What do parents and children in the Czech Republic believe about women's roles?

How do African American women make moral judgments?

What are the precursors to male youth joining a gang?

What do community organizers do?

Just how depressed is my client?

Is my intervention working?

other chapters in this book discuss how to turn questions like these into procedures for getting answers.

Characteristics of Scientifically Useful Questions

Here are five simple rules that can be used to construct questions that could usefully guide scientific inquiry in social work. Let's look at all five here and then discuss each in more detail:

1. The question must be posed in terms of observables.
2. The question must be expressed in terms for which nominal definitions are available.
3. The scope of possible answers should not be arbitrarily limited.
4. The question should be testable in principle.
5. The answer should be important—it should matter to someone.

The requirement that **researchable** questions be referenced in terms of observables simply means that a researchable question contains a proposition or inquiry about the state of the empirical world under some conditions. Identifying **referents** for things that have a physical existence—like age, gender, and income—is fairly easy. However, when our questions concern mental constructs like loneliness or oppression, finding referents can be a bit more challenging. Referents are the real-world things—observables—that allow us to accurately infer that the quality indicated by a mental construct is present. The topic of conceptualization—that is, working out meaning systems—will be taken up in more detail in Chapter 4, "Measurement." For now, it is enough to remember that researchable questions make reference to observables or ideas that can be defined unambiguously in terms of observables.

Is it just to refuse education to children of undocumented workers? This is an example of a question that is not researchable in its present form. "Just" does not have an empirical referent. (It reflects a value.) Resolving this question would be primarily a matter of political, religious, or philosophical discourse. Researchable alternatives might include: What proportion of the population thinks that refusing education to children of undocumented workers is a desirable social policy? or What are the costs of educating children of undocumented workers? or What are the ways that the presence of children of undocumented workers influences communities? Many other possibilities exist, and providing answers would help us understand the phenomenon of children of undocumented workers, but none of the possible researchable questions would answer the initial question, which is phrased in terms of values.

The nominal definitions referred to in the second criterion are social conventions about the classes of experiences that are associated with a particular word/symbol. Ideas that are so subjective and personal as to be impossible to define in ways recognizable by others are seldom researchable. If you can't explain the question in ways that are meaningful to others, you probably do not have a researchable question. In fact, many areas of research emerge only after some enterprising social scientist resolves definition and measurement problems to the satisfaction of most of her or his peers. In order for a question to be researchable, it must be expressed in terms that are understandable to other persons with an interest in the answer. This doesn't mean that unconventional questions are not researchable, just that researchable questions tend to be consciously phrased in words that have conventional meanings to persons interested in the question.

The requirement that the elements of a research question reflect shared definitions and meanings is not meant to suggest that there are "real" definitions for ideas that are the absolute standards of meaning. In fact, consensus around meanings in any cultural context tends to be incomplete and evolving. What is needed here is enough shared meaning that the domains to be tapped by the question can be approximately identified. For example, pollsters have found that asking questions about "welfare" has produced unexpected results, in part because of the negative stereotyping in the word, but also because of its ambiguity. Different patterns of response result when a more precise label, such as AFDC (Aid to Families with Dependent Children), is referenced in the question. In areas of interest where many ideas are not yet worked out at a conceptual level, expressing the question clearly may include some explanation and definition. For example, research questions involving concepts like homelessness, underemployment, or at-risk clients usually require some explanation of what is meant by these terms as part of the research question.

The requirement that research questions use terms for which nominal definitions exist or potentially exist plays out similarly in research activities designed to uncover meaning systems of clients or populations. "How do the people in this community think about crime?" is a perfectly valid ethnographic question. So is "What do fights with her spouse mean to my client?" However, in this type of research, the definitions of terms such as *crime* and *fights* that are assumed by the social worker asking the question are only starting points. Activities designed to answer questions like these would most likely involve the social worker looking for differences and similarities between conventional uses of the terms and the way they are used by the community members or clients germane to the study.

The third criterion proposed is that questions must be phrased in such a way that answers other than the one favored by the researcher are permissible. This is actually a difficult criterion to meet because the very act of asking questions tends to limit the range of acceptable answers. One operating rule is that a question that permits only one acceptable answer is too restrictive to ever be useful. A research question cannot be phrased as a statement (Proving the value of treatment X) but rather as an interrogatory concerning classes of alternatives (Whether or not treatment X works under specified conditions). Beyond the criterion that a question that permits only one answer is too restrictive, any question that eliminates classes of plausible answers by rhetoric and definition is problematic. For example, "Do children of the poor learn the successful coping strategies of successful families or do they remain stuck in the maladaptive strategies of the culture of poverty?"

unnecessarily restricts the answers to the question of coping strategies by assuming that the strategies of successful families are adaptive and those of poor families are maladaptive. This particular example also gets close to the issue of values implicit in questions. The tendency to assume that behaviors of the poor are necessarily maladaptive arises from a value base that sees the poor as personally responsible for their fate. We will return to the issue of values implicit in questions shortly. The point here is that values tend to narrow the range of answers that are logically possible. This is also true of exploratory questions if the structure of the question leads the investigator to overlook the unexpected.

Even if the first three conditions (posed in terms of observables, nominal definitions available, not arbitrarily limited) are met, the question may still not be scientifically useful if it is not answerable in principle. This criterion requires that the questioner be able to specify the conditions under which an answer may be obtained. If it is possible to envision conditions under which a credible answer to the question can be obtained, then the question is probably researchable. This criterion is tricky, because technical, ethical, and resource concerns may make some questions very difficult to pursue and thus blur the boundary between answerable and nonanswerable questions. For example, ethical considerations may make an experiment involving comparing emerging therapies infeasible, or lack of cultural contact may make it difficult to test some propositions in cross-cultural settings. However, if there exist some conditions under which it is possible to address the otherwise sound question, then it probably meets our definition of a researchable question.

The final characteristic we propose is that the question be important and that the answer matters. As an aspiring member of a helping profession, you recognize that empirical studies often compete with direct services for time and resources. Therefore, your research should put something back into the system for the good of clients. Even if the research requires very little beyond your own time and energy, you should be able to justify its value to the profession and to the clients we serve—for your time and energy are valuable resources that should not be squandered on trivial research. Of course, the degree of importance of a question is, once again, not purely an objective matter. The question of who gets to define the criteria for "important" and the like are sociocultural concerns. To some individuals, a very narrow experimental hypothesis that tests a critical implication of a theory is very important; to others, this may seem trivial. Research questions that focus on the unique viewpoints of individuals or nondominant groups sometimes have been unenthusiastically received by the scientific community and power elite reflecting a bias toward generalizing statements. The requirement that a researchable social work question be nontrivial includes implicitly the view that importance is the result of social consensus, not the application of fixed criteria.

Sociocultural Origins of Research Questions

Fashion and Fad as Influences on Research Questions.   The kinds of questions that are addressed by scientists and the way those questions are expressed tend to reflect the preoccupation of the individuals conducting the research and their culturally learned assumptions about the world. Numerous scholars have made this point, perhaps none better than Thomas S. Kuhn in his landmark history of science (1970). Despite the assumed existence of an empirical world filled with objects and energy, people do not experience these directly, but rather experience a process in which the senses interpret environmental information (visual, auditory, tactile, olfactory, and taste) through cultural lenses. Which sensation is important enough to attend to, and how that sensation is classified and attached to meanings, are the result of the various processes of socialization and enculturation. We learn what is what, and what is nothing, by watching others, having experiences, and through formal education. Thus, as social workers, we have inherited a cultural preoccupation with particular classes of events, culturally determined ways of structuring experience, and also a capacity for our own personal experience to allow us to dissent, but not disconnect, from those cultural influences.

What are some examples of the scientific and sociocultural fads that might influence social work research questions? Preoccupation with integration of human services during the Nixon presidency led to many studies of linkages between human service agencies, a line of research that received little attention before that time. This macro focus was related to national legislation, the Allied Health Services Act. Longstanding cultural beliefs that raising children is women's work led to a large body of socialization research that ignored caregivers other than mothers and other female relatives. Only recently has the role of fathers in children's adjustment and maladjustment become the focus of broad scholarly interest. Expanded research interest in gerontology has accompanied the aging of the front wave of the "baby boom" generation. Current national preoccupation with law enforcement and drug abuse has led to an interesting combination of research and social experiments in these areas. Because money and related resources tend to follow cultural preoccupation, these are likely to influence what questions seem worthy of study and how those questions will be phrased. Even the ability of individual social workers to challenge existing ways of thinking about social events is influenced by this flow of resources, because your ability as a social worker to have certain classes of experiences (and thus be prompted to ask certain questions) is shaped by the availability of work contexts.

Influence of a Preferred Research Paradigm on Question Formulation.   Although the interplay between the scientific and social work communities and the rest of society tends to shape both the topics and form of questions, preferences for certain kinds of research methods also tend to influence questions. Modern sociology of science identifies the tendency for researchers to express strong preferences for various research methods. Some researchers prefer predominantly laboratory research, others prefer field experiments, and still others prefer exploratory studies. Some prefer designs that use extensive mathematics, whereas others prefer data expressed in words, pictures, artifacts, and the like. These preferences are important because many of the research methods are designed to address only a limited set of research questions. For example, methods such as ethnography are primarily involved with inductive processes, that is, answering questions about the nature of meaning systems. Other methods, such as laboratory experiments, require that meaning systems be worked out in advance and are associated largely with testing one or a few specific hypotheses. A preference for surveys over interviews is likely to influence the degree of openness or preconceptions in questions. Surveys tend to feature simple questions with simple answers, often in precoded categories. Persons who favor this kind of research tend to phrase questions in very focused formats. Conversely, interviews tend to provide many more opportunities to spontaneously follow leads and seek clarification. Although many interviews are highly structured, the potential flexibility allows questions to be phrased in ways that are more open and allows adjustment of response categories and questions as needed. These are only a few examples out of many different approaches to research methods. We discuss these in more detail in the chapters on design and data collection.

The social worker who is attempting to turn a vague concern into a researchable question is likely to try to shoehorn the concern into a form that fits the research methods that he or she knows or prefers. The relationship between preferred methods and the kinds of questions asked is likely to occur at an unconscious level. When faced with a task such as program evaluation, the ethnographically oriented evaluator is likely to ask how the program works, and the experimentally oriented evaluator is more likely to ask whether it produces measurable outcomes. The emphasis on process does not necessarily exclude interest in outcome, any more than interest in outcome precludes interest in process. However, in practice, the tendency to think about research questions in terms of the tools at hand is pervasive.

Identification of the Value Base of Questions.   It is hoped that the foregoing has convinced you that useful social work research questions arise from cultural processes and personal interest. Because all cultural processes are linked to implicit values, all researchable questions thus reflect personal and cultural values and beliefs. These values and beliefs define the domain within which allowable answers can be found. Answers that do not fall within this domain will not be allowed. Therefore, in considering the adequacy of a social work research question, it is appropriate to ask about the value base of the question in order to determine what is likely to be included and excluded in the set of possible answers. That is, is the diverse range of values around this question adequately integrated or are certain viewpoints arbitrarily excluded?

The existence of a value base is not necessarily a deficiency. In fact, it is necessary if a research question is to meet the criterion for importance. However, given the diversity of values across various cultures and classes, it would be foolish not to inquire how the values implicit in a particular question limit the range of applicability of the question. Furthermore, a divergence of basic values between the persons studied and the persons doing the studying, and perhaps the ultimate consumers of the study findings, is likely to result in miscommunication and error. After all, the choice of whose values determine the question is a matter of power and potentially an avenue of oppression. It is important to be clear that (1) a particular set of values underlies every research question, (2) those values limit the range of possible answers allowed, and (3) the interpretation of the results of a study of a research question is influenced by the values of both the persons doing the study and those interpreting the findings.

Decoding values implicit in a research question or any text is not a simple matter. Aside from looking for obviously biased language that would signal belief and value systems, there are few rules that always work. Often, the values are reflected in the tone of the question in a holistic sense. A research question on parenting such as "Is parental use of corporal punishment predictive of acting out behavior of children?" may reflect a perspective on parents as sources of children's maladjustment. "Does the presence of a warm, supportive caregiver help children in disadvantaged families to cope with school failure?" sounds like an inherently parent-friendly question and may reflect the value that parents be viewed as potential, positive coping resources for a maladapted child. A question about the effectiveness of couple therapy may reflect a perspective that maintaining a marital union is a high goal, whereas phrased another way, the underlying value may be on personal self-actualization. Can you see how the values that underlie the question limit the range of answers that may be found and the context in which the answers may be applied?

The Role of Stakeholders in Question Formulation.   One way to limit problems related to unexamined and conflicting values is to involve stakeholders in question formulation. Social work researchers, like many modern social scientists, are acutely aware that in research involving people as participants, these participants have a stake in the outcome of that research and thus deserve a share of the power to influence both the question and the methods through which it is answered. This position is probably easier for persons trained in ethnographic methods to accept, but valid across the continuum of research methods.

Just how to involve stakeholders in the question formulation process varies from one situation to another. As we discuss in Chapter 10 ("Practice Evaluation in Single and Multiple Systems"), in single-subject research designs problem identification, goal setting, and research questions are negotiated jointly between the practitioner/researcher and the client. Standards for large-scale program evaluation activities include stakeholder involvement in the conceptualization of research questions as an ethical standard (Sanders, 1994). Typical techniques for stakeholder involvement in research questions involve formal negotiations with clients or key informants, focus groups, interviews, or surveys. The social work practitioner/ researcher must guard against unexamined values and beliefs implicit in research questions that may inappropriately narrow the ranges of questions asked or answers allowed.

Question Formulation for Student Projects.   Students often are in a unique position regarding the selection of a research question in conjunction with their academic work. As we discussed earlier, most researchable questions arise from substantive interests of social scientists and other professionals. They arise from the work we all do and have a history and context. The student role is unique in that the student assigned to select a research question may be lacking this context or perhaps thrust into an unfamiliar context (by being assigned a topic). This may be complicated by a lack of understanding of the implications of the form of the question for research design.

Now that you have some idea what a researchable question looks like, you are on your way to being able to find one. In general, we see two sources of research questions. First, the question may arise deductively from theories you have been studying. Although it is a myth to think that research questions arise exclusively as a logical extension of existing theory, the questions underlying much student research, especially experimental theses and dissertations, often do arise deductively from existing theory. Second, research questions may arise from the experience of the student. A student intern placed in a shelter for battered women may develop research questions concerning socialization for violence. Excellent questions concerning the lifeways of persons in the United States who are from nondominant groups have been raised by persons who themselves are from nondominant groups (Matsumoto, 1994).

In our experience, the applied researcher often starts with some personal interest in an area or with an opportunity to study a particular situation, rather than starting from a theoretical basis. The empirically oriented social worker is then likely to search the literature, find theories that bear on the topic of interest, and generate a researchable question that makes sense in the light of existing theory. Thus, it is often some personal or professional concern that initiates the process, rather than some kind of insightful and researchable question that emerges from focused attention to some theory. If the research primarily tests a theory, so much the better, but theory testing is often secondary to some other preoccupation.

What this means for you as a student is that you need to develop the ability to connect your interests with the empirical database of the profession. This usually means asking, "How do social scientists talk about the constructs of interest to me?" "What theories seem to account for the areas of interest to me?" "Has anyone developed and tested a model of causes and effects that includes the constructs of interest?" We recommend to our students that they employ a two-step process. First, try to be specific about what your interest or question is and write it down. Writing is a great way of determining if you have a clear idea. Be mindful of the criteria for good social work research questions described earlier. Next, hit the books and journals looking for nominal definitions of terms and most likely the specialized vocabulary that scientists use to discuss the topic of interest to you. It may take some time to find the scientific synonyms for the everyday words you use. A recent article that attempts to review everything known about your topic often can be found.

Use your reading to accomplish three tasks. First, find out how other persons conceptualize the important ideas in your question. More about conceptualization is presented in Chapter 4 ("Measurement"). The main point here is to recognize the meaning systems that other people are using to understand the phenomenon of interest to you so that you can benefit from the head start that prior work might provide. Second, try to identify populations or settings in which the phenomenon of interest is likely to be found. Those settings are the places where answers to your question will be found also. Third, try to find a causal model of the forces that seem to influence the phenomenon you wish to study. This might seem most relevant to largely deductive questions, such as the probability that increasing social support depth will improve adjustment. However, this is equally applicable to inductive questions in which models of socialization forces, economic process, or political process will help guide meaning identification. Use all this information to fine-tune your research question.

You are probably starting to see why some beginning students find such difficulty in choosing a question. At the beginning of your career, locating a researchable question is in part asking you to develop the art of empirical thinking, perhaps before you know what that is. The student with little training in the social sciences, and particularly in empirical reasoning, may have had insufficient time and opportunity to develop this list of personal interests. It seems artificial to us to force the issue by requiring beginners to invent questions. A better strategy is to ask students to learn what empirical thinking is, read in their areas of interest, and let the questions flow! Ultimately, the topics you study will come from personal experience, social concerns and conflicts, or as an extension of some theory of interest to you. However, in order for such questions to flow effortlessly, it is necessary to first cultivate the habits of critical thinking. The mental habits involved with critical thinking give you a whole new perspective through which to view your professional practice and cause those researchable questions to flow faster than time allows you to pursue. Helping you to develop those habits is part of what this book is about. As your scientific thinking skills and education progress, you will have no difficulty finding researchable questions without getting hung up on the artificiality of producing questions on demand.

When you are seriously considering investigation of a research question, you should determine whether your question fits into the priorities of persons and organizations that control resources needed to conduct studies. One of the most hotly debated aspects of science these days is its sociocultural origins. To be sure, the way that scientists conceptualize the things they study, the questions that are asked, and the resources dedicated to finding answers form a thoroughly cultural and political process. The kinds of information in the scientific literature suggest that a rather whimsical collection of initiatives arising from direct experience, personal beliefs, and social and political forces is emerging, along with valuable information about our strongest theories. What does this mean? It means that social scientists study what is of interest to their cultures and themselves. As the people who do empirical social science research have become more diverse, the questions have changed to reflect this diversity. We see this as a very positive change in the culture of social research. For example, fewer researchers study mothers as an exclusive source of socialization, preferring to define socialization as the result of caregiver systems. The plight of the poor is seldom conceptualized as "the culture of poverty," but is more likely to be studied as complex adaptive systems in response to power distribution. Very limited views of women and non-Europeans that characterized earlier work have yielded to more refined explorations due in no small part to greater diversity among scientists.

Occasionally, one encounters tracts written under the banner "postmodernism" that view these sociocultural origins of social science ideas as evidence for the fundamental futility of the science enterprise. If all knowledge is cultural and political, so the argument goes, and there are no absolute grounds for choosing one belief over another, then knowledge based on scientifically tested questions are no better than any other political or faith statements. In Chapter 1, we dealt with this criticism, but it bears some repeating. Propositions about empirical states and events that are tested by scientific methods are logically superior to all forms of conjecture without evidence if the criteria for superiority are prediction, control, and replicability. Although empirical tests of questions are potentially vulnerable to many kinds of distortions related to who is asking and observing, the very nature of the scientific method is designed to limit the sources of such bias and allow the questioner to transcend, even a little, the limits of his or her sensory and cultural limitations.

Summary

Researchable questions are those that are posed in terms of observables, expressed in nominal and operational definitions of variables, do not arbitrarily limit the range of possible answers, are answerable in principle, and are important. Some of the sociocultural forces that influence question formulation include fashion and fad, preferred research paradigms, and values. Although all questions are cultural and personal in origin, involvement of relevant stakeholders can help forge a consensus and allow meaningful work to proceed.

4 Measurement

Representing the Empirical World

Relationship of This Chapter to the Whole

One characteristic that makes scientific activity different from other ways of knowing is the requirement for empirical verification. This means that although much of the work of science involves logic and reason, at some point, we are required to conduct observations of the empirical world and note what we find there. Measurement is the word we use to refer to the process of representing observations in terms of organized symbol systems. Although the word *measurement* is sometimes associated only with the process of attaching numeric symbols to observations of quantities (e.g., Nunnally, 1978), we offer our more general definition because observations that can be represented as quantities are only a portion of the interesting things to know about the empirical world. In fact, numbers may also be used to represent attributes of experience that are not quantitative, as in the case of **nominal measurement** scales. In such cases, the choice of a number or a word to represent concepts such as group membership is purely arbitrary. It is not quantification or number systems that delineate scientific measurement from other ways of knowing, but rather unique processes of conceptualization, operationalization, and observation.

A second reason for our more inclusive definition is that we wish to emphasize that measurement involves the development of meaning systems that underlie symbols, as well as the act of assigning those symbols to represent a measured quality. It is important to understand the development of meaning systems because these provide the structure by which we determine what aspects of experience are relevant and how we think about these aspects. **Meaning systems** determine how experience is organized into units, variables, attributes, the ranges of these that we experience, and the boundaries among them. Modern views of science see the development of meaning systems as essential to the scientific process and worthy of rigorous treatment. Therefore, this discussion of measurement considers both the meaning systems that provide the mental structures through which we filter our experiences as well as rules for representing experiences through symbol systems.

An important characteristic of scientific measurement is the presence of a clear, easy-to-follow trail from the symbolic representation back to the events the symbols represent. That is, given a symbolic description of some event—be that description words, numbers, or some yet-to-be-developed symbol system—it should be possible to specify exactly how sensory experiences and logical rules led from the event to the choice of that symbol. This trail is important because it is a necessary condition for generating verifiable statements about the empirical world. As discussed in subsequent chapters, maintaining the link between abstract symbols and the empirical events they reflect is a necessary first condition for all scientific attempts to abstract meaning from sensory experience.

Maintenance of the clear path from experience to symbols is the task of measurement techniques. The integrity of this path is threatened by errors introduced by limitations of human perception and cognition. The formal procedures of scientific measurement discussed in this chapter seek to limit the influence of human error through clear definitions of concepts, precise coding rules, and selection of conditions of observation that are less vulnerable to errors and deceptions. These techniques seldom completely resolve the problem of human error, but when correctly applied tend to render these errors less troublesome than they are under conditions of casual observation.

This chapter summarizes the basic principles that underlie scientific measurement of all types. Specific techniques designed to maximize the quality of measurement are discussed in Chapters 5 ("Research Designs") and 7 ("Data Collection").

Relationship of This Chapter to the Roles of Social Workers

Competent measurement skills are important in nearly every aspect of social work practice. "Measurement is as much a part of social work practice as relating to clients," wrote Reid and Smith (1989, p. 191). Bloom, Fisher, and Orme (1999) noted that social work practice involves assessment of states of clients and social environments, evaluation of the outcomes of interventions, and providing evidence of effectiveness. To accomplish these tasks, social workers need to know how to think clearly about states of clients and social environments, how to conduct unambiguous observations, and how to symbolically represent the results of those observations. These are measurement tasks. Additionally, social workers are called on to be knowledgeable of the body of empirical evidence on which social work interventions are based. This task also involves understanding the goals, techniques, and pitfalls of measurement in the empirical world. This chapter helps social workers to understand the principles of scientific measurement and how these techniques facilitate various social work tasks.

Learning Objectives

After reading this chapter, you should be able to:

1. list limitations of human perception and cognition related to measurement procedures
2. describe how ideas progress from personal concepts to public constructs
3. describe the components of an operational definition of a construct
4. describe and define validity and reliability
5. describe how validity of a measure is assessed
6. describe how reliability of a measure is assessed

Key Terms and Concepts

Measurement and Limitations of Human Perception and Cognition

Scientific procedures designed to assist measurement can be thought of as attempts to extend human capacity, in much the way that microscopes, telescopes, glasses, and contact lenses are used to extend the human visual system. The analogy is an apt one because all of these optical devices use curved lenses to bend light, but their use ranges from correction of deficient vision (e.g., contact lenses, eye glasses) to extension of vision far beyond its normal range of sensitivity (as in the case of telescopes and microscopes). Measurement techniques have the same range of applicability. A good measurement scheme often allows the person using it to measure some experience of interest with greater accuracy and completeness than would be possible with ordinary informal observation. For example, a good depression inventory or carefully designed clinical interview can provide a much more complete indication of subjective states than casual observation. Also, good measurement technique cuts down on the range of variability associated with individual differences in observational powers or the effects of extraneous elements of the environment in which the observations are conducted. That is, good measurement practice improves the interobserver agreement concerning the state of the empirical world. All of these attributes—accuracy, completeness, and interobserver agreement—are consistent with the goal of creating a shared body of scientific evidence on which to base our profession.

In addition to extending human observational capacity, a primary reason for measurement techniques is to compensate for flaws in the ability of most humans to process information about the empirical world. What is the nature of those flaws? As wonderful as our sensory and cognitive systems seem to us, humans are prone to many types of systematic and random errors when we process our experience of the empirical world. Susceptibility to optical illusions, hallucinations, forgetfulness, selective attention, propaganda, false beliefs about causal sequences, and tenacious retention of demonstrably false ideas are all manifestations of our potential for error. Where do these errors arise? Some errors are rooted in the human sensory apparatus. Other measurement errors are rooted in cognitive apparatus, such as limitations of human memory and attention. Still other errors are introduced when beliefs, values, customs, and experiences interact with cognitive and sensory limitations. Whatever the source, errors introduced by human limitations have great potential to subvert our ability to create knowledge that is both culturally meaningful and subject to verification.

It is important to note that errors related to expectations may occur either outside of awareness or as part of a conscious strategy of deception. Perceptual errors such as those revealed in the familiar Muller-Lyer illusion are examples of errors that occur outside of awareness. Thomas Gillovich, in his delightful little book *How We Know What Isn't So* (1991) lists the cognitive determinants of a long list of common misperceptions and illusions. For example, humans seem to automatically seek out information confirming expectations with more zeal than disconfirming information. Likewise, in making judgments concerning classification of experiences, information consistent with expectations is given more weight than disconfirming evidence. Ambiguous situations (poorly defined situations or those in which sensory information is incomplete) are special problems for humans. In these cases, blanks caused by missing or hidden information are filled in by cognitively programmed expectations (Gillovich, 1991). Experiences that may cause us to doubt cherished beliefs are especially prone to distortion. Paraphrasing Sir Francis Bacon (as quoted by Gillovich, 1991): People "prefer to believe what they prefer to be true." Mental representations of experience tend to be distorted along lines of human hopes, fears, and beliefs.

The reader who thinks that these dire warnings are overstated need only look at some common examples, such as intergroup conflicts based on stereotyped perceptions of outgroup members. Matsumoto (1994) provides an excellent short summary of how culture and social class shape personal perception and impression formation. Often, a few features (such as cultural rules governing physical attractiveness) are transformed by meaning systems into a set of expectations that cause us to start seeking confirmation. Thus, an almost endless list of things like hair texture or color, skin complexion, body weight, even foot size, are transformed into the standards by which "beauty" is defined. Having created the definition of "beauty," "beautiful people" are identified who personify the definition. In turn, the recognition of who these "beautiful people" are confirms the definition of what is beautiful—and the cycle goes on. Remembering our human tendencies to look for data that confirm expectations and undervalue disconfirming data, is it any wonder that disfavored outgroup members so often are found to be consistent with negative stereotypes?

Not all errors of observation and measurement arise from unconscious distortions. In addition to improving the accuracy and intersubjectivity of our measurement, scientific measurement strategies can help protect us from the results of frauds, wishful thinking, and deceptions. Stage illusions, confidence games, and propaganda campaigns are conscious strategies designed to produce deception. Editors and contributors to the journal *The Skeptical Inquirer* have investigated hundreds of claims on the fringe of science, many of which have involved active deception. However, even the formal procedures discussed in research texts are sometimes insufficient to prevent distortions. In her book *Tainted Truth*, journalist Cynthia Crossen (1994) notes that financial and political interests often seem to distort findings about seemingly factual events, such as the efficacy of antibiotics, safety of food and water, and the like. For example, scientific research into the effects of antibiotics on middle-ear infections revealed that industry-funded pharmaceutical research was more likely to find antibiotics to be beneficial than was government-funded research, sometimes at the same institution. One case involved a prestigious medical journal that received two papers on the subject of antibiotics and middle-ear infections in the summer of 1986 from the same institution, but that reached opposite conclusions concerning the effect of antibiotics on middle-ear infections (Crossen, 1994). The messy controversy did not subside for years until a larger body of research ruled that the treatment was in fact ineffective. Although no evidence of active deception surfaced, in this case, as others that involve large sums of money and prestige, it is worth being concerned about deception as well as accidental sources of systematic error.

In addition to the individual problems listed, attempts to report experience to others are also likely to be complicated by differences in language and experience, as well as internal distortions introduced by both the sender and receiver. Knowledge-generating activities in the social sciences nearly always involve interpersonal interaction that can alter what was believed to be present and what is recorded. The process of recording or assigning codes is not immune from cultural patterns of influence and authority. For example, Rohner (personal communication) reported efforts to develop codes of mother-child interaction for the Human Relations Area Files (HRAF) from ethnographic descriptions of diverse cultural groups. In a pilot test of the coding protocol, whenever male and female coders (both American university students) disagreed concerning the interpretation of sequences of mother-child interaction, males consistently altered their codes to be consistent with their female partners. Presumably, the male coders believed that the female coders were more expert in mother-child interactions. This was not altogether surprising because as we attempt to fine-tune perceptions, we often seek verification from others, particularly with those assumed to have expert knowledge (Carlson, 1985). Although it is not clear if men or women were more accurate coders, it is apparent that not only will coders with different socialization histories rate narratives differently, but contemporary social interactions can cause them to change their codes. The codes that were ultimately published (Rohner & Rohner, 1982) were based on a formal protocol for applying evidence to resolve coding disputes.

Because many of the errors of perception and memory are specieswide, it is reasonable to think that observations of experience will always be composed, in uncertain proportions, of attributes of the actual empirical event and distortions added—intentionally or not—by the observers. This relationship between the true portion of a score and the distortion or error portion is called **observed score** and is illustrated in Equation 4.1.

$$\text{score}_{\text{observed}} = \text{score}_{\text{true}} + \text{score}_{\text{error}} \tag{4.1}$$

That science is only partially successful in overcoming this potential should not be a cause for abandoning all efforts to build knowledge, but for a reasonable skepticism. From the perspective of minimizing human errors, many would argue that science gives us our best hope of understanding empirical events. The consequence of abandoning efforts at systematic measurement—that is, to avoid being too scientific—is to allow free rein to wishful thinking, frauds, and unconscious distortions.

Scientific efforts to overcome human error in measurement date back at least to the scientific revolution of the sixteenth century when techniques such as providing precise operational definitions of key variables, better control of the context of the observation, and the use of specific rules to govern assignment of symbols (numbers or words) to observations began to receive acceptance. All these techniques tended to limit the opportunities for human cognitive limitations to distort the representation of experiences. Whereas the conceptualizations behind scientific inquiry remain the products of culture, the knowledge resulting from scientific measurement is potentially more trustworthy than casual observation because it transcends, at least somewhat, limitations of individual differences in human perception and cognition. In the sections that follow, we will examine modern perspectives on how personal experiences are translated into public cultural knowledge and the principles that have been found to be helpful in reducing the effects of human error on measurement.

Conceptualization: Development of Meaning Systems

All knowledge about the empirical world ultimately originates in meaning systems carried by persons. Contemporary social scientists are in general agreement that the meaning systems we all use are reflections of our personal experience, including our socialization into particular sociocultural systems; that is, the meaning systems through which we conduct inquiries have no "real," material, or "objective" existence, but are abstractions that originate in personal experience and cultural discourse. This is not to say that scientific ideas are no better than casual speculation. However, it is an error to treat the labels we attach to our experiences as if those labels were direct extensions of the empirical world. To confuse our mental representations with the events they symbolize is sometimes labeled **reification,** a clearly faulty thought process.

The degree of specificity and agreement about conceptualizations that is needed varies with context. For example, vague, personal definitions that seem to work fine for many personal, internal thought processes are often not adequate for explaining ideas to others. Interpersonal communication requires greater specification and consideration of alternative viewpoints. Likewise, slight differences in definitions are not generally much of a nuisance when communicating with persons in our reference group, but create problems as we attempt to communicate to a more broad and varied audience. The demands for specificity and agreement are even greater in the case of a science that hopes to generate knowledge that is true and useful at a cultural or even specieswide level. It is these greater demands for specificity and agreement that lead scientific conceptualizations to be more formal than those ideas that we employ in our daily living.

The steps through which personal ideas are transformed into forms that can be shared with others are labeled the **conceptualization process.** Although there are many ways to describe this process, it is convenient to think of **conceptualization** as the process of associating specific personal experiences and ideas about the world (conceptions) with culturally recognizable symbols (words, numbers, pictures, sounds), developing public constructs with shared meanings (nominal definitions), and finally specifying the empirical referents of those constructs (operational definitions). These acts are connected in a continuous process of mutual influence. Meaning systems both arise from language and influence language's development. Meaning systems and words cause persons to look for certain empirical events, and sometimes empirical events lead to changes in meaning systems including new words and symbols. This process occurs both informally in the everyday life of people and formally in the cycle of science.

Table 4.1 lists three types of ideas: personal conceptions, public constructs, and empirical referents. Each of these is specified through a different strategy. For example, personal conceptualizations are defined in terms of mental categories and symbols. Public concepts are specified by nominal definitions. Finally, **empirical referents** of ideas are specified through operational definitions.

Personal conceptions refer to definitions, beliefs, and feelings individuals associate with experiences. Personal conceptions exist in the minds of individuals. Literally every thought that an individual has exists mentally as some kind of

TABLE 4.1   Components in the Conceptualization Process

Types of Ideas	Specification by
Personal conceptualization	Mental category and symbol
Public construct	Nominal definition
Direct observables	Operational definition

personal conception. Personal conceptions are an amalgam of highly personal sensory experiences organized into clusters that reflect cultural learning; that is, the structure of personal conceptions is determined by culture, but the contents of these clusters reflect individual sensory experiences and interpretations as well as culture. Personal conceptions of any individual may or may not bear close resemblance to the personal conceptualizations of other individuals.

Many personal conceptions, and all those intended for communication to others, are associated with abstract symbols used as a proxy for the elements of the conception. For example, the symbols "RED ROSE" may be used to represent a mental category that includes defining characteristics of a certain kind of plant part, memories of the sensory features of certain experiences, the social context of the experience, affective impressions, and more. The choice of the symbols "RED ROSE" is culturally determined and reflects access to language and the existence of similar conceptions across persons with similar cultural backgrounds. It is important to note that the connection between most words and the conceptions they connote is arbitrary and the product of acculturation rather than any necessary connection. (Words like "hiccup" that attempt to mimic sounds may be the exceptions to this rule.) Although personal conceptions associated with symbols such as "RED ROSE" will vary even within a narrow reference group (due to individual differences in experience), commonalties across individuals allow us to develop working rules for assigning this label and distinguish the conceptions behind this symbol from others. Language and shared experience provide us with many labels and rules for connecting labels to personal conceptions and for distinguishing one conception from another.

Swiss psychologist Jean Piaget called the mental categories used to represent personal conceptions "schemas." It is useful to think of schemas as mental shoe boxes that contain all our memories and associations about some class of experience. These boxes are labeled with cover terms, word symbols used to identify the conception. Although personal conceptions are highly idiosyncratic, cover terms and included experiences are culturally determined, forming the basis for communication and sharing of ideas. As personal conceptions take on this kind of shared meaning, they take the form of public constructs.

Public constructs are meaning units that reflect agreements of individuals concerning rules for assigning a label to experiences. Public constructs are the intersection of the private conceptions of many individuals. That is, public constructs tend to be defined in terms of those elements of individual schemas that are common to many individuals. Public constructs are often expressed in **nominal definitions,** a label for rules describing how a particular symbol should be assigned to a collection of ideas. For example, the dictionary defines aggression as "an attack or assault,...especially unprovoked" (Williams, 1977). This nominal definition implies that experiences associated with unprovoked assaults should be labeled as aggression. Dictionaries are not the only source of nominal definitions. In fact, it is probably useful to think of dictionaries as works that collect and attempt to identify consensus that really emerges from cultural processes. These processes include formal and informal efforts at communication, teaching, and learning.

Clustering ideas into constructs seems to be a fundamental human way of dealing with the need to establish meaning and avoid overload from too much unstructured stimulation. Public constructs can be thought of as the interpersonal equivalent of Piaget's "schemas." Clustering our public knowledge into categories with convenient labels makes it possible for communication to take place without constant repetition of all the communication sender's relevant personal conceptions and endless debates over definitions. Complex and sophisticated ideas may be communicated quickly by using public constructs. Take, for example, the term "clinical depression." The term refers to a specific mental health condition that requires special training to accurately diagnose. Yet, because "clinical depression" is also a widely understood public construct—at least among professional social workers—all readers of this book will be able to differentiate clinical depression from related, but distinct, constructs.

When a public construct contains meaning units that themselves are clustered around several smaller ideas, it is common to describe that construct as multidimensional. Dimensions, also known as domains, are clusters of ideas that relate to only one aspect of a construct. For example, Rohner's (1986) definition of the construct "perceived parental rejection" includes parental behaviors grouped into four domains: warmth/affection, hostility/aggression, neglect/indifference, and undifferentiated rejection. Although the construct "perceived parental rejection" has been shown to be a meaningful construct in many cultural and linguistic groups (Rohner & Cournoyer, 1994), the construct is multidimensional, defined in terms of four domains, each of which refers to a different aspect of the perceived parental rejection.

Before proceeding to a discussion of operational definitions, it may be useful to put this discussion of conceptualization back into context. The professional literature that you consume, first as part of your formal education and later as continuing professional development, can be thought of as an aid to the development of a set of public constructs covering aspects of experience that many contemporary social workers find important and meaningful. These constructs facilitate communication between social workers about their craft, and also provide links between the individual social worker and parts of the collective experience of social workers and related professionals. The professional literature provides social workers with meaning categories that facilitate thinking about clients and social environments, cause-and-effect models to facilitate discovery of intervention strategies, and specifications for measuring the states of individuals and social environments. This body of constructs also allows individual social workers to share their specific experiences and thereby influence the profession.

One of the first steps of professional social work practice, as well as scientific inquiries in general, is to connect personal experiences with relevant public constructs. Facility in this process may be one of the most important consequences of professional education. Although all of us experience our lives in unique personal ways, correctly identifying the class of experience to which a particular experience belongs allows the social worker to connect with a wealth of shared experience and knowledge. This connection enhances our ability to explore and more fully comprehend the experiences that a client system is undergoing, as well as to identify avenues for adjustment that may be appropriate. Often, some of the most useful professional writings are those that give us rich public conceptualizations. These writings may broaden our understanding of the dimensions of a concern, cause us to seek more information, or to look for previously unexpected avenues for intervention. These public constructs are designed to shape our thinking about empirical events in ways that provide the best connection with previous study.

It is important to note that the conceptualization process is not exclusively in the scientific domain. Artists, poets, mystics, and philosophers often provide very useful and provocative conceptualizations of constructs. These conceptualizations may provide fascinating and empowering ways of extracting meaning from experience. However, it is also possible for such elegant conceptualizations to generate false or misleading statements about the empirical world. Rationalism or any other form of argument without data lacks an element that is always present in scientific inquiries. In order to be part of a scientific process, concepts must be definable ultimately in terms of empirical events and subject to verification. Useful conceptualizations must also provide necessary specifications for actually assessing states of the empirical world. These specifications are the operational definitions that we discuss shortly.

Development of useful conceptualizations about the world is an important aspect of science. Discussions of the deductive, experimental side of social science research often treat meaning systems as givens. However, other forms of scientific inquiry focus primarily on the development of meaning systems. Library research is an exploratory research technique that is used to help the scientifically oriented social worker to enhance the meaning systems used to structure experience in practice settings. Other kinds of exploratory studies such as ethnography, oral history, and the like are directed toward the goal of developing public constructs that adequately capture the meaning systems of individuals or groups in social settings of interest. Unlike the experimentalist, the social worker engaged in conceptual work tends to make only weak assumptions concerning the constructs that are adequate to capture the phenomenon of interest. Instead, the social worker engaged in the scientific process at the conceptual level tries to identify meaning systems by observation and questioning. This is an active feedback process that includes observation, synthesis, more observation, more synthesis, in repeated cycles until agreement is reached that the social worker's cognitions about meaning systems are congruent with those of the person(s) under observation. Glaser and Strauss (1967) have called this process **grounded theory** development. For convenience, we will delay discussion of specific techniques for discovering meaning systems until the chapter dealing with nonnumeric data analysis. However, suffice it to say here that the formation and discovery of meaning systems are as much a part of the scientific measurement process as is collecting observations and assigning codes.

Operationalization

Once a meaning system has proceeded to the level of adequate nominal definitions, it becomes possible to go a step further and explicitly specify how the construct in question is experienced in the empirical world. **Operational definition** is the label assigned to these more precise specifications of a construct. Operational definitions take nominal definitions a step further toward consensus and specification by describing (1) the classes of empirical events that map to the construct, (2) social situations in which such events can be unambiguously observed, and (3) precise coding rules for converting observations into symbols. The empirical events consist of direct observables that reflect critical features of nominal definitions. The social situations are arrangements such as interviews, direct behavior observation, responses to questionnaires, or observation of records or artifacts that are designed to minimize the opportunity for human error, deception, or fraud. Finally, the coding rules specify the various states that the empirical events can take and how the states present will be represented through symbols.

An example of an operational definition might be in order here. Corporal punishment is a label that refers to a construct nominally defined as "the use of physical force with the intention of causing a child to experience pain, but not injury, for the purpose of correction or control of the child's behavior" (Strauss, 1991). An operational definition of corporal punishment used to guide an empirical study of the consequences for children's development might be written as "beating with objects, hitting, kicking, slapping, shaking, biting of children for the purpose of correction or control of behavior (empirical indicators) as measured by the Physical Punishment Questionnaire, a self-report questionnaire administered by a research associate at the child's school (social setting)." The test manual for the Physical Punishment Questionnaire provides the specific rules for converting responses into codes (Rohner, Kean, & Cournoyer, 1991). This definition contains the three components of a clear operational definition: empirical indicators, social settings, and coding rules (by reference to a test manual).

The language used to discuss operational definitions varies somewhat both within and between the various social sciences, but several ideas seem to be of general interest. Who or what is observed is generally called the **unit of observation.** Units are defined in ways that establish the boundary between units of interest and other entities that are not the units of interest. Some units have clear self-evident boundaries. The boundaries between persons (when person is the unit) are fairly clear. However, other units, family for example, have less clear boundaries between units. (Is my cousin part of my family or part of another family?) It is worth noting that the units that are observed are not always the units about which we seek knowledge. For example, we may be interested in studying families and generating knowledge about families. However, we obtain our description of families from individual family members. In this case, the individual family member interviewed would be considered the unit of observation and the family would be considered the unit of analysis when we processed our findings. The **unit of analysis** is the unit whose characteristics are of primary interest.

The distinction between units of observation and units of analysis is important in order to avoid an interpretation error called the **ecological fallacy.** This error involves mistakenly attributing characteristics of one unit to another. For example, observing that a neighborhood in a city (unit of analysis) has a high rate of personal crime does not mean that residents of that neighborhood (units of observation) are all perpetrators of personal crime. Stereotyping is one possible manifestation of falling prey to the ecological fallacy.

The characteristics, aspects, or traits of units that we study are called **variables**. The label for a variable actually is a cover term for a set of **attributes,** a collection of concepts that defines the range of states that the variable may take. For example, the attributes that map to the variable "marital status" might include single, never married, married/cohabiting, widowed, and divorced. The attribute list and the definitions used to specify how to distinguish one attribute from another define the variable. A proper attribute list covers the full range of variation of a variable; that is, the list of attributes must be **exhaustive.** Another requirement for attributes is that they be defined in nonoverlapping ways, generally referred to as being **mutually exclusive.** The need for these requirements should be obvious. An exhaustive list of attributes is needed so that regardless of the state of the variable, it is possible to find an attribute that matches what we observe. Second, mutually exclusive definitions for attributes are needed so that we can make an unambiguous match between the state of the variable and our attribute list. If the definitions of two or more attributes overlap, it may impossible to determine which attribute label to apply.

Often the foci of our research are latent constructs that have no direct material reality. The variables that we study are often *indicators* of some latent construct. That is, whereas some concepts are directly defined by direct observables (e.g., the concept "table"), many other concepts refer to abstractions or patterns among observables and do not have a direct material referent. Concepts such as "self-esteem" or "depression" are examples of such abstract concepts, sometimes called **latent constructs.** Whereas it is possible to specify observable empirical events that are manifestations of concepts like these, the concepts themselves have no direct material reality. We call the proxy variables that we use to measure concepts such as self-esteem and depression **indicator variables.** Many of the constructs of interest to social workers are *multidimensional* and may be defined by multiple indicator variables. Sometimes, rather than explore all expressions of a construct, one or a few variables believed to strongly represent the construct are studied. Sociological research (Lazarsfeld, 1959) has led to the proposition that a complex construct often can be measured equally well by any one of a large number of possible indicators. This idea is generally labeled the **interchangeability of indicators.** We return to the idea of indicators when we discuss test construction in Chapter 7.

Rules for actually coding observations are rooted in the definitions of the attributes of variables. **Coding rules** tell us what to look for in the empirical world and what symbol to use to represent what we experience. Coding rules consist of an arbitrary symbol system (generally, words or numbers) that specify how symbols are matched to each attribute that a variable might take. That is, each attribute may have its own word label or be represented by a number. It is useful to note that the information carried by such symbols is determined by the dimension that underlies differences between attributes. In the language of mathematics, the qualities that underlie the differences between the attributes of a variable are called **levels of measurement.**

For example, the dimension that separates the attributes of the variable "marital status" is a qualitative difference in the partner situation. Although at first glance, "single, never married" may seem "less partnered" than "married," there appears to be no dimension of quantity that divides the attributes "divorced" or "widowed." In fact, the logical relationship that exists between all attributes of this variable is simply mutually exclusive partner arrangements. Marital status is an example of a **discrete variable** in that each attribute defines a different status that is separated from other statuses in an "is not equal to" relationship. Discrete variables are coded at a *nominal* level of measurement. That means that when numerals are used to code discrete variables, the numerals are simply substitutes for the names of the attributes. In contrast, the variable age is a **continuous variable,** where the attributes that define the variable differ from each other in quantity. For continuous variables, the attributes may be distinct from each other on up to three dimensions. The definitions of the attributes may be based on rank order (is more than/is less than), unit difference (how much more or less than the adjacent attribute), or absolute quantity (how much relative to zero quantity). **Ordinal measurement** refers to variables whose attributes reflect ranking (is more/less than) and numerals used to code the attributes reflect rank order. **Interval measurement** occurs when the unit difference that separates adjacent attributes is used to distinguish attributes. Finally, **ratio measurement** occurs when each attribute is defined as a specific distance from a zero point that reflects a true absence of the quality.

An example might be in order. A person observing activity at a school playground might code the children's gender and record this using numerals in place of words. The attributes that define the variable *gender* (e.g., girls and boys) are separated by identity, and thus the measurement is on a nominal scale. In addition, our observer might note the *ranked outcome* of a foot race involving all of the children (i.e., first, second, third,..., last). These finishing ranks would be an example of a variable measured at an ordinal level of measurement. An astute observer might be able to assess accurately the varying increments between the finishing racers, much as a horse racing aficionado might note a horse winning by "two lengths." Such a variable, margin of victory, is an example of coding at the interval level of measurement. We don't know how fast a runner was, just the incremental distance between runners. Finally, a variable called elapsed time would contain attributes that reflect the time each runner took to complete the race. This variable would be coded at a ratio level of measurement. Ratio measurement is distinctive in that one of the attributes in the list is defined as having none of the quantity (a true zero point) that underlies the attributes (i.e., no time elapsed = 0).

The distinction between discrete variables measured at the nominal level of measurement and continuous variables measured at the ordinal, interval, or ratio levels of measurement is important, especially when observations contain both discrete and continuous variables. The codes "1, 2, 3,..." mean something quite different when applied to a discrete variable than when applied to a continuous variable. For one thing, the range of mathematical operations that can be done on the symbols is radically different. This will become more obvious when we discuss data analysis a little later. Suffice it to say now that it would be meaningful to subtract the numerals in a variable called *elapsed time* to compute the difference in different runners' finishing times, but it would be meaningless to add the numerals corresponding to gender to determine anything about gender. The different properties of the three types of continuous measurement (ordinal, interval, ratio) place limits on what can be done statistically with variables, although the degree of restriction has been a matter of debate among applied statisticians for at least thirty years or more. Since these issues are largely related to data analysis, we will not pursue this discussion further here.

Desirable Characteristics of Measures: Reliability and Validity

Operational definitions of constructs often include collections of indicator variables. It is common to speak of these organized collections as scales, instruments, or tests. Scales, as organized measurement systems, include all the elements of a good operational definition. They reference empirical events, define a social setting designed to produce unambiguous observations, and provide precise coding rules, often in test manuals or scoring aids. Although the particulars of the test administration may allow wide latitude, the better instruments have been found to be highly consistent across many settings. The most common image of scales is the questionnaire, a paper-and-pencil question list designed to elicit responses that map to one or more constructs. Much of the literature concerning validity and reliability is directed at evaluation of such instruments. Although the following remarks could apply equally to any collection of indicators, for the sake of clarity, we discuss validity and reliability in the context of scales and instruments.

Our presentation of the concepts of reliability and validity varies somewhat from the traditional approach found in most research texts. Traditionally, consideration of measurement reliability precedes that of measurement validity. That approach almost certainly flows from the mathematical reality that an instrument's level of reliability sets an absolute ceiling on the level of its validity. Instead, we offer an instructive approach that reflects the logic that people use to actually think about and develop new measurement systems. This approach also produces a continuity in the methods used to assess reliability and the various forms of validity—moving from criteria that are based in logic and expert opinion to those driven by theory and statistical evaluation.

Measurement **validity** is a multidimensional construct. Over the years, social scientists have tended to group the dimensions of validity into four classifications. These are face validity, content validity, construct validity, and criterion-related validity. Reflecting this, our approach is organized around answering five basic questions: (1) What should the instrument content "look like"? (2) What actual content domains should the instrument include? (3) Can the instrument assess the selected domains consistently? (4) Will the assessment, or scores, produced by the instrument correlate with other variables in patterns that are predicted by relevant theory? and (5) Will the scores produced by the instrument accurately reflect the level of the characteristic being assessed? Collectively, these five questions address the evaluation of reliability and the four traditional classifications of measurement validity. Each of these five questions is addressed in what follows to fully elucidate these core concepts.

Face Validity: What Should the Instrument Content "Look Like"? To claim **face validity** for an instrument is to say that the items on an instrument appear to be logically related to the construct that the instrument is intended to measure. Whether they do so appear, rather than whether the instrument performs as it should, is the basis of a claim to face validity. We can draw a rough analogy with an old folk saying: Face validity is the psychometric equivalent to the expression, "Beauty is only skin deep." Personal beauty is a pleasant aspect in interpersonal relationships, but it is a weak claim if the deeper and more abiding personal characteristics are lacking. So it is with a measurement instrument; face validity is only "skin deep." Although it is not strictly necessary that the items of an instrument actually do bear an obvious resemblance to the construct being assessed, it is reasonable that such an expectation exists. In the absence of some compelling reason for disguising an instrument, the requirement of face validity seems reasonable.

Although face validity is the weakest form of validity and some measurement researchers choose to disregard it completely, we believe that it has a practical psychological value for both social work practitioners as well as those people who are completing the items of a measurement instrument. Sometimes an instrument that does not appear to be what it claims distorts the measurement through a process called **reactivity.** In these cases, the apparent incongruence between what a participant was told about an instrument and what it appears to be may create the impression of deception or incompetence, and the negative affect may influence responses to the instrument.

Content Validity: What Actual Content Domains Should the Instrument Include? After having developed some sense of what an instrument should look like—that is, an idea of face validity—the developer of a new instrument turns to the question of *content domains* to be included in the instrument. **Content validity** concerns the degree to which a measurement instrument includes the full range of meaning found in the nominal definition of the construct being measured. An instrument designed to measure a particular construct incorporates a number of different items. It is often literally true that the items used are selected from a larger pool of potential items that were considered for inclusion. Even this larger pool of items has been implicitly selected from an even larger set of potential items. This largest set of items is called the item domain for the construct. High content validity is present when the items on an instrument are representative of the construct's item domain.

Of course, we can never know for sure that any set of items truly does accurately represent the theoretical item domain. In practice, the claim of content validity is one of judgment. We generally rely on informed opinion. Often, you will read that a panel of experts was used to generate items or that items were generated from a thorough review of the literature. These are both efforts to legitimate a claim of content validity. In the final analysis, such a claim can never be proven. Instead, it rests on how clearly the method by which individual items were selected ensures the inclusion of all key aspects of the construct's item domain.

Reliability: Can the Instrument Assess the Selected Domains Consistently?

Having identified the appropriate content domains for inclusion and specific indicators to reflect those domains, the instrument developer must address the issue of measurement consistency, or reliability. **Reliability** refers to the consistency of a measure. The reliability of a measure is generally operationalized in one of three domains: interchangeability of indicators, stability of scores over time, and stability across observers. These three are labeled, respectively, as (1) internal consistency and parallel forms reliability, (2) test-retest reliability, and (3) interrater reliability.

All measures of reliability are intended to estimate the proportion of scores that reflect the "true" value of the characteristic being measured in contrast to the portion of a score that represents random error. Reliability is a necessary but not sufficient precondition for all forms of validity. If any instrument is unable to produce consistent measurement (reliability), it is a logical impossibility that it is able to reflect true meaning (validity). Whereas the claims of face and content validity are based on logical arguments as described before, the claim of reliability and the two classifications of validity that are addressed in the discussion that follows rest on empirical demonstration.

Measurement Error.   To better understand this discussion of reliability and the subsequent discussions of construct and criterion-related validity, we refer the reader to Equation 4.1 earlier in this chapter and its expansion here as represented in Equation 4.2. As is indicated in Equation 4.2, the error component of any measurement can be subdivided into random error and systematic error. The random and systematic error components of an observed score are

$$\text{score}_{\text{observed}} = \text{score}_{\text{true}} + \text{score}_{\text{random error}} + \text{score}_{\text{systematic error}} \qquad (4.2)$$

The goal of developing good measurement tools or assessment instruments is to maximize the portion of the observed score that is "true" and to minimize the error portions of the observed score. Unfortunately, some degree of error is present in all measurements. Error in a measurement can come from many sources—the person making the measurement can be inattentive to proper procedures, an instrument may carry a cultural or gender bias so that it may be accurate for some groups but overrepresent or underrepresent the measurement for others, or the subject of the measurement may intentionally or unintentionally misrepresent some aspect of their behavior. Every measurement instrument will have its own limitations on how accurate it can be. All these kinds of errors, as well as others that you might be able to think of, can be classified as being either *random or systematic sources of error*.

Random error is defined as error that occurs without any underlying pattern. Random error is just as likely to make an observed score larger than its true score as it is to make the observed score lower. Precisely because it is random, one can never be sure in which direction it is operating. Unfortunately, some degree of random error is present in all measurements, even the most precise scientific ones. Random error interferes with an instrument's reliability. As random error increases, an instrument's reliability must necessarily go down. That is because the random error produces a sort of a "wobble," or inconsistency, in the measurement. And inconsistency is the opposite of reliability.

Systematic error in a measurement happens in some regularized way. Think of systematic error as *bias*. Reliability, like validity, is strongly context-dependent. Earlier, we noted that the social setting in which the measurement is conducted provides important contributions to validity and we promised to return to that topic in Chapter 7 when we discuss data collection strategies. It is also true that validity and reliability are likely to differ across populations. It should be easy to see why this must be true. If an instrument is to be reliable and valid for persons from a certain population, the distinctions that underlie the attributes of the variables must be recognizable and meaningful to those persons. If they are not, the epistemic relationship between the indicators and constructs they are intended to reflect becomes suspect. Once this relationship is threatened, both reliability and validity are also likely to be threatened. Empirical tests of validity and reliability are only as useful as the match between the population from which the validation sample was drawn and the sample with which you intend to use the instrument.

When the error portion of a measurement consistently happens in the same direction—either erroneously raising or lowering a score—we say that the measurement instrument has an upward or downward bias. Obviously, if one *knows* that such an error consistently occurs, appropriate adjustments can be made to counteract the systematic error and remove the bias. However, it is often true that a systematic error only occurs for some subgroups in a population. When this happens, we say that the measurement instrument is biased in favor of or against the group or groups for which the systematic error is present. Imagine a measure of intelligence that produces higher scores for people with life experience in a modern postindustrial society and works to the disadvantage of people from traditional agrarian societies. Many psychological scales are criticized for producing more socially desirable scores for males, Caucasians, and those from postindustrial societies. To the degree that an observed score on an "intelligence test" has this kind of systematic error, the measurement really doesn't measure "intelligence," but rather other qualities such as life experience in a modern postindustrial society. In this way, systematic error is directly related to validity.

Assessing Reliability: Internal Consistency and Parallel Forms. The underlying logic of **internal consistency reliability** is that all of the items in an instrument should be assessing the same construct. Internal consistency reliability has traditionally been assessed using the *split-half* approach. The items of an instrument are divided into two halves. After administering the instrument to a group of subjects, each half of the instrument is scored separately. Finally, a correlation is computed for the two halves. In Chapter 8 ("Numerical Data Analysis"), we will examine the concept of correlation in detail. However, a brief explanation at this point will facilitate interpretation of reliability and validity coefficients. **Correlation** is a statistic that expresses (amongst other things) the accuracy with which one score can be used to predict another. Correlations are statisics with an absolute value between 0 and 1. A correlation of 1 indicates a perfect correlation and a 0 indicates the absence of a correlation. In the context of split-half internal consistency reliability, it is convenient (if not altogether accurate) to think of a correlation as a number reflecting the tendency for a person to respond to corresponding test items on the two halves with exactly the same score. Raw correlations are frequently translated into other numbers to provide more understandable indicators. For example, because instruments with a greater number of items tend to have higher reliabilities than shorter ones as a matter of mathematical necessity and the number of items in each split-half scale is only half the number in the actual scale, the computed correlation is corrected using the Spearman-Brown Prophecy equation (Nunnally, 1978). This corrected correlation serves as the split-half correlation coefficient. The closer this number is to 1, the greater the internal consistency.

Modern computing opens the door to an alternative approach to assessing internal consistency referred to as **Cronbach's alpha.** Conceptually, Cronbach's alpha is an index of the extent to which test items are all pulling in the direction of the construct being measured. Cronbach's alpha is computed from the inter-item correlations for all of the items in a scale. This is a little like using individual items instead of the two halves to compute the correlation. Many computer statistical packages include routines for assessing reliability using Cronbach's alpha, and it is one of the most frequently encountered measures of internal consistency found in the professional literature.

Parallel forms reliability involves the correlation between the instrument of interest and another equivalent or parallel form of the instrument. Parallel forms reliability assessments are seldom seen due to the simple fact that the procedures for developing parallel forms are quite cumbersome. We include it along with internal consistency to highlight the concept of *interchangeability of indicators*. In short, this concept suggests that there are multiple equivalent ways of assessing a construct. As the multiple items of a scale each contribute to accurately assessing the measured construct, it is possible to think that each item *individually* could be taken as a measure of the construct. Likewise, the notion of parallel forms advances the reasoning of interchangable indicators as well. Why then should one bother with multiple indicators at all? Recall that all measurement contains some portion of error. By using multiple assessment strategies or indicators, we are able to obtain a more accurate estimate of the true score. This process is called *triangulation,* from the ancient travelers who took multiple bearings from the stars in order to more accurately establish their own geographic position.

Assessing Reliability: Test-Retest Reliability.   **Test-retest reliability** concerns a measurement's stability over time. The assessment of test-retest reliability is based on the logic that any fairly stable client trait assessed over repeated measurements within a reasonable time frame should yield the same score, assuming that no real change has taken place. If this assumption can be accepted, any difference between the two administrations should reflect random measurement error. Test-retest reliabilities are quite common because of the relative ease in collecting the data.

Assessing Reliability: Interrater Reliability.   **Interrater reliability** involves the degree to which two independent judges using the same instrument arrive at the same score. Assume that you are in a practice setting that requires one of two intake interviewers to make an assessment of new clients with respect to the new clients' need for immediate service. How can you know if both of your intake workers are exercising consistent judgment in this process? This is a question of interrater reliability and can easily be assessed by having both interviewers assess the same group of clients. The correlation between the ratings of the two intake workers represents the interrater reliability. If it is acceptably high, say, .80 or more, you have the assurance that these intake decisions are being made in a consistent manner. If the reliability coefficient is unacceptably low, the interview has low interrater reliability and may not produce consistent, valid results.

Interpretation of Reliability Coefficients.   Reliability is generally estimated either by Cronbach's alpha in the case of internal consistency reliability or as a correlation in the case of test-retest and interrater reliabilities (Hudson, 1982). Because both indicators come from the same family of statistics (correlation), it is possible to offer rules for identification of good or adequate reliability. According to Hudson (1982), the rule to apply depends on how the measurement is to be used. The standard for clinical work with individuals is a bit higher than that for basic research with groups of subjects. This is because unreliability tends to be more troublesome in estimating individual scores than it is when the task is estimating group averages. Hudson (1982) has proposed that measurement tools with reliabilities of at least .60 be used for basic scientific work, whereas instrumentation with reliabilities of at least .80 or greater be used in clinical work. Nunnally (1978) is a bit more demanding by proposing that reliabilities in basic science be at least .80, whereas those in some practice settings should be .90 or even .95. We find ourselves split between these two. All would agree that higher reliabilities are better than lower reliabilities. However, scales with published reliabilities of .90 or .95 are difficult to find in some areas. Rather than rely on measures with unknown and possibly much lower reliabilities, we recommend using scales in clinical work with reliabilities as low as .80 as a matter of practical necessity. Because these same scales are available for basic research with groups, we do not see a practical need to appreciably lower the standard from .80 for this research. Thus, our final recommendation of a minimum of .70 for reliabilities in basic research and .80 for clinical work reflects a practical balance for social work practice.

Construct Validity: Will the Assessment or Scores Produced by the Instrument Correlate with Other Variables in Patterns That Are Predicted by Relevant Theory?   **Construct validity** concerns the way scores from an instrument compare to expectations provided by relevant theory about how it should perform

statistically. Specifically, the instrument should yield similar scores to other valid measures of the same construct, and scores on the instrument should differ appreciably from valid measures of dissimilar constructs. As with the assessment of reliability, the evaluation of construct validation is dependent on actually applying the measure, and possibly several other measures, and statistically examining the relationships among the scores. Construct validity is heavily theory-driven and was initially addressed in a classic paper by Donald Campbell and Donald Fiske (1959).

Campbell and Fiske (1959) proposed a multitrait-multimethod approach to construct validation in which the researcher proposed in advance which measures should correlate significantly with the measure being validated and which should not, and then measure these constructs using at least three independent methods. The key to understanding this approach is to appreciate that any construct necessarily exists in a conceptual matrix with other constructs that are predicted by theory to have stronger or weaker relationships with the construct of interest. These relationships can be efficiently expressed as correlations between pairs of constructs. Construct validity is present when two conditions are met. First, the construct of interest must be well-correlated with other constructs that are *measured by independent means* and are *predicted by theory* to be closely related to the construct of interest. Campbell and Fiske called this **convergent validity** because measurements of the construct of interest are seen to *converge* with the other theoretically related constructs. Second, construct validity requires that the construct of interest be poorly correlated with other constructs that are *measured by independent means* and that are *predicted by theory* to lack any relationship with the construct of interest. This quality is called **discriminant validity** because the construct of interest is discriminated from these other theoretically unrelated constructs. (A note of caution: This use of the term discriminant validity should not be confused with that sometimes used in criterion-related validity discussed later in this chapter.)

Measures of convergent and discriminant validity strengthen the argument for an epistemic relationship between the instrument and the construct it is believed to measure in two ways. Convergent validity is demonstrated when different measures of the same construct yield the same results for each person. Convergent validity is strongest when widely different methods are used. Discriminant validity is demonstrated when constructs that are predicted by theory not to be related are not related. Discriminant validity is strongest when all constructs are measured using the same or similar methods. An additional benefit of this approach is that although not directly addressing the issue of reliability (discussed previously), high convergent validity would not be possible if the instrument was not at least somewhat reliable since unreliability places a cap on statistical correlations. Therefore, strong evidence of convergent validity (high correlations) suggests that the instrument is reliable also.

The foregoing discussion assumes that we are considering a unidimensional scale, that is, a scale that is seeking to assess one and only one construct. The importance of construct validation also applies to the subscales within a multidimensional instrument. If we think about the subscales within a multidimensional scale as a set of unidimensional scales, it would be appropriate to apply the logic of Campbell and Fiske to see if the correlations with one another occur in predicted ways. However, a mathematical technique called factor analysis is typically applied to assess the "factor structure" of the instrument.

Factor analysis provides much information about patterns of responses. Two types of information are of interest in the context of this discussion of validity. First, factor analysis can confirm that individual items contribute to, or *load* on, the individual subscales with which they are expected to be associated. Second, factor analysis can assess the correlations among the subscales producing information similar to the Campbell and Fiske logic described before. Construct validity as reflected in factor analysis studies is an advance over face and content validity in that the techniques of factor analysis directly confirm by empirical test that the desired domains are present and that the items do in fact map to those domains, whereas face and content validity rest on argument without empirical verification.

Criterion-Related Validity: Will the Scores Produced by the Instrument Provide Useful Insights in Terms of Accurately Identifying the Characteristics of Interest? **Criterion-related validity** reflects how well a measurement instrument compares with some external measure of the same construct—a criterion. There are two subtypes of criterion-related validity that are defined by their temporal relationship to the external criterion—*concurrent* criterion-related validity and *predictive* criterion-related validity. **Concurrent validity** is estimated by comparing scores on the instrument being evaluated and with scores on a criterion that measures the same construct taken *at the same point in time*. **Predictive validity** is estimated by measuring the construct *before the criterion event has happened* and then waiting for the predicted event. The outcome is then compared to the instrument score to see how accurate the prediction was. An example of each clarifies the difference.

Assume you supervise an agency and are interested in establishing the criterion-related validity for an instrument to be used at client intake that identifies high-risk clients in need of immediate service. Your current system requires that new clients be assessed by one of the professional social workers who makes this determination. Although you are well-satisfied with the quality of these decisions, you are concerned that services to high-risk clients are being delayed because of the time it takes to assess all incoming clients. If your new instrument is valid, you can identify high-risk clients and refer them for immediate service by the professional social work staff.

Without interrupting the existing flow and pattern of work in the agency, you ask the intake workers to administer the new, brief high-risk assessment scale to all incoming clients. The completed high-risk assessment scales are forwarded to you. At the same time, clients are referred to the professional social work staff for complete assessments, as in the past. After an adequate number of new clients have completed the high-risk assessment and have been assessed by the social workers, you compare the recommendations that would have been made using the high-risk assessment scale to those actually made by the professional social workers. Note that this comparison can be represented by a simple correlation. If the correlation, known as the validity coefficient, is satisfactorily high—say, .60 or higher—you have evidence of *concurrent criterion-related validity* that supports a decision to use the new scale to more efficiently connect high-risk clients to service. Note that in this example, the agency's existing professional social work staff provided the concurrent "external" criterion—their regular assessment of all new clients. Because there was satisfaction with the quality of this professional decision making, it made a fine criterion that could be used without any disruption to the agency.

A variation on this assessment of criterion-related validity starts with two client groups, one of which is known to have a relatively high level of the problem being measured (e.g., an immediate need for service) and the other is relatively free from the problem. The measurement instrument could be completed by both groups and the results compared. The tendency for scores in the high-risk group to be higher than scores in the low-risk group reflects the test's *known groups validity*. Sometimes the utility of a test score as a means of categorizing persons into two or more groups is estimated by a statistical procedure called discriminant function analysis. In such cases, the known groups' validity is sometimes called *discriminant validity*. Note that discriminant validity as used here is a subtype of criterion-related validity and is different than discriminant validity in construct validation discussed earlier.

Let's now turn to a similar example illustrating *predictive criterion-related validity*. This time you are concerned about the number of teens dropping out of a primary prevention health and well-being program. If potential dropouts could be identified in advance, staff could intervene to postpone or avoid their premature departure. As before, you are interested in assessing the criterion-related validity of an instrument that seeks to identify those at high risk of dropping out. The instrument is administered to new clients at intake. We then wait until an adequate number of clients have either dropped out or completed the program. The measurement of predictive criterion-related validity would be the correlation between the new instrument score and the actual discharge status of the clients. This time, because the criterion was a future event—the actual event of dropping out—we have assessed *predictive criterion-related* validity.

Table 4.2 classifies measurement validity along with the various subtypes that are discussed in this chapter. As the table illustrates, it is useful to think of validity as having four main conceptualizations, and two of these, content- and criterion-related validity, each can be subdivided into three additional types.

Interpretation of Validity Coefficients.   As should be clear at this point, each kind of validity is interpreted in a slightly different way, reflecting the conceptualization behind the validity type. Only construct and criterion-related validity can be evaluated using a mathematical coefficient. Face and content validities do not provide specific coefficients for interpretation, but rest on the strength of the logical argument that can be made in their support.

Interpretation of the adequacy of validity from a correlation requires consideration of statistical significance, intended use of the measure, and risk-taking strategies of the persons using the measure. First, a correlation between a measure and its criterion or some other valid measure of the construct should be nonzero,

**TABLE 4.2   Categories and Subtypes
of Measurement Validity**

Face validity
Content validity
Construct validity
     Convergent validity
     Discriminant validity
     Factor analytic validity
Criterion-related validity
     Concurrent validity
     Known groups validity
     Predictive validity

as indicated on some test of significance, and preferably much higher than zero. Second, the validation correlation should be relevant to the use to which the score is put. For example, if the measure is used to predict some criterion (such as success in treatment, risk of injury), some form of predictive validity would be appropriate. Alternatively, if the measure is being used to detect differences between groups of individuals in various program components, a form of construct validity such as convergent and discriminant validity would be appropriate. Finally, when the measure is used as a broad screen for potential risk, quite small validities might be acceptable.

Relationship of Reliability to Validity.   You may have concluded by now that reliability and validity are related. An instrument that does not produce consistent measurement (reliability) is not likely to reflect any particular class of observations, including reflecting what we think we are measuring (validity). For example, if a test is described as measuring scholastic ability, but test and retest of the same individual produces widely different scores (a test of reliability), how can we say that the test is a valid measure of scholastic ability? Furthermore, it is a mathematical necessity that unreliability of the scores pushes all validity coefficients computed as correlations toward zero. Thus, conceptually and mathematically, it is not possible to have a valid measure if it is not first reliable.

In short, reliability sets an absolute upper limit on validity. Hudson (1982) provides a simple mathematical formula for this relationship. The relationship between reliability and validity is

$$\text{validity}_{\text{upper limit}} = \sqrt{\text{reliability}} \qquad (4.3)$$

In practice, it is very rare that any measurement instrument approaches this theoretical upper limit; most fall considerably short of it. The practical implications of this equation are very important for professional social workers. In the extreme cases of perfect reliability (i.e., $r = 1.0$), it would be theoretically possible to obtain perfect validity since the square root of 1.0 is 1.0. In the total absence of reliability (i.e., $r = 0$), there could be no validity because the square root of zero is zero. In the space between these extremes, where social work practice takes place, it is important to remember that any reduction in an instrument's reliability is likely to produce a corresponding reduction in the validity of the instrument. As our validity shrinks, we have a smaller and smaller claim that our measurements carry any real meaning at all. Thus, seek out and avoid those sources of random error as a part of your commitment to providing clients with meaningful measurement.

The relationship between validity and reliability notwithstanding, reliability and validity do reflect different ideas. First of all, recall random and systematic error. High reliability depends on eliminating all of the possible sources or random error—or at least keeping them to an acceptably low level. The techniques of developing observation protocols and asking questions discussed in Chapter 7 ("Data Collection") consist of procedures designed to maximize reliability.

Whereas reliability is influenced only by random error, validity is influenced by both random error (unreliability) and systematic error (bias). Because validity concerns accurately labeling what an instrument measures, any bias must necessarily reduce the measure's worth as a true reflection of the intended object of measurement. Sources of bias influence validity by moving scores away from the construct the test was intended to measure. For example, a test of intelligence that requires familiarity with Western urban environments is likely to push the scores of rural non-Western persons in a common direction, decentering the score from intelligence and toward Western urbanalization.

Summary

Scientific approaches to measurement are designed to facilitate communication between diverse individuals by clarification of meanings and linking ideas to empirical referents. Scientific measurement can be thought of as a conceptualization process that starts with individual concepts and ends with operational definitions and observation. Conceptualization refers to the process of building consensus concerning the meanings and symbols used to represent experience. Operational definitions specify direct observables, social situations, and coding rules through which experiences will be observed and recorded. Two important attributes of any measure are validity and reliability. Validity refers to the meaningfulness of a measure, that is, its conceptual clarity. Reliability refers to the consistency of a measure, that is, the tendency to obtain the same result when we measure the same phenomenon under different conditions, including different indicators, observers, settings, or over time. The degree of validity and reliability that is adequate depends on the use of the measure. In the case of standardized measures, reliabilities of .80 or higher are recommended for individual assessment and .70 for group comparisons. Minimum standards for validity include empirical demonstration of a nonzero correlation between the measure of interest and either other measures of the same construct or a suitable external criterion in a population that matches the population for which the test is to be used. In order for a test to be valid, it must first be reliable.

CHAPTER

5 Research Designs

Drawing Inference

❧ Relationship of This Chapter to the Whole

This chapter is organized around the concept of making inference. **Inference** means drawing meanings from experience through reasoning. Scientific knowledge consists largely of inference; that is, guesses or suppositions about the empirical world gleaned by our careful use of reason, method, and emphasis on intersubjectivity. **Research design** refers to the organization of the specific acts that scientists do into patterns that support the strongest inference possible given the question being posed.

Earlier, we noted that developing description, prediction, and explanation concerning empirical events are three of the aims of science. However, a single study seldom is intended to provide all three. In fact, description, prediction, and explanation all reflect different kinds of inference and therefore require different approaches if we are to build a strong case for some statement about the empirical world. In this chapter, you can see how scientists and scientifically oriented practitioners combine the basic tools of science into research designs that support various kinds of inference.

We start this chapter by discussing some general issues related to making inference. Next, we look at each type of inference (description, prediction, explanation) and describe tools that can be employed in support of making strong inference. We then discuss threats to internal and external validity that operate to produce erroneous inference. Finally, we provide examples of designs that are useful in providing strong cases for each type of inference.

Contrary to some of the historical debates among scientists, we don't see any particular design or class of designs being superior in any absolute sense. A superior research design is that which is matched to the particular question that is being posed. Here, *matched* means capable of providing inference strong enough to support the reasons why the study was undertaken, as well as being feasible and cost-effective. The design reflects the capacities and constraints that one may face with measurement, sampling, and the methods of data collection that are available. This often involves making compromises in design strength to accommodate the realities of a given research setting. The superior design is the one that maximizes all three criteria—strength of inference, feasibility, and cost-effectiveness—regarding a particular research question. In some ways, research design sits at the center of the research enterprise. Designs take all the complex acts that we discuss in this book, such as ways of sampling, measurement, data analysis, and the like, and combine them into organized wholes that guide scientific study. Understanding these wholes is a bit like reading recipes. Understanding designs gives you a better idea of what the final product will look like and should help you avoid becoming lost in the minutia of research tools. However, just where to provide such a panoramic view of science in this book was a bit of a dilemma. Many of the acts that are organized into designs are not fully discussed until later chapters. Yet it is difficult to understand why some of these acts (e.g., random sampling) are important unless you can see the big picture provided by a discussion of design. We have sometimes wished we were able to transmit the core body of research knowledge to our students in a single, whole experience. Unfortunately, all of our experiences in teaching research methods suggest that learning this content is a more linear process that starts at one point and moves through to a logical conclusion. The fact is, however, that there are various routes from the beginning to the end of this process. We have traveled a number of them and, to some degree, have always found ourselves teaching content that draws on an understanding of material yet to be covered. Such is the interrelationship among the pieces of the research puzzle. More than any of the topics in this book, research design provides an integrated view of science.

Relevance to the Roles of Social Workers

Social work is an applied profession, and, as such, social work research questions must have relevance in the lives of the people served by social workers. It is important for social workers to be able to describe people and things, predict relationships, and explain likely outcomes given particular actions. Whether we are concerned with the actions of clients that might result in untoward consequences for them or with the actions that we employ in our interventions to ameliorate existing difficulties in their capacity to be fully functioning people within a particular social environment, we are best equipped when we are able to describe, predict, and explain the phenomena of interest and the relationships among them from the standpoint of strong inference.

Social workers need to be familiar with a broad range of designs because they are involved in all aspects of the scientific process. Wallace (1971) suggested that one of many ways to categorize scientific activity was the intersection of two dimensions, an inductive-deductive dimension and a theorizing-testing dimension. Table 5.1 illustrates this view of science. Operating in the deductive, theorizing quadrant, social workers make guesses (hypotheses) about consequences of various courses of action in the context of their professional practice by using their knowledge of theory and logic. In the deductive, testing quadrant, social workers are likely to mount empirical tests of theory-derived propositions, such as the effectiveness of interventions or policies. Moving to the inductive, testing quadrant, social workers are constantly, at individual and group levels, trying to attach meanings to observations; that is, listening to clients and attempting to understand their viewpoints. Finally, in the quadrant combining induction and theorizing, social workers participate in the creation of new theories.

The three forms of inference discussed in this chapter—description, explanation, and prediction—are not evenly distributed throughout these quadrants, but do tend to be present in all four quadrants. For example, the ability to describe is dependent on theorizing to tell us what to describe, as much as theorizing is dependent on observation to tell us what to theorize about. Prediction may be accomplished in the context of weak explanation, but good description is needed for accurate prediction, and good description rests on good theory, which is in fact good explanation. What this means for social workers is that you need to be comfortable with acting in any of the quadrants of the scientific process. Arguments that social workers need to be more inductive, deductive, theory using, or theory testing are misguided in that these things are pieces of the whole, separable for purposes of analyses, but intimately bound up in practice.

TABLE 5.1 Modes of Using Science

	Constructing Theory	**Applying Theory**
Theorizing and Using Logic	Forming propositions and concepts, understanding, explaining	Making hypotheses about particulars from general theory, deduction
Doing Empirical Research	Estimating population parameters from measures, using research methods, looking for associations	Using scales, instruments, sampling in practice, describing individuals and samples

Some practice-oriented examples of different forms of inference might be in order. If you have been hired as a community organizer, you need to accurately describe your community of interest in terms that have consistent meaning for the people with whom you are involved. You probably make some inference about the whole community based on experience with some smaller portion of the community. Data for this "smaller portion" may be drawn from a sample of people, the use of key informants, or other sources. Each possibility involves deciding on a specific research design to gather data so that your inference is supported.

Once our practice interests have been adequately described, we are usually interested in being able to predict outcomes based on conditions or events that might be present in the social environment. Note carefully that we have said only that outcomes are to be predicted by these other conditions or events. This is quite different than saying that these other conditions or events caused the outcome. For instance, you might reasonably notice that as the weather warms in the summertime, teenagers are more likely to be involved in mischief that ranges from adolescent pranks to serious criminal behavior. Whereas it would be appropriate to predict that these behaviors will probably occur when the next summer arrives, it would be inappropriate to suggest that summer *causes* these behaviors. There are many things in social work practice that we are able to predict with reasonable accuracy even though we may not be able to identify the causes with equivalent accuracy. Accurate prediction is supported by using research designs that produce the kind of data that support predictive inference. This goes beyond what was needed for accurate descriptive inference.

Explanation, the third and final kind of inference that we wish to make in social work practice, involves moving beyond prediction to an understanding of the underlying causes that result in behaviors of interest. We call this explanatory inference and it requires us to rule out any of the other alternative explanations that might account for an outcome. In addition to ruling out all other alternative explanations, strong explanatory inference requires that we are able to show a correlation between the suspected cause and its precipitant outcome, as well as appropriate time ordering between the cause and its outcome. (Causal variables are required by logic to precede the outcomes they produce.)

In doing social work, most practitioners incorporate a large number of specific behaviors into their helping interventions. We perform a series of theory-driven behaviors to facilitate the therapeutic relationship that we are employing. Although it is possible that every one of these behaviors/actions contributes equally to the helping process, it is likely that some more than others actually *cause* client change. Practice is most efficient when we are able to maximize our presentation and facilitation of these *causal factors*. In order for this to be done, we need to be able to explain the relationships between specific actions in the social work intervention and the resultant outcomes in the client system. This kind of explanatory inference requires the use of research designs that allow us to recognize which of our actions are the true causes of client change.

Each of these parts of knowledge is important as we are engaged in the role of social worker. The kind of practice that you are interested in pursuing may call on one type of knowledge more than the others. Nonetheless, you are well served to be able to apply the design tools appropriate to all of them. In that way, not only are you prepared to meet the demands of your own practice, but you are also equipped to read and evaluate the published work of others as you seek to apply the best available information to your practice.

Learning Objectives

After reading this chapter, the student will be able to:

1. use the vocabulary and concepts of research design
2. describe the functions of research designs
3. describe the tools of research design for descriptive, predictive, and explanatory inference
4. describe common threats to inference of each type
5. give examples of designs that tend to yield strong inference of each type

Key Terms and Concepts

The Nature of Research Design

Research design is organizing acts to maximize the strength of inference possible. We think of research design very much as manipulating a set of tools in different combinations in order to allow different kinds of inference to be made. Although we have said that the different kinds of inference are really cumulative, it does not necessarily follow that one is better than another. When description is necessary, it seems to us that it is an unnecessary expenditure of research resources to mount a study that is capable of providing explanatory inference. Thus, in practice, you should always strive to employ research designs that are appropriate to your question—nothing more and nothing less.

In truth, there are not that many of these tools to learn to manage. In this section, we review the kinds of inference that were introduced earlier, as well as the tools that can be employed to provide appropriate data to support necessary inference.

Inference Related to Description and Prediction. The logical process that leads to description is largely inductive. **Induction** involves reaching general conclusions by reasoning from specific cases. Although sometimes we may be describing only a specific set of cases that are all available for our examination and resultant description, more often we wish to draw a **descriptive inference** that allows us to say something about a larger class of phenomena when only a subset has actually been observed and studied. When we make such descriptive inference, we are applying inductive logic.

Predictive inference is also initially based on induction. It is quite common in practice that observations of specific cases are made over time that allow the skilled practitioner to predict with sometimes remarkable accuracy that a particular client outcome is likely to occur. This is an application of inductive logic that produces what has been called "practice wisdom" in the literature. Klein and Bloom (1995) proposed that to be truly "practice wise," practitioners should endeavor to apply the kinds of tools that are described in this chapter in order to strengthen the quality of the predictive inference that is being made.

Sometimes predictive inference involves the use of deductive logic. Deduction involves reasoning from a general principle, through a particular case covered by the general principle, to a conclusion. In using deductive logic to support predictive inference, the social worker is seeking to make accurate predictive statements about specific cases based on what can be predicted for the class of such cases more generally. The existence of the prediction allows the theory to be confirmed deductively by testing it against outcomes found in specific cases. Whenever we make practice decisions about the efficacy of a particular type of practice intervention with a client system of a specific nature, we are drawing predictive inferences based on deduction.

Our caution about grounding these and other deductive processes in inductive research concerns the need to avoid a costly deductive "guessing game." Remember, whenever we use deduction, we are seeking to make an inference about the specific case based on what is known about the general class. Ask yourself, "From where does this understanding of the general class come?" At its best, it is from the painstaking application of inductive research. When we fail to ground our deductive questions in this kind of research, we run the significant risk of being caught up in a series of wasteful "maybe-it's-this-maybe-it's-that" deductive questions. By drawing our questions from well-grounded, inductively generated principles, we vastly enhance our chances of producing a strong deductive inference—be it predictive or explanatory. Sometimes these inductive processes involve nonnumeric data as in many qualitative research studies, whereas other times the induction is based on heavily quantitative or numeric data. The issue is not the form that the data takes, but rather the form (and quality) of the logical process employed.

Inference Related to Explanation.   Explanatory inference is almost always based on deductive logic. Strong explanatory inference allows us to identify *causal patterns* in our data. *This causal inference requires us to meet three specific conditions.* First, we must be able to show that the causal variable and its outcome are *statistically correlated.* That means that when one of the variables occurs, it is statistically likely that the other variable will also be present. Note that correlation must also be present when we take one variable as predictive of another. Second, we must meet the requirement of **time ordering.** Logically, variables that cause change in other variables must precede those changes in time. Although students have occasionally tried to convince us that a test to be given later in the semester has caused them to study earlier in the term, it is actually their anticipation of the exam and their motivation to do well that has caused them to study. The long and short is simply that if we are to infer cause and, by extension, explanation, we must be able to demonstrate that our causes precede our outcomes in time. Finally, we must be able to eliminate all of the spurious pseudo-causes that might explain the phenomenon. In the language of research, we most often refer to this process as eliminating all of the rival hypotheses. A rival hypothesis is any statement that might be offered as an alternative explanation for the apparent relationship between a cause and an outcome. For example, one of the authors has had experience (as a consumer) with "therapeutic touch," an intervention that is similar in some ways to therapeutic massage. The premise of this intervention is that by the proper placement of the therapist's hands, the client's body is enabled to overcome the target problem. Friends and colleagues have challenged the idea of "therapeutic touch" and have offered "therapeutic suggestion" as a potential rival explanation for the supposed efficacy of the intervention. If all we are seeking is predictive inference, it makes little difference whether the "touch" or the "suggestion" is actually responsible for the outcome since both are present. However, when we truly desire to explain the nature of the intervention, simple prediction is not enough. Explanatory inference requires that we can identify the actual causes of an outcome, and this requires a more powerful research design. These designs will almost always employ deductive logic as their fundamental process. (By the way, neither "therapeutic touch" nor "therapeutic suggestion" produced the desired therapeutic outcome for the author!)

Optimal Design Is Determined by the Nature of the Research Question.   It bears repeating that the optimal design is determined by the kind of research question that is being asked. Too much time has been spent in the literature arguing about the relative merit of inductive designs or deductive designs, or of qualitative or quantitative data. We believe that science is about the business of providing accurate description of the changing world (including an acknowledgment of the perspective from which the description was generated), allowing predictions that serve to guide practice and building explanations so that practice can be made more effective. Although every social worker is not likely to be involved in all of these knowledge-building activities, every social worker is involved in asking some of these questions. The quality of both your questioning and your social work more generally is enhanced by allowing the characteristics of your question to drive the form that your research might take.

Designs Involve Manipulating a Small Group of Research Tools.   We have said that research design involves the manipulation and organization of a small group of research tools. Although each of these tools provides some specific quality in its own right, it is in combination that the tools produce the logical arrangements that allow strong inferences to be made. In general, the more tools that one uses in a design, the stronger the inference that is capable of being made. By the same token, our preceding admonition to let the question being asked determine the form of the research design should make clear that "more is not always better." We have learned the sometimes difficult lesson that "using a large hammer to drive a small nail often results in a bruised thumb!" As with all craft, the skilled practitioner has the tools that are necessary to cover all of the likely contingencies and then employs those that are necessary to achieve the task at hand.

All research design depends on the presence of *good measurement* (that which can be consistently and meaningfully applied within the social context in which the measurement is made). In many kinds of designs, the researcher is able to specify nominal and operational definitions in advance of the implementation of a particular design. However, in other cases—most notably qualitative inductive studies in which truly open exploration is being made—this is not possible. Nonetheless, even in these latter cases, quality inference depends on quality measurement. In these cases, a design tool called *triangulation* is used.

Our inclusion of triangulation as a tool of research design rather than treating it in its more limited interpretation as an issue of measurement stems from our inclusion of all inference as a function of research design. In designs where a priori operationalization is not possible or appropriate, the use of triangulation should be explicitly incorporated into the research design as a way of improving the inference that is ultimately produced. This would be the prevailing situation in most research designs involving nonnumeric data.

A second research tool called grounding is similar to triangulation in that it relies on multiple informants for its strength. **Grounding** refers to the process of checking or confirming insights drawn from the research process with multiple people from within the social environment being studied. Like triangulation, the strength of grounding derives from the consistency of the confirmation (or refinement, or disconfirmation) that is produced. However, grounding is focused on the validity (context-specific meaning) of the inferences that will be drawn.

Random selection for participation in a research study is a procedure that employs a random process to identify subjects in a research design. As you learn in detail in the next chapter on sampling, a random process is one that ensures that each and every member of the population from which we are sampling (more technically, the sampling frame) has an equal chance of selection. This tool provides two important qualities in a research design. First, by using random selection from a population about which you are interested, you are better able to apply the inferences that you draw to that larger population. In other words, you are able to *generalize* your findings beyond the limits of the study itself. This is a major portion of what is often called external validity. **External validity** is limited to the degree that findings within a study are not able to be generalized. We must be concerned with external validity whenever descriptive, predictive, or explanatory inferences are being made. Although external validity may also be limited whenever the study conditions differ from those that are found in the nonstudy environment, failure to randomly select from the population is probably the most common limiting factor in generalizing.

In addition to external validity, random selection eliminates the likelihood that the **selection bias** might operate in favor of one group or another. When selection biases are present, both external validity and internal validity may be compromised. **Internal validity** concerns the degree to which we are able to eliminate the rival hypotheses or potential alternative explanations for our findings. As such, the concern with random selection in relationship to internal validity is limited to selection biases in research designs that are attempting to support explanatory inference.

A different random process that may be confused with random selection is called random assignment. **Random assignment** is one of the most powerful research design tools available for drawing explanatory inference. It is always present in the strongest designs intended for explanatory or causal inference. Random assignment involves separating the subjects in a research study into two or more groups by any *random process.* Similar to the random selection process defined before, a random process for assignment to groups is defined as any procedure that ensures that each subject has an equal chance of being assigned to any particular group. This process need not be elaborate. If the need is to establish two randomly assigned groups, you could start by assigning the initial person to the first group by the flip of a coin and then taking every other person in the sample after that. After all of the participants have been assigned, each group can be given its designation as an intervention group or a control group by a final flip of the coin. The important thing to understand and remember is that after groups have been created by random assignment, they can be assumed to be *generally equal* on all dimensions *within the bounds of sampling error.* The logic of random selection and random assignment as well as the procedures that can be employed to achieve them are presented in some detail in the next chapter.

The *selecting times for taking measurements* in a research study is a tool of research design that is much more powerful than one might initially think. Whether you are doing inductive or deductive research, understanding the timing of your measurements in relationship to other variables is an important consideration. In a phenomenological study (employing inductive logic), you might wish to accurately describe the experience that people have following their abrupt termination from employment. It seems reasonable that the data you would accumulate if you conducted your interviews within days or even hours of being notified of termination would likely differ from the data drawn from interviews that were conducted weeks or even months later. The point is not to say that one time is "correct" and the other is not. Rather, it is important for the researcher to understand the relationship that the timing of measurement or assessment has to the research question and the research process more generally. The very same logic applies in more deductively designed research studies involving pretests and posttests. Although it tends not to be explicitly stated in many published research papers, **pretests** are assumed to be given shortly before the introduction of the intervention (the independent variable) and **posttests** are assumed to be taken shortly after the impact of the intervention is believed to have occurred. These two measurements are timed to provide the best comparison of the "before" and "after" states of research participants. A posttest that occurred years later would be of little value in drawing a precise explanatory inference. Recognize also that the term *test* in this context refers to *any measurements* that occur before and after an intervention that are taken to facilitate an evaluation of the change that was produced by the intervention. They are not limited to the more narrow interpretation of a *test* as a pencil-and-paper assessment.

The ability to *manipulate the independent variable* is another tool that is vitally important in research designs that seek to provide explanatory inference. Manipulation of the independent variable allows the researcher to introduce the independent, or causal, variable into otherwise controlled settings in order to evaluate the effect that it has. When two research settings are arranged such that the only difference between them is the presence or absence of the independent variable, very strong evidence regarding the causal force presumably exerted by the independent variable is produced. In fact, along with random assignment to groups and the timing of measurements, the ability to manipulate the independent variable is the third benchmark of a group of research designs called **true experiments.**

We offer **statistical control** as our final research design tool. Statistical control goes beyond the use of statistics that is generally suggested by the more inclusive term of statistical analysis. Statistical control is achieved through the use of a number of statistical procedures—most commonly analysis of covariance (ANCOVA) and a whole family of multiple regression techniques. The skillful application of statistical control allows the researcher to approach the three requirements for inferring causality and explanation by analyzing the effects of an independent variable after separating the influences of identifiable alternative explanatory variables. Although these procedures can never produce inference that is as strong as that produced by true experiments (involving the use of random assignment to group, manipulation of the independent variable, and control over the timing of measurements), they are also not burdened with some of the onerous procedural requirements of true experiments. As a consequence, the use of statistical control in social work research is an important and powerful design tool.

The Qualitative versus Quantitative Distinction at the Level of Design.

We have alluded to a simmering controversy in social science research involving the use of qualitative and quantitative research "methods." To the degree that this controversy slows the advancement of social work knowledge building activity, we find it disheartening. More importantly, we believe that the controversy is more apparent than real. Before we move to our discussion of research designs to support explanatory, predictive, and descriptive inferences, we want to make our position with respect to these issues clear.

First of all, we are troubled by the blurring that has occurred between two sets of descriptors—inductive and deductive logical methods, and quantitative and qualitative data. As we have described in this chapter and elsewhere, induction and deduction are the logical processes involved in moving from specific observations to general classes and from general classes to specific cases, respectively. Because it is the nature of inductive questions to involve concepts and variables that may not have been fully understood previously, it is most efficient to use methods of data collection that rely on open-ended or free form responses. These methods of data collection have often been called "qualitative research methods" and do indeed produce data that are oftentimes qualitative in nature. That is, the data reflect experiences, sensations, understandings, and the like that are not *readily* amenable to quantification; hence, the label qualitative. However, it is equally possible that these same data collection methods might yield data that are quite readily quantifiable. In such a case, we would be wasteful to not record these data with the highest level of precision available. In any case, "qualitative" data frequently can be coded with numbers so that they look like and sometimes can be manipulated like numbers, that is, quantitative data.

On the flip side, because deductive questions are best drawn from existing theory, these studies tend to allow the use of previously explicated variables that are capable of being reliably and validly operationalized. When such concepts are well understood, it is generally possible that they can be studied using closed-ended questions that are readily coded with numbers to represent various levels that a respondent might report. Such data are traditionally referred to as "quantitative," although they are clearly intended to communicate something about the underlying qualities of the research subjects from whom the data were collected. Indeed, one can argue that all "quantitative" data is only as valuable as the essential qualities that they represent. Thus, for us, the adjectives "quantitative" and "qualitative" are most apt as descriptions of the form that our data might take—either numeric or nonnumeric—and not so much about the methods of data collection.

As convenient as it would be for inductive questions to be answered by qualitative data and deductive questions to be answered by quantitative data, that is an oversimplification of reality. Inductive questions are informed by both qualitative and quantitative data. Our favorite example of an inductive study that depends on high levels of quantification and statistical analysis is the large-population epidemiological survey. The purpose of such a study is to establish the cause of disease, including the transmission vectors, vulnerable populations, and a wide range of other important information. In cases of large-scale epidemiological studies, huge quantitative data sets are generated and subjected to very sophisticated analyses. Such a study is appropriately labeled *quantitative induction.*

We could go on with examples of mixing these descriptors. All of the combinations are possible. This means, for us, that when we set aside the "quantitative-qualitative" controversy, two distinctive features remain. First, social workers need to recognize when the nature of the research question calls for an approach that is either inductive or deductive. When we have little (or weak) theory to guide us in making prediction or offering explanation, we should be drawn to more inductive procedures. The fact is that in these cases, we may not know enough to allow us to move deductively from the general class of the phenomenon of interest to the specific case (that is often represented by our practice client). On the other hand, when there is a strong literature about what has been done in the past that can serve to guide us as we shape the future (with small or large client systems), we are wasteful to disregard this knowledge by failing to utilize deductive approaches that draw fully from the theory describing the general class of the phenomenon.

Second, social workers need to fully appreciate that our inductive and deductive questions can be informed by data that take either numeric or nonnumeric forms. When we lack the kind of specific understandings that are often required to generate "quantitative" questions, we are foolish to guess about the forms that our subjects' responses might take by asking them to "check a box." When the kind of understanding required to legitimately construct closed-ended questions does exist, we must take advantage of this expediency to advance our understanding of human behavior by testing the predictive and explanatory capacities of our theories. Armed with an understanding that accepts both forms of logic and all forms of data collection as having potential to contribute equally to the scientific process, we now turn to the construction of research designs for explanation, prediction, and description.

Designs to Support Explanatory Inference

Threats to Inference Related to Explanatory Questions.   There are two funda-mental classes of errors that can be made when we are seeking to draw an explana-tory inference. The first concerns *external* validity. For a number of reasons, whereas the conclusions that we draw may be perfectly legitimate *within* the group of sub-jects that we have actually studied, those conclusions may not be applicable to people outside the groups studied or in situations other than the study environ-ment. Because this class of errors concerns the application of the study findings to a social environment that *goes beyond the limits* of the actual study (i.e., different people and/or different contexts), the potential causes of these errors are called threats to *external validity.* The primary **threats to external validity** involve interac-tions between the outcome variable and the testing/assessment procedures (i.e., testing) or other unique characteristics of the study's sample (i.e., selection) and the reactions that subjects have to the study's unique conditions (Campbell & Stanley, 1963). Because the threats to external validity all involve a reaction to some stimulus (testing procedures, subject characteristics, or the study environment), they have been called **interaction effects** by Campbell and Stanley.

In contrast, the other class of errors in making explanatory inference con-cerns the degree to which we can rule out other possible causes for the outcome behaviors that we are studying. The errors in this class operate within the proce-dures of the study and are hence called **threats to internal validity.** Threats to internal validity operate to potentially produce changes that are mistakenly taken to be caused by the independent variable(s) of interest. Thus, since the primary purpose of making explanatory inference is being able to explain the change mechanisms (that is, *causes*) that are operating in a social work intervention, it is essential that we are able to rule out these threats to internal validity that present themselves as alternative explanations or rival hypotheses.

The classic work explicating both threats to internal and external validity was written by Donald Campbell and Julian Stanley in 1963. Along with the three primary threats to external validity that we have indicated before, Campbell and Stanley identified eight threats to internal validity. We will address each in the paragraphs that follow.

History is a cover term for all factors *external to the study participant and the study itself* that may influence research subjects. In spite of the past tense implied by the name, these factors most commonly operate concurrently with the research study. In fact, history becomes an increasing threat as the time between pretest and posttest measurements are made. You may think of history as all those known and unknown factors that have the potential for causing change in the research subjects. Although some history effects may operate on only some individuals in a study, generally, these external influences are operating on a scale that potentially impacts most or even all of the research subjects. Imagine an educational program designed to encourage young adolescents to resist drug-using behaviors that is conducted *at the same time* as a major television campaign designed to encourage young adolescents to avoid drug taking. Assume further that at the conclusion of the program, the graduates take a behavioral assessment inventory that indicates an increase in their drug-avoidance tendencies compared to a comparable measure taken before the educational program. Could you attribute this change to the impact of the educational program. No! An equally plausible explanation is that the media campaign produced the change. To conclude otherwise would be to ignore the role of history as a threat to internal validity.

In contrast to history, which involves factors operating outside of the research subject, **maturation** represents the changes that take place internal to the research participant. These influences would include all of the physical, psychological, and social changes that take place in a person's life as a function of the passage of time. However, the social work researcher should also take note of the possible influence of fatigue or boredom on study participants. Although these processes are not what we would think of as maturation in a developmental sense, they are included as maturational threats to internal validity because they operate *within* the individual.

The possibility that any *pretesting* can have an effect on the measured outcome is yet another threat to the internal validity of a study. **Testing** as a threat to internal validity involves the sensitization that can occur with subjects as a result of their exposure to the constructs or ideas that are involved in the study. For instance, suppose you were interested in the effect of a training intervention on a nursing home staff that was intended to correct erroneous stereotypes about the aging process that you believed were held by the staff. In order to measure the changes that take place in staff persons, you decide to measure the knowledge of the staff before the training begins and again after the training has been completed. People are generally curious beings, and after the pretest, they are likely to think about the issues raised, and perhaps even discuss those issues with friends and colleagues. It is quite possible, even probable, that exposure to the content of the pretest can produce changes in the knowledge measured at the posttest, even without the training intervention. To the degree that this process results in an independent change in the outcome variable, it is a threat to the internal validity of the research design that was implemented.

An additional threat that occurs between a pretest and a posttest is called **instrumentation.** Unlike the testing effect discussed immediately before that involved an unintended change in the subject as the result of exposure to the pretest, instrumentation involves an unintended change in the measurement instrument itself. In a mechanical sense, such a chance could be represented by the fatiguing of a spring in a scale or the like. More commonly in social work research, instrumentation as a threat to internal validity results from changes in the views or interpretations of the people doing the measurement. Of course, it could also involve an actual change in the person doing the measurement or in the measurement instrument used. Any time there is a potential that the observed change in a subject's scores between the pretest and the posttest is really a reflection of a change in the measurement technology rather than an actual change in the subject, our design suffers from instrumentation, a threat to internal validity.

When we measure characteristics of people who are participating in our study precisely because they have extreme levels (high or low) of the characteristic in question, we must guard against **statistical regression** as a threat to inferring cause. Statistical regression involves the universal tendency for every person's measurements on any characteristic to cluster around his or her own norm, or average. If, for instance, you took the Graduate Record Exam (GRE) and achieved a score that you felt was much higher than you anticipated, you probably wouldn't take the GRE again. Why? Because you know intuitively that you would likely receive a lower score on the next attempt. In the language of research, you would tend to regress toward your own (lower) norm. Quite often in social work research, we face a similar situation. People are involved with our interventions *because* they have reached an extreme level on some characteristic that is deemed unacceptable to themselves or to significant others in their social systems. People don't seek social services because everything in their lives is going along normally. Instead, the decision to seek services is much more likely to be the result of some atypical feeling such as, "I've never felt worse than I feel now" or "I simply can't go on this way." Whenever we have such a situation in research, we are facing regression as a likely threat to internal validity. The fact is that whenever people are "at their limits," they are likely to improve (at least somewhat and at least temporarily) with or without an intervention. When this spontaneous improvement reflects one's movement toward a more personally normative level, it is called statistical regression.

Sometimes we take advantage of existing groups when we are trying to evaluate different approaches to addressing problems in client systems. When we do so, we run the risk of **selection** as a threat to internal validity. Selection, sometimes called selection bias, reflects the fact that any existing groups (i.e., any groups that were not explicitly constructed to be equivalent to one another) differ from each other in ways that may be recognized or unrecognized. Thus, returning to our preceding brief example of aging stereotypes held by a nursing home staff, suppose that you wanted to assess the impact of your training by comparing the knowledge following training in one nursing home to the knowledge levels among staff in another similar but *untrained* nursing home. You could not be sure that any differences that you found were not present before your intervention. Depending on the nature of the preexisting differences, your training could appear to be *either* more or less effective than was actually the case.

Mortality is a dramatic sounding threat to internal validity that refers to the tendency for research participants to drop out of the study for any reason. The threat to internal validity arises when participants' withdrawal creates differences between the groups. When subjects withdraw from a study, we can never be certain that those terminations are not related to our outcome variable. Perhaps subjects withdraw because our intervention has been so successful they no longer are motivated to seek additional change. On the other hand, it is possible that subjects withdraw because they perceive the intervention as being a waste of time. The effect that this mortality has on the outcome cannot be assessed without adequately controlling for it as a threat to internal validity.

A different kind of threat to the internal validity of a research study is produced when an interaction between selection and one of the other threats is possible. In the case of a selection-history interaction, people who are selected for participation in different research groups (comparison groups, treatment and control groups, etc.) may be exposed to different external conditions (i.e., history) for any number of reasons. For example, a state regulatory quality assurance survey may occur in a facility that was assumed to be equivalent to another in which a new intervention technique is being tested. The interaction between this effect of history and the intervention may produce differences in the outcome variable that can be mistakenly assumed to have been caused by the intervention alone. Similar conditions arise when selection-maturation or selection-instrumentation interactions are possible.

In addition to these eight threats to internal validity, Cook and Campbell (1979) have identified a small number of others. Most important among these are causal time ordering, the potential for diffusion of the intervention, and a set of potential influences related to withholding the intervention from a control group.

Recall that the first requirement for inferring causality is that the cause must precede its effect or outcome. Although this seems obvious on its face, it is a common error to confuse a relationship that is characterized by correlation alone (the second requirement for inferring causality) with causality, especially in studies of naturally occurring phenomena. We might notice, for instance, that adolescents in residential drug-treatment programs who have more scheduled visits from family members progress through the treatment steps more quickly. Although we may interpret such a finding as evidence that family interaction facilitates treatment progress, it is equally plausible that increased treatment progress encourages a higher level of family interaction. This is the "chicken or egg" problem that characterized *causal time ordering* as a threat to internal validity.

The potential for **diffusion** of the intervention as a threat to internal validity is present whenever the intervention is able to be "shared" between study participants who have been exposed to the experimental intervention and those who have not. When interventions are organic in nature (i.e., dependent on physiological processes, as in the case of a drug being ingested), the threat of diffusion is minimal to nonexistent. However, in many behavioral interventions, the techniques involved are able to be taught to others not receiving them directly or to be successfully imitated by those who have not had direct exposure. For example, if an economic cooperative was developed in a community as a means of combating economic dependency for residents, it is not unreasonable to think that enterprising people in neighboring communities might observe the successful efforts and develop their own cooperative ventures. Any hoped for comparison between the communities to show the impact of the intended economic cooperative would be minimized by the similar improvements demonstrated by the "imitator" community to whom the intervention had diffused.

The final class of threats to internal validity involves the tendency for people to make **compensatory adjustments** that are not incorporated into the research design with respect to the control group's status of having the intervention withheld. We will note three distinct possibilities. First is the possibility that administrative *adjustments are made to equalize the treatments.* One of the authors was involved in a randomized study of a specific case management program. Other administrators who were aware of but uninvolved in the study had a tendency to want to allocate new program resources to community populations, including the control group members, since the intervention clients were known to be already receiving the "goodies" involved in the intervention. (Note, however, that the research was being done precisely because the value of these "goodies" was uncertain.) These compensatory actions have the effect of potentially diluting the intervention effect.

The other two common reactions when control groups are used involve *compensatory rivalry* and *resentful demoralization* by control group members. Knowing that they are members of a control group (as must generally be the case in any ethical research), control group members may respond by either putting forth an especially strong effort to achieve a positive intervention outcome status or they may simply "give up" and accept their perceived disadvantaged status. In either case, the comparison between the control group and the group receiving the intervention is altered by these nonintervention influences.

In summary, we have identified eleven threats that can operate to jeopardize the internal validity of a study. Any one of these can cause us to infer that an intervention has a measured effect when, in fact, no such effect exists. By the same token, threats to internal validity can operate so that we conclude that our intervention fails to produce the desired outcomes when the real (and valuable) effect of the intervention has been masked beyond our recognition. We turn now to a number of research design tools that we can employ so that these threats can be minimized or excluded altogether.

Research Tools That Strengthen Explanatory Inference.   The first tool used to strengthen explanatory inference (as well as the other types of inference to be discussed) is **random sampling.** As indicated in the overview of research tools, random sampling involves a selection process that ensures that each subject in the sampling frame has an equal chance of selection. A table of random numbers or a computer-generated listing of random numbers can facilitate this process, which is discussed more fully in Chapter 6 ("Sampling and Generalization"). As it applies to the process of drawing correct inference from data, random sampling provides the assurance that selection biases are not operating in the identification of subjects to be included in the study. In addition to this protection against the threat to internal validity presented by selection biases, random sampling is also the strongest tool for protection against selection as a threat to external validity. Remember that external validity involves making generalizations from the people and conditions actually studied to the wider social environment in which most social work practice takes place. With respect to external validity (generalization), it is always important to remember that you cannot generalize to a population from which you have not sampled. Thus, *random sampling is a key tool in ensuring both internal and external validity.*

Use of random assignment furthers the protection against selection bias as well as several other threats to internal validity. **Random assignment** involves the process of designating study participants to groups in such a manner that every participant has an equal chance of assignment to each group. In this way, *equivalent* control groups and intervention groups can be created. Sometimes additional groups are constructed using random assignment, as when different forms of the intervention may be studied. The essential value of random assignment is that it serves to *equate* the groups on all characteristics—known and unknown. As the size of the groups increases, the degree to which random assignment can work to increase their equivalence also increases.

Although each of the research design tools discussed in this chapter is important with respect to controlling against some threat to the validity of a study, random assignment to groups is probably the single most important control against threats to internal validity. If you do not already have an intuitive sense for the power of random assignment, consider the following mental experiment. Suppose you have 200 people who have been randomly selected for inclusion in your study of an intervention to produce a favorable attitude toward parental involvement in the academic activities of their school-age children. Half of these people will be provided with your intervention immediately (the intervention group), and the other half (the control group) has been told that it will be provided with the intervention services in a second wave. This allows you to make comparisons between your intervention group and the control group after only one group has received the intervention. You anticipate that the parents' own educational level may be a conditioning factor in the way that your intervention affects the research subjects and rightly use a random assignment procedure to equate the two groups. Consider how the process works. Would you expect one group to have more college graduates than the other group *by chance*? Would you expect one group to have more high school dropouts than the other group *by chance*? No. Since chance is the only influence operating in a random assignment procedure, you should expect the distribution of education between the two groups to be about equal. Furthermore, you should expect the distribution of *every other characteristic of the group members to be distributed about equally.* This is the power of random assignment. The important factors as well as the mundane are equally represented in both groups. Thus, the naturally occurring attitude in one group can be expected to be about the same as in the other group. In this way, random assignment offers protection against many of the identified threats to internal validity.

The *ability to manipulate the independent variable* provides a research design tool that works along with random assignment to allow the researcher to control who experiences the intervention variable and who does not. Consider the difficulty in proving that the experience of being abused as children "causes" adults to become abusers of their own children. Although research has suggested this causal relationship, the inability to manipulate the independent variable by "assigning" the status of "adult survivor of childhood abuse" to one group limits our ability to "prove" the relationship. The same is true with many of the social problems that are of interest to practicing social workers. In contrast, when we are able to control the delivery of the independent variable (typically, the intervention) to a preselected group of study participants, we are able to glean considerable insights into the causal relationship that might be there (i.e., rule out threats to internal validity).

Timing of measurements is the final tool that we discuss here for strengthening the explanatory inference that we are able to draw. Our ability to choose when to take measurements can be important in several ways. Most basically, since all science involves making comparisons, the ability to time measurements to occur both before and after an intervention allows us to compare the client states that existed prior to and following the intervention. This alone doesn't provide much protection against the many threats to validity that have been discussed; however, if we make such comparisons repeatedly (e.g., in an exploratory inductive study), we may have the beginning theoretical support for mounting a stronger examination. In another application, a series of measurements extending over a considerable period may be "interrupted" by the occurrence of the independent variable in such a way that we are able to infer the causal influence of the independent variable. This design is called an **interrupted time-series design** and is often used in assessing the impact of large-scale policy changes like seat belt laws. Timing of measurements is used differently in a deductive study in which we are concerned about the possibility of a pretest influencing outcomes (i.e., the threat of testing). Here, our ability to avoid pretesting by the timing of other measurements (as in the posttest only or Solomon four-group designs to be discussed in the next section) allows us to eliminate or test for this possible threat.

These four tools—random selection, random assignment, the ability to manipulate the independent variable, and the ability to define the timing of measurements—seem to be a modest arsenal against the many threats to internal and external validity in designs intended to produce explanatory inference. But be assured, they can produce powerful control over these threats when they are knowledgeably combined. The result of those combinations is a family of research designs called *true experiments.*

Examples of Designs That Support Inference Related to Explanatory Questions.
The essential qualities of all true experiments involve three of the four research design tools discussed before, and the fourth is a very desirable addition. *All true experiments require random assignment to groups, manipulation of the independent variable, and the intentional timing of measurement.* Brought together in intentional combinations, these three tools can be organized to protect against all of the threats to

internal validity. The fourth tool, random selection, provides additional support for external validity.

Unfortunately, some of the very power that protects against threats to internal validity creates potential limitations on external validity. In a nutshell, the rigid control required for random assignment and manipulation of the independent variable create an artificial research condition that does not mirror prevailing reality outside of the research setting. This artificiality interferes with external validity in that the conditions found in the research setting may not be readily reproduced (generalized) in the nonresearch setting. With this cautionary note, true experiments still remain the best way to confirm causality and advance explanatory inference.

The most commonly used true experiment is called the classic **randomized pretest–posttest design.** We will use it as the foundation for the discussion of all true experiments. In its basic form it involves (1) randomly dividing the research participants into two groups, (2) evaluating both groups (the pretest) with respect to their levels on the dependent variable, (3) administering the independent variable (usually some kind of intervention in social work research) to one group, and, finally, (4) reevaluating both groups (the posttest) with respect to the dependent variable. We have illustrated the classic randomized preposttest true experimental design in Table 5.2, where R represents randomization, O represents the measurements of the dependent variable (remember "O" standing for observation), and X represents the independent variable.

First, note that by creating the two groups by using a random assignment process, a strong protection against any selection bias has been created. There is no reason other than chance that any individual (and by extension, any subgroup of individuals) should be over- or underrepresented in either group. By eliminating any serious threat of selection bias in the assignment process, the likelihood of

TABLE 5.2   **True Experimental Designs**

Randomized pretest–posttest design

R	O1	X	O2
R	O3		O4

Randomized posttest-only design

R		X	O1
R			O2

Solomon four-group design

R	O1	X	O2
R	O3		O4
R		X	O5
R			O6

any interactive effects between selection and other threats such as maturation has also been generally eliminated. In short, $O1$–$O3$ differences should be negligible if not zero. Beyond the commonly accepted assumption of equivalence between the two groups created by random assignment, the design offers the pretest as additional assurance of equivalence on the dependent variable ($O1$–$O3$).

We want to take advantage of your focus on this $O1$–$O3$ comparison for a moment while we jump to the right-hand side of the randomized pretest–posttest design illustration. The correct final comparison to be made in this analysis is between the two posttest measurements ($O2$–$O4$). A too common error in analyzing data from this design is to compare the $O2$–$O1$ and the $O4$–$O3$ contrasts for differences. This is a mistake that negates all of the control and power that was introduced by the creation of randomized groups in the first place. Just as the pretest comparison ($O1$–$O3$) should have shown no differences between the groups, the posttest comparison ($O2$–$O4$) should reflect the differences produced by the independent variable—to the degree that threats to internal validity have been eliminated.

Returning to the role of the random assignment process, note that it also protects against all of the threats to internal validity that can be reasonably expected to be naturally operational. Consider maturation, for example. To the degree that maturation may account for the observed differences (i.e., $O2$–$O1$ and $O4$–$O3$), research participants should experience the maturation processes equally. Thus, any difference observed in the $O2$–$O4$ comparison cannot be the result of maturation (or other influences that are uniform across groups).

Although the randomized preposttest true experiment is extremely robust, it does not control for every threat automatically. Instrumentation, for example, involves changes in the measurement apparatus between the pretest and the posttest. If the same measurement apparatus is used for both groups, the design provides appropriate control against instrument decay. However, if different methods are used, careful attention by the researcher is required to assure that measurement differences are not allowed to masquerade as true effects of the independent variable. This is especially true when independent judges are used to make assessments. Sometimes, it is possible to randomly assign the judges to different observations; other times, video or audio recordings are used so that pretest and posttest measurements can be mixed. The point is to exercise appropriate caution that the researcher has not introduced possible threats to internal validity that are not controlled by the design alone.

The one threat to internal validity that is not controlled, but actually introduced by the use of this design, is an interaction between testing and the independent variable. Testing involves the reactivity that research participants may have to the use of a pretest. A pretest can be a sensitizing or educational experience. If the reaction to the pretest causes the participant to experience the independent variable (i.e., the intervention) in some unique way, internal and external validity are compromised. Internal validity is threatened because the posttest comparison will reveal differences that are assumed to result from the independent variable in spite of the possibility that they result from the interaction discussed. External validity is threatened because the intervention may only produce its observed effects in the presence of a pretest.

The **randomized posttest-only design** protects against the testing-intervention interaction effect as well as all of the other threats to internal validity that are addressed by the classic prepposttest experimental design. An illustration of the randomized posttest-only design is presented in Table 5.2. By simply eliminating the pretest, the randomized posttest-only design eliminates the possibility of an interaction with the independent variable. So why, you might reasonably ask, should the randomized prepposttest design ever be used? That's a good question. The one thing that the posttest-only design sacrifices is the pretest. The purpose of the pretest is to ensure equivalence on the independent variable between the randomly assigned groups. To the degree that you have confidence that the random assignment produced equivalent groups, the pretest is unnecessary. Now, the caveat. Random assignment, like all random processes, works best with larger numbers. If you are able to randomize relatively large groups of research subjects and have any concern that there might be reactivity to the pretest, a posttest-only design should be used. On the other hand, if reactivity is not likely to present a threat or the number or research participants you are able to use is small, the protection provided by the pretest is probably worth the risk of reactivity.

The "Cadillac" model of true experimental designs is the **Solomon four-group design.** Notice in Table 5.2 that the Solomon four-group design is actually a combination of the randomized prepost test design with the randomized posttest-only design. In this way, the assurance of pretest equivalence on the independent variable offered by the prepposttest design and the ability to eliminate a testing interaction effect provided by the posttest-only design are both realized. The Solomon four-group design provides the maximum protection against all threats to internal validity. The Solomon four-group design extends all of the demands present in any true experiment to all four groups, however. As a result, the use of this design is fairly uncommon in social work research.

A final class of research designs that is able to support the inference of causality, at least in a preliminary way, is strong **quasi-experimental designs** that rely on extensive statistical controls to rule out recognized alternative hypotheses. These designs cannot provide the causal certainty of true experiments, but because they do not require the use of random assignment to groups and the manipulation of the independent variable, they are much better suited for many of the kinds of social problems that are the subject of social work research. For example, we may be interested in knowing whether drug abuse *causes* domestic violence. However, it would be ethically and practically impossible to randomly assign research participants to groups and then to require one to "abuse drugs" (i.e., manipulate the independent variable). Thus, as in all research, we must consider the trade-off between using a stronger design and the practical benefits of a more "useable" design. Most of the strong quasi-experiments that support explanatory inference depend on the various statistical techniques to "control" for identified variables that may also influence the dependent variable. Some of these techniques include path analysis, factor analysis, discriminant analysis, and time-series analysis. A full discussion of multiple regression techniques would typically involve several courses on the subject and far exceeds the scope of this book. The reader is strongly encouraged to explore appropriate statistical courses to acquire an introductory exposure, however.

Designs to Support Predictive Inference

We begin this discussion of research designs that support predictive inference with the admonition that these should not be thought of as lesser designs. Instead, we invite you to think of them as being qualitatively different than the true experiments discussed earlier. Although it is almost always of value to understand the causal relationships that are involved in a full explanation of some phenomenon, it is often adequate to be able to accurately predict outcomes without a full explanation. In very practical terms, predicting the weather with a barometer is worthwhile even if we don't understand why it works. With an appreciation for the value of prediction, we turn to the threats that may interfere with our ability to accurately predict and those research designs that allow such inference to be made.

Threats to Inference Related to Predictive Inference.   The important distinction in understanding the difference between explanation and prediction is that explanation requires the attribution of cause, whereas prediction requires only that we are able to identify an association between two variables. In statistical terms, association is often called *correlation.* You will recall that correlation is a necessary but insufficient condition for inferring causality—the elimination of alternative explanations and an assurance of time ordering are also required. Thus, the necessary design tools that allow us to eliminate all of the alternative explanations as possible causes for an outcome can be eliminated from our designs when predictive inference is the goal. Prediction involves only correlation and *not* the elimination of all other possible causes. Remember, however, that any study that is able to support explanatory inference is also able to support predictive inference, since the correlations on which predictions are based are also required for explanation.

   The principal threats to making predictive inference are related to a general concern with external validity. This should make sense, since internal validity is associated with identifying causes and external validity is associated with the accuracy with which research findings can be replicated in the larger population. As such, predictive studies must be based on an accurate reflection of the population of interest and hold to appropriate standards for reliable and valid measurement. If the measurement systems utilized are not able to perform consistently to support reliable observation or those observations do not explicitly represent some particular phenomena within a given meaning system, it is unlikely that we will be able to make accurate predictions based on our data.

   In order to draw inference that supports accurate prediction in a population beyond the sample that was studied, *the study sample must be representative of the larger population.* As discussed in the next chapter, there are a number of strategies that can be employed to enhance the likelihood that a sample is actually representative of a population. Depending on the ends to which the predictive inference is put and the resources that are available to support the study, different levels of rigor may be acceptable in assuring that a sample is representative. However, as one is less certain that the sample is legitimately representative, one must also be less confident that the predictions supported by the correlations found *in the sample* are equally valid and true in the larger population. When our sample is haphazard, predictions based on that sample are equally haphazard.

A second factor threatening the validity of our predictive inference involves **measurement error.** You already know that any measurement is really composed of two portions—that which represents the true level of some characteristic and another that is made up of measurement error. In turn, measurement error includes both random and systematic influences. When our measurements contain high levels of random error, the relationships (i.e., correlations) on which prediction is based are difficult to identify at all. When our measurements contain high proportions of systematic error, we can identify relationships in the data, but these relationships are based on phenomena that are not necessarily what we thought we were measuring. This latter situation is illustrated by the association commonly found between "race" and a number of social problem variables—when, in fact, the measurement of "race" contains a very high proportion of systematic error that actually represents "economic status." Recall that systematic error is also sometimes called *measurement bias.* When large portions of any kind of measurement error exist, our ability to draw predictive inference is severely limited.

We call the third threat to drawing sound predictive inference **premature closure.** Premature closure involves stopping short of the number of observations necessary to draw clear inference. Premature closure is represented by special cases of both nonrepresentative sampling and inadequate measurement. We illustrate each briefly.

When a representative sample is sought, a sampling plan is generally employed that applies a specific strategy designed to produce a sample reflective of the larger population. Random selection processes are generally accepted as the best, although not necessarily the most feasible, strategies available. Imagine that you start taking a random sample from a population of potential voters in a large city (like drawing every nth name from the voter registration list), but stop after selecting only five names. How representative can your randomly selected sample of five voters be? Do you think you have represented all of the diversity in the city? It would be highly unlikely in any contemporary city. Your sample is simply too small to capture any measure of the full complexity and diversity of social life in the population. This is premature closure of the sampling procedure and results in an ability to draw predictive inference.

In the second case, imagine that you are conducting an in-depth inductive study of family caregiving patterns among middle-class families. During the first week of your data collection phase, you and the other members of your research team notice that significant amounts of care for frail, elderly family members seem to be provided formally—that is, by paid care providers. You are intrigued by the apparent division of labor since all of the available professional literature has indicated that family members are overwhelmingly the source of long-term care for frail, elderly people. Fortunately, you are also wise enough to quickly recognize that your data collection efforts during that first week were made during the day-time "working hours." Although much informal long-term care takes place during these hours, it is also the time during which the overwhelming majority of formally provided care takes place. If you were to make a prediction based on such limited observation (without considering evening, nighttime, and weekend hours), it would be a case of radical premature closure. Sound measurement also requires that an adequate number of representative measurements be taken to avoid the threat of premature closure.

In addition to these three threats, some of the threats to internal validity discussed with regard to explanatory inference can threaten predictive inference. For example, the threat to internal validity labeled *history* can operate to jeopardize predictive inference. Imagine that you have employed appropriate measurement techniques with an adequately representative sample to predict population atti-tudes toward the requirement of harsh punishment for adult children found guilty of failing to provide adequate support for their aging parents. Just as you initiated your study, an especially horrendous example of such disregard by adult children was brought to light. It is probable that your data would lead to errone-ous prediction in the months after the public attention of the media case waned. Short of expanding your study into one that could support causal inference, there is no general protection for such threats. Instead, it is incumbent on the researcher to be aware of these potentials so that they can be acknowledged in the data col-lection or analysis processes.

Research Tools That Strengthen Predictive Inference.   First and foremost, the threat to any inference that is presented by poor sampling is addressed by utilizing sampling procedures that are recognized as producing representative samples and to ensure that the size of the sample is large enough to provide the degree of preci-sion that is required. Strategies to achieve both of these ends are presented in detail in the next chapter. Although some may argue that less stringent approaches may be adequate, the fact remains that all scientific prediction rests on assessed relation-ships in the data. Those relationships are all based on correlations, and correlation is a statistic that requires an adequately large sample to be sure that the relationship is not just a one-time anomaly. The tendency for people to base their predictions on less than adequate data is precisely the threat to good inference against which we are seeking to protect ourselves. When small samples or samples of unknown rep-resentativeness are used as the basis for predictive inference, we must recognize that such predictions are exploratory or preliminary and proceed with caution.

There are three specific research tools that we offer for protection against the threat posed by poor measurement as discussed before. The use of these depends, in part, on the degree to which previous work with the phenomena of interest exists. When considerable previous research exists, we are more likely to protect our infer-ence by using *validated measurement techniques*. Validated measurement techniques represent explicit operationalization of variables that have been found to be reliable and meaningful within a given meaning system. When such tools already exist, it is imperative that their use be fully explored. To fail to do so is extremely wasteful. The use of existing validated instruments is not only efficient within a given study, but allows the new knowledge generated to be integrated more fully into that which is already recognized or understood. This is especially true in deductive research that is seeking to confirm the application of general principles to specific cases.

When we are seeking to identify new phenomena or relationships through inductive research, our ability to use previously validated measurement instruments is typically more limited. Although the use of validated instrumentation should be pursued when they are available and appropriate, the intended function of most inductive research designs is to explore new meanings. Consequently, it is not always possible or appropriate to rely on previous measurement instruments. In such cases, the use of *triangulation* is an appropriate strategy to increase the likelihood of accurate measurement.

Triangulation involves the use of multiple indicators to assess or measure some phenomenon. In history, the concept of triangulation comes from the ancient mariners who used three points—usually two stars and the horizon—to determine their position. You may recall from high school geometry that as long as three points are not all on a single straight line, they can be used to define two lines and that the intersection of two lines defines a point or position in space. In social science research, we are not quite so precise. Our use of triangulation might be adequately employed by remembering that "if something walks like a duck, talks like a duck, and looks like a duck, it probably is a duck!" When we find multiple independent indications that some phenomenon is present at a given level, our confidence that we are measuring the intended phenomenon with some level of reliability increases.

Moreover, when new insights are drawn from data and confirmed by different actors within the meaning system being employed, we can have some confidence in a level of validity as well. The process of confirming preliminary findings with research participants who are a part of the meaning system from which our findings are drawn is called **grounding.**

The tool of grounding is most likely to be employed in research designs that rely on more nonnumeric data. While numeric measurements rely on both logical and statistical arguments to support their claims of reliability and validity, arguments in support of the reliability and validity of nonnumeric measurements rest solely on logical procedures including triangulation and grounding. As such, grounding really boils down to the process of asking data sources within the meaning system if our descriptive or predictive inference is correct. Imagine that you have been studying the impact of recent changes in public assistance policies (some have called these changes "welfare reform") by living in a low-income neighborhood and interviewing residents within the community about the impact that these policy changes have made in their lives. When you believe that you are able to make a strong predictive inference, the tool of grounding would lead you to share your insights with members of the community to see if they concur. Through the process, you are seeking to anchor your insights in the meaning system from which they are drawn.

Examples of Designs That Support Predictive Inference.   Recall from the scientific cycle that inductive processes move from specific observations toward generalizations. These generalizations operate as predictions by suggesting that sets of operations seem to "go together." In their highest form, these generalizations/ predictions are embodied in theories. When we move from these theories to test the predictions or explanations that are drawn from them, we are employing deduction. Thus, the designs that we use to make predictive inference can be of either an inductive or deductive nature, depending on whether we are attempting to contribute new insights to a developing theory or confirm the predictive power offered by an existing theory.

The most commonly used research designs to test predictive propositions drawn from existing theory are correlational studies sometimes called *quasi-experiments*. These designs need to employ sound sampling and measurement strategies and to avoid premature closure as protections against the threats to drawing predictive inference that have been discussed. Once those procedural safeguards have been implemented, these designs rely on the computation of correlations among the variables measured to suggest predictive relationships. Although this process may seem simple or even simple-minded to some, the value of such research can be substantial.

One very important use of this logic is demonstrated in the special case of interrupted time-series designs called *single-system designs* (SSDs) (Bloom, Fischer, & Orme, 1999). These designs provide one of the most important tools for evaluating social work practice with individual clients or small systems (although they can be used with large systems as well). All SSDs involve a series of client-system measurements made over time. Change behaviors in the client system are identified and operationalized so that they can be validly assessed. The selected behaviors are generally referred to as target behaviors. The intervention process is also well specified in order to allow replication and (potentially) preliminary inference about possible causal patterns to be drawn. Multiple measurements are taken prior to the introduction of the intervention (the baseline phase), and others are taken after the intervention process has been initiated (the intervention phase). Comparisons over time provide information on the changes that are occurring in the target behaviors. The most common SSD has been labeled the AB design to reflect the baseline phase (represented by the A) followed by the intervention phase (represented by the B). Various combinations of baselines (or nonintervention phases more generally) and intervention phases are common. These variations represent alternative manipulations of the independent variable (the B phase) and other patterns of measurement timing. Even modifications in the intervention can be incorporated, in which case the altered intervention phase is labeled with a new letter (e.g., C then D and so on). The application of SSDs is further discussed in Chapter 10 "Practice Evaluation in Single and Multiple Systems").

A second essential use of well-executed studies supporting predictive inference is in confirming the predictions that are made by prevailing theory. If the expected correlations among variables are found, the theory is strengthened by this partial confirmation. If the expected predictions are not found in the data, the theory or the particular study is thrown into question—a question to be settled by additional research. As these kind of correlational designs are structured to control for additional influences, they evolve into the kind of quasi-experiments that were identified as appropriate to preliminary explanatory inference. Such is the continuum of science!

When we do not have strong theory on which to base our predictions, we are confronted with the need to make careful observation on which to base clear generalizations. In turn, these generalizations are formalized into preliminary theory from which we might draw tentative predictive hypotheses for testing in correlational studies as before. However, this sector of the scientific cycle is also best served when logical research designs are employed to advance our knowledge. One of the best known and widely respected research designs for use in inductive science is called "grounded theory" development (Glaser & Strauss, 1967). As a research design, **grounded theory** involves the careful preliminary identification and analysis of the concepts, activities, and other meaning units that are identified in inductive field work. In the process of this analysis, the relationships and threads of theory are allowed to "emerge." As this emergence takes place, the findings are grounded (as before) with research participants from within the meaning system being studied. When the grounding process fails to confirm our findings, the fault could be located in our poor sampling of the phenomenon or inadequate definition of the construct (measurement at the nominal level). As the individual themes are confirmed through grounding, new theoretical understandings are identified. It is this kind of insightful yet disciplined sensitivity to the nuances of a more full understanding of phenomena that allows clear theory to be constructed and sound prediction to be made.

Designs to Support Descriptive Inference

Often, our interest in describing things involves the relationship between two or more variables. When this is the case, one actually needs a design that can support a predictive inference. This is because the description of a relationship between two variables requires prediction—a prediction that as one variable increases or decreases the other will behave in the predicted fashion. Consequently, we limit our discussion in this section to designs that support descriptive inference about variables as single entities within a population.

As with our caution that designs supporting predictive inference should not be thought of as "inferior" to those supporting explanatory inference, we stress that designs supporting descriptive inference should not be considered the weak siblings of these other designs. Although research designs supporting explanation and prediction are also generally able to provide clear description, each type of design is valuable in its own right. To use a stronger design than is necessary to achieve the intended purpose is not "better"; it is wasteful. We hope that we have been both clear and consistent in our commitment to this view.

Threats to Inference Related to Descriptive Questions.   The influences that can threaten our ability to produce accurate description are the same as those that limit predictive inference. These include *poor sampling, poor measurement, and the special* *case of each labeled premature closure.* Whenever we base our descriptions on inadequate samples that were assessed using questionable measurement procedures or when we terminated either the sampling or data collection prematurely, we run the risk of producing erroneous descriptions.

Research Tools That Strengthen Inference Related to Description.   In general, the protections that we employ in making sound descriptive inference follow those that are used in making predictive inference. However, because much descriptive research is conducted in the *exploratory phases* of understanding new phenomena, we tend to be much more tolerant of the possible threats. For example, one of the authors studied the experience of nursing homes in providing treatment for people with AIDS (Klein & Botticello, 1997). Based on a previous study, long-term care facilities serving residents with AIDS were identified and invited to participate in the research. Even with overwhelming agreement to participate in the research interviews by representatives of these facilities, the number of facilities involved was fewer than 30. Should research based on such small (an oftentimes much smaller) numbers be discounted? We believe that as long as such studies are intended for the purpose of preliminary description and the uses to which their findings are put are consistent with this intention, they can make a valuable contribution to our scientific knowledge. When we, as principal researchers or as consumers, seek to push findings to ends that are not supported by the tools employed in the original designs, we run a considerable risk of making faulty inference.

Examples of Designs That Support Inference Related to Description.   The specific design features of studies intended to support descriptive inference closely parallel those of predictive studies. This is reasonable since the threats to descriptive inference also parallel those of predictive inference. Descriptive designs are recognized not so much by the tools that they employ, as in the analysis that is conducted on their data. Descriptive analysis is much more heavily dependent on *descriptive statistics*—those that simply describe things. Descriptive statistics most commonly include the various *measures of central tendency* (i.e., means, modes, and medians), *measures of dispersion* (e.g., standard deviations, ranges, and variance), *frequencies,* and *percentages.* These are the basic tools of description. Any study that utilizes them is likely seeking to provide descriptive inference.

Summary

This chapter introduces research designs that support scientific inference. Scientific inference is made whenever we extend the findings from samples of data to larger groups or populations from which the data were drawn. Three kinds of scientific inference can be made: descriptive inference, predictive inference, and explanatory (or causal) inference. As implied by the names, these inferences serve to describe the characteristics of populations of people or phenomena, predict relationships between two or more variables, or explain the pattern of causes that underlie specific phenomena, respectively.

All research designs involve the intentional use of a small group of design tools in order to eliminate threats to internal and external validity and consequently strengthen the inference made. In general, the greater number of tools that are incorporated into a design, the stronger the inference that can be drawn from the design. By their nature, explanatory designs require the strongest kind of inference, and the family of research designs that are able to support explanatory or causal inference is called true experiments. All true experiments incorporate the design tools of random assignment to groups, manipulation of the independent variable, and the intentional timing of measurements. Quasi-experiments are a family of research designs that do not involve random assignment or the manipulation of the independent variable, but rely instead on statistical controls to rule out identified threats to internal validity. Although quasi-experiments are sometimes used to provide preliminary explanatory inference, they are more commonly used to support predictive inference. Predictive and descriptive designs require less control and depend most heavily on appropriate sampling and measurement techniques.

Although it is tempting to automatically assume that the research design that supports the strongest inference is "the best," it is essential to doing good science that the research design that is used be matched to the nature of the question asked. This is in part dictated by the previous research and level of understanding that exist with regard to the research question. When research designs are employed that are excessively robust with respect to the question asked, we are being wasteful of resources that could be better used in support of focused research or client services.

6 Sampling and Generalization

Representing Populations

Relationship of This Chapter to the Whole

Arguably, all empirical generalizations are based on sampling of one sort or another. The ability to extract meaning from limited experience and apply those ideas in similar settings is probably one of the keys to the success of humans as a species. For some kinds of phenomena, generalizing from whatever events present themselves yields knowledge that is sufficient. However, careful study of the logic of generalization reveals that the process is fraught with difficulty. Stereotyping, self-fulfilling prophecies, gullibility, and ignoring exceptions and individual differences are some of the potential hazards of a generalization process gone awry. In response to these difficulties, scientists have developed techniques to limit the impact of logical errors on the generalization process. In this chapter, we discuss techniques collectively called sampling.

Sampling techniques are procedures designed to provide one of the conditions required before accurate and useful generalizations can be made from observations. That one condition is called **representativeness.** Representativeness refers to the adequacy with which a collection of observations represents the variability in some population of interest. The concept of representativeness is crucial to generalizability. Before we can generalize from one set of experiences to another, we need to know if the experiences have anything in common, that is, whether both are representative of the same or similar phenomena. Sampling methods are largely about choosing the persons, events, or observations (the units) in ways that allow us to specify the class of persons, events, or behaviors of which our observations are representative. For phenomena that are widely and evenly distributed, nearly any group of units is representative of the entire class of units. However, when the phenomena are unevenly distributed, probability samples can be very useful in assuring representativeness and also have the advantage of allowing us to estimate the limits of errors in some of our generalizations.

In this chapter, we discuss both nonprobability and probability sampling as approaches to assuring representativeness. Although much sampling theory deals with the mathematics of samples for hypothesis testing research, we discuss representativeness in the context of case studies, exploratory research, and practice-related observations.

Application of This Chapter to the Roles of Social Workers

Much of what social workers do involves generalizations. Although our primary concern in doing social work is generally to facilitate change in client systems and the social environment within which those client systems exist, we are often concerned with making accurate generalizations. Sometimes those generalizations take the form of asking what the professional literature might provide in the way of guidance for practice with this client or efforts to intervene in a social system. Other times, we wish to use our practice insights gained with earlier clients in shaping our interventions with subsequent client systems. After all, that is a large part of what gaining experience and developing "practice wisdom" (Klein & Bloom, 1995) is all about. Still other times, we seek to share our successful practice experience with colleagues. For example, if we have been successfully employing a particular intervention strategy with an identifiable client group, we have a professional responsibility to make this successful approach available to others to utilize with their own clients (NASW, 1997).

All three tasks—applying the experience of others, generating new knowledge from experience, and sharing new knowledge with others—involve generalizations. In the first, we are taking the experience of others and generalizing it to our own client or clients. In the second case, we are generalizing from our own past experience to the present or even into the future. In the last case, we are recommending the generalization of our own successful experience to the practice of others. Certainly, effective practice and the advancement of professional knowledge depend on such generalizations. Otherwise, each one of us would need to rediscover every bit of practice knowledge, our own as well as others, for every application.

Many of the tasks students face involve sampling. As a student, you have no doubt been required to conduct library-based research on any number of topics. Sometimes these papers are developed to argue a specific point; articles and other literature sources that support your argument are persistently sought. However, sometimes your goal is to review a complete literature on a client problem area or the like. In these latter cases, the literature review that results is intended to reflect the range of opinions that exist in the literature. But what happens when your search of the library's CD-ROM-based bibliographic reference system produces 60 or 70 *good* sources related to your topic? Do you read them all? Quite honestly, we doubt it. (Furthermore, in some cases, we wouldn't even recommend it!) Instead, most of us probably quickly review the abstracts and then seek to pull a *representative* set of the articles. Fair enough. But notice that this process really involves two different kinds of sampling. First, each article's abstract is essentially a sampling of the article. When the actual article doesn't seem to follow the abstract, we say something like, "The abstract wasn't *representative* of the article." Obviously, good abstracts provide an accurate representation of what might be found in the entire article. In the second phase of our sampling, we are selecting some of the abstracts but eliminating others. In this process, we are trying to represent a sense of the whole by selecting abstracts with varying perspectives, perhaps some that are empirical and others that are more conceptual, and so on. The degree to which we are successful in collecting this sample is reflected in the degree to which our review is *representative* of the entire literature.

In professional practice, our routine sampling behaviors may include sampling the experiences of a single system or sampling caseloads. We ask clients to describe a specific behavioral incident as a sample of all related behavioral incidents. We might even ask, "How *representative* was this fight with your mate (or whatever behavioral incident is at issue) of all fights between you two?" We might ask an adolescent how many times drugs have been used in the last week to make a generalization about drug use over time. We might inquire how often a client cries as a sample of the many behaviors that are reasonably related to the client's complaint of depression. We may decide to try a new program intervention with *only some* of our agency's clients to see how it works before instituting the change programwide—if we are convinced that the positive results will *generalize* to all or at least most of the agency's clients. We may need to evaluate an agency program in order to secure continued funding, but we do not have the time or resources to contact all former clients, so we draw a representative sample.

Social workers are sampling things all of the time. We are seeking a better understanding of the world in which we live and work. Sometimes the strategies used to obtain those samples are strongly limited by practical matters such as time and access to people and behaviors of interest. At other times, such as when our interest is in expanding our understanding of some domain, more formal and precise sampling methods may be employed. Any time the focus of our attention is a group that is too large or too geographically dispersed, or we are interested in regular client behaviors that cannot all be observed or related by clients, we are likely to sample. Understanding the basic logic of sampling helps make these generalizations more accurate and helpful. Figure 6.1 illustrates the relationship between representative sampling and accurate generalization.

As the foregoing illustrates, sampling is certainly not some esoteric process that is reserved for quality control experts in manufacturing or for highly paid political pollsters. To be sure, these professionals use carefully selected sampling procedures. However, social workers—including social work students—are in the process of using implicit forms of sampling much of the time. One of the goals of this chapter is to make those regular practice applications of sampling more explicit so that the generalizations based on them might be more fully representative.

Learning Objectives

After reading this chapter, you should be able to:

1. distinguish between populations and sampling frames
2. define external validity
3. describe the logic of probability sampling
4. give descriptions of the basic types of probability sampling—simple random, systematic, stratified, and cluster

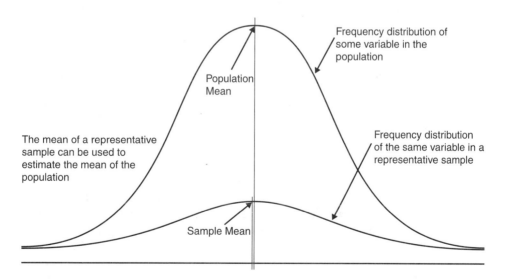

FIGURE 6.1   Estimating Population Characteristics from a Representative Sample

5. be able to use a table of random numbers
6. differentiate between probability and nonprobability sampling
7. give examples of nonprobability sampling and when it would be acceptable to use it
8. describe techniques for establishing optimal sample size
9. evaluate the appropriateness of a sampling plan as a part of the assessment of published social work articles

Key Terms and Concepts

The Act of Sampling

In everyday life, the act of sampling is nothing more than taking a small portion of some group and using it to represent the larger group from which it was taken. We follow this general procedure when we try a small sample of some new food or when we search the radio dial, listening for small samples that might suggest the station is one that we'd enjoy. In social work practice and in research, we are similarly sampling. However, in these professional contexts, we hold higher standards for judging what represents an adequate sample. Because practice decisions that influence the lives of clients are based on such sampling, it is very appropriate that we hold to the highest possible standards in making decisions about how we will be sampling.

Goals of Sampling.   The goal of any sampling strategy is to obtain observations that adequately represent the variability in some population of interest. We define *population* more completely later, but for now, consider a population of some large group of people, organizations, or events about which we desire description. In a classic work, Cochran (1977) lists five different approaches to drawing samples. First, **convenience sampling** involves simply selecting a portion of the population that is easy to access, say, the next 10 new cases or last month's discharges. Second, **haphazard sampling** involves picking a sample without conscious planning, such as the people on our caseload, behaviors we can easily observe, or an organization that is convenient. (Note that in this sense, haphazard sampling is almost always convenient sampling.) Third, **purposive sampling** involves conscious selection of typical units, those that meet the sampler's impressions of the average, or that represent some specific aspect of the population that is being studied. (Sometimes, the rare or unusual elements in a population are sought out for inclusion in a purposive sample.) Fourth, **volunteers** can be sought to constitute the sample. Fifth and finally, **probability sampling** can be drawn using sampling frames and random procedures (Cochran, 1977).

All the sampling procedures just mentioned can yield adequate results in certain situations (Cochran, 1977). For relatively homogeneous populations, convenience and haphazard samples should produce relatively representative samples. A person with detailed knowledge of a small population can use purposive techniques such as quota samples to produce representative samples. In contexts where the processes under study are likely to be unrelated to willingness to participate in research (such as biochemical studies), volunteer samples are likely to be representative. Any of these approaches can generate useful samples under the right conditions. In particular the nonprobability sampling methods (the first four) are often easier to employ and with small homogeneous populations yield useful results with minimal intrusion and cost. Although nonprobability samples have many uses, as we will see, the one area in which probability samples excel is the ability to estimate the limits of sampling error, a characteristic that is limited to probability samples.

Each of the five approaches to sampling places different constraints and demands on the sampler. Convenience, haphazard, and volunteer samples require little advance knowledge of the population units and perhaps little planning as well. However, these techniques will produce representative samples only in very special situations, such as when a population has very little variability. Sampling to fill quotas specified by expert guesses about the population and probability samples both require the sampler to know quite a lot about the population to be sampled. In the case of probability samples, it is required, at least in principle, that a list of all the units in the population be known and available for selection. Another important constraint presented by probability samples is that unusual units with low frequencies in the population may rarely be found in samples unless the sample size is very large. This limitation has serious consequences for a profession such as social work in which small disadvantaged segments of the population are often the units of interest.

Whatever sampling strategy seems to provide the right mix of advantages and disadvantages, the sampler must be able to make a case for representativeness if the results of the inquiry are to generalize beyond the units studied. With probability samples, that case is made through mathematics and probability theory. For the other forms of sampling, the case must be made through the application of observation, argument, and reason. For example, anthropologists have often made the case that the characteristics of a culture that can be understood by an outsider during a short period of field work are present in a very large proportion of the population, therefore justifying small convenience or haphazard samples. Likewise, use of nonprobability sampling in populations assumed to be homogeneous on some characteristic of interest should be accompanied by evidence that the population is homogeneous with respect to relevant characteristics. The degree to which a convincing argument for representativeness can be made establishes outer boundaries on the confidence with which we may generalize from findings on samples to other samples from the same population or, moreover, to the population itself.

From a practical standpoint, choose the sampling technique best suited for the reasons you have undertaken the observations. Despite the emphasis on probability samples in the scholarly literature, they are not always optimal. Probability samples are superb techniques when the goal is testing quantitative hypotheses and in situations in which sampling error is likely to be an important obstacle to drawing inference. Otherwise, one of the other techniques may yield credible results.

Optimal Sampling.   A good sample is one that is minimally fit for the purpose for which it was drawn. That is, to be optimal, the sample must contribute an appropriate level of confidence concerning the representativeness of the units studied and also not use more time or money or be more intrusive than is necessary to accomplish the purposes of the study. Selecting a sampling strategy and targets for sample sizes are, in part, an exercise in maximizing the marginal utility of a study. Choose a sample that engenders weak confidence concerning representativeness, and the results will be difficult or impossible to interpret and therefore of low utility. Choose a too complex or expensive sampling strategy and the study may be disproportionately costly or intrusive or not allow the phenomenon of interest to be explored in enough depth.

The optimal sampling strategy for any given study is determined by the nature of the populations involved, questions to be asked, and resources available. Studies of characteristics with very little variability in a population often can be maximized with small, informal sampling strategies. For example, ethnoscientists attempting to discover shared meaning systems have made persuasive cases for studying a handful of convenient informants because, presumably, general meaning systems are distributed within populations with little variability. Likewise, a study of specialized knowledge in a population might involve a sampling technique that takes referrals from persons known to possess that knowledge. In both of these cases, it may be possible to draw a very large random sample of persons in a target group, but in the first case, the costs of asking an obvious question of many people may not be justifiable, and in the latter case, asking inappropriate questions of a large group would seem equally unreasonable. In both cases, the cost in terms of timeliness, intrusiveness, and money may be too great or prohibit the researcher from studying the phenomenon in enough depth to yield valid conclusions. As we discuss sampling procedures that range in complexity from informal "go ask one of them" approaches to probability multistage cluster samples and in size from a full census to small fractions of large populations, consider that the correct strategy depends on the characteristics of the population of interest and resource demands on the persons conducting the study.

The Vocabulary of Sampling

It has become conventional among social scientists to discuss samples in terms of a small set of concepts. It is useful to think of these concepts as characteristics that can be used to specify the "pedigree" of the sample. That lineage provides important information about constraints on the generalizability of findings from one sample to another. The concepts we discuss here are *universe/population, sampling units, sampling frames,* and *elements.* Some related terms that are also relevant to data collection and data analysis are also discussed, including *units of observation,* and *units of analysis.*

Population or Universe.   The **population** or universe, refers to a theoretical aggregate that includes all possible members of some group. A population is defined by the rules for determining what elements are included in the population. A population might consist of people sharing certain characteristics, but, alternatively, a population might consist of other entities, such as objects, localities, groups, organizations, programs, or anything else that may be studied. A population may even be defined as a set of particular behaviors of one person or a small system—for example, all fights involving physical contact between members of a marital dyad. As another example, let's suppose that we are interested in the level of AIDS prevention awareness among social workers in a given state. In this example, the population would be the group that included all social workers in the state of interest. To more clearly specify this population, we would define "social workers" as those people working in human service positions and who have a BSW or an MSW degree from an academic program accredited by the Council on Social Work Education (CSWE).

Note that you do not need to be able to identify or otherwise name all of the members of a population. Instead, the important feature is that you are able to conceptually define the population such that any single entity (person, organization, family, what have you) could be clearly identified as either belonging to or not belonging to the population. Some authors distinguish between a sampling universe and a sampling population, but we believe that for practical purposes, the distinction is unnecessary and prefer the term population.

Sampling Unit.   A **sampling unit** is a part of a population that is selected at some stage in a sampling procedure. A sampling unit may consist of the smallest entity in the population or clusters of such entities. In a population consisting of people as the smallest entities, individual persons might be the sampling unit, families might be the unit, as might neighborhoods or some other grouping. The designation of the sampling unit, like the designation of the population, is a matter of definition and the objectives of the researcher. In some cases, different sampling units may be used in subsequent rounds of sampling. For example, social workers are often found in clusters called NASW state chapters. If our research interest was in all social workers in the United States, it might be convenient to first take a sample of state chapters (a state chapter would be the sampling unit), then obtain membership lists for the states chosen, and finally sample the members within each state chapter (now an individual social worker would be the sampling unit).

Sampling Frame.   A **sampling frame** is a list of some or all of the units in a population. The sampling frame, in fact, might be a physical list, such as a phone book, voter registration list, roster of clients, and the like. However, a "virtual" sampling frame may exist in principle only; that is, it is possible to construct the sampling frame if needed. Sampling frames are handy in general but are absolutely required for drawing probability samples. Ideally, a sampling frame would include all the units in a population. In practice, however, readily available sampling frames such as rosters, phone lists, and membership lists often contain only partial listings of the units. Omissions from sampling frames are often due to errors or changing populations and sometimes due to difficulty identifying members of the population. The quality of the sampling frame is important in our efforts to develop representative samples because the quality of the sampling frame places constraints on the representativeness of probability samples, and the effect of errors in the sample frame are not easily estimated.

In our preceding sample, the sampling frame might be the membership roster of the state chapter of the National Association of Social Workers (NASW). An obvious limitation of such a sampling frame is that it is incomplete. It is highly likely that some people who meet the requirements of being a "social worker" as defined earlier have not joined their professional association. To the degree that some social workers have not joined NASW, the sampling frame does not represent the full range of variability that might be present in the population. (The non-NASW members may differ from their NASW member colleagues in more ways than just membership status.) Nonetheless, the NASW membership probably represents the best sampling frame available. The point here is this: In spite of the fact that many sampling frames don't perfectly represent the population of interest, the more completely a sampling frame can represent the full diversity of a population on every dimension, the better will be the generalization based on a sample drawn from that frame.

We stated earlier that the list that comprises the sampling frame can be a *virtual list* in the sense that it does not literally need to exist—only that it could be constructed as necessary. Here is an example of a virtual sampling frame. If we were interested in the level of AIDS prevention awareness among social workers in the whole country, for example, the sampling frame might be the combined membership rosters for all state NASW chapters. It is not a difficult mental task to imagine a combined listing of all states' membership that could serve as our sampling frame, but we are not likely to gather all these lists and combine them into one master list. Later in this chapter, we discuss a multistage sampling procedure that would produce a probability sample by selecting a sample of state NASW chapters in a first round of sampling and then social workers from within the selected states at a second round of sampling. This procedure avoids expending the effort to actually construct a national list. The sampling frame is virtual in that the first stage of the sampling is done on a symbolic description of the list, not the actual list.

The concepts of populations, universe, units, and frames are all terms in which specifications for samples are written. Although these concepts are most often associated with probability samples, it is equally important to be as clear as possible what populations, units, and frames were assumed when nonprobability samples are drawn.

Elements, Units of Observation, and Units of Analysis.   Discussions of observations made on samples often include a group of related terms that are not properly characteristics of samples, but are more about data collection and analysis. These terms include *element, unit of observation,* and *unit of analysis.* Although these refer to other parts of the research process (measurement and data analysis), these terms are more easily understood in the context of samples, so we digress briefly here to discuss these.

An **element** is the individual entity that has been selected as a member of the sample. In a sampling procedure involving only a single round of sampling, elements and sampling units are synonymous. However, in procedures involving multiple rounds of sampling (as in the example immediately preceding), the use of "element" is usually reserved to describe only those sampling units in the final round of sampling. The research proceeds by investigating the individual elements that comprise the sample. In this sense, elements are sometimes referred to as the **units of observation.** Observations of the elements may take the form of interviews, pencil-and-paper questionnaires, direct observations of behavior, or any other form of data collection. We typically make these observations—or collect these data—for the purpose of making generalizations about the elements. However, there are occasions when the element that serves as the unit of observation serves as the source of information about some other unit. Say, for instance, that you are interested in studying families and making comparisons among them on particular dimensions. We often use an individual family member as the source of information about a family. In such a case, the element that is selected from a sampling frame (a particular family member) would be the unit of observation, whereas the family about which data were being collected would be the **unit of analysis.**

It is important to maintain the distinction between units of observation and units of analysis so as to avoid falling into the **ecological fallacy.** The ecological fallacy is an error that is made when characteristics of units at one level of aggregation are ascribed to units at a different aggregation. Returning to our example of a survey of social workers, characteristics of NASW chapters (potential units of analysis) are not necessarily the characteristics of members (likely units of observation). Chapters may be very politically liberal, for example, but any individual member may be more conservative. Likewise, we could be studying neighborhoods (units of analysis) and find that they vary with respect to the amount of litter that is observed along public streets. If we inferred that neighborhoods (a higher level of aggregation) with high levels of litter were populated by people (a lower level of aggregation) who littered a lot, we would be making an ecological error. An alternative explanation for the high volume of litter might be that tourists frequented a fast-food restaurant and threw all of their waste out of car windows before they returned to their own homes. Alternately, the relative cleanliness of some other community might result from the efforts of a small but active group of residents that organized to pick up litter scattered by their own litterbug neighbors.

Random Sampling Error.   **Sampling error** is the discrepancy between the characteristics of a sample and the characteristics of the population from which it was drawn. Sampling error is the result of random processes. All samples are only approximations of the populations from which they are drawn and are subject to random fluctuations. Why this is so might be a little difficult to understand, but it is probably safe to conclude that all human attempts at knowledge acquisition involve random error at several points. An example might help illustrate how sampling error works.

We consider sampling error in more detail as a part of the following discussion of probability. For now, however, we'd like to do a little mental experiment. Imagine that you have an old wool hat that contains 100 colored chips—50 red, 25 white, and 25 blue. If you blindly reach in and select 40 chips, the most likely color distribution to occur would be 20 red chips, 10 white chips, and 10 blue chips. Indeed, if you blindly reach in and select 4 chips, the most likely color distribution to occur would be 2 red chips, 1 white chip, and 1 blue chip. That's what probability theory tells us quite simply. However, if you brought out 4 chips and found that 3 were red and only 1 was blue, would you suspect that the drawing was necessarily rigged? We doubt it. Instead, you'd probably say that it was only chance drawing and sometimes it just works out that way. Exactly! And that's an example of sampling error. If everything was perfect all of the time (i.e., there wasn't *any* sampling error), every drawing of 4 chips from our hat would produce 2 red, 1 white, and 1 blue chip.

In practice, every sample contains some sampling error. All else being equal, larger samples produce smaller errors. You can see that intuitively in the hat example by thinking about the color distribution of your sample as the sample size moves from 4 to 100. When you've "sampled" the entire population (technically not a sample at all), there is no room left for error. How much error is tolerable is a function of the purpose to which you wish to put your results. For now, it is more important for you to know that all samples have some sampling error and that in probability samples (discussed later), the amount of the sampling error can be estimated.

Systematic Sampling Error: Bias.   Another kind of sampling-related error, called **sampling bias,** consists of error that systematically distorts the characteristics of a sample. When sampling error is a function of probability, sample bias is often a function of the selection of a sampling frame. If you were interested in studying all high school students and selected a sampling frame that included only public high schools, your sample would carry a bias to the degree that parochial and other private high school students differed from their public school counterparts. Bias is one of the typical shortcomings of nonprobability samples, but can also be present in probability sampling. Sample bias may be best avoided by correctly specifying the population of interest and utilizing a probability sampling procedure within a sampling frame that accurately represents the population of interest.

Nonprobability Sampling

Properties of Nonprobability Sampling.   **Nonprobability sampling,** as implied by the name, involves sampling procedures in which random selection processes are not utilized. Casual nonprobability samples employ no organized sampling strategy, as in the case of convenience, haphazard, and volunteer samples. Purposive nonprobability samples such as quota samples, key informant samples, and snowball samples specify either the type of units to be selected (quota and key informant samples) or rely on a network of referrals (snowball samples). Samples drawn by any of these procedures can yield representative samples under the right conditions. However, the chief limitation of nonprobability samples is that it is difficult to estimate the degree of sampling error in the sample. Also nonprobability samples do not contain the protections against unconscious sampling bias that random selection provides. Both the inability to estimate sampling error and the loss of protections from bias can erode our confidence that the sample we observe is representative of some population of interest. However, in many instances, it is possible to make a credible case for representativeness, albeit without mathematical precision associated with probability samples. There are many research situations and research questions for which a nonmathematical claim of representativeness is either acceptable or an unavoidable circumstance given the constraints of resources or other limitations.

Convenience Sampling.   *Convenience sampling* involves selecting units on the basis of accessibility. Selecting an existing group of clients with which to test a new therapy or testing for child abuse by polling the children in a classroom whose teacher is friendly and willing to let you administer a questionnaire are two examples of convenience samples. The chief advantage of convenience samples is that exploiting units that are easily accessed tends to reduce the cost and complexity of drawing a sample and conducting observations. Also, actual or virtual lists of all elements of the sampling frame are not needed as they are in the case of probability samples. Convenience samples yield representative samples in populations in which the phenomenon of interest is believed to be widely and homogeneously distributed. Samples where entrance into the group involves screening (a diagnosis, admissions requirement) can be thought of as homogeneous with regard to the screening criterion. Anthropologists have long claimed that the cultural beliefs that an outsider is likely to be able to comprehend in a year or so of field work are so general that they are carried by nearly everyone and, therefore, nearly anyone is able to provide a representative response.

Convenience sampling should be limited to homogeneous populations or preliminary studies that are of an exploratory nature; and even then, the effort should be made to sample so as to represent various dimensions of the population that might be especially relevant. For example, in a preliminary study of the use of an adjunct faculty in schools of social work in which one of the authors was involved (Klein, Weisman, & Smith, 1996), the participation of schools was solicited largely on the basis of convenience; however, schools were sought that provided geographic diversity as well as a mix of public and private institutions.

Haphazard Sampling.   *Haphazard sampling* involves grabbing a few units unsystematically from a collection of units. Haphazard sampling has the feel of a random process without the assurance of randomization procedures. A unit is grabbed here and another there with no particular pattern. If the population of interest is small and the units homogeneous, haphazard samples may be representative. It is possible that haphazard sampling may avoid some of the bias related to convenience sampling, in that the sample is not all drawn from one place in the population.

Volunteer Sampling.   **Volunteer sampling** involves building a sample around individuals who self-select into the sample. Such sampling is widely employed in medical research and can yield useful samples when volunteerism is not likely to produce selection bias, as in the case of biochemical processes. Volunteer sampling may also be useful in populations that are homogeneous with regard to the characteristics of interest, such as access to widely available cultural knowledge. However as soon as the variables of interest include psychosocial factors that may predispose persons to volunteer or not volunteer, a potential source of selection bias is introduced.

Purposive Sampling.   *Purposive sampling* employs systematic procedures to the selection of a sample. For example, **quota sampling** involves identifying categories of individuals believed to incorporate the diversity in the population, setting targets for the number of individuals in each category to be sampled, and selecting individuals who match the set of categories until the targets are met. For example, a national quota sample of social work students based on race could be drawn from the proportions identified in *Statistics on Social Work Education in the United States: 1996* (Lennon, 1996). The sample should contain 12.5% African Americans, 1.0% American Indians, 2.9% Asian Americans, 3.3% Mexican Americans, 1.5% Puerto Ricans, 2.5% "other" minorities, 1.4% foreign nationals, and 74.9% white non-Hispanic students. The actual means of selection may be haphazard sampling or volunteerism, but quota sampling provides a degree of representativeness that is added by requiring that all strata be represented in some logically defensible proportion.

   Snowball sampling may also be thought of as a purposive sampling technique when applied to studying networks by asking earlier subjects to nominate candidates to be included in the sample. Snowball sampling refers to a methodology that starts with a single element and then grows and grows, like a snowball getting bigger and bigger as it is rolled through the snow. More specifically, as you conclude your data collection with your first element, you inquire, "Can you suggest others to whom I might speak about this topic?" After getting names and contact information for additional people, you follow through and incorporate them into your sample. You continue in such a manner until you reach your desired sample size or until you are getting no additional new names to contact.

   An obvious problem with snowball sampling is that most people tend to associate with others who share similar perspectives, values, and other relevant psychosocial variables. As a result, biases that may be present in your sample tend to get confirmed and amplified as the "snowball" keeps rolling. Suppose a social worker wanted to survey parents of schoolchildren about a new policy that imposed a strict curfew and dress code on students. If the first parent selected for interviewing felt very favorably about the new policy, the people to whom this person referred the social worker would likely be positive as well. The more salient and the more public the issue, the more likely such segregation is to occur. Note that the larger your "snowball" becomes, the less likely these strong systematic biases are to be maintained.

On the other hand, there are limited occasions when snowball sampling offers an appropriate sampling procedure. Early in his career, one of the authors was assigned as a VISTA (*Volunteers in Service to America*) to develop a program for volunteers working with parolees and probationers. Knowing little about operating a formal volunteer program and less about corrections (VISTA tended to be like that in those days), the young VISTA talked with a supervisor from the host agency. With copious notes and a head swimming with new details, he remembered to ask, "Is there anyone else that you think I should talk to about corrections or volunteerism?" After several full weeks of interviewing all of the people identified by the snowballing procedure, no new names surfaced. Used in this way, snowball sampling can offer an appropriate mechanism for sampling a well-defined population—in this case, local people who knew about volunteerism and/or corrections.

The choice of experts may also be a special case of purposive sampling in that such individuals are chosen because they are believed to possess special knowledge. **Key informants** are persons selected because of their access to key observations and willingness to share their observations with an investigator. In addition to describing their own characteristics, key informants are sometimes asked to describe general characteristics of a population. Under these conditions, the key informants themselves may not constitute a sample at all, but an expert judge. Although key informants can be excellent sources of information about their own direct experience, when asked to make generalizations to other persons or situations, key informants and expert judges are not very reliable (Rossi & Freeman, 1993).

It should be obvious that the choice of precisely whom the key informants might be in a particular study depends on the subject matter of that study. Consider this example. You have been hired by a consortium including the local United Way, a neighborhood business persons' association, and a regional planning council to do "community development" work in a particular neighborhood. One of your first tasks is to try and get an accurate assessment of macro characteristics of the neighborhood. You could use the census data and draw an excellent probability sample to accurately represent the neighborhood in a well-designed survey. However, you need your results rather quickly and you don't have the budget to develop and administer a survey. A key informant or small group of key informants seems a tempting alternative.

Because the goal of sampling is always to accurately represent a larger population, you would want to select key informants whose perspectives would offer insights into all segments of the neighborhood. Often, when key informants are selected, we would include local officials. Their positions offer a unique view of neighborhood functioning. Other people in formal positions of leadership are also often included—members of the clergy, perhaps educators, or representatives of civic clubs. Social workers and other professionals working in the neighborhood are probably able to provide additional insights. But if we really want to represent all neighborhood views, who else should be included? Social workers reading this book are probably quick to notice that we haven't sampled any key informants who might offer a "street-level" view of the neighborhood. Of course, the identification of these people will vary widely from neighborhood to neighborhood, but, in general, we would caution the beginning community researcher not to overlook people like beauty shop operators, neighborhood tavern keepers, youth gang leaders, or others who wouldn't traditionally be thought of as key informants. Remember the goal—to accurately represent the whole neighborhood by sampling some portion of it. Key informants can do this, but only if they are very carefully selected. An added benefit of using key informants is to connect you as a social worker with a number of people who are likely to be significant actors in the functioning of the neighborhood.

Understand that none of these methods provides the kind of sample that is strictly necessary in order to draw strong inference to a more general population—that is, inferences drawn from such samples may lack sufficient external validity. Additionally, it is technically inappropriate to use most common inferential statistics with nonprobability samples. However, there are clearly circumstances in which nonprobability sampling offers an appropriate choice in social research.

Sampling in Single-System Designs and Other Case Studies.   Most of the foregoing discussion assumes that the element to be sampled consists of persons. However, it is frequently the case that the element is an entity such as a particular kind of behavior. Such situations would obviously include those in which you are evaluating the outcomes of your work with specific individual clients, as is mandated by the NASW *Code of Ethics* (1997). Single-system designs (Bloom, Fischer, & Orme, 1999), or SSDs as they are often abbreviated, offer an appropriate tool for such evaluation. In such cases, the logic of sampling is employed by selecting particular client behaviors from a population of all behaviors to be *representative* of the client's biopsychosocial state or by asking the client to take self-assessments at multiple preselected times to gain a representative image of the client's behavior.

Social workers most often employ single-system design research in the evaluation of their own practice. The "subjects" of this research are first and foremost clients and are probably never even thought of as research subjects, much less sampling elements! In fact, they were not selected by *any* sampling procedure. Nonetheless, it is quite likely that the practitioner/researcher will employ sampling as the therapeutic relationship is evaluated.

Most of the life challenges with which social workers become involved can be represented by an array of circumstances or behaviors. Indeed, client assessments often involve, in part, checklists of behaviors that are taken collectively to represent the client's particular challenge. Thus, when client movement toward the contracted goal is assessed, the practitioner usually selects some subset of the problematic behaviors or even feelings related to the problem area and records the frequency, magnitude, duration, or switch in these indicators. Similarly, a client may be asked to note the frequency of all instances of a particular behavior or psychological state and to record every *n*th instance in detail. These choices obviously involve some behaviors and not others, and should also involve the application of sampling logic. As in all sampling, the goal is to represent the larger population—in this case, a population of behaviors, feelings, circumstances over time.

Case studies, or idiographic research, are similar to SSDs in that they are also likely to record and reflect a subset of all case behaviors and circumstances. Unlike SSDs, however, case studies are often intended to represent a more general class of circumstances. In this case, the social worker would likely select a research subject that offered the greatest likelihood of a rich and varied experience. Just as a researcher conducting an exploratory study might purposively sample in order to represent multiple, important dimensions in the population of interest, the case study subject also might be selected to represent multiple, important dimensions. Sampling logic is invaluable in seeking to fully represent the case. But the kind of external validity and statistical generalizability provided by probability sampling is not the goal of the case study. Instead, it seeks to explicate a particular kind of case situation on which insights and future research might be based.

Techniques of Probability Sampling

Properties of Probability Sampling.   *Probability sampling* uses a random selection process to determine what elements will be observed. Probability sampling procedures are designed to assure that every unit in the population has an equal, or at least *known,* chance of being selected and that the frequencies with which various types of units appear in the sample are proportionate to the frequencies of those units in the population.

Probability sampling produces two major advantages. First, using the tenets of probability theory, the degree of sampling error can be estimated. Estimates of sampling error can be of great value to consumers of research, particularly when the phenomena of interest tend to fluctuate in the same magnitude as sampling error. For example, knowing that a community policing referendum supported by a coalition of social workers and neighborhood groups is leading in the polls by four percentage points is of little comfort if the sampling error in the poll is ±5%. Although the best estimate of the lead is four percentage points, a sampling error of this magnitude (i.e., ±5%) means that the lead may be as high as 9% (4% + 5%) or that the referendum may be trailing by 1% (4% − 5% = −1%). The second advantage that probability sampling offers is protection against any systematic bias (sample bias) that may be interjected into the selection procedure (unintentionally or otherwise) by any less rigorous selection measures. As we will show, the procedures through which random samples are drawn explicitly assure that every element in the sampling frame has an equal (or known) chance to end up in the sample, thus avoiding systematic sample bias.

Simple Random Sampling.   **Simple random sampling** consists of drawing elements from a population in a lottery format in which each element has an *equal* chance of selection. Thus, if you were to first assign numbers to all of the elements in your sampling frame, then write these numbers on identical slips of paper, and mix them thoroughly in a bucket, you could reach in and blindly select a set of elements that would represent a simple random sample. In many states, you see this process demonstrated regularly on television as the state-sponsored lottery numbers are drawn. State-run lotteries are excellent examples of random sampling and arguably equally fine examples of poor social policy. Although other forms of probability sampling are more convenient, simple random samples are conceptually the simplest form of probability samples.

Tables of random numbers provide a symbolic alternative to actually conducting a lottery to select a sample. In practice, we have only rarely gone to the trouble of actually preparing slips of paper with numbers on them so that we could conduct a simple random sampling procedure. Instead, we generally turn to a table of random numbers in the back of a research or statistics book (see the Appendix) to facilitate the process. Notice that a table of random numbers is nothing more than block after block of numeric digits. Actually, these are numbers that have been selected according to an algorithm, so that there is no predictable pattern among the numbers.

Here is how to use a table of random numbers. Let's say that you want to select a 10% sample of 300 clients at your agency. These 300 clients represent your sampling frame. Create a list of these clients numbered from 1 to 300. Because the largest numbers in the sampling frame require three digits (e.g., 300), we will need three-digit random numbers. You use a table of random numbers by randomly picking a starting point. We generally close our eyes and bring a pencil point gently down to the page to select the first number. From this number, you simply move down the column (or up, across, or any other *consistent* pattern that you find convenient) of numbers recording the first 30 numbers (10% of 300 clients) that fall between 001 and 300. Clients with numbers corresponding to the 30 random numbers will be included in the sample.

Many personal computer statistics programs and spreadsheets include the capacity to produce random numbers. In fact, the random numbers in the Appendix were generated using a personal computer. Most of these programs will provide you with a set of random numbers that fit your specifications. For the preceding example, you could request 30 random numbers between 1 and 300 inclusive. You need only connect the 30 numbers provided with the corresponding clients on your master list. For example, to generate a random sample using a widely available spreadsheet program, Microsoft Excel, this procedure would be conducted by first selecting the "TOOLS" menu option. From the drop-down menu, select "DATA ANALYSIS...." From the data analysis dialog box, select the "RANDOM NUMBER GENERATOR." In this final dialog box, set the number of variables to 1, indicate the number of random numbers that you'd like (in our example, we'd like 30), select "uniform" from the various distribution options offered, and set your parameters from a low of 1 to a maximum value of 300. (This is equal to the number of sampling units in your sampling frame.) Click on "OK" and Excel will present you with 30 random numbers.

Systematic Sampling. **Systematic sampling** involves dividing the sampling frame into arbitrary groups called sampling intervals and selecting the first element in each group. Systematic sampling is a modest variation on simple random sampling and is appropriate with any sampling frame list in which there is no meaningful periodicity or pattern. First, a **sampling interval** is determined by dividing the number of elements in the sampling frame by the number desired in the sample. In our preceding simple random sampling example, we would establish a sampling interval of 10, the result of dividing the number of elements in the sampling frame (300) by the desired sample size (30). After picking a random start between 1 and 10 (10 being the *range* of the sampling interval), we would pick the unit corresponding to the random start and continue to select every tenth element (i.e., our sampling interval) until we reached a sample of 30. Systematic sampling with a random start produces probability samples with a minimum of hassle.

We need one cautionary reminder, however. On some occasions, the sampling frame is constructed according to some pattern. It is possible that this pattern and the sampling interval come together in such a way that a strong sampling bias can result. As an extreme illustration, imagine a sampling frame of schoolchildren who have been arranged and listed in a boy-girl-boy-girl fashion. Any sampling interval that is an even number will produce a sample that is comprised wholly of either boys or girls. Such a problem can be avoided if the elements in the sampling frame are randomly ordered initially. However, if such a cyclical pattern exists in the sampling frame, we suggest that it would be easier to use a simple random selection process rather than the systematic procedure.

The chief advantage of systematic sampling is that the method is easier to use than simple random sampling and results in fewer errors. Systematic sampling does not require that all the elements in the sampling frame be numbered or converted to a uniform selectable form (e.g., slips of paper). Also, systematic samples may be more precise than simple random samples because samples drawn by this method are evenly spread over the sampling frame.

Proportionate Stratified Sampling. **Proportionate stratified sampling** involves grouping a sampling frame into subsets called strata and the application of a random selection process within the stratum of a sampling frame. A stratum of a sampling frame refers to a nonoverlapping subset of the sampling frame. For example, in a study of political behavior, the voter lists are often grouped by street. The list of voters on a particular street would constitute a stratum. There are two sets of circumstances when **stratified sampling** is particularly advantageous. The first occurs when there is a critical variable that you want represented in your sample with as little error as possible—say, for instance, educational level. You might determine that 15% of your sampling frame has less than a high school education; 25% has a high school diploma as the highest degree earned; 50% has a baccalaureate degree as the highest degree earned; and the remaining 10% has a graduate degree. By selecting these same proportions of your elements from *within* the educationally homogeneous strata or groups, you have represented each group in your sample in the exact proportions in which it existed in the sampling frame.

Stratified sampling is a valuable strategy to employ when (1) estimates are wanted for specific subsets of the population, (2) the elements are naturally organized in strata, (3) people in some strata require different approaches to sampling, or (4) improved estimates of the population as a whole are sought. However, stratified sampling is only possible if the data needed to create the stratified groups exist. For example, if you do not know the race and gender of all the people in your sampling frame, you cannot stratify your sample on these variables. Further, the variables on which you are stratifying should be important to your overall research question. There is no point in going to the trouble of stratifying your sample for variables that may be of only marginal importance.

Disproportionate Stratified Sampling. **Disproportionate stratified sampling** involves selecting a number of elements in some strata that is different (disproportionate) than the percent of the sampling frame that is in that strata. Disproportionate sampling is an especially valuable tool when one of your strata or classes is particularly small because this method of sampling allows one to specify the number of elements that will be in each stratum. Think back to your general sense of sampling and probability. Two facts are likely to be fairly obvious. First of all, larger samples are likely to produce more accurate results—they have less sampling error. Second, elements that are quite rare in the sampling frame are more likely to be missed completely or to be significantly underrepresented. Now, think about sampling professional social workers when you have a special concern with race and gender. If you use the membership of your state chapter of NASW as a sampling frame, you are likely to find the unfortunate reality that men of color make up a very small percentage of this group. However, if gender and race are important variables for your research, you must have a sample of men of color that is large enough to allow accurate estimation. The solution is to "oversample" elements from classes that may be too small if left to chance alone.

Remember that probability sampling procedures require that each element have a *known* chance of selection. This is not to say that it is necessarily *equal* as in simple random sampling. In the case of disproportionate sampling, an element's chance of selection is increased by a known degree. This allows adjustments to be made in the analysis so that the improved estimates that result from oversampling are not also overrepresented when considered with the rest of the sample.

In a nutshell, disproportionate sampling involves analyzing the subsets of your sample separately when considering variables *within* groups (e.g., comparing the years of professional experience by gender and race in our NASW example), and "unweighting" the cases that were oversampled for any *across*-group analysis. For example, if men of color had been oversampled by a factor of 4, computation of "average years of professional experience" for the whole sample would require first that the analyst compute the average number of years for men of color separately. Then, this value would be substituted into the computation of the overall mean. However, it would be used only in this computation for the number of men of color who would have been present in the sample if they had not been oversampled.

Cluster Sampling. **Cluster sampling** follows precisely the same procedure as any simple random procedure with the proviso that your sampling unit is actually a group of elements. You may be studying children in elementary schools and, from all the classrooms, randomly select a set of classrooms of children to provide your elements. This is a situation in which a sampling unit and an element are *not* the same thing. That is, the classroom is the sampling unit and the elements are children. Another example would be the selection of families in which all family members would be elements of the sample. Cluster sampling can be especially valuable in situations in which the cluster represents the unit of analysis and the elements within the cluster are the units of observation.

Multistage Sampling.   Cluster sampling is perhaps most commonly used as one stage in a **multistage sampling** procedure, which, as the name implies, involves more than one round of sampling. Typically, the first stage involves the random selection of some kind of group (cluster) and the second stage involves the random selection of individuals from within the chosen group. So, for example, as a program planner for a state department of human services, you might be interested in a statewide assessment of the satisfaction of home-delivered-meal program participants. Although these individuals are known to the local program staff, a statewide listing of them that would provide the necessary sampling frame for a simple random sampling procedure does not exist. However, you do have a listing (sampling frame) of the many individual meal programs as well as the number of consumers served by each. This is a perfect situation for multistage cluster sampling. First, a random sample of meal programs would be selected, and, next, a random sample of clients within the selected programs would be drawn.

Sampling with Clusters of Different Sizes.   Unfortunately, when the clusters that you select in the first stage of a multistage procedure vary appreciably in size, an extra wrinkle is added to the procedure. Remember that in all probability samples every element needs to have either an *equal* chance of selection or, in disproportionate sampling, a known chance of selection so that computational adjustments can be made. If you select clusters of differing sizes and then plan to draw *the same number* of elements from each, the elements from smaller clusters have a higher probability of selection than those from larger clusters.

Let's review the arithmetic behind joint probabilities briefly. If you flip a fair coin, the chance of its landing on "heads" is $1/2$. If you flip it a second time, the chance of its landing on "heads" is $1/2$. A fair coin always has a $1/2$, or 50%, chance of coming up "heads" on any given toss. Now, what is the probability that the coin comes up "heads" on both the first and second toss? The rules of probability say that you must multiply the probability of "heads" on the first toss by the probability of "heads" on the second toss, that is, $1/2 \times 1/2 = 1/4$. So, the probability of getting "heads" on both the first and second tosses (a "joint probability") is $1/4$.

Now, back to our home-delivered meals. Let's imagine that we have 50 local programs delivering meals and half of them (25 programs) have 100 participants and the other half (25 programs) have 200 participants. The chance that any one program is selected as a cluster in our first stage of sampling is $1/50$. So far, so good. Now imagine that you want to select 20 people out of each program. In the smaller programs (100 participants), the chances of an individual being selected is 20/100, or 1/5, whereas in the larger programs, an individual's chance of selection is 20/200, or 1/10. Thus, the overall probability of a participant in a smaller program being selected is 1/250 (i.e., $1/50 \times 20/100$), whereas a participant in a larger program has a 1/500 (i.e., $1/50 \times 20/200$) chance of selection. Whoops, we've given participants from small programs twice the "opportunity" to be in our study.

The solution to this common problem is to sample the clusters in a way that is proportionate to their size. If we are going to select the same number of people from each cluster, the larger clusters need a relatively larger chance of selection in the first stage of sampling. By computing the joint probability of selection (the chance of a cluster's selection multiplied by the chance of an individual from within that cluster being selected), you can confirm that each individual has an equal chance of being selected for the final sample. We demonstrate a very mechanical procedure for achieving this end (see Table 6.1).

First, in table form, list all of the programs in a column. In the next column, write the number of participants that are involved in that program. In the third column, write the cumulative range of the number of participants. That is, if the first program had 77 participants, its range would be 1–77. If the second program had 92 participants, its range would be 78 (the first number above the high point of the preceding range) to 169 (the sum of the participants in the preceding programs plus the number of participants in the current program). In a similar manner, a third program with 51 participants would have a range of 170–220. Following this pattern for all of the programs will result in the high point of the final program's range being equal to the total number of participants in all programs combined.

Let's assume (without justification for the moment) that you have determined that a sample of 200 is adequate for your purposes. By dividing your total sampling frame (4,000) by your sample size (200), you get a sampling interval of 20. Using a random-number table or a suitable computer program, select a random number between 1 and 20 inclusive (your sampling interval). Starting with this number, select every twentieth number through the entire range of participant numbers (1–4,000).

Finally, put your selected sample numbers into the fourth column of your table on the line parallel to the range in which they fall. So, element numbers 16, 36, 56, and 76 fall in the range associated with Program 1. Element numbers 96, 116, 136, and 156 fall in the range associated with Program 2, and so on. Now you are prepared to approach each of the meal programs and, using a local listing of their program participants that has been renumbered to reflect the range that you have assigned (column 3), identify the actual person selected for inclusion in the study. Table 6.1 illustrates this procedure with an initial randomly selected starting number of 16.

A modest but somewhat easier alternative to the last step of matching the numbers in column 4 with the multiple-program participant lists is available. The underlying logic of this alternative is that the essential point is the *random selection* of the correct number of elements given the relative size of the cluster. Thus, in

TABLE 6.1   Proportionate Sampling from Clusters of Varying Sizes (Using a Sampling Interval of 20 and a Random Start at 16)

Program Name	Number of Participants	Cumulative Total of Participants	Selected Participants	No. of Elements per Program
Program 1	77	1–77	16, 36, 56, 76	4
Program 2	92	78–169	96, 116, 136, 156	4
Program 3	51	170–220	176, 196, 216	3
Program 4	107	221–327	236, 256, 276, 296, 316	5
Program 5	83	328–410	336, 356, 376, 396	4
Program 6	73	411–483	416, 436, 456, 476	4
Program 7	67	484–550	496, 516, 536	3
Program 8	68	551–618	556, 576, 596, 616	4
Program 9	73	619–691	636, 656, 676	3
Program 10	131	692–822	696, 716, 736, 756, 776, 796, 816	7
Program 11	75	823–897	836, 856, 876, 896	4
Program 12	54	898–951	916, 936	2
Program 13	76	952–1027	956, 976, 996, 1016	4
Program 14	54	1028–1081	1036, 1056, 1076	3
Program 15	111	1082–1192	1096, 1116, 1136, 1156, 1176	5
Program 16	127	1193–1319	1196, 1216, 1236, 1256, 1276, 1296, 1316	7
Program 17	74	1320–1393	1336, 1356, 1376	3
Program 18	101	1394–1494	1396, 1416, 1436, 1456, 1476	5
Program 19	62	1495–1556	1496, 1516, 1536, 1556	4
Program 20	123	1557–1679	1576, 1596, 1616, 1636, 1656, 1676	6
Program 21	58	1680–1737	1696, 1716, 1736	3
Program 22	38	1738–1775	1756	1
Program 23	56	1776–1831	1776, 1796, 1816	3
Program 24	74	1832–1905	1836, 1856, 1876, 1896	4
Program 25	114	1906–2019	1916, 1936, 1956, 1976, 1996, 2016	6
Program 26	77	2020–2096	2036, 2056, 2076, 2096	4
Program 27	72	2097–2168	2116, 2136, 2156	3
Program 28	61	2169–2229	2176, 2196, 2216	3
Program 29	107	2230–2336	2236, 2256, 2276, 2296, 2316, 2336	6
Program 30	63	2337–2399	2356, 2376, 2396	3
Program 31	73	2400–2472	2416, 2436, 2456	3
Program 32	104	2473–2576	2476, 2496, 2516, 2536, 2556, 2576	6
Program 33	58	2577–2634	2596, 2616	2

(continued)

TABLE 6.1   Continued

Program Name	Number of Participants	Cumulative Total of Participants	Selected Participants	No. of Elements per Program
Program 34	33	2635–2667	2636	1
Program 35	111	2668–2778	2656, 2676, 2696, 2716, 2736, 2756, 2776	7
Program 36	65	2779–2843	2796, 2816, 2836	3
Program 37	67	2844–2910	2856, 2876, 2896	3
Program 38	56	2911–2966	2916, 2936, 2956	3
Program 39	64	2967–3030	2976, 2996, 3016	3
Program 40	121	3031–3151	3036, 3056, 3076, 3096, 3116, 3136	6
Program 41	117	3152–3268	3156, 3176, 3196, 3216, 3236, 3256	6
Program 42	74	3269–3342	3276, 3296, 3316, 3336	4
Program 43	101	3343–3443	3356, 3376, 3396, 3416, 3436	5
Program 44	51	3444–3494	3456, 3476	2
Program 45	146	3495–3640	3496, 3516, 3536, 3556, 3576, 3596, 3616, 3636	8
Program 46	48	3641–3688	3656, 3676	2
Program 47	68	3689–3756	3696, 3716, 3736, 3756	4
Program 48	56	3757–3812	3776, 3796	2
Program 49	75	3813–3887	3816, 3836, 3856, 3876	4
Program 50	113	3888–4000	3896, 3916, 3936, 3959, 3976, 3996	6
			Total Sample Size	**200**

Program 1, it is not so important that participants 16, 36, 56, and 76 are selected, but that *four* participants are *randomly* selected from this program. Consequently, we find it easier to simply select four participants (using a table of random numbers or a computerized random-number generator) from the 77 people who receive services from Program 1. Likewise, four participants are randomly selected from Program 2 and three are randomly selected from Program 3. The number of participants to be selected from each program is given in column 5.

Setting Probability Sample-Size Targets

Although sampling strategies (convenience, haphazard, purposive, volunteer, or random sampling) establish the representativeness of the sample, sample size establishes the cost, sensitivity, and precision of population estimators derived from the sample. Therefore, choosing a sample size involves striking a balance between the desire to keep sample sizes small (lower cost) and to keep sensitivity and precision high (usually associated with larger samples). With probability samples, the random selection methods provide a very strong argument in support of a claim of representativeness. When nonprobability samples are used, representativeness becomes a characteristic of a sample that must be supported on the logic of the nonprobabilistic sampling procedure. As a result of this important distinction, the procedures for determining sample-size targets that we provide are based on the assumption that a probability sample is being employed. That said, it is also reasonable to use these methods with nonprobability samples that are being used as "substitutes" for probability samples—say, perhaps, an initial exploratory study that samples from convenient clusters of sample elements. Although it is still technically inappropriate to use certain analytic tools like inferential statistics with such sample data, the intentional determination of an appropriate sample size (in probability sampling terms) may provide some degree of comfort in the generalizations that are to be made.

Very often students' concern with sample size is limited to the desire to avoid having too few subjects to allow proper inference. Their concerns are voiced in questions such as, "Will it be enough if I have such-and-so-many subjects in my research?" Although their concern is well based, it reflects only half of the issue. Samples can be too large as well as too small. When samples are too large, they are wasteful. Regardless of the method by which research data are collected from the sampling elements, sampling more of them will cost more. With face-to-face interviews, each interview can cost a considerable sum of money. Surveys are usually much less expensive, but including more sampling elements than are needed is still wasteful. After sampling and data collection, there is a continuing unnecessary cost associated with coding and entering unneeded data. We would much rather see those wasted dollars used for direct client services or for more quality research.

To err on the "too-small" side of optimal sample size is to weaken the conclusions that can be drawn from research. In the extreme, research based on too-small samples is more wasteful that using samples that are too large because the results of that research do not support inference at all. Indeed, when small-sample research is subject to large-sample analysis, we run the risk of discarding practice interventions that may have actually offered clients real relief.

Probability Theory.   **Probability theory** allows us to estimate in advance the sensitivity and precision associated with population descriptions drawn from samples of various sizes. Probability concerns the likelihood that something will happen. Every event that you can imagine is either possible or impossible. If some event is impossible—that is, it will literally *never* happen—we say that it has a *zero* probability of occurring. Everything else, in contrast, has some nonzero probability of occurring. When things are quite unlikely to happen, we say they have a low probability, whereas we say that other things that are extremely likely have a high probability.

Now, some things that have a nonzero chance (probability) of occurring have causes that we recognize and that allow us to predict the probability of the event's occurrence with some range of accuracy. For instance, if you know that your best friend *always* has carrot sticks as a snack before research class, you can predict with reasonably high probability that your friend will have carrot sticks as a snack before research class again tomorrow. Maybe tomorrow will be the day that this culinary habit is broken, but if you needed to make a wager, carrot sticks would be a good bet. Obviously, our knowledge about influences in human life allows us to make much more important predictions than snack food. For instance, we know substance abuse increases the probability that a range of untoward outcomes will occur in an individual's life. On the positive side, we know that exercise and calcium supplements reduce the probability that osteoporosis will occur as we grow older.

Probability theory is a large body of mathematics that allows us to assess the likelihood that an event will occur. You don't need to worry about much of this arithmetic because most of the work has been done and is conveniently summarized in tables. What we do need to know to be competent in social research is some of the very basic logic of probability and how to make it work for us as we practice social work. In the next few paragraphs, we review the fundamentals of the **binomial sampling distribution** as a way of better understanding sampling, and, in Chapter 8 on numeric analysis, we return to some of this logic as we consider hypothesis testing and the precision of making estimates about populations.

Let's start by imagining a machine that does nothing but flips a penny 10 times every minute, hour after hour, day after day. The penny is a "fair" penny, which means that on any one flip, it has a 50–50 chance of landing "heads" up as opposed to "tails" up. You'd be correct in guessing that if we were to count all of the heads and all of the tails for a week (that would be 100,800 flips), the number of heads and the number of tails would be very nearly equal. If we did our counting at the end of a single day (14,400 flips), you'd be accurate to say the number of heads and tails would be about equal. Likewise, even after an hour (600 flips) the number would be about equal. But how about after just one minute? That would be only 10 flips. If we watched the machine and counted 6 heads and 4 tails, would you say that the coin wasn't fair? That the machine was "fixed"? Probably not. How about if we counted 7 heads and only 3 tails? Even at seven 7 and 3 tails, you probably wouldn't be so surprised as to accuse someone of "fixing" the experiment. You'd likely just say, "Things happen. Everyone knows that just because the probability of getting heads on one flip is 50–50, it doesn't mean that the next flip will be heads just because the last one was tails." Exactly! Let's continue this mental experiment and then apply some probability theory to drawing probability samples in social work.

You know that the probability of heads on a single flip is 50–50, and you know that "over the long haul" the distribution of heads and tails approaches 50–50. Imagine that you take a representative "sample" of the next 10 consecutive coin flips. Your result comes out 4 heads and 6 tails. Fair enough. After a few minutes, you take another sample of 10 flips and get an even 5 and 5. If you were to keep at this for several hours and keep track of the various distributions of heads and tails that you got on each sample of 10 flips, the frequencies of heads in these sampling distributions would look something like those reported in Table 6.2. Indeed, you'd find that the 5 heads and 5 tails outcome was the most common, but that most, perhaps even all, of the other possibilities also occurred. In fact, if you did this experiment long enough (say, about 10,000 samples—that would be

100,000 flips), you'd find the various outcomes very closely approximate the proportions listed in Table 6.2). (We used the "binomial distribution function" in a spreadsheet program to produce these probabilities instead of spending a fair portion of our semester flipping a penny!)

The degree to which any one of these samples varies from that which should be expected (i.e., 50–50) due to random variation is called sampling error. We can see in Table 6.2 that 5 heads out of 10 flips is the most probable outcome in our 10-flip experiment, but that it is only likely to happen a little less than 25% of the time. However, if we consider the middle 20% of the range of outcomes (i.e., 5 heads ± 1 head), we would likely see "success" (defined as the number of heads) about 65% (20.51% + 24.61% + 20.51% = 65.63%) of the time. So, in samples of 10, the probability of getting heads 4, 5, or 6 times would be about 65%. Is there anything that we can do to increase the probability of making a particular prediction? Certainly, probability theory tells us that as we increase our sample size, we decrease our sampling error. Consider what happens with our coin-toss experiment if we increase our sample size to 20 tosses, or even 100 tosses. The sampling distribution probabilities for the middle 20% of each of these ranges are presented in Table 6.3 on page 140.

There is something of a paradox evident here. Note that in samples of 100 flips, the likelihood of getting exactly 50 heads and 50 tails is only about 8%. This is much lower than the 25% probability of getting the exact 50–50 outcome in a 10-flip sample. And, yet, the likelihood of obtaining one of the more extreme outcomes, say, 30% heads, is dramatically reduced (.00% versus nearly 12%). How is it possible that a larger sample is simultaneously less likely to reflect the perfect

TABLE 6.2 Binomial Sampling Distributions Showing Probabilities of Outcomes on a 10-Flip Coin-Toss Experiment

10-Flip Experiment	
No. of Heads	**Probability**
0 out of 10	0.10%
1 out of 10	0.98%
2 out of 10	4.39%
3 out of 10	11.72%
4 out of 10	20.51%
5 out of 10	24.61%
6 out of 10	20.51%
7 out of 10	11.72%
8 out of 10	4.39%
9 out of 10	0.98%
10 out of 10	0.10%
Total Probability	**100%**

TABLE 6.3   **Binomial Sampling Distributions Showing Probabilities of Outcomes for the Midpoint ±10% on 20-Flip and 100-Flip Coin-Toss Experiments**

	20-Flip Experiment		100-Flip Experiment	
	No. of Heads	Probability	No. of Heads	Probability
	8 out of 20	12.01%	40 out of 100	1.08%
			41 out of 100	1.59%
			42 out of 100	2.23%
			43 out of 100	3.01%
			44 out of 100	3.90%
	9 out of 20	16.02%	45 out of 100	4.85%
			46 out of 100	5.80%
			47 out of 100	6.66%
			48 out of 100	7.35%
			49 out of 100	7.80%
	10 out of 20	17.62%	50 out of 100	7.96%
			51 out of 100	7.80%
			52 out of 100	7.35%
			53 out of 100	6.66%
			54 out of 100	5.80%
	11 out of 20	16.02%	55 out of 100	4.85%
			56 out of 100	3.90%
			57 out of 100	3.01%
			58 out of 100	2.23%
			59 out of 100	1.59%
	12 out of 20	12.01%	60 out of 100	1.08%
Cumulative probability of midpoint ±10%		**73.68%**		**96.48%**

50–50 outcome and less likely to reflect the more extreme outcomes? The key to understanding how this works is in recognizing that larger samples have smaller sampling errors. This is why the middle 20% of each of the previous three sampling distributions (i.e., 4, 5, or 6 heads out of 10 flips; 8, 9, 10, 11, or 12 heads out of 20 flips; or from 40 to 60 heads inclusive out of 100 flips) captures an increasing proportion of all possible outcomes as the size of the samples is increased. From Tables 6.2 and 6.3, it can be seen that the range of outcomes from 10% below the most probable outcome (50% heads and 50% tails) to 10% above this point reflects a probability of 65.6% (in the 10-flip samples), to 73.7% (in the 20-flip samples), to 96.5% (in the 100-flip samples).

Probability theory allows us to evaluate how far off an estimate of a population characteristic derived from a random sample might be. Further, probability theory enables us to establish a *confidence interval* for each estimate. A **confidence**

interval is a range within which the "true" population value has a known probability of falling. As will be seen, confidence intervals can be specified in advance
and, by working backwards, used to determine the sample size needed to achieve
a desired level of precision or accuracy.

Factors Influencing Optimal Sample Size.   The determination of sample size
and, by extension, statistical power is an often neglected aspect of social work
research (Orme & Combs-Orme, 1986). This is probably true because the mathematics that underlie this determination are quite complex. Fortunately, tables are
available that allow the researcher to avoid struggling with these calculations. This
allows us to offer a nonmathematical discussion of the factors that are involved in
deciding just how many subjects you need for your research. Set aside whatever
math phobias you may have and focus on an intuitive understanding in the discussion of sample size that follows. Three concepts central to choosing a minimum
sample size are (1) the magnitude or size of that which we wish to observe (*effect
size*), (2) the certainty that we want to have in our observations (*confidence level*),
and (3) the desired certainty that our sample is large enough to allow us to detect
effects of the size of interest (*statistical power*).

Imagine that you are taking an afternoon walk down a lovely forest path on
a beautiful autumn day. You happen under a huge old maple tree that is dropping
its many leaves of stunning fall colors. You bend and retrieve one leaf that seems
especially exquisite. With your unassisted eye, you observe its color, shape, and
smooth surface. Wishing to examine it more thoroughly, you slip on your reading
glasses and appreciate the major and some minor veins, as well as some small
spots of blight. With a second look, you realize that some of the blight is really just
bits of dirt. You take a small magnifying glass from your pocket and train it on the
leaf. You are now able to see irregularities in the color and in the fine patterning
that suggests the cellular structure. With your interest more thoroughly piqued,
you decide to take the leaf home to study it even more closely using the hobby
microscope belonging to your visiting niece.

Okay. We could go on with this story and suggest that you even beg your
aunt to subject the leaf to observation using the electron microscope in her lab in
the university physics department, but we think you already get the point. Quite
simply, we make choices about how carefully we want to study things. Most of us
settle for appreciating the color of leaves en masse; however, for those interested in
the intricacies of tree biology, much closer observation is essential.

So it is in social work. Most people are probably content to say that adolescents who study hard make better grades, but how much improvement needs to be
detected in order to be considered "better"? Are we only interested in fairly large
grade changes or should we be using more powerful techniques—such as the magnifying glass or microscope in the preceding example—to discern smaller changes
in the students' performance? In research language, the decision about how large
an effect (e.g., the grade change) must be in order to be considered important is
called **effect size.** If a community organizer finds that the amount of substandard
housing stock decreases by 2% as the result of a massive organizing effort, is that a

large enough effect size to be considered important? If the number of adolescents accessing confidential HIV testing increases by 6% after the elimination of a parental-consent requirement, was the effect size of the policy change important? If a depressed client reports feeling "a little better" or has a score change on the Beck's Depression Inventory of five points, has the effect size suggested that our intervention has been successful? These are all questions of *effect size.*

After we have specified an effect size of a magnitude that we judge to be important, we must specify how confident we want to be about our estimates when we actually measure the effect in a sample. By specifying a **confidence level,** we indicate how much of a chance we are willing to take that the real value falls outside of our estimates. If we made the observation again, would things change—as did some of the blight on our leaf, turning out to be bits of dirt instead? In our everyday language, we are accustomed to saying things such as, "I'm 95% certain." What does that really mean? Aren't we really saying that if we made our assessment again and again, we'd come out with the same conclusion 95 times out of 100? That's the level of *certainty,* and in research language, we call it the *confidence level.* We can communicate the same level of certainty by indicating the likelihood of our results being wrong. In this case, we refer to the *statistical significance level* and would say that our results are significant at the .05 level. This .05 refers to the 5% chance that our findings are in error, in contrast to our 95% confidence that our findings are correct. We continue the discussion of statistical significance in Chapter 8 in the consideration of inference.

Statistical power is represented in our story by the use of the increasingly powerful methods of observation—the naked eye, a pocket magnifying glass, and the varying powers of microscopes. Statistical power simply refers to the ability to detect characteristics or effects when they are actually present. As higher powers of magnification were needed to observe the finer aspects of the maple leaf's configuration, so, too, is greater statistical power required to detect relatively smaller changes in client systems.

These three concepts—effect size, confidence level, and statistical power—are all related. Simply stated, statistical power limits our ability to detect smaller effect sizes at a given level of confidence. We have seen that determining the effect size is largely a matter of our deciding how much change is important enough to be considered minimally important and that the confidence level reflects our need for certainty. These are usually established by considering the relevant theory that guides our intervention and by referring to what others have done in the related literature. With effect size and confidence level determinations being made on the basis described earlier, we turn to a more detailed discussion of *statistical power.*

Principles of Statistical Power Analysis.   In studying our autumn leaf, we recall that it took more and more powerful visual aids (the reading glasses, magnifying glass, hobby microscope, and, finally, an electron microscope) to detect smaller and smaller leaf characteristics. In exactly the same way, you can see that it takes more and more effort (statistical power) to be increasingly certain (*statistical significance*) that more subtle changes (small *effect sizes*) really do result from the multiple factors that you think (with the support of theories of human behavior) influence adolescents' school achievement. This is the role of statistical power. Greater statistical power allows us to detect smaller effect sizes and to be more certain of our results. Power represents the likelihood that we are successful in demonstrating an intervention that is, itself, successful. In more technical language, as statistical significance indicates the likelihood that we erroneously reject a (true) null hypothesis, statistical power indicates the likelihood that we correctly reject a (false) null hypothesis. This is admittedly a very basic description of the relationship between these three concepts—effect size, statistical significance, and statistical power. For the purposes of using the concepts to determine sample size, we believe that it is adequate. We turn now to two approaches to setting sample-size targets.

Setting Sample-Size Targets for Hypothesis Testing.   Although the application of power analysis requires a greater treatment of statistical hypothesis testing than can be included here, the general principles are quite simple. In research designed to test hypotheses, the optional sample is one that provides reasonable protection against concluding erroneously either that there is some effect when there is none (a **Type I error**), or that there is no effect when in fact there is one (a **Type II error**). These errors are caused in part by sampling error and may be managed by selecting a sample size that is large enough to keep sampling error under control. Determining the minimum sample size that meets this need is largely a mathematical process, once we set the level of risks of Type I and Type II errors (also known as alpha and beta errors, respectively) that we are willing to tolerate and estimate how large an effect we expect to find (or would be large enough to be important).

For many common hypothesis testing statistics, the sample sizes have already been worked out for various combinations of effect sizes, and assumptions concerning Type I and Type II errors (Cohen, 1969; Cohen & Cohen, 1983). The tables contained in these sources provide sample-size recommendations covering many combinations of alpha, beta, and effect sizes. For the present purposes, a few practical guidelines may suffice. First, conventional levels have been established for both Type I and Type II errors. The accepted limit for Type I (alpha) errors is generally .05, and the limit for Type II (beta) errors is recommended to be set at .20 (Cohen, 1969). Second, effect sizes are often expressed in terms of correlations (discussed earlier and destined for further description in Chapter 8). Rubin and Babbie (1997) report that in psychology, sociology, and social work, evaluations of interventions tend to produce effect sizes resulting in correlations in the small to medium range corresponding roughly with simple correlations in the .1 to .3 range. Given the conventions for Type I and Type II errors and common effect sizes, it is possible to form some simple guidelines for sample sizes. For example, a sample size of 783 is needed to detect a small effect size (say, a correlation of .10) with alpha set at .05 and beta at .2 (Cohen & Cohen, 1983). If the expected effect size were medium (a correlation of .30), the sample size needed would decrease to 84. For a truly large effect size (a correlation of .50), the sample size needed would be 28. Although various combinations of alpha, beta, and effect sizes produce different sample-size needs, these values should give a rough idea of what an adequate sample size should be. What the social work researcher needs to do is carefully consider what effect size is reasonable or important. A study with only a few subjects reliably detects only the largest effects related to major interventions. Much larger sample sizes are needed to detect effects of minor interventions. If conditions (say, conventions among persons conducting research in a given area) require a more stringent .01 cutoff for Type I errors, the minimum sample size will be larger. The minimum sample size changes any time one of the three parameters—alpha, beta, or effect size—is changed.

The implication of all this for practice-related research is that conducting research with too few subjects is likely to lead to Type II errors. That is, real but less dramatic effects may be missed because our research is insensitive to them. Given what was said earlier about the ethics of incompetent research, it is not enough to conclude post hoc that "I should have used a larger sample" when power analysis would have allowed that concern to be addressed at the design phase. On the opposite extreme, selecting a sample that is much larger than needed can introduce unjustified expense and intrusion.

Setting Sample Size Targets for Precision in Estimating. Many times, social workers are concerned about drawing a sample in order to make an estimate about some characteristic in a population. For instance, when we are interested in conducting a community survey to determine the perceptions of needed services or the satisfaction with existing services, we would want to assess these views in a representative sample in order to estimate with **precision** the prevalence of those views in the population from which the sample is drawn.

An excellent guide to setting target sample size in such a situation is provided by using the binomial sampling distribution. Many of the kinds of questions that social workers ask involve a choice between two answers, for instance, to approve or disapprove. Variables that have only two possible attributes are called binomial variables. In using the binomial distribution to set sample-size targets, the use of the confidence level is maintained from the previous approach. The idea of a **margin of error** is used instead of the minimum effect size to be detected. (You can see that whenever estimates involving a large margin of error are made, small effect sizes would be impossible to detect with certainty.) Finally, an estimate of the variability in the population is incorporated. The sample size is estimated using the following equation:

$$N = z^2 PQ/c^2 \tag{6.1}$$

where

N = sample size

z = z score associated with the confidence level

c = margin of error

P = expected proportion of one outcome

$Q = 1 - P$

This equation is really quite easy to use because a number of its elements can be chosen from a relatively small set of possible choices. Let's consider each.

Although one could look up z scores for any possible confidence level, most social work research uses a confidence level of 95%. The z score for a 95% confidence level is 1.96. (For a confidence level of 90%, the appropriate z score is 1.645.) Thus, the equation calls for squaring this quantity, which in the case of the 95% confidence level would be 3.8 (1.96 × 1.96 = 3.84).

The margin of error (represented by c in the equation) is a limit of how much error can be tolerated in percentage terms. You are probably familiar with this from seeing political polling data reported in the newspaper for likely voters' preferences between two candidates, plus or minus three percentage points. This "±3%" is the margin of error in the research. The margin of error can be set at whatever level the researcher deems appropriate. Note, however, that as the margin of error increases, it is increasingly difficult to be sure of small changes (effect sizes) that may have occurred. Obviously, a study that is conducted with a sample that allows a margin of error of ±10% is not able to reliably detect changes of 5% in the population because these changes are below the accuracy of precision of the estimator.

Finally, the equation requires that you have some estimate of the real variability in the population. Students often ask, "How can I know that? If I knew that, I wouldn't be doing the study." Perhaps. Often, you have estimates based on previous research that can be helpful, but in the final analysis, you must often make your best educated guess. In the absence of knowing anything about how the two possible outcomes of P and Q might be distributed, our best guess would be 50–50. This is exactly the same as if you were to flip a coin 100 times and record the number of heads and tails. Although it might vary somewhat, your best guess of the final outcome in your coin-toss experiment would be 50 heads and 50 tails. Let's accept this "guess" for a moment. The equation calls for the expected probability of one outcome to be multiplied by the expected probability of the other; and this provides a convenient approach. Consider Table 6.4. Note that as the

TABLE 6.4   Binomial Probability Cross Products

P	Q	P × Q
.0	1.0	.00
.1	.9	.09
.2	.8	.16
.3	.7	.21
.4	.6	24
.5	.5	.25
.6	.4	.24
.7	.3	.21
.8	.2	.16
.9	.1	.09
1.0	.0	.00

quantity P is multiplied by the quantity Q, the product reaches its maximum value when each is equal to .5 (and the product PQ is equal to .25). Thus, if you have no basis to assume anything else about the expected outcomes of P and Q, the best guess is 50–50 and the product (i.e., .25) can be substituted into the formula for the quantity PQ.

At this point, you are able to do the final arithmetic to calculate the target sample size. Multiply the squared z score for the selected confidence level (e.g., 3.84 for a confidence level of 95%) times the product of P and Q (e.g., .25) and divide that quantity (i.e., $3.84 \times .25 = .96$) by the squared value of your selected margin of error (e.g., ±5% would be $.05 \times .05 = .0025$). The target sample size would be 384. This method proves a quite adequate technique for setting sample-size targets in this kind of research.

As with the power analysis approach to setting sample size discussed earlier, the parameters used in the binomial approach can be adjusted to reflect varying standards and interests. For example, to relax the confidence level to 90% and the margin of error to ±10% results in a sample size target of 68! Understanding these trade-offs is important in designing and interpreting research to the maximum benefit of our clients.

Summary

This chapter highlights the primary goal of sampling, which is to obtain a representative subset of a population from which to make generalizations about the larger population. Sampling strategies discussed here are techniques designed to improve the representativeness of samples and thus the generalizations that social workers and other researchers make from studies of subsets of populations. In addition to formal large-group research, sampling and sampling logic are used in exploratory studies, single-system designs, case studies, and even in such activities as library-based literature reviews.

Sampling involves defining a population of interest by describing elements that belong in that population. A sampling frame is a list of the elements in a population and may be an actual list or virtual list. A sample is a subset of the sampling frame drawn by a variety of methods. The sampling strategy is designed to maximize representativeness and convenience and minimize cost and intrusiveness. Nonprobability samples tend to be easy and inexpensive (when compared to probability samples), but may be weaker in protection from bias and contain unknown levels of random sampling error.

The major advantages of probability sampling are that it allows an accurate estimation of the degree of sampling error and the protection against any systematic bias that may be interjected into the sampling procedure. The distinguishing characteristic of all probability samples is that every element in the sampling frame has a known chance of selection. With any of the proportionate probability sampling techniques, every element has an equal chance of selection. Tables of random numbers and generation of random numbers by common personal computer software are described as valuable tools in probability sampling. In dispı portionate probability sampling, the chances for selection of each element are noı equal, but are altered in a known way so that special subpopulations might be more accurately sampled. These alterations must be readjusted in the analysis of the data collected.

By employing the basic principles of statistical power analysis, every social worker can identify an optimal size for a given research situation. Equally importantly, if deviations from the optimal size must be made, the social work researcher knowledgeable of these principles can make adjustments in an intentional and rational way.

ER

Data Collection

Observing the Social World

Relationship of This Chapter to the Whole

Reliance on observation is one of the features that distinguishes science from other ways of knowing. However, it is not merely the reliance on observational confirmation that makes science different from mysticism, rationalism, and authority-based knowledge systems. As Wallace (1971) noted, the use of deliberate methods of observation designed to improve intersubjectivity and reduce the likelihood of errors is an important part of what makes science a different way of knowing. One way to think about the deliberate methods to which Wallace refers is as social situations carefully crafted to produce the clearest, most replicable observations about human behavior in the empirical world. This chapter is concerned with these social settings, their dynamics, characteristics, and some common strategies for getting the most out of data collection procedures.

Relevance to the Roles of Social Workers

The social situations we call data collection are natural extensions of social work activity. As applied professionals, social workers are constantly gathering information to facilitate decision making. This information is collected in the context of direct and indirect person-to-person interactions as well as observation of individuals and larger social systems. In all of our professional social work roles, we are constantly involved in collecting information, processing it, and deciding on professional actions based on that processed information. This chapter looks at various modes of data collection as specifications for particular kinds of social roles. Roles provide norms for behavior that specify how people will act. By being conscious of the special social relations and tasks of data collection, it should be possible for the social worker to obtain the needed answers and at the same time see how good methods are consistent with traditional value positions of social work, such as respect for clients and responsibility for our actions.

Learning Objectives

After reading this chapter, you will be able to:

1. describe three social settings in which most observation occurs
2. describe criteria to be optimized by choice of a data collection strategy
3. describe three examples of flexible-response data collection procedures
4. describe three examples of fixed-response data collection procedures
5. design questions and questionnaires that provide valid, reliable data

Key Terms and Concepts

Data Collection Procedures

Important Characteristics of Data Collection Procedures.   The act of making observations and collecting data does not occur in a social vacuum. It is useful to think about data collection activities as constituting social roles. Like all roles, these involve implicit knowledge concerning norms, rules, power designations, and the like. The social roles designated by labels such as interviewer, tester, and observer imply social situations designed foremost to allow the researcher to obtain desired information, but also to meet reciprocal needs of participants and not create too much conflict with the values and norms of other overlapping social roles. These role designations determine to some extent what demands can be placed on both the social worker and other participants in scientific study by specifying patterns of communication and norms for action. These in turn create both motivation and opportunities for cooperation, competition, and even deception. Because of the potential for the social context to influence objectivity (defined as intersubjectivity), it is reasonable to ask how procedures can be designed to maximize the quality of observations in a variety of social settings.

You will recall that the goal of science is to generate culturally relevant, intersubjective knowledge about the world. Consistent with that goal, a good data collection strategy should (1) provide the opportunity to actually observe the phenomenon of interest, (2) permit valid and reliable measurement of states of persons and groups of interest, (3) be replicable, (4) minimize cost and intrusion, and (5) fall within conventional guidelines concerning ethical treatment of persons. A good observation procedure should maximize all these characteristics.

Fixed/Flexible Response Continuum.   Data collection strategies vary in the extent to which data must be fit into preexisting categories (**fixed-response strategies**), or are free to evolve into new meaning structures (**flexible-response strategies**). For example, a mailed questionnaire survey with multiple-choice questions severely constrains the set of possible answers that are allowable. Contrast this with a typical ethnographic interview in which the respondent receives very general probes and the interviewer waits for promising leads to be produced by the interviewee. The difference between structured survey questions and ethnographic interviewing is the use of closed (i.e., fixed-response categories) questions as opposed to open (i.e., flexible-response categories) questions. Because even open-ended questions are constrained by the meaning categories of the questioner, it is useful to think of the fixed/flexible dimension as a continuum on which every question fits somewhere.

It is important to note that fixed and flexible strategies vary in usefulness depending on the question and context, and neither approach is inherently a better or poorer data collection strategy. In general, flexible-response strategies are more likely to produce data reflecting knowledge that is firmly grounded in the meaning systems of the respondents. However, such data are potentially imprecise, poorly focused, and difficult to replicate. Fixed-response strategies tend to produce more reliable data, but at the risk of being less grounded than the more flexible-response strategies. The choice of the flexible response or the fixed response, or some combination of the two, is based on the observers' assessment of use of the data and quality of existing knowledge about the phenomenon of interest.

Under ideal conditions, the choice of flexible versus fixed settings will be determined by the nature of the questions being asked. However, custom, personal preference, and training are likely to influence the approach taken as well. Also, it is common for applied research to include a combination of fixed- and flexible-response strategies. This can provide a form of triangulation of method that some claim to be indicative of the strongest of research approaches (Campbell & Fiske, 1959; Rohner, 1986). Here, as elsewhere in the text, we urge the social work researcher to begin with a focus on the demands of the task and then proceed with a full toolbox that includes competence in both flexible- and fixed-response data collection methods.

Social Settings in Which Data Are Collected

Regardless of where on the fixed versus flexible continuum a researcher ends up, the actual data collection occurs in a social context. Table 7.1 lists some of the methods that have been developed to facilitate data collection in various contexts. These are classified in terms of social setting (dialogue, written questioning, direct observation) and the degree to which response categories are fixed or flexible. In this chapter, we examine the purposes served by the selection of a strategy and describe each of the methods mentioned in Table 7.1. However, let us first discuss the dynamics of each of the social settings.

Dialogues. **Dialogues** are a common social situation in which data collection is conducted. By dialogue, we mean two-way communication between the social work researcher and a participant for the purpose of finding answers to the researcher's questions. Generally, one person takes the role of interviewer and the other that of respondent. In an interview, questions flow from one party and answers from the other. Power to direct the dialogue varies depending on how flexible or fixed the protocol is. In open, flexible-response approaches to dialogue, the respondent has much power to control the direction of the conversation. In fixed-response approaches, the interviewer exerts more control over the dialogue. The various kinds of dialogues used by social scientists may include face-to-face interviews or interviews mediated through technology, such as telephone, computer, or video interface.

Dialogues are prized for their value in examining the conceptual agreement between the interviewer and person being interviewed. This is because, even in the most structured form, the social situation permits the interviewee to take some control of the scope and content of replies. The more open approaches to interviews involve considerable power on the part of respondents as they are encouraged to ask for clarification or even to argue about the conceptualizations of the researcher. However, the extent to which an interviewee is able to direct the scope of the interview varies with the observer's choice of a fixed- or flexible-response strategy.

TABLE 7.1 Strategies for Data Collection

	Dialogues	Written Questions	Direct Observation
Flexible-response strategies	Open-ended (ethnographic) interviews	Projective tests, storytelling, essays	Field work, naturalistic observation
Fixed-response strategies	Structured interviews	Questionnaires, surveys, standardized assessment instruments	Behavioral checklists, observation protocols, logs

Interviews and other forms of dialogue have great potential to maximize the goals of scientific observation in that the researcher can collect data concerning a large variety of phenomena. Being interviewed by a social scientist is a commonly defined social role that most people can understand. Checks for validity and reliability of measurement can be applied, and opportunities to check for agreement in conceptualizations abound. Further, ethical procedures for interviews have been established. On the negative side, idiosyncrasies of a particular dyad may reduce intersubjectivity; interviews can be highly reactive, which potentially distorts the responses; and interviews can be time-consuming, expensive, and intrusive. These considerations help determine the selection of interviews or sometimes the choice of another approach to data collection.

Written Questioning.   Written approaches to data collection constitute a distinct social context for data collection characterized by limited social interaction between the interviewer and interviewees. Written questions can take the form of self-report inventories, questionnaires, checklists, projective tests, essays, and storytelling techniques. The questions and necessary stimulus materials may be prepared on paper or with electronic media. The balance of power is in the direction of the person providing the questions in that the respondents are assigned the task of responding to the written material and are not free to respond to anything else. The written instruments are intended to be self-contained and may be prepared to exacting specifications designed to ensure the validity and reliability of the data collected by standardizing the response set. However, written questions, such as checklists and multiple-choice items, need not be fixed; they may be flexible and ask general questions that permit a broad range of free-form responses. It is often the case that written surveys contain both fixed-format (closed) and flexible-format (open-ended) questions.

Written questions provide excellent strategies for maximizing the goals of data collection. Written instruments are relatively inexpensive to administer, can be less reactive than interviews (improving validity and reliability), and can be administered to large samples in a very short period of days. The technology for writing fixed-response-format questions that produce valid and reliable responses is very well developed. On the negative side, written self-report instruments have the potential to be less grounded if the questions reflect unique conceptualizations of the question writer that are not shared by the respondents. Also the quality of responses will reflect the respondent's comfort and skill with written communication in the language of the instrument. These are important concerns to professionals like social workers who have questions for clients who may be less comfortable with the written language of Western scientists.

Direct Observation.   **Direct observation** is a form of data collection characterized by clearly delineated roles of observer and subject, often including the least amount of interaction between observers and participants of the three social settings discussed. Direct observation requires the legitimization of the role of a "watcher." The role of early anthropologists as observers of the Third World was legitimized by the authority of European colonial powers—although the legitimacy of colonial power itself has more recently been challenged. Social scientists observing in their own cultures may rely on the power and prestige of their occupation to legitimize observing. At an individual level, social scientists may negotiate a role as a participant observer to legitimate their activities. In these cases, the scientist provides something of value to those being observed (participation) in exchange for a role definition that allows observing and recording. Much social work research observation is legitimated through a combination that may include authority, occupational status, and negotiation.

Direct observation is an appealing source of data for social work research. Many interesting social phenomena can be observed directly without the need for questioning. In fact, for some kinds of behaviors, particularly those concerning acts that are subject to social disapproval, direct observation is more likely to generate accurate information regarding actual behavior than would direct questioning through either interviews or written questions. Direct observation also reduces problems related to the relative level of self-awareness of respondents. Particularly for habitual behavior, people are often not the best reporters of their own actions. Therefore, in at least some cases, direct observation may yield data that are more valid and reliable than that obtained from self-reports.

Direct observation can occur in natural, open settings or controlled settings. Ratings of marital couples playing a competitive game in a laboratory setting is one example of a controlled setting. Recording interaction of children on a playground is a more open setting. Although persons being observed may not even be aware of the observers, these settings nonetheless are governed by culturally prescribed rules. In participant observation, the observer negotiates a modification of existing social roles with participants. In laboratory settings, the roles of the observer and the observed tend to be proscribed by the observation protocol. Once again, the choice of fixed or flexible strategy is a function of the nature of the question and perhaps the power available to the observer. For phenomena over which it is unlikely that the observer will have control, direct observation of the world of the participant in its natural setting may be the only feasible approach. Conversely, for events that are easily controlled and reproduced in standardized settings, the approach that yields the clearest results may be to study these phenomena in the laboratory.

Examples of Flexible-Response Data Collection Procedures

Flexible-Response Approaches to Dialogues: The Ethnographic Interview. James Spradley (1979) provides an excellent summary of the procedures of open-ended interviewing. Clearly operating on the inductive, meaning-generating side of the cycle of science, Spradley describes the **ethnographic interview** as a technique for developing a description of the beliefs and customs of another. He emphasizes the role of the person being questioned as the teacher or guide and the observer as the student or a person to be socialized. Persons conducting an ethnographic interview maintain their own cultural perspective, but attempt to discover or be "taught" the perspectives of the other. This is the essence of open-ended interviewing, the willingness to allow the respondent to exert strong control of the transaction. To be sure, the observer starts with culturally determined ways of asking questions and assigning meaning to answers and probably starts with specific interests to which the dialogue may be redirected. However, ethnographic interviewing techniques are designed to encourage the respondent to provide the response categories and meanings, tending to produce more well-grounded observations.

Open-ended interviews in general are cultural events with beginnings and endings and rules for asking questions, taking turns, and using time and space. Open-ended interviews for professional purposes have the following characteristics. There is a purpose for the interview that the interviewer must communicate to the interviewee. This includes the purpose for the overall social activity in which the interview is a part (in the case of clinical social work practice, this may be helping a client to achieve some goal) and purposes for specific activities during the interview. For example, it is necessary to explain the reasons for recording information. Reasons for returning to a particular topic may need to be shared. Feedback from the interviewer to the interviewee concerning the interviewer's (hopefully) deepening understanding of the viewpoint of the interviewee is essential. Pauses on the part of the interviewer are a tacit acknowledgment of the interviewee's control of the direction of the interview and encouragement to freely express thoughts. Open-ended interviews cannot be rushed. In open-ended interviewing, informants are encouraged to explain things in their own language and ideas and not to translate into forms they think the interviewer wants to hear. The interviewer must continuously emphasize the importance of the informant's viewpoint and check out the interviewer's interpretations directly.

The open-ended interview will also contain beginnings and endings that match local customs. Greetings are used to help establish the norms and roles. Rules governing interpersonal conduct concerning use of space, tone, turn taking, and the length of comments are the purview of the interviewee, and the interviewer needs to be very conscious in the "use of self" in such contexts, rather than responding in the natural, unexamined ways to which one was socialized. Finally, some appropriate form of leave-taking is needed to end the social interaction.

Spradley identified more than thirty types of questions that can be asked in ethnographic interviews. Three major types include *descriptive questions, structural questions,* and *contrast questions* (Spradley, 1979). **Descriptive questions** ask the interviewee to describe some phenomenon in his or her own language. Often, the reason for asking descriptive questions is to obtain examples of the language of the interviewee as a clue to how reality is structured and organized as much as it is to obtain a description of something. For example, one of us interviewed a social worker about his experience at a two-month summer camp for troubled youth located in a wilderness area. "Could you tell me what a counselor at camp does?" is an example of a descriptive question. When the object of interest is the mental categories a person uses to structure experience, structural questions are a logical choice. A **structural question** is intended to discover the categories a person used to classify their experience. "What are all the different kinds of workers at summer camp?" is one example of a structural question. Finally, clues concerning content that is important enough to create a distinction can be obtained by asking contrast questions. **Contrast questions** are used to explore meaning systems by discovering the basis for classification of objects into different classes. "What are the differences between night workers and day treatment staff?" is an example of a contrast question.

Open-ended interviews are excellent examples of flexible dialogues. Keep in mind that what is unstructured is the client's responses, not the social roles or behaviors of the interviewer. The interviewer still needs to start with specific objectives; adopt a role of interested ignorance; urge interviewees to use their own language to respond; ask descriptive, structural, and contrast questions; and use recording methods that capture the natural speech of the persons being interviewed. Good open-ended interviewers are careful to avoid biasing responses and are constantly reflecting on what they have heard. As we discuss more fully in Chapter 9 ("Analysis of Nonnumerical Data"), another feature of open-ended interviews is minicycles of asking questions, analyzing replies, and feeding back understandings to interviewees for confirmation or clarification. Open-ended interviewing often involves two or more sessions separated by enough time for the interviewer to reflect on what was said and form more focused questions. Actually, all forms of open-ended interviews are actually very structured from the standpoint of the role of the interviewer. However, what makes flexible-response approaches different from fixed-response approaches is that flexible-response approaches place fewer constraints on the respondents.

Flexible-Response Approaches to Written Questioning: Essays and Stories. Despite the prevalence of standardized tests, multiple-choice questionnaires, and the like, flexible approaches to written questions also abound. Projective tests such as the Rorschach inkblots (Rorschach, 1921) and pictorial techniques such as the Thematic Apperception Test (Murray et al., 1943) were early attempts to elicit information through the use of pictures and simple open-ended questions. Various forms of storytelling techniques (e.g., Costantino, Malgady, & Rogler, 1988) and essays are examples of written questioning techniques in which the range of responses are flexible and largely unbounded. Historically, these techniques (like more fixed-response techniques) have presented problems when structured, largely culture-bound, scoring systems were applied to the responses of members of nondominant groups. However, when such material is scored from an ethnographic perspective (the perspective of the respondent), cultural bias can be minimized.

Descriptive, structural, and contrast questions of ethnographic interviews also can be adapted for written use. These can provide very flexible forms of written questions. Of course, the degree to which answers are guided by the question varies. In the case of questions such as "What is there to know about living on the street?" the boundaries are fairly broad. In other cases, the boundaries may be tighter. Some authors (Denova, 1979) suggest breaking down broad unfocused questions into several more focused ones. For example, it is possible to replace the question, "How satisfied are you with services provided?" with a collection of more focused questions such as "What was your experience with the scheduling of appointments?"; "Did you get everything you expected from your counselor?"; and "Did what we provided resolve the problems that led you to seek our help?" In fact, one could go as far as Reid and Gunlach (1983) who developed a structured questionnaire that asked about 34 aspects of client satisfaction, grouped into three factors. How far you go down the continuum toward very precise questions with standard response options is partly a matter of taste and partly a matter of how much you know about your respondents and the phenomenon of interest.

Like open-ended interviews, what is flexible and unstructured about open-ended written questions is the range of responses that are possible. However, the actual administration of projective tests is highly formalized, as may be the scoring. The role of tester and test taker are well established. Interpretation of such material poses many challenges to the observer. Analytic approaches such as those Spradley proposed for open-ended interviews are helpful in avoiding bias, but written approaches do not provide the opportunities for the observer to verify conclusions with the person being observed. The result may be a stereotyping of interpretation in the direction of the observer's biases as every vague response is interpreted in the observer's frame of reference. This poses a serious threat to the validity of the data.

Flexible-Response Approaches to Direct Observation: Field Work. We have chosen the term field work to label observation in natural settings with little or no control of the context and no direct or indirect questioning of those being observed. It is rare to find strictly observational methods that do not also involve some form of interviewing and questioning, but sometimes it is instructive to simply watch and observe unobtrusively. For example, students in our practice evaluation course often conduct unobtrusive observations of social work agencies by watching various public behaviors. One student observed clients approaching the door of a social work agency in an inner city. She saw people glance nervously around, press a button that summoned a person to a speaker, provide information through the speaker so that the door would be opened, and finally go inside. Another observed clients passing time in a waiting room. One watched parents of seriously ill children in the pediatric ward of an acute care hospital interact with various staff members. These direct observations were used to evaluate practice-related questions without any form of direct questioning.

Flexible-response observations often start with the observer recording as much of the behavior as possible, and then after lengthy observations, noting regularities in behaviors and making tentative descriptions and explanations of the patterns. For example, the student observing waiting-room behavior kept a narrative journal that described a large number of behaviors. Later, during data analysis, she noted a string of observations related to use of reading materials provided by the agency and concluded that the reason magazines were not read by clients had little to do with literacy, but rather was a poor match in language and culture between the persons buying the magazines and the needs of clients. She speculated that this might constitute a pattern of cultural insensitivity in the agency and began to look for other evidence of this in interactions between staff and clients.

Flexible-Response Approaches to Data Collection: A Summary.   In general, flexible-response observation techniques are best suited to situations where it is important that the range of responses be as unbounded by the researcher as is possible. Written testing and direct observations are generally preferred when there is concern that asking questions directly will distort responses due to reactivity. On the other hand, dialogues have the advantage of allowing impressions and interpretations of the observer to be verified by reflection back to respondents. Although flexible data collection strategies are intended to minimize constraints on responses, the behavior of observers is often highly constrained. In the case of direct observation, observers are often expected to have little or no direct contact with those being observed to avoid influencing the behaviors under study. Likewise, the use of written questions and similar stimuli are intended to reduce reactions to the observer by controlling the degree of interaction between the observer and participant. In all cases, validity of responses is maximized by recording what is said or written verbatim and describing observations with as little interpretation as is possible. Thus, use of photography and tape recordings are very popular in such work.

What flexible techniques gain in groundedness, they tend to lack in precision and reliability. Although the open techniques allow the observer to detect patterns rooted in the life ways of the respondents, individual differences in response may mask other trends. The next set of data collection strategies, fixed-response procedures, are capable of providing very precise, reliable measures.

Examples of Fixed-Response Data Collection Procedures

Fixed-response data collection strategies are greatly valued because of their high potential to generate data that are both valid and reliable. That is, a well-designed fixed-response strategy produces data that are credibly linked to the conceptualizations of interest and also produce consistent responses, increasing the objectivity of scientific and professional generalizations. When researchers honestly have a clear understanding of the range of possible answers that might be provided to a question, it is most appropriate to use a closed question. Because of the familiarity with the topic, the response set can meet the necessary requirements of being *exhaustive* and *mutually exclusive*. *Exhaustive* means that the response set must contain the complete set of possible answers for any potential respondent, and mutually exclusive means that any respondent would be able to select *one, and only one,* response. We sometimes tell students to remember that every respondent needs to be someplace, but they can only be in one place at any one point in time.

Standards for such procedures arose in the middle of the twentieth century. In 1954, the American Psychological Association issued recommendations for psychological tests. In 1955, the American Educational Research Association and the National Council on Measurement in Education issued their standards for achievement tests. In 1966, both these documents were merged into the first APA standards for both educational and psychological tests (American Psychological Association, 1974). These and subsequent documents laid out the scientific and social responsibilities of persons who devise instruments designed to be used to influence intervention and decision making around the lives of persons. These standards mostly assured the reliability and validity of instrumentation, but also protected the helping profession from potential abuses of educational and psychological tests. Grossly simplified, the standards require persons who develop and use instruments to demonstrate empirically that (1) the tests measure what they claim to measure and (2) the measurement is stable enough to yield the same or similar values under different conditions of measurement. An excellent and detailed treatment of the issues and procedures provided in Anne Anastasi's (1954) classic *Psychological Testing*, currently in its seventh edition (Anastasi & Urbina, 1997), remains the authoritative source of practical interpretation of the scientific standards for measurement in the social sciences, particularly as it relates to fixed-response instruments.

Fixed-Response Approaches to Written Questioning: Questionnaires and Standard Tests.   We start this section on fixed-response approaches by examining written tests because these illustrate most clearly the principles behind all types of fixed-response data collection. One of the most useful ways to approach this material is from the standpoint of a test developer. Although we describe in detail how scales are constructed, our advice to you is don't construct your own scales unless you truly need to. It is far more efficient to conduct a reasonable search for existing assessment tools than to develop your own. Putting together the items for your scale is only the beginning of having a measurement tool. If you are proposing a new instrument for ongoing use with client populations, we believe that there is an ethical imperative that you demonstrate that your instrument is both reliable and valid. Because this complete process usually demands more time and effort than most practitioners are able to give, we fall back on our initial advice.

There are those occasions, often within the context of agencywide planning, monitoring, or assessment, when developing a scale is warranted. Other times, there is a need for a one-time survey of a client population regarding needs, satisfaction with services, or other practice-relevant information. When this is the case, you set about the exciting and creative process of instrument design and construction. In the sections that follow, we provide some overview comments about measurement instruments in general. Then we review some of the common item formats and discuss their use in social work research. Finally, we offer a fairly extensive list of do's and don'ts for you to consider as you develop your own instrumentation.

Some General Instrument Design Issues.   Some instruments are intended to gather general information from a sample for the purpose of developing a profile of a population. We refer to these instruments as "survey-type" instruments. The standards for establishing adequacy of this type of instrument are found in sociological survey method texts such as Sudman and Bradburn's *Asking Questions* (1982). The standards are similar to those of standardized tests that follow, but less rigorous.

Survey instruments are generally intended for only one or two administrations. Needs-assessment surveys, political polls, and client satisfaction surveys are all of this type. The primary tool for assessing quality of such instruments is a *pretest*. A pretest involves the administration of the instrument to a small sample of respondents who are typical of the population with whom the final instrument will be used. The purpose of a pretest is to identify areas of the survey instrument that might adversely influence the reliability of the instrument. Sometimes, the results of a pretest administration are analyzed to identify anomalies in the response patterns. Other times, respondents are interviewed following completion of the instrument so that they can verbally explain their own interpretation of the various items. Still other times, respondents are invited to write questions or otherwise "mark up" their survey to indicate items that were troublesome. Confusion, jargon, and other sources of "unreliability" can be identified and eliminated through pretesting.

Other instruments are intended for more in-depth assessment of individuals. Examples of these include diagnostic tests such as the MMPI and rapid assessment inventories such as those found in Hudson's clinical assessment package (1982). For instruments such as these, it is imperative to go through the methodological steps to establish psychometric properties—the instrument's reliability and validity scoring, interpretation, and intended use—described in the APA standards. The standards for this type of instrument tend to be more demanding than that for surveys and generally involve multiple administration to groups under controlled conditions, in addition to pretests, before compliance with standards can be demonstrated.

Kerlinger (1973) offers the **maxmincon principle** to improve research instrumentation. This little mnemonic refers to *maximizing* the individual variation along the dimension of interest, *minimizing* the sources of error that reduce reliability and/or validity, and *controlling* other extraneous sources of variation. Beyond the maxmincon principle, he offers three additional suggestions. First, write items as unambiguously as possible. Ambiguity produces confusion and confusion reduces reliability. Second, when you need to raise an instrument's reliability, add more items that are of comparable quality. As a general rule, more items produce an instrument with higher reliability because the random fluctuations that are the source of unreliability tend to cancel one another out. Finally, write clear instructions. Comprehensible results are unlikely to be produced by incomprehensible instructions.

Measurement instruments for client assessment are referred to by a number of different names—scales, inventories, and indices among others. Although there are some technical differences, for all practical purposes, these are equivalent. It is useful to distinguish between unidimensional and multidimentional instruments. Unidimensional instruments are those that seek to assess one and only one quality, for example, depression or emotional instability, but not both. In contrast, multidimensional instruments simultaneously assess two or more qualities. Most typically, multidimensional instruments are really composed of a set of short unidimensional instruments, often referred to as *subscales*. Multidimensional instruments tend to be very efficient when there is an interest in assessing the range of qualities that is included in the instrument. However, if only one or a small number of these qualities are of interest, it is probably more efficient to use carefully selected unidimensional instruments.

The importance of understanding the difference between uni- and multidimensional instruments is especially important in designing an instrument. Although you may be interested in ultimately having a multidimensional instrument, you will be far better served by constructing the dimensions one at a time. In that way, you can clearly focus on each distinct quality and capture its essential meaning to the fullest extent possible. Then, when you have constructed the necessary unidimensional components, they can be combined into the composite multidimensional instrument.

Common Item Formats.   Formats for fixed-response questions tend to fall in one of several standard types. These include Likert-type, semantic differentials, and Thurstone and Guttman scaling formats. Each is discussed in what follows. Likert-type and semantic differential questions are common in social work research and are discussed more extensively. Because the Thurstone and Guttman formats are fairly uncommon in social work research, the discussion of these is limited to a brief overview.

Likert-type scales are among the most commonly used in social work research. These items are designed to allow respondents to indicate an agreement or disagreement with a given position and to indicate some level of intensity with which their position is held. Thus, we commonly see the response set including strongly agree, agree, neutral, disagree, or strongly disagree. It is important that the response set be balanced. That is, that the number and intensity of choices in each direction are equal. Multiple variations on this format exist, for instance, using a measure of frequency instead of agreement. Likert-type scales are often employed in instruments that are *summated-rating scales*. A **summated-rating scale** is one in which the responses to individual questions are added to produce one score that reflects the underlying attribute of interest. Of course, it is important that the investigator establish the scoring key so that all items are scored in the same direction. For example, assuming a five-point response set scored one through five, an item score of five should consistently represent the extreme favorable (or unfavorable) response position. This is sometimes accomplished by writing the original items so that a person with an extreme position would consistently answer with choice 1 (or consistently, with choice 5). Sometimes, however, the wording of half of the items is reversed (so that a strongly positive response becomes 1 rather than 5) to reduce the respondents' tendency to form a **response set** bias. In this case, the consistency must be reestablished in scoring by *reverse scoring* the portion of items that were reworded.

Students often ask how many choices should be included in a Likert-type response set and whether this number should be odd or even. There is no magic to these decisions, but there are a couple of guiding principles. First, with regard to how many choices should be included, we remind you that in the final analysis, science is about the business of observing order and difference. If people are presented with only two choices, there is a limit to how much variation (or difference) there can be. Everybody is required to *either* agree or disagree—to order either vanilla or chocolate ice cream, so to speak. There simply is no opportunity for any wider variation. This doesn't offer the potential for a realistic reflection of most of social life. On the other hand, if a very large number of choices exist, most respondents probably are overwhelmed and mentally reduce the selections to a more manageable number of categories. If we may be permitted the comparison to ice cream flavors, most of us do not truly consider all of the choices that are available to us in the neighborhood ice cream parlor. The fact is, with Likert-type questions, most respondents do not need more than five or so categories to give a reasonably full reflection to their practical range.

The consideration of an odd or even number of responses is a bit more clear-cut. With an even number of choices, there is no possibility for a respondent to take the neutral middle ground or be a "fence sitter." If the investigator is concerned about a significant central tendency bias—that is, the propensity of respondents to resist reporting their position and opting for the "safe" neutral ground instead—having an even number of response choices can be advantageous by eliminating this possibility. On the other hand, many respondents become quite frustrated if they legitimately feel undecided and are not given the opportunity to accurately report their position. We lean toward providing respondents with the full response set represented by an odd number of choices, including the possibility of a neutral answer, unless there is a strong belief that central tendency bias is likely to be a problem.

Two general assumptions underlie summated-rating scales. The first is that each of the items on the scale is of an approximately equal value. Thus, two respondents may have the same score on a ten-item Likert-type scale even though they may answer individual items quite differently. The second assumption is that the distance between each of the choices within a single-response set is approximately equal, that is, that the responses are measured at an interval level of measurement. For a number of years, Likert-type scales were considered to produce ordinal level data that were not appropriate for analysis using parametric statistics. However, it has become generally accepted that if the intervals between choices within a response set do not appear to be grossly unequal, Likert-type scales can be treated as if they produce interval-level data (Kerlinger, 1973; Nunnally, 1978). It is this assumption and the psychometric research that has taken place to support it that permit the use of certain classes of statistical analyses with summated rating scales.

Osgood semantic differential scales present the respondent with pairs of polar opposite words. Respondents are asked to consider their position with respect to some social object and then to identify their position by placing a mark on a continuum between two polar opposite words. Like Likert-type scales, Osgood semantic differential scales depend on dividing the response set into a range of levels or partitions (e.g., from positive to negative). For this reason, both are sometimes called **category partition scales**—the response category is partitioned into the various levels. The number of points that is provided on the continuum is guided by the same principles as with Likert-type scales. In contrast to Likert-type scales, the response set categories are usually not individually labeled in semantic differential scales. Instead, only anchor points are provided by the polar opposite words. Consider the following example based on questions asked Rosencranz and McNevin (1969).

I think most aging people are (place a check on the line that best represents your position)

Progressive	_____	Old-fashioned
Active	_____	Passive
Tolerant	_____	Intolerant

| 1 | 2 | 3 | 4 | 5 | 6 | 7 |

Here, each point on the continuum would be associated with a particular item score, generally, one through seven. As with Likert-type scales, care must be taken to establish scoring codes for all of the items in the same direction. Because Osgood semantic differential scales are also summated-rating scales, they are scored by adding the individual item scores to produce a total score for the whole scale.

Thurstone scales require respondents to either agree or disagree with each of a series of statements. Unlike Likert-type and semantic differential scales that assume equal value of all the items in contributing to the respondent's total score, Thurstone scale items are explicitly weighted when scored. These weights are generally established by "expert" panels and confirmed with empirical research. Some items on a Thurstone scale represent a very low level of the quality being studied and others very high levels of the quality. Although the logic of a Thurstone scale is extremely appealing, in practice, it is very difficult to establish meaningful weights for each of the items. Without carefully establishing these weights, any resultant scale's validity would be questionable at best.

Guttman scales are similar to Thurstone scales in that they also ask respondents to indicate agreement/disagreement with a series of statements. The essential quality of Guttman scales is that the items are arranged in a decreasing order of intensity or complexity. Thus, if respondents are able to answer a more difficult question, it is assumed that they will be able to answer less complex subsequent questions. Guttman scales have been used quite successfully to measure things like social distance or acceptance of various behaviors. If a respondent indicates that he or she accepts the use of severe corporal punishment in disciplining a child, it might be reasonably assumed that that respondent would also accept less severe punishments like verbally scolding a child. The key to successfully constructing a Guttman scale is the valid ordering of the items. In that sense, both Thurstone and Guttman scales involve variations on scaling the items themselves, rather than relying on summing the scores of equally contributing items of the category partition variety. Although Thurstone and Guttman scales can be powerful measurement instruments, each can be very laborious to construct and validate. It is for that reason that they are relatively uncommon in contemporary human services research.

Guidelines for Writing Questions. The characteristics of questions that produce valid and reliable data vary somewhat with the subject matter and social setting of the questioning. The best advice we can offer to those starting out to write questions is to familiarize yourself with related scales and instruments. This helps both with the conceptualization of the meaning domains behind questions and also with developing conventional and unambiguous wording. In our experience, the authors of many rapid assessment instruments are quite willing to allow (for proper recognition) and even to assist you in the modification of items for a related purpose. We have encouraged our students to contact scale authors and have found, with very few exceptions, that a letter or e-mail to the developer of an instrument generally elicits a helpful response. However, if you are writing original items, the following suggestions are related to enhancing reliability and/or validity.

Questions are likely to produce the most valid and reliable responses when they (1) concern topics that are interesting (salient) to the respondents, (2) maintain a low or managed threat value, (3) include aided recall techniques to compensate for forgetting and related distortions, (4) are about specifics rather than summary judgments, (5) are about phenomena to which the respondent has direct access, (6) designate a time period when asking for a count of some event or behavior, and (7) use simple, ordinary words. These criteria apply equally to survey questions and those on assessment instruments.

Clarity. It cannot be overstated that questions must be clear to the respondent. This means more than that the respondent thinks the item is clear. The understanding that is gleaned from a question by a respondent must be the same understanding that is intended by the investigator. When a respondent understands a question differently than is intended by the investigator, the respondent is essentially answering a different question. If such misunderstandings go by undetected, the validity of the instrument is seriously compromised. The best overall advice to achieve clarity in writing a question is to keep it simple. Care must be taken, however, to ensure the inclusion of all necessary information. Take, for instance, a seemingly straightforward question about income. We might ask, "What is your income?" It seems clear. But consider the many ways this simple question might be interpreted by reasonable respondents. Are we asking about annual income or some other time period? (Understand that it is quite possible to confuse high weekly incomes with low monthly or even annual incomes in this society.) Are we asking about the actual number of dollars earned during a specific 12-month period or should the respondent report the current annual *rate* of income—after including that large raise given just last week? Are we asking about personal income or household income? Gross income or "take-home" income? The list of possible confusions goes on. Suffice it to say that when respondents misunderstand our questions, it is not their problem, it is ours.

Length.   Length of questions is partly related to keeping them simple. At the risk of being too lengthy, a bit more deserves to be said. Short items are easier to read. Most respondents are willing to give a reasonable bit of time to the research task, but the longer our items become, the more likely it is that respondents will be skimming along with a reduced level of comprehension. Short items tend to be less confusing—assuming that necessary clarifying detail is present. Finally, for respondents who may be less familiar with the research process or for whom reading may be a less comfortable activity, longer items can be intimidating. On the other hand, there are situations "especially in verbal interviews" where longer questions may be better. Longer questions may serve as memory cues, provide respondents (to verbal interviews) more time to think about their response, and encourage longer open-ended responses (Sudman & Bradburn, 1982).

Double-Barreled Questions.   **Double-barreled questions** really incorporate two different questions into one. Consider the question: Should clinical social workers be licensed and have the associated costs passed on to clients? Although the question may appear to be clear, how to respond to such closed-ended categories is often not. An individual respondent could either favor or oppose the licensure of clinical social workers and *independently* favor or oppose passing on the costs associated with licensure to clients. Because the respondent only answers once, it is impossible to be certain which question is being answered. If the investigator actually wanted to know if licensure was favored *under the condition of costs being passed on to clients,* a better approach to the question would be to ask: If costs associated with licensure of clinical social workers were passed on to clients, would you favor licensure? Because of the potential for misunderstanding, double-barreled questions should always be avoided. The little word *and* should be a red flag that a double-barreled question may be present.

Negative Form.   Another little word that should raise the red flag of potential misinterpretation is *not,* or, more generally, a negative form of a question. As respondents are quickly reading through your questionnaire, little words may be lost. Although missing any little word in a question might be problematic, missing *not* has the effect of misdirecting the question to mean exactly the opposite of what was intended. This situation can be remedied by clearly rewording the question to avoid the use of this word.

Social Desirability.   Most people want their attitudes and behaviors to be perceived as socially acceptable. Of course, what is acceptable is very context-sensitive. It is influenced by all sorts of cues from the social environment. Some of those cues are embedded in the language we use to ask questions. When we ask questions in ways that communicate that some answers are more acceptable than others, we are, in effect, guiding respondents' answers. This obviously interferes with validity. Related to this is concern with the use of prejudicial language in questions—it is no more acceptable in research than in any other form of social work practice. We must scrupulously avoid using **biased language** or other subtle ways of manipulating answers from respondents.

Jargon.   Closely related to the use of biased language is the use of jargon—language whose meaning is unique to specific circumstances. All of us in professional work are guilty at some level of using jargon. One of the seeming goals of graduate education is to become facile in the use of this "professional" language. Among professionals, jargon may improve communication efficiency with no cost to clarity. However, when we extend the use of that in-group language to others, we invite misunderstanding. Acronyms and other jargon can be easily misunderstood by lay people. In constructing items, this misunderstanding leads directly to a reduction in reliability and validity. Pretesting all items with a small sample of folks similar to the intended sample is the best way to identify confusing jargon.

Some uses of jargon may actually improve the understanding of questions among particular subpopulations for whom unique jargon, or slang, is commonly accepted. Incorporating some of this language into questions can be clarifying. At the same time, appropriate use of some respondent-appropriate jargon or slang may enhance the credibility of the research. Extreme care must be taken to ensure, however, that the inclusion of such language does not come across to respondents as artificial. When in doubt, the better course would be to avoid jargon completely.

In addition to these principles for constructing research questions, there are a number of other guidelines that can improve the overall instrument. Even well-constructed items can lose their value if they are muddled by a disorganized or otherwise unappealing instrument. Attention to these matters can help to ensure the production of an overall quality instrument.

Response Sets.   Earlier in the chapter, the two required characteristics of closed response sets were stated as being *exhaustive* and *mutually exclusive.* These qualities deserve repeating. If a respondent is unable to find a personally relevant choice in a response set because the set is not exhaustive, the result is frustration, a nonresponse, or a "wrong" second choice. Investigators often try to cover this contingency by including an "other" category. Although this is an appropriate inclusion, it should not be used as a shortcut for developing a thoroughly exhaustive response set. Respondents are less likely to indicate an "other" response than they are to select a meaningful choice when it is offered. The flip side of being exhaustive is that a response set must be mutually exclusive. If a respondent must select one answer from a response set that contains two or more answers that are "correct" for the individual, the researcher has a problem. There is no way of knowing that the respondent has self-selected into one or another of the categories. As we have said before, everyone needs to be someplace, but it must be only one place. One common approach to obtaining valid and reliable responses when it is not possible to create a response set that is mutually exclusive is to ask respondents to provide the one "best" or "primary" answer to an item.

Response Formatting.   Although it may seem an unimportant matter, the format or space provided for respondents to indicate their choice is critically important. Nothing is more frustrating than receiving a completed research instrument and being confronted by unintelligible markings. In some cases, formats seem almost designed to produce predictable confusion. In other cases, the clean and professional format facilitates an error-free response. We feel strongly that the availability of computers and quality word processing software makes the technical creation of professional-looking research instruments possible for every social worker. Obviously, a professional appearance cannot guarantee high-quality content. However, it should be unacceptable that high-quality content be diminished by a poor presentation.

Contingency Questions.   **Contingency questions** that ask respondents to follow a skip pattern depending on their answers to previous questions can be a very efficient tool. However, they are also more complex to follow by their nature. In verbal interviews, contingency questions do not represent a significant problem because trained interviewers can easily negotiate skip pattern. On the other hand, with pencil-and-paper instruments, skip patterns must be clearly indicated. We recommend using contingency questions only when absolutely necessary. When they are used, clear instructions should be provided in writing and accompanied by graphic aids like arrows in the margin to indicate the point of resumption.

Item Order.   Much has been said about item order, and, indeed, there are many variables that influence the best order for a particular set of items. Even the method of administration—verbal or pencil-and-paper—can influence item ordering. In general, initial questions should be interesting and engaging to the respondent. However, care should be taken to avoid especially sensitive questions early in the instrument. Demographic questions are generally best left to the end of an interview. If items refer to a topic of high salience, it is usually better to ask the general or overall questions first, followed by more specific questions as necessary. However, in topic areas of relatively lower salience, it is better to focus respondents by first asking the more specific questions and moving to the summary questions. There is extensive literature on this topic.

Respondent Instructions.   One of the least considered components of instrument construction is the instructions provided to respondents. Instructions communicate three important pieces of information. First, instructions introduce the research. Respondents start with a natural curiosity about the research. The instructions can respond to this reasonable curiosity by explaining in a few clear sentences the general purpose of the research. Second, instructions can facilitate the transition between sections of the instrument. Sometimes question formats may change as well, but even a change in the content or focus of the items can be made more sensible with a brief narrative transition statement. Third, instructions must provide the necessary "how-to" information to respondents. Graduate students and others with a college education are familiar with test-taking situations. Such respondents are usually very good at producing the expected response types for various kinds of questions. Other respondents may not be so savvy and may require clear explanations about filling in an instrument. As always, it is the investigator's responsibility to meet the needs of the respondent and not vice versa. If you want a clearly understood and properly completed instrument, provide easily understood and complete instructions.

Overall Presentation.   With pencil-and-paper instruments, the overall "look" or presentation of the instrument is often the respondent's first introduction to the research. As with all social exchanges, first impressions are important. Commonly available word processing software make the production of high-quality instruments easy to accomplish. Spacing, font size, the use of fancy or unique fonts all contribute to the presentation. However, just because we have these tools, do not be tempted to overuse them. Too many different fonts can make a document appear busy. Unnecessary changes in font size can be distracting. In the attempt to make an instrument appear shorter, investigators sometimes use a smaller typeface to reduce the number of pages, whereas the use of larger type or more white space would produce an instrument that appears more readable and manageable. On the positive side, using a boldface or italic type can emphasize and clarify content. Our overall recommendation for instrument presentation is to be reasonable. Design an instrument that has visual appeal to you and your colleagues—and then pretest!

Fixed-Response Approaches to Dialogues: Structured Interviews.   At one extreme, **structured interviews** are merely standardized questionnaires delivered orally. The conceptualizations and response formats tend to be largely if not completely worked out in advance. The questionnaire becomes the script for the interviewer. Other structured interviews slip back down the continuum toward less fixed strategies by providing options for respondents who have trouble responding to questions using the standardized formats. In these cases, a standard set of probes or clarifying comments may be built into the interview schedule to guide even these short digressions from the standard plan.

Structured interviews have the potential to combine some of the groundedness of flexible-response strategies with the validity and reliability of written fixed-response data collection using standardized tests and instruments. Structured interviews are the data collection strategy of choice when administration of a written instrument is likely to introduce unreliability, either because of literacy-related problems or because of reactivity to the social conditions of test taking. Such situations would arise in the case of data collection with young children, persons whose primary language is not that in which the instrument is written, persons who may lack the concentration due to illness to complete a lengthy written questionnaire alone, and the like.

Fixed-Response Approaches to Direct Observation: Behavior Checklists and Logs.   Direct observations can yield very useful data concerning social phenomena. The flexible-response approaches described earlier were intended to take in as much behavior as possible to be used later to determine patterns. Fixed-response strategies, on the contrary, start out with an interest in specific behaviors and seek to assess the presence or absence, type, frequency, duration, or intensity of specific events. These data collection strategies often take the form of behavior checklists or logs. **Behavior checklists** consist of lists of behaviors to be scored, often by an outside observer. Formats may include any of the aspects mentioned earlier: presence, type, frequency, duration, or magnitude. **Logs** tend to be self-reports and may use one of several formats to allow individuals to record behaviors or events as they occur in real time or soon after.

The main requirement for fixed-response (or perhaps fixed-coded would be a better label in the case of observation) protocols is that the conceptualizations of the variables of interest have been worked out in advance. That is, the progression from personal conceptions, through public, nominal definitions, to operational definitions can be completed to the satisfaction of the persons who have a stake in the data (at the very least, you and some client system in which you are working). Once a set of indicators is agreed on, it is necessary to consider if a social context can be found in which observations can be made. This context is one in which the behaviors of interest are likely to occur with reasonable predictability, and it is possible for an observer to be present in the situation without changing the phenomenon in any meaningful way.

Armed with a clear idea of what you are looking for and the context in which it is likely to be found, the next task is to deal with the problem of sampling. Sampling here has several levels of meaning. In the context of group designs such as experiments, sampling concerns certainly include drawing a representative sample from the population of interest. The why and how of this is discussed in Chapter 6 on sampling. Here, the issue of sampling deals more with the idea of **time sampling.** Over what time period do the observations take place? Are the events during that time period representative of other time periods? Are several time periods sampled? Once that is determined, what will be recorded—the presence of some behavior, the duration, magnitude, or frequency of the behavior? The answers to these questions are by no means fixed. Largely, they reflect the conceptualization of the behaviors under study and the uses to which the data are to be put. For example, homelessness can be conceptualized as not having a dwelling in which to sleep on a particular night, as the number of such nights in the last six months, or as the adequacy of housing arrangements by some defined standard.

The choice of a sampling and coding strategy largely reflects how the data are to be used. Knowing the average number of homeless persons on any given night may be helpful in planning shelters. The adequacy of housing and frequency of homelessness would be more appropriate for individual interventions. Consideration of the decision context when operationalizing variables is taken up in Chapter 10 in the context of practice evaluation.

Often, observation can be conducted by a trained individual who is already a participant in the social situation of interest. For instance, in a study concerning student conduct while receiving a drug-prevention curriculum, teacher's aides who were regular attendees made the observations. The only danger in the use of such individuals is that if the behavior checklists and protocols have any ambiguity or room for interpretation, the observations are likely to be slanted in the direction of the hopes, wishes, or biases of the observers. This can be alleviated to some extent by focusing on very specific behaviors and avoiding items that call for observers to summarize or interpret sequences of behaviors. Bloom, Fischer, and Orme (1999) have an excellent discussion of behavior observations. Although their remarks are made in the context of single-systems evaluation, the principles are applicable to direct observation in a variety of contexts.

Behavior checklists that ask observers to report behaviors retrospectively blur the line between written tests and checklists. For example, the family of child-behavior rating scales developed by Achenbock and Edelbrock (1983) include written standardized tests used by parents, but also include direct-behavior rating versions of some scales.

Summary

Data collection strategies in social work contexts typically take place in three social situations: dialogues, written testing, and direct observation. In any of these, the data collection may employ flexible-response strategies or fixed-response strategies. The flexible-response strategies allow the researcher to code the widest range of responses without imposing categories a priori. These strategies are used when the researcher is operating in an inductive mode, with a subsequent desire not to restrict the range of responses. Fixed-response strategies channel responses into a coding structure that is developed in advance. These strategies are more common in studies employing deductive logic, such as hypothesis testing.

Ethnographic and other forms of open-ended interviews are examples of *flexible response to dialogues*. Projective tests and storytelling techniques are examples of *flexible response to written questioning*. Field work, including unstructured participant observation, is an example of *flexible response to direct observation*. Structured interviews are largely closed-coded questionnaires delivered verbally and examples of *fixed response to dialogues*. Diagnostic testing and surveys represent examples of *fixed response to written formats*. Finally, structured behavior observations using checklists and logs are examples of *fixed response to observational techniques*.

Data Reduction, Patterns, and Generalizations

Relationship of This Chapter to the Whole

Data analysis is the phase of inquiry in which we begin to abstract general meanings from collections of observations. It is useful to think of data analysis as a meaning assigning activity that lies between measurement on one side and deriving conclusions and implications on the other. During data analysis, the focus is still largely on the products of the measurement process (data). However, preoccupation with systematic coding of the attributes of individual observables, which was the emphasis of data collection, is replaced with an emphasis on systematically abstracting attributes of collections of observations as a whole.

Data analysis is intended to convert observations into forms that facilitate thinking, communicating, and deriving conclusions and implications. Even the most modest scientific inquiry results in so many observations that our minds would be quickly overcome by the volume if we attempted to deal with the observations in their raw form. As a consequence, humans seem compelled to reduce experience to shorthand representations as aids to memory and thinking. Scientific data analysis strategies are simply procedures designed to convert data into forms that are more "mind-friendly" while minimizing the influence of logical errors and other limitations of human cognition. The procedures of data analysis presented in this chapter and the next represent efforts to keep generalizations linked closely to actual observations by manipulation of data in systematic ways.

All forms of data analysis are intended to accomplish one of three broad tasks: data reduction, pattern identification, and estimation of generalizability. However, the actual techniques of data analysis are strongly tied to the form of the data. In this chapter, we discuss techniques intended for use with numerical data.

Most, if not all, scientific inquiries involve some observations coded as numbers. In ethnography and some case studies, only a few numbers may be encountered. In the case of quantitative-descriptive and hypothesis-testing studies, most or all of the observations of interest may be represented in numbers. In either situation, it is important to understand that the numbers, like words, are just symbols used to remind us of an attribute of a variable that we observed. Numbers are preferable to words when the attribute of interest consists of ranking, quantities, or ratios because the procedures for assigning numbers can be stated precisely and communicated easily, maintaining a strong connection between the observations that give rise to the numbers and higher-order abstractions and generalizations about what we observed. Although the ability to maintain strong links between generalizations and observations is a desirable characteristic of numerical data analysis, there are also some limitations. Even the most complex numerical analysis greatly oversimplifies empirical events by failing to code potentially important context variables. This limits the value of numerically-oriented research as a tool of early exploration. In exploratory contexts, nonnumerical data, the subject of the next chapter, are often of greater value. A hallmark of the competent postpositivist social work practitioner is to recognize the value and limitations of both numerical and nonnumerical data.

As you read, keep in mind the linear nature of the scientific method. In this chapter, we assume that the numbers in a data set reflect observations of the empirical world at least somewhat accurately and that the persons, organizations, or situations (units) from which the observations are made represent classes of units of interest. However, such veracity is not automatically a characteristic of number sets. Flaws in conceptualization, measurement, sampling, design, and coding of observations may result in collections of numbers that lack strong connection to the phenomena of interest. Numbers representing poorly conceptualized variables are likely to produce only confusion. Well-conceptualized variables that are poorly measured are likewise of little value because the numbers may provide a poor reflection of the empirical world. Measures taken on samples that are not representative of a population of interest are of little value in describing that population. And so it goes. The point at which a study is so flawed that data analysis is futile is not always clear, but sometimes a pile of numbers is just a pile of numbers. A good rule to keep in mind is that no amount of manipulation and analysis can extract meaning that isn't coded into the numbers in the first place. As you proceed with numerical data analysis, it is wise to be mindful of how those numbers were obtained and stop the analysis when you lose sight of a clear logical link between the numbers and the phenomenon of interest.

This chapter is written for the person who needs a basic review or has had little prior exposure to numerical data analysis. The topics we cover here should help a beginner to adequately manage the numerical analysis of a simple data set and also provide some statistical insights that may be useful in deciphering scientific literature related to social work practice. To keep matters simple, we have selected a small number of simple but robust statistical procedures that are likely to be of value to the beginning social work researcher. Sections dealing with advanced significance testing statistics are intended primarily to help the reader to understand the meaning of these techniques as they are encountered in the literature of the profession. Advanced study beyond this chapter would be required for the student who aspires to use advanced techniques in his or her own research.

Application to the Roles of Social Workers

Observations expressed in numbers and subjected to statistical analysis are a mainstay of Western science for the professions. Although it should be clear that numerical data are not optimal for all scientific tasks, the student, practitioner, and social scientist encounter so much numerical information, that to be ignorant of the proper handling of such information would be unthinkable. This chapter provides you with a description of common practices of statistical analyses to help you to conduct simple numerical analyses on your own data sets using commonly available spreadsheet programs. Discussions of advanced hypothesis testing statistics are based on an informed consumer perspective and assume that the reader has encountered these in peer-reviewed journals in which many of the fine points of statistical assumptions and application have been resolved between reviewers and the authors, leaving the reader simply trying to decipher the implications for practice.

Learning Objectives

After reading this chapter, you will be able to:

1. describe three general tasks of data analysis
2. describe, calculate, and interpret common data reduction techniques
3. describe, calculate, and interpret common bivariate pattern identification statistics
4. describe, calculate, and interpret procedures for estimating population parameters
5. describe, calculate, and interpret the results of simple significance tests
6. describe the logic of advanced multivariate statistics

Key Terms and Concepts

Purposes of Data Analysis

Data analysis is the process of extracting general meanings from a collection of symbols representing observations. The social work researcher is faced with several tasks before reasonable generalizations can be extracted from a collection of symbols representing observations. In our experience, it is useful to think of data analysis as an activity designed to accomplish three general tasks: (1) reducing information overload (data reduction), (2) discovering patterns among variables, and (3) estimating the generalizability of findings. These tasks are true of both numerical data, the subject of this chapter, and also nonnumerical data to be discussed in Chapter 9.

Scientists have developed many techniques designed to facilitate data analysis tasks in response to bottlenecks and limitations that characterize human information processing. For example, data reduction techniques are used to convert myriad observations into a smaller set of easy-to-remember symbols in order to compensate for the low capacity of human conscious memory and related problems. Likewise, humans appear strongly motivated to search for cause and effect and other patterns of relationship between variables, but prone to a series of logical errors when they do so (Carlson, 1985, Gilovich, 1991). Data analysis procedures designed to facilitate pattern recognition are designed to help us minimize the influence of such errors as we look for relationships among observations. Likewise, one goal of social work research is to develop understanding in one social context that can be applied to other contexts. However, the generalizability of findings is influenced by many factors, including precision in measures, variability in observations, and sampling error. Procedures designed to estimate confidence intervals and significance tests are intended to help determine the generalizability of findings.

Previously, we referred the reader to a short discussion of how the limitations of the human perceptual and cognitive apparatus influence clinical decision making (Carlson, 1985) and everyday reasoning (Gilovich, 1991). In the context of data analysis, we consider solutions to additional problems related to logical errors in the way we generalize and extract meaning from experience. Specifically, the tendency to ignore observations that are inconsistent with expectations, the tendency to see patterns in random systems, and errors of memory related to information overload are three logical errors that provide significant obstacles to abstracting general meanings from collections of observations. Regardless of the source, if unchecked, these limitations tend to create confusion and make it difficult to agree on findings and on the implications of findings. As we discuss various statistical procedures, it is useful to keep in mind that these procedures are intended to limit the influence of such logical errors.

Procedures associated with data analysis are powerful aids to extracting meanings from experience because these procedures help maintain the critical logical link between observations and generalizations about those observations.

Statistical procedures make it possible to trace generalizations back to the data and procedures from which they arose by standardizing the meaning extraction process through clearly defined, logically sound techniques. This trace is an important component in the process of separating fact (intersubjectively verifiable experiences) from fiction (mental activity without shared empirical referents). Data reduction techniques help maintain the connection between abstractions and observations by allowing the researcher to represent an entire collection of raw data with a few numbers, a simple picture, or a table. Not only is it easier to think about a few general principles than thousands of data points, but the presence of the statistics that define the concepts behind descriptive statistics reduces the risk that we will "reify" our generalizations, that is, fail to recognize that they are abstractions. Likewise, procedures for identification of patterns and determining the generalizability of findings are intended to maintain the critical link between abstractions and data. That is, in all cases, the logical connection between a statistical generalization and the data from which the generalization arose can be precisely specified. Each statistical procedure is really the operational definition of a concept used to integrate observations into our meaning systems. This link between abstractions and data is part of what makes science different from other ways of knowing.

At the onset of this chapter, we proposed that data analysis is generally conducted to achieve one or more of three purposes. These include data reduction to reduce information overload, pattern identification to detect relationships between variables, and testing the generalization of findings to other populations or situations. Now we look at techniques designed to facilitate each of these in cases in which the data consist of numerical codes.

Data Reduction

Data reduction is the process of describing the characteristics of a collection of numbers. It is often the case that we must keep track of or respond to large sets of numerical data. Imagine the volume of information obtained on an initial assessment interview with a client. The data from a single interview could easily exceed thousands of values. Now consider attempting to describe in detail the thirty or more persons on a typical caseload or the thousands served by a single agency over a brief period of time. The logical solution to situations like these is to look for commonalities across experiences, situations, and persons and develop shorthand, generalized descriptions. Informal efforts to develop general descriptions of experience are examples of data reduction and a necessary part of our existence. Through data reduction, sets of numbers are described by a few descriptive statistics that represent attributes of the collection.

The need for data reduction lies in the way human memory and attention work. Early cognitive research (Miller, 1956) suggested that the part of the mind where conscious thought occurs is capable of holding seven plus or minus two simple ideas at the same time. Try to add more and something is bumped out, forgotten, or ignored. Contemporary views see human information processing as a bit more complex, but whatever the actual capacity of the mind is, observations of the way people remember and forget make it clear that it is impossible for most of us to keep dozens of numbers (or anything else) in our consciousness at the same time. One way that people naturally circumvent the bottleneck in memory is to group information into chunks. Swiss psychologist Jean Piaget devised the label "schema" to refer to mental categories that contain clusters of related observations, principles, feelings, and meanings. Category labels for the schema help us avoid the bottleneck in conscious memory because they take up only a single place in memory and yet connect us to a rich array of experiences in long-term memory.

Descriptive Statistics.   **Descriptive statistics** perform a task similar to the idea of chunking information or organizing it in schemata. Descriptive statistics are procedures for compressing a large collection of numbers into a smaller set of numbers that reflect attributes of the entire collection. Descriptive statistics are useful in that they are easy to communicate across persons, allow us to recover much of the detail from the original set of numbers, and serve as the basis for abstracting general meanings from observations.

Univariate descriptive statistics are numbers used to create short descriptions of a single variable. Remember from our previous discussion that a variable is a characteristic of the units we are studying. A descriptive statistic is not a characteristic of the units studied, but a characteristic of a group of scores. What is there to know about a group of scores? When the scores represent quantities, the characteristics that are generally of interest include indicators of **central tendency** (representative score) and indicators of **dispersion** (also known as *variability*). Statistics representing central tendency are attempts to locate a score that is typical or representative of a group of scores. Statistics representing **dispersion** attempt to describe the diversity in the group of scores, often in terms of the extent to which the actual scores differ from what has been identified as typical. We could probably come up with many more characteristics of groups of scores that are interesting, but custom and demonstrated value in maintaining the connection between abstractions and data have led to widespread interest in a small number of well-defined ways of expressing central tendency and dispersion as characteristics of groups of numbers.

Several different approaches to operationally defining central tendency exist, including the *mean* (average), *median* (middlemost score), and *mode* (most frequently occurring score). Each of these three defines "typical" in slightly different ways. The **mean** defines *typical* as the arithmetic average, that is, the sum of all the scores divided by the number of scores. The mean is a good indicator of central tendency in **quantitative variables** that have frequency distributions that are symmetric around some midpoint, such as the familiar bell-shaped curves. Variables with frequency distributions that are markedly different from bell-shaped curves often are not usefully described by means. Personal income in the United States is an example of a variable in which the mean is not a good measure of central tendency. In the case of income, a small proportion of very high scores tends to inflate the mean to an extent that it is not very typical at all. In cases like these, the median produces a measure of typical income that is more useful than the mean. The **median** is the score that divides a distribution of scores in half. That is, 50% of the persons (units) have scores below the median and 50% have scores above the median. The median is less influenced by a few extreme scores than is the mean and thus more useful when the frequency distributions of a variable are not symmetric.

In some cases, neither the mean nor the median is the most useful operationalization of "typical." Another measure of central tendency, the mode, might give the most useful indication of what is typical when reporting findings related to quantitative variables that seem to group into clusters, a nominal variable, or ordered discrete scales (such as a Likert-type scale, 1 = strongly disagree, 2 = disagree, 3 = agree, 4 = strongly agree). The **mode** is simply the number that appears most often in the data set.

The key in selecting a measure of central tendency is to exercise some judgment concerning the likelihood that the measure will produce a score that truly meets the idea of "typical." For variables that are quantities and have frequency distributions that are symmetric around a single score or small range of scores, the mean is a good choice. For variables that have frequency distributions characterized by a pile up of scores at one end or a few extreme scores, a median would be a good measure of central tendency. Finally, when the numbers represent discrete categories, a mode would yield a good measure of central tendency.

Dispersion, or variability, can also be operationalized in various ways. In the case of quantitative variables, three common **measures of dispersion** include the *range, variance,* and the *standard deviation.* The **range** is calculated by subtracting the lowest score from the highest and tells you how many units there are between the highest and lowest scores. This is a fairly crude measure of dispersion and vulnerable to distortion by even one unusually large or small score, but useful if the need is to identify the range of values that is possible. The variance and standard deviation are defined in terms of how different each score is from the mean. The **variance** is calculated by first computing the mean for a variable, then subtracting the mean from the actual score for each person (unit), and squaring the difference. After calculating the squared distance from the mean for each person's score, all the squared deviations are added together (summed) and divided by the number of scores. The final measure of dispersion we present, the **standard deviation,** is simply the square root of the variance.

Table 8.1 contains a column of age scores extracted from a study of child socialization (Rohner, Kean, & Cournoyer, 1991). The table contains two columns of data extracted from a large matrix of scores: the identification number and age of the youth in years. The other numbers in the table are the result of calculations based on the age scores. At the bottom of the age column are a collection of descriptive statistics calculated from the 30 age scores. The third column contains squared deviation scores that could be used to calculate the variance and standard deviation. The final four columns contain frequency data used to identify the mode and median. Although calculation of descriptive statistics is usually left to computers (Lotus 1-2-3 was used to check the values shown in the table), it would

TABLE 8.1   Common Descriptive Statistics for 30 Age Scores

ID #	Actual Age	Squared Deviation $(AGE - Mean)^2$	Age Score	Frequency	Percent	Cumulative Percent
1	18	4.41	13	5	16.67	17
2	15	0.81	14	3	10.00	27
3	17	1.21	15	4	13.33	40
4	17	1.21	16	4	13.33	53
5	18	4.41	17	7	23.33	77
6	17	1.21	18	6	20.00	97
7	18	4.41	19	1	3.33	100
8	16	0.01	Sums	30	100.00	
9	15	0.81				
10	17	1.21				
11	17	1.21				
12	16	0.01				
13	17	1.21				
14	18	4.41				
15	16	0.01				
16	19	9.61				
17	15	0.81				
18	15	0.81				
19	17	1.21				
20	16	0.01				
21	18	4.41				
22	18	4.41				
23	13	8.41				
24	13	8.41				
25	13	8.41				
26	14	3.61				
27	14	3.61				
28	14	3.61				
29	13	8.41				
30	13	8.41				

Sum of Age	477	100.70	Sum of squared deviation scores
Mean of Age	15.90	3.36	Variance (sums of squares divided by $n = 30$)
Minimum	13.00	1.83	Standard deviation (square root of the variance)
Maximum	19.00		
Median	16.00		
Range	6.00		
Mode	17		

be useful for you to follow the instructions in this text and calculate each of the statistics just to see how they arise from simple manipulation of the data.

The standard deviation and variance, although less commonsensical than some other measures of dispersion, are important because they reflect the amount of variability across the entire data set and also because these two statistics are useful in accomplishing other statistical tasks related to pattern identification and testing generalizability. Later, we illustrate how means and standard deviations can be used to create **standard scores,** a way to facilitate comparisons between variables measured on scales that differ in range and variability. Also, we see how a special type of standard deviation, called a **standard error,** can be used to estimate the limits of sampling error when using descriptive statistics calculated on a sample to estimate the characteristics of the population from which they were drawn. With a few exceptions, representing dispersion through variances and standard deviations is done to facilitate pattern recognition and testing the limits of generalizability of findings, not because they provide strong insights into collections of scores.

Means, standard deviations, and variances are among the most common descriptive statistics and generally yield useful descriptions of variables that are quantities, that is, variables coded at interval or ratio scales. However, descriptive statistics that are based on the mean simply don't make sense when the numbers we seek to analyze reflect classification (nominal measurement) or rank ordering (ordinal measurement). For example, given a variable in which the names of five different political parties are recoded into numbers, what would an average of those numbers mean? What would be the meaning of a standard deviation calculated on rank data? Clearly, nominal and most ordinal variables require alternative methods of data reduction.

The solution to the problem of data reduction in nominal and ordinal variables is to calculate frequencies. Frequencies are the number of units in the data set that have a particular value on a variable of interest. In the earlier example of the four-point Likert scale, a group of scores might be adequately described by counting the number of persons who checked one, two, three, or four. Frequency counts provide a shorthand description of the variable by simply noting all the possible values that a nominal or ordinal variable can hold and counting the number of units that hold each value. Frequencies can be represented in tables or graphs, and are often converted to percentages to facilitate comparisons. In addition to purely nominal variables such as religious preference, political preference, occupation, diagnosis, and the like, ordinal variables employing Likert scales and variables such as social class may be effectively described in frequency tables and graphs. Frequency tables and charts make it easy to identify the mode and median on a variable, as well as the range.

To summarize, univariate descriptive statistics are used to develop a short description of certain properties of a single variable. Reducing a large number of observations to a few descriptive statistics provides relief from information overload. Measures of central tendency provide information about what is typical, and measures of dispersion show, to some extent, how typical "typical" really is. The goal we seek when calculating descriptive statistics is a smaller package of numbers that help us to keep in memory and communicate the essence of the original set of raw scores without exceeding our capacity for thought. The measure of central tendency and dispersion actually used is determined in part by the level of measurement of the variable, the shape of the frequency distribution of the scores in the sample, and the presence of extreme scores.

Calculation of Descriptive Statistics Using Spreadsheet Programs.   Often, one of the first steps in analyzing the numerical portion of a collection of observations involves calculation of measures of central tendency and dispersion and/or frequency tables for all variables. Even if not all of these statistics are contained in a final written report, it makes sense to calculate means, ranges, standard deviations, frequency tables, or bar charts for all quantitative variables and frequency tables, medians, and percentages for nominal and ordinal variables. In addition to simplifying the reporting of your findings to others, these statistics give you an efficient mental representation of the observations to help you distill meaning from the data.

Calculation of univariate descriptive statistics is almost always accomplished electronically. Computer programs dedicated to statistical analyses are widely available, even in pocket calculators. SPSS, SPPC, SAS, and SYSTAT are only a few of the many programs available for personal computers. If you don't have access to one of the specialized statistical data analysis programs, a good resource for analyzing numerical data is a computer spreadsheet program. Virtually every office or home computer has access to some spreadsheet program, Microsoft Excel and Lotus 1-2-3 being two of the most common for personal computers.

Before calculating statistics using a spreadsheet program, it is necessary for you to become familiar with the general procedures for opening and closing files, entering data and formulas, and marking ranges of data. The excellent tutorials that are built into most of these programs are a good place to start exploring a spreadsheet program. The discussion that follows assumes that you have some familiarity with how a spreadsheet program works.

Spreadsheet programs have many statistical functions built into them. These statistical functions are actually little programs that solve the formulas that define statistical concepts. This means that once your data are keyed into a spreadsheet, you only need to find the name that your program uses to call in a particular statistical formula, paste that formula into a cell, and tell the spreadsheet program the range of cells that contain the data. To calculate descriptive statistics in Microsoft Excel, you first need to enter the set of observations into the rows and columns of a spreadsheet. When a spreadsheet is being created to facilitate data analysis, it is conventional to type the data into rows and columns, in which each row represents all the values for a person or particular unit and each column represents all the values for a particular variable.

Once a data set has been typed into a spreadsheet and checked for accuracy, it is time to start the analysis. First, open the spreadsheet with the data set you wish to analyze. Move the cursor to an open cell. Next, click on the icon for statistical functions. In Excel, this is called the function wizard. A menu will pop up. Scroll down the menu until you find the statistic you want. In Excel, the function names of interest here are AVERAGE (the mean), MEDIAN (median), MODE (mode), VAR (variance), and STDEV (standard deviation of a sample). The statistics MIN (smallest score) and MAX (largest score) can be used to calculate the range. After clicking on the name of one of these statistics, just type in the addresses of the first and last data cells in the column to which the statistic is to apply (or mark the cells with the mouse). As fast as you can press the enter key on the statistical function, enter the range and press the enter key again; you will have calculated the desired descriptive statistic. You may ask for measures of central tendency and dispersion for other variables in the same way. A note of caution: Be sure to place labels somewhere near the cells where the descriptive statistics are printed because it will soon become unclear what variables a particular collection of statistics describes. Because spreadsheets contain many features to facilitate copying of statistical commands and data ranges, it is possible to produce descriptive statistics for many variables with a minimum of typing, but it takes practice to get the ranges right and avoid overwriting statistics with new values. Table 8.2 lists the names of some common descriptive statistics available in Microsoft Excel and Lotus 1-2-3.

Spreadsheets can also automate the process of calculating frequency counts. Obtaining frequency counts requires two steps. First, a list of the values permitted for the variable of interest (called the bin range) must be typed into a column of

TABLE 8.2   Generating Descriptive Statistics in Common Spreadsheet Programs

Here are the names of some common statistical functions in Lotus 1-2-3 and Excel:

Statistic Common Name	Lotus 1-2-3 Name	Excel Name
Average (mean)	AVG	AVERAGE
Standard deviation (pop.)	STD	STDEVP
Variance (pop.)	VAR	VARP
Smallest score*	MIN	MIN
Largest score*	MAX	MAX
Median	MEDIAN	MEDIAN
Mode	—	MODE

Note: Microsoft Excel and Lotus 1-2-3 produce descriptive statistics by operating on lists of scores typed into a spreadsheet.

To obtain statistical functions in Lotus 1-2-3, click in a cell in which you want the statistic to be printed. Next, click on the function icon in the tool bar marked with the "@" sign. Choose "list all" to see all the functions alphabetically or "statistical." Click on the name of the desired statistic. When prompted, enter the range of cells in the spreadsheet containing the values for which the statistic is desired.

In Excel, click on the function wizard icon marked with the "*fx*" sign. Choose "statistical" from the menu of functions in the left window and then click on the desired statistical function in the right window. Next click OK and enter the range of cells to which the statistic is to be applied. Be sure to type some identifying label (such as "mean of age") in an adjacent cell to document the source of the statistic.

*Used to calculate the range: maximum − minimum = range.

cells somewhere in the spreadsheet. For a four-point Likert-type scale, this may be the numbers 1, 2, 3, and 4. In Excel, click the function wizard icon, and select FREQUENCY from the menu. You will be asked to specify the bin range (the place where you typed the expected values) and an input data range (the column containing the variable for which you desire frequencies). The frequency counts are printed in the cells just to the right of the bin range (called the output range). When you execute the frequency command, Excel counts the number of instances each of the values in the bin range appears in the input range and prints the frequency in the cells adjacent to the bin values. The number of cells that had scores other than those specified in the bin range or blank cells are printed in the bottom cell in the output range. It is a good idea to type some form of label near the output range to remind you of the variable to which the frequencies pertain. The procedure is similar in Lotus 1-2-3.

Table 8.3 was created using Lotus 1-2-3 and combined the automatic features of built-in statistical functions and the report-generating features of a spreadsheet. To obtain the frequency table contained in Table 8.3, the MIN and MAX functions were used to find the beginning and end of the range of values the variable social class could take. These were typed into a bin range in a part of the spreadsheet

TABLE 8.3   Sample Frequency Table Generated Using Lotus 1-2-3

Labels	Code	Social Class Frequency	Percent	Cumulative Percent
Highest	1	8	26.67	26.67
—	2	5	16.67	43.33
—	3	7	23.33	66.67
—	4	5	16.67	83.33
—	5	2	6.67	90.00
Lowest	6	3	10.00	100.00
	Missing	0		
	# valid	30		

Labels	Code	Frequency	Formulas Used to Create the Frequency Table	
			Percent	Cumulative Percent
Highest	1	8	(F21/$F$15)*100	(H22)
—	2	5	(F22/$F$15)*100	@SUM(G21...G22)
—	3	7	(F23/$F$15)*100	@SUM(G21...G23)
—	4	5	(F24/$F$15)*100	@SUM(G21...G24)
—	5	2	(F25/$F$15)*100	@SUM(G21...G25)
Lowest	6	3	(F26/$F$15)*100	@SUM(G21...G26)
	Missing	0		
	# valid	@SUM(F21...F26)		

next to the raw data. This bin range is contained in Table 8.3 under the title "Code." Next, the frequencies were calculated by selecting RANGE from the toolbar and then ANALYZE and DISTRIBUTION from the subsequent menus. Lotus 1-2-3 then prompted for the range containing the actual data and a bin range containing the possible score values. The frequencies were printed into the column labeled "Social Class Frequency." To obtain percentages, it was necessary to enter additional formulas in adjacent columns to produce cumulative frequencies, percentages, and cumulative percentages. The lower half of Table 8.3 shows the formulas combining cell addresses and mathematical operations that produced the percentages. In addition, options to center cell entries, forcing the number of values after the decimal point to a maximum of 2 and other matters of style and presentation were set. All of the entries not seen as formulas in the bottom half of the table were typed directly into the spreadsheet.

Using spreadsheets to calculate statistics requires some care and attention. For instance, if you specify only part of a column containing a variable (e.g., you entered the range from memory and forgot that you added 50 cases at the end of the column), the descriptive statistics will be wrong and there will be no obvious way to catch your error. Spreadsheet programs do not immediately show what columns produced the result (that information is in the formula, but not displayed). Correct labeling of the source of the descriptive statistic is up to you. Also, if you reuse the bin range without moving it, the output range will be overwritten by the new frequencies. This all adds up to a potential for errors and a corresponding amount of work to carefully check results.

Dedicated statistical packages such as SPSS generate elegant frequency tables that contain good documentation and percentages with much less work than is required in a spreadsheet program. Generally, dedicated statistical packages such as SPSS and many others greatly simplify the whole process of numerical data analysis. Elegant, well-documented tables can be obtained by simply choosing a statistic name and specifying a variable all with the click of a mouse. The output is formatted and it is not possible to accidentally overwrite the mean for column 5 with the mean for column 6, as it is easy to do in a spreadsheet program. Dedicated statistical programs also have a much greater range of statistical routines available and built-in options for tailoring the analysis to your data. Such programs take much of the labor out of generating descriptive statistics and reduce the probability of errors related to mislabeling variables or incorrect specification of data ranges. For most students, the downside is usually the cost and learning a new program that serves only one purpose.

Despite the care needed, spreadsheets are well suited to the data analysis needs of the social work researcher. We like spreadsheets for three simple but practical reasons. First, spreadsheet programs are widely available and therefore may eliminate the need to purchase additional software. Second, spreadsheets keep you close to your data, reinforcing the notion that descriptive statistics are simply shorthand descriptions of larger groups of numbers. Third, most word processors are capable of directly importing spreadsheets, eliminating the need to retype statistical tables and simplifying report writing. With a little practice and care, spreadsheets are handy tools for generating descriptive statistics. An advantage of spreadsheet programs is that they serve functions other than data analysis and thus potentially provide more return on the time and money invested.

Pattern Identification

Research questions frequently go beyond simple description of each variable. Often, our most interesting questions involve relationships between variables. **Bivariate descriptive statistics** allow us to abstract information about relationships between two variables in samples. **Multivariate statistics** can be used to look for patterns involving two or more variables. Let's look at bivariate descriptive statistics first.

A common pattern of relationship between two variables can be examined by asking if the two are correlated in some way. **Bivariate correlation** refers to a class of statistics used to estimate the extent to which pairs of variables seem to "go together." For example, the belief that numerous social support networks protect against depression (Lin, 1986) implies that persons' scores on measures of social support and measures of depression "go together" in the sense that finding a high score on social support leads us to expect or predict, on the average, a low score on depression. A correlation coefficient is a statistic that represents the strength of such a pattern in the numbers representing the experiences of a sample of persons. We continue to use the word *statistic* to refer to a number that represents a characteristic of a group of numbers, but now the numbers of interest span two variables.

Pearson's Product/Moment Correlation Coefficient.   At the end of the nineteenth century, Karl Pearson published a formula that provided a precise mathematical definition of the concept of correlation. Pearson's **correlation coefficient** is a number that quantifies the correspondence between scores on two variables as described before. The correlation coefficient has a lowest possible value of –1 and a highest value of +1. The sign of the correlation, + or –, carries one bit of information, and the absolute value of the numerical portion contains another. First, considering the sign, a positive correlation (+) indicates that high scores on the first variable tend to go with high scores on the second variable, and low scores on the first variable tend to go with low on the second variable. Another way of saying this is that when the sign of the correlation is positive, persons who are unusually high on some variable compared to other persons in the sample tend also to be unusually high on a second variable, and those persons low on the first variable tend to be low on the second variable. A negative correlation (–) indicates that high scores on one variable tend to be associated with low scores on the other. In the example given before concerning social support and depression, the correlation is said to be negative in that persons who are higher than their peers in social support tend to be persons with depression scores lower than peers. Please be clear that positive and negative in this context are mathematical terms and do not carry conventional meanings such as beneficial or detrimental. In this case, the negative correlation suggests a beneficial effect of social support.

The number portion of a correlation (absolute value) has a range of 0 to 1. When $r = 0$ (r is the symbol used to denote correlation), we conclude that there is no correlation between the two variables, that a person's score on one variable carries no information about the other variable. At the opposite extreme, when the absolute value of a correlation equals 1, we say that the relationship is perfect, that is, knowing a person's score on one variable allows an exact prediction of that person's score on the other variable.

You may have guessed that in our complex social world, perfect correlations of $r = 1$ are pretty rare and usually reflect some mistake of coding or correlating a variable with itself. Although it is mathematically possible for a correlation to have an absolute value of 1, correlation coefficients calculated on numbers representing observations are generally decimal values less than 1. The magnitude of these decimal values is a little difficult to interpret without a digression into statistical theory, although r does have a precise mathematical meaning. Specifically, the value of r is the increase in one variable associated with a one-unit change in the other variable, both variables being translated into standard scores (see a discussion of standard scores in what follows). Our experience is that this concept is a little difficult to get across to clients and agency executives who quickly become impatient with such mathematical trivia. Increasingly, applied social scientists are finding that a slight transformation of the correlation coefficient yields a conceptualization of correlation that is much easier to communicate to nonspecialists. This more useful statistic is the quantity r^2 (**r-square**), which is literally the correlation coefficient r multiplied by itself (i.e., squared). The reason that this version of the statistic is preferred in many contexts is that its interpretation is more sensible. The **coefficient of determination,** as r^2 is called, is the proportion of the variance in the outcome variable, Y, that can be accounted for by X in a regression equation.

Continuing with the social support and depression example, assume that we found that $r = -.40$ and therefore $r^2 = 16$. The interpretation is that 16% of the variability in depression in the sample can be accounted for by variability in social support (and vice versa). This is not precisely the same conceptualization as r, but it is much easier to communicate. Correlation conceptualized as r^2 is useful when the question is something like, "Just how important is social support in the prevention of depression?" Answer, "Well, in our study, 16% (–.40 squared) of the differences in depression could be accounted for by differences in the level of social support."

Although there are many ways to calculate a correlation coefficient, the standard score formula gives many people the clearest understanding of the concept behind correlation. The standard score formula for **Pearson's r** is

$$r = 1 - \frac{1}{2}\left(\frac{\Sigma(z_x - z_y)^2}{n}\right) \tag{8.1}$$

The essence of correlation is revealed by the symbols in parentheses. The expression $(z_x - z_y)$ is the comparison (subtraction is a comparison operation) of a person's standard score on the X variable with that person's score on the Y variable. A *standard score* is a transformation of the original score into a number that reflects not the original units of the variable, but how far a particular score is from the mean in standard deviation units.

By using standard scores, correlation defeats the problem of variables measured on very different scales. Direct comparison of raw scores would be difficult to interpret because variables are often measured on scales with different numbers of points and different amounts of variability. For example, it is commonly observed that years of education and income are correlated. But, education is measured on a scale that may range from 0 to 20 years and income on a scale that extends into millions of dollars. How do you compare the income and education scores of a person who is $13,000 above the mean in income and 4 years over the mean in years of education? Standard scores eliminate the problem by changing the raw score from a measure of some attribute to a score representing how far the score is from the sample mean expressed in standard deviation units. Standard scores can be compared directly because (for variables that are normally distributed) a group of standard scores will have a mean of zero and a standard deviation of 1. In a distribution of standard scores, most (as many as 99.7% according to the rules governing the properties of normal curves) of the scores fall between -3 to $+3$ no matter what the original scale of measurement was. This allows us to compare variables measured on dissimilar scales, because we are not comparing social support to depression, but "typicalness" on social support with "typicalness" on depression.

Pearson defined correlation in a way that allows prediction of one variable from another with the greatest accuracy. For Pearson, greatest accuracy meant a formula that kept the sum of the squared distance between values predicted and actual values as small as possible. This "least squares criterion" is used to define optimum formulas for several statistics. Pearson was able to prove that the r value from his formula could be used to predict Y from X such that the smallest squared errors of prediction would be produced and thus meet the least squares criterion.

Returning to Equation 8.1, we are instructed to subtract the standard scores for Y from the standard score for X for all persons, squaring and summing any differences found and dividing the total squared differences by the number of persons in the data set (n). Think for a minute about the mathematics of this. When a person has the same standard score on X and Y, the difference is zero. If this happens to everyone in the data set, the expression in the parentheses would equal zero and the value for r would be 1, a perfect correlation. Does this give you an inspiration concerning what a correlation represents? Correlation can be thought of as a measure of the extent to which persons tend to occupy the same position relative to their peers on both variables.

A brief hand calculation of the correlation coefficient might help illustrate the process. Table 8.4 contains portions of a data set describing child-rearing practices on St. Kitts, West Indies (Rohner, Kean, & Cournoyer, 1991). The two variables coded in Table 8.4 are the age of the youth being interviewed and a score reflecting the frequency and severity of physical punishment received in the last two weeks. The first step in calculating a correlation statistic is to find the mean and standard deviation for the each of the two variables. The formulas for the mean and standard deviation have been defined previously, and the values for these are shown at the bottom of the columns containing the raw scores for age and punishment. Next, the means and standard deviations are used to create two columns of standard scores, one standardizing the age scores and one standardizing the punishment scores. Recall that a standard score is a raw score minus the mean and divided by the standard deviation, that is, how far the raw score is from the group mean measured in standard deviation units. The table shows the process of obtaining the deviation scores (x) and then converting these into standard scores (z_x and z_y) by dividing the x and y deviation scores by the appropriate standard deviations. The final column shows the squared differences between the z scores. At the base of the column, the squared differences are summed, divided by n, and finally multiplied by ½ and subtracted from 1. The resulting value, $-.38$, is a moderate negative correlation, indicating that older children (high age scores) tend to have lower physical punishment scores. The final value in the last column of Table 8.4, is r^2, indicating that about 14% of the variability in physical punishment in the sample was related to the age of the child.

Sometimes the percentage of variance in common (r^2) is not really what we want to communicate. A practical question like, "If we can increase social support by two points, what will be the probable effect on stress?" requires that we work with an aspect of correlation and regression that deals with developing prediction equations. Several times in the previous section, we referred to correlation being used to predict scores on one variable from another. Although r^2 provides an estimate of the proportion of variability that can be accounted for, the r value can actually be used to develop a function rule that allows us to predict one variable from the other. Look at Figure 8.1 on page 188. This figure is a scatter diagram and shows the scores of the same 30 children in Table 8.4 on the amount of physical punishment received and age. Each dot on the graph represents one individual in the data set. The position of the dot represents the age (x axis) and punishment scores (y axis).

The line drawn through the cloud of points is called a regression line (regression is what the r stands for). Once we have a value for the correlation coefficient, r, we can use our knowledge of the sample size, means, and standard deviations of the two variables being compared to draw the line that goes through the "cloud" of points as close as possible to all the points. Straight lines on graphs have equations of the form $\hat{Y} = a + b(X)$, where $\hat{Y}$ is a predicted score for Y, a is the value of $\hat{Y}$ when $X = 0$ (also known as the Y intercept), b is the slope (rise or fall) of the line, and X refers to any raw score for variable X. Because the formula says to multiply X by b, each time X goes up one unit, $\hat{Y}$ goes up by b units. Because b is calculated as $b = r\,(\text{std}y/\text{std}x)$, that is, the correlation coefficient multiplied by the standard deviation of Y divided by the standard deviation of X, the correlation r, reflects the change of Y predicted from X. The regression line in Figure 8.1 was drawn based on the observed correlations and standard deviations reported in Table 8.4.

Correlation is one way of exploring or confirming the possibility that two variables are related. The correlation coefficient condenses a tremendous amount of scores and comparisons into a compact little expression such as $r = .50$. With a little practice, you will remember that this means that scores on the two variables

TABLE 8.4   Standard Score Computation of Pearson's *r* for the Relationship between Age and Frequency and Severity of Corporal Punishment

ID#	AGE X	Deviation X – mean = x	Standard Scores x/std = zx	PUNISH Y	Deviation Y – mean = y	Stardard Scores y/std = zy	Compare $(zx - zy)^2$
1	18	2	1.15	7	–10.97	–0.72	3.50
2	15	–1	–0.49	25	7.03	0.46	0.91
3	17	1	0.60	16	–1.97	–0.13	0.53
4	17	1	0.60	7	–10.97	–0.72	1.76
5	18	2	1.15	7	–10.97	–0.72	3.50
6	17	1	0.60	7	–10.97	–0.72	1.76
7	18	2	1.15	8	–9.97	–0.66	3.26
8	16	0	0.05	65	47.03	3.11	9.32
9	15	–1	–0.49	49	31.03	2.05	6.46
10	17	1	0.60	10	–7.97	–0.53	1.27
11	17	1	0.60	8	–9.97	–0.66	1.58
12	16	0	0.05	7	–10.97	–0.72	0.61
13	17	1	0.60	40	22.03	1.46	0.73
14	18	2	1.15	14	–3.97	–0.26	1.98
15	16	0	0.05	7	–10.97	–0.72	0.61
16	19	3	1.69	7	–10.97	–0.72	5.84
17	15	–1	–0.49	8	–9.97	–0.66	0.03
18	15	–1	–0.49	15	–2.97	–0.20	0.09
19	17	1	0.60	8	–9.97	–0.66	1.58
20	16	0	0.05	23	5.03	0.33	0.08
21	18	2	1.15	10	–7.97	–0.53	2.80
22	18	2	1.15	8	–9.97	–0.66	3.26
23	13	–3	–1.58	15	–2.97	–0.20	1.92
24	13	–3	–1.58	35	17.03	1.13	7.34
25	13	–3	–1.58	7	–10.97	–0.72	0.74
26	14	–2	–1.04	7	–10.97	–0.72	0.10
27	14	–2	–1.04	13	–4.97	–0.33	0.50
28	14	–2	–1.04	31	13.03	0.86	3.60
29	13	–3	–1.58	29	11.03	0.73	5.34
30	13	–3	–1.58	46	28.03	1.85	11.80
Mean	15.90			17.97		sum	82.80
std	1.83			15.13		/n	2.76
						1–1/2(2.67)	–0.38
						r^2 =	0.14

Source: Rohner, Kean, & Cournoyer, 1991.

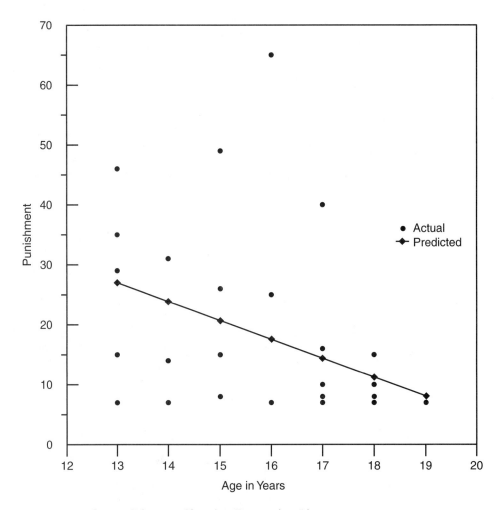

FIGURE 8.1   Scatter Diagram Showing Regression Line

tend to differ from the mean in the same direction (positive correlation) and that 25% of the variability in each of the two variables can be accounted for by the other (r^2 = .25). A correlation of this size between variables of interest to social workers would be high enough to potentially be of practical interest.

Computation of Correlations Using Spreadsheets.   Thanks to electronic computing devices, the mathematics involved with computing a correlation is painless (almost). As we mentioned earlier, dedicated statistical computer programs tend to be the easiest to use, but your handy spreadsheet already has correlation built in as a statistical function. Excel and Lotus 1-2-3 both provide built-in functions for a correlation called CORREL. To use this function, be sure your data are typed into the spreadsheet. Then, place the cursor in a blank cell and call up the function menu by clicking on the tool bar. From the list of statistical functions, click on CORREL. When prompted, specify the column range of the first variable (i.e., the Y variable) in the CORREL function and then the column range of the second variable (the X variable). The spreadsheet produces a correlation coefficient in the expected range between +1 and –1 and puts it in the cell in which you have entered the formula. This process can be repeated with as many pairs of variables as are of interest. The more detailed information concerning slopes of regression lines and the like can be obtained from regression routines. In Lotus 1-2-3, click on RANGE, then ANALYZE, and then REGRESSION. When prompted, fill in the X range, Y range, and output range. In Excel, the SLOPE and INTERCEPT functions are used to obtain regression statistics.

Correlation and regression constitute the simplest level of multiple regression and correlation analysis, a complete analytic system. Although we have introduced Pearson's correlation as an example of a bivariate correlation, a group of related statistics, specifically partial correlation, multiple regression, and factor analysis can be used to look at relationships between two, three, or more variables. After a brief discussion of correlation among nominal variables, we discuss more advanced correlation and regression statistics.

In this section, we have discussed correlation as a bivariate descriptive statistic used to identify patterns in sample data. Later in this chapter, we see how to use a correlation computed from data in a sample to estimate what the relationship is probably like in the population from which the sample was drawn and to estimate the likelihood that a particular correlation arose due to random sampling error in a population where the true correlation is zero (no correlation).

Correlation among Nominal Variables: Lambda and Chi-Square.   Sometimes the variables we believe to be correlated are not quantities, but discrete variables. Although Pearson's r can also produce interpretable results when applied to nominal variables in some cases (Cohen & Cohen, 1983), the conceptualization behind r yields the clearest results with variables that are coded on interval, ratio, and some kinds of ordinal scales. When the correlation of interest is between nominal variables, other operational definitions of correlation yield results that are more easily grasped. Many useful approaches exist. We review two here, lambda (λ) and chi-square (χ^2).

The **lambda** statistic (Bohrnstedt & Knoke, 1988) defines correlation between nominal variables as the degree to which classification on one nominal variable can be used to predict classification on another nominal variable. Like Pearson's r and many statistics, λ starts with an assumption concerning what errors would look like if there were no association between the two variables and then measures the extent to which information contained on a predictor variable can be used to reduce the error rate in predicting classification on the second variable. Earlier, we said that the value of r^2 reflected proportionate reduction in prediction errors when X was used to predict Y instead of just guessing the mean of Y. Lambda produces the same kind of information, but uses modes and frequencies rather than means and variances.

When two nominal variables, X and Y, are uncorrelated, the best guess concerning the classification of any person on variable Y, the one that would produce the fewest wrong guesses over many trials, would be to guess the mode of Y, regardless of the person's classification on variable X (from earlier in this chapter, the mode is the classification that appeared most frequently in the sample). For example, if we know that most clients at an agency achieve planned discharges (planned being the mode) and we want to guess the treatment outcome as clients walk through the door for the first time, the guess that would minimize our errors over the long term would be "planned." If we use the mode as our guess for all subjects, the error rate would be n (the total number of persons in the sample) minus the frequency of the modal group in the whole sample. By using this error rate as a standard, λ is used to determine whether we would make fewer errors if we first sort the sample into subgroups determined by their classification on another nominal variable, X, and base our guesses on the mode of the *subgroup* instead of the whole sample mode. That is, maybe some kinds of clients are more likely to achieve a planned discharge than others. In general, the formula for λ is

$$\lambda = \frac{\text{errors using the whole sample mode} - \text{errors using subgroup modes}}{\text{errors using the whole sample mode}} \quad (8.2)$$

Lambda varies in magnitude between 0 and 1.00 like r^2 and provides similar information. Specifically, λ is the proportionate reduction in classification error on some outcome variable that occurs when the prediction is adjusted based on the classification of some predictor variable. A good brief discussion of λ and related measures of association among nominal variables is contained in Bohrnstedt and Knoke (1988).

An example might best illustrate λ. Table 8.5 summarizes data from 110 adolescents discharged from treatment for delinquency (Cournoyer, 1996). The table contains a cross-tabulation that shows the status of the 110 boys on both discharge status and minority group status. As the table shows, the mode for discharge type

TABLE 8.5   **Cross-Tabulation of Ethnicity and Discharge Status**

Was Client Minority?	Discharge Status		
	Unplanned	Planned	Row Totals
No	25	39[1]	64
Yes	29[2]	17	46
Column totals	54	56[3]	110

[1]Planned is the nonminority mode.
[2]Unplanned is the minority mode.
[3]Planned is the whole-sample mode.

was "planned" based on the total in the planned column of 56 individuals. However, if we compute modes separately for "minorities" and "nonminorities," we find that although the mode for nonminorities is still "planned" (39 planned versus 25 unplanned), the mode of minorities is "unplanned" (29 unplanned versus 17 planned).

If we simply predict the group mode "planned" for each of the boys, we would make 54 classification errors (the total 110 – 56 actual planned discharges). Lambda asks whether we could reduce our misclassification rate and instead of guessing the mode for the whole 110, guess the mode of the subgroups (minority and nonminority). In the case of Table 8.5, the errors of prediction resulting from using modes for minority status would result in 25 errors for nonminorities and 17 errors for minorities for a total of 42 classification errors. Subtracting these 42 misclassifications from the 54 misclassifications associated with using the whole-sample mode, we find that our predictions contain 12 fewer misclassifications than when we guess the whole-sample mode. To compute λ, we simply divide the error reduction (12) by the misclassification rate using the whole-sample mode (54) resulting in a value of .229. The λ value of .229 indicates that consideration of minority group status improves the classification accuracy by 22.9%. At a practical level, this suggests that 22.9% of the differences in discharge status have to do with factors related to minority group membership. Lambda is equally useful with nominal variables with more than two levels.

Despite the conceptual simplicity and clarity of λ, it is useful only in those situations in which the modes of subgroups differ from the mode of the sample as a whole. If all the subgroups have the same mode as the entire sample, then λ equals zero. This approach does not detect the situation in which the modes of all subgroups are the same, even though the proportion of individuals in the modal category varies systematically. In the foregoing example concerning minority group status and discharge status, if 99% of the nonminority clients achieve planned discharges and 51% of the minority clients also receive planned discharges, $\lambda = 0$; but we would still have some valid concerns about an association between discharge status and minority group status. What would be useful is a statistic that took into account the proportions of frequencies in cells, not just modes. After a brief digression to discuss some other useful calculations involving contingency tables, we explore *chi-square,* a statistic that uses more of the information about frequencies.

Contingency tables like Table 8.5 are used to simultaneously represent frequency data on two variables. Interpretation of these tables is greatly simplified by calculation of row and column percentages for each cell. By expressing the frequency in each cell as the percent of the row and column totals contained in a cell, it is possible to look for trends that may be hidden by uneven numbers of individuals in the rows and columns. To calculate these percentages, first, totals called *marginals* are calculated for all rows and columns. The column marginals are simply sums of the frequencies contained in each cell in a column and row marginals are the sums of the frequencies contained in each cell in a row. In Table 8.5, the column marginals are shown at the bottom of each column and the row marginals are to the right of each row. Row percentages for each cell are calculated by simply dividing the cell observed frequency by the total of the frequencies in the row in which the cell in question lies and multiplying by 100. Column percentages are calculated by dividing the cell observed frequency by the total frequencies in the column in which the cell in question lies and multiplying by 100. Thus, each cell would contain, in addition to the actual frequency of persons who fall in the cell, two additional numbers, a row, and a column percent. Table 8.6 expands the cell entries shown in Table 8.5 to include the raw frequencies first, row percentages second, and column percentages third. The fourth entry, expected frequencies, is discussed more in what follows.

Interpretation of these cell percentages are fairly straightforward. Look at the cell in the upper left-hand corner of Table 8.6. This cell contains frequencies for nonminority clients who received unplanned discharges, 25 in all. The row is labeled No, for not minority, so the row percentage indicates that among all nonminorities, 39.1% received unplanned discharges. The column percentage associated with this cell indicates that of all the unplanned discharges, 46.3% of these were to nonminority youth. Comparison of the row and column percentages is much more revealing concerning the relationship between the two classification variables. Although the agency served fewer minority clients and therefore expected fewer planned discharges for minority clients, in proportion to their numbers, minority clients were less likely to receive planned discharges. Specifically, 60.9% of the nonminority clients received planned discharges, but only 36.9% of the minority clients received planned discharges. The column percentages tend to confirm this also, for although only 41.8% of the clients were minority, 53.7% of the unplanned discharges were to minority clients.

This exploration of the frequencies contained in Table 8.6 illustrates an important property of data analysis. Data analysis is not just about representing and reordering observations, it is also an active process of abstracting new information. The data contained in Table 8.6 were identified as part of a routine data

TABLE 8.6   Cross-Tabulation Showing Row, Column, and Expected Frequencies

Minority?	Discharge Status		
	Unplanned	Planned	Row Marginals
No—frequency	25	39	64
Row %	39.1	60.9	58.2
Column %	46.3	69.6	
Expected frequency	31.4	23.4	
Yes—frequency	29	17	46
Row %	63.1	36.9	41.8
Column %	53.7	30.4	
Expected frequency	31.4	23.4	
Column marginals	54	56	110

reduction step during a program evaluation that was not primarily focused on ethnic differences. Here, as is often the case, efforts to reduce data to simpler descriptive statistics and cross-tabulations led to deeper understanding and allowed the agency to take corrective action.

The entries in Table 8.6 labeled **expected frequencies** deserve a bit of explanation. Expected frequencies are those in each cell that we would expect if minority group status and discharge status are not associated. The expected frequency for a cell is computed by determining the marginals for the row and column within which the cell in question lies, multiplying those row and column marginals together, and dividing the product by the total sample size. The logic behind this math is the idea of equal proportionality. That is, the expected frequency reflects only the relative frequency of the two variables as seen in the row and column marginals. In the case of Table 8.6, the fact that most of the clients are nonminority results in the expectation of a higher frequency in cells in the column labeled "No" (nonminority), simply because there are more clients who meet this condition. Expected frequencies are the frequencies that should have appeared in this cell if no correlation is present.

Once the table includes both observed and expected frequencies, it is possible to calculate the difference between the two. The difference between the expected and observed frequencies is the basis for another measure of relationship between the two nominal variables, the **chi-square test** (χ^2). Chi-square is simply the squared differences between the observed and expected frequencies, divided by the expected frequency for each cell, summed across all cells. The larger the value for χ^2 becomes, the greater the discrepancy. Unfortunately, interpretation of χ^2 is not straightforward because χ^2 becomes larger when the number of cells increases, even when there is no correlation. Chi-square is seldom used as a descriptive statistic, but is very useful as a significance test to determine if the observed frequencies differ significantly from those expected under the hypothesis of equal proportionality. We hold further discussion of this use of χ^2 until we cover significance tests.

Generating Cross-Tabulation Tables Using Spreadsheets. With small data sets, it is entirely reasonable to calculate the observed frequencies in a cross-tabulation by hand, but for most samples, using a computer is preferable. Dedicated statistical programs such as SPSS, SAS, SPPC, and many others automate this function so well that four or five clicks of a mouse can produce a cross-tabulation table complete with row and column percentages, observed and expected frequencies, lambda, chi-square tests, and several other measures of correlation. If you don't have access to a dedicated statistical program, but have some skill with spreadsheet programs (or an adventurous spirit), cross-tabulations can be computed fairly effortlessly. Routines for generating cross-tabulations are a little more complicated to use than the statistical functions but numerous Help screens are available. In Microsoft Excel, cross-tabulations are called Pivot Tables. To access the correct routine, choose the Data menu, and then Pivot Table Report from the pop-up menu. The Pivot Table Wizard then takes you through a four-step process of specifying where the data are in the spreadsheet, identifying the rows, columns, and a data field, and options. The resulting table contains cell counts and row and column marginals. To generate a cross-tabulation using Lotus 1-2-3, choose the Create command and select Database from the pop-up menu, and then Dynamic Crosstab from the next pop-up menu. Next you are asked to specify the data range, including the column labels. After the data cells are specified, the Crosstab Assistant takes you through three steps to specify the rows, columns, data, and type of summary function. Choose Count as the summary function to get frequencies. Finally, click on the word Done. Here is a hint for both Excel and Lotus 1-2-3. The logic of these tables allows for a third *data* variable to be specified in addition to the variables specifying the rows and columns. However, when computing frequencies, just enter the name of the row or column variable in the data field and ask for Counts as the summary function. Unfortunately, row and column percentages are not computed automatically, and it is necessary to calculate these, and chi-square or lambda, by manually entering formulas into other cells. Our experience is that the learning curve for these routines is only slightly longer than that for dedicated statistical programs.

Pattern Recognition Involving Two or More Variables (Multivariate Statistics). The last group of pattern recognition statistics that is mentioned here is *multivariate statistics*. Multivariate statistics are used to examine patterns among two or more variables. These are the ultimate pattern detectors in numerical data analysis. Many multivariate statistics are based on the logic of Pearson's correlation coefficient. It would be difficult to master the use of these statistics without intensive study, but the concepts behind each are fairly straightforward. Here are brief descriptions of three common multivariate statistics.

Multiple regression analysis is used to examine patterns of relationship between a single-outcome variable and a group of predictor variables (Cohen & Cohen, 1983; Lewis-Beck, 1980; McClendon, 1994). Multiple regression/correlation analysis actually refers to a family of statistical routines that are used to generate a collection of statistics describing and estimating significance of relationships among a group of variables. The **multiple R-square**, a squared correlation coefficient representing the extent to which a group of predictor variables is correlated with a single quantitative outcome variable, is interpreted similarly to the simple r^2, the coefficient of determination. The unique contribution of each of the predictor variables to reducing prediction errors in the outcome variable is estimated through calculating **partial regression weights.** The partial regression weights (b weights if in raw score form or β weights if in standardized form) reflect the correlations between each of the predictor variables and the outcome variable when the correlations between all the predictor variables in the model are taken into account. Calculating a correlation while holding constant all other variables in the model is commonly called *statistical control* and is one of the techniques used to strengthen inference from quasi-experimental data in which significant variables were not controlled by random assignment. The mathematics of multiple regression allows the researcher to examine the plausibility of threats to internal validity posed by factors such as uncontrolled selection, diffusion of treatment, and others. Although statistical control is not as logically conclusive as is experimental control, multiple regression analysis allows the social work researcher to rule out at least some of the alternative explanations and makes study of naturally occurring phenomena that can't be subjected to true experiments more rigorous.

Because multiple regression analysis is a complete analytic system, there is quite a bit more to know than this brief exposition can provide. For example, multiple regression analysis can be used to examine curvilinear correlation, combinations of nominal and interval variables, joint effects (interactions), and others. The interested reader is directed to such classic works as Cohen and Cohen (1983), an excellent short treatment of correlation and regression by Lewis-Beck (1980), or application to causal modeling by McClendon (1994) for a more through description of this family of statistics.

Spreadsheet programs such as Microsoft Excel and Lotus 1-2-3 contain built-in functions for calculation of multiple regression. In Excel, this function is accessed through the function wizard and allows the researcher to enter multiple data ranges (one range for the Y outcome variable and ranges for each of the X variables). Once the data are in the active worksheet, the researcher pastes the function and data specifications to a blank cell and Excel provides a group of statistics. The problem with using Excel to do this is that a cluster of secondary statistics used to diagnose potential problems is not easily obtained unless the researcher enters the formulas into a table cell. Likewise, Lotus 1-2-3 contains a regression statistic that provides rudimentary statistics only. The Statistical Package for the Personal Computer (SPPC), a specialized (and affordable) statistical package developed by Walter and Kirk Hudson, has one of the best PC-based multiple regression programs we have seen. The popular SPSS also has a credible and very easy to use multiple regression program.

Factor analysis (Rummel, 1970) is a multivariate statistic that is conceptually similar to correlation and is used to identify tendencies for groups of variables to cluster together. As mentioned in our discussion of measurement (Chapter 4), factor analysis is often used to examine construct validity of scales within multidimensional test batteries. Among other statistics, factor analysis helps the researcher identify groupings of variables that tend to go together (the factors), statistics showing how much each variable contributes to the factor to which it belongs (factor loadings), and measures that reflect the portion of variance accounted for by a given factor. Factor analysis is a specialized statistic not preprogrammed into spreadsheets and is often an add-on to even dedicated statistical packages. Although it is potentially applicable to many aspects of practice-related research, the most common use is in test validation.

Structural equation modeling (Jöreskog & Sörbom, 1993) is a very powerful statistical technique gaining popularity among social work researchers. The technique conceptually can be thought of as a combination of multiple regression and factor analysis (although the mathematics are quite different). In a nutshell, structural equation modeling uses something like multiple regression to test for a relationship between a group of proposed causes and effects. However, the causes and effects need not be measured directly, but scores can be derived from the factor scores among three or more indirect measures of each cause or effect of interest. This form of data analysis is usually applied to testing causal models (as is multiple regression). By triangulating through multiple measures of all the predictor and outcome variables, structural equation models develop scores believed to reflect latent variables (the factors) and then use these scores rather than raw scores to test causal models. This is a very serious statistical tool. A small group of social work researchers are pioneers in the application of this statistic to social work questions. Computer programs designed to conduct structural equation model analysis tend to be highly specialized. LISREL (Jöreskog & Sörbom, 1993) is among the most common.

Generalizing from Samples to Populations

At their simplest form, all of the statistics we have discussed thus far are descriptive; that is, they are intended to communicate characteristics of variables in a sample of units. However, social work researchers are seldom interested in the characteristics of merely a small sample of observations. More often, our primary interest lies in determining whether what was observed in one context, and perhaps with one group, can help predict what happens in some other context, time, or with different persons from the same population. This section takes up some problems of using data from samples to predict characteristics of larger populations or other samples. These are the topics most textbooks discuss under the heading of "inferential statistics" and "significance testing."

All of the procedures discussed in this section help us to address sampling error as a plausible explanation for the magnitude of some statistic. Specifically, inferential statistics allow us to use probability theory and create mathematical models reflecting the likelihood of certain values appearing due to sampling error (or chance). Once these models are worked out, it becomes possible to calculate a range called a *confidence interval*. A confidence interval is a range of scores between which the "real" population value could be expected to fall with a certain degree of certainty. Confidence intervals are used in two ways. First, confidence intervals can be used to estimate the range of values within which some descriptive statistic could be expected to fall if we take repeated samples. Second, the application commonly called **significance testing** asks if the value found for a particular statistic could have arisen, due to sampling error, in a population in which the real value is zero. This is really all that most significance testing comes down to. This logic can be extended to all the forms of statistics discussed thus far, from univariate to multivariate statistics. Let us first look at the use of confidence intervals for descriptive statistics and then consider how such statistics can be used in tests of statistical significance.

Calculating Confidence Intervals around Descriptive Statistics. Random sampling allows the researcher to use probability theory to establish estimates of population parameters based on the characteristics of samples. Population parameters are simply estimates of the descriptive statistics we would expect to find if we measured the entire population. Generally, the best estimate of the characteristics of a population is a descriptive statistic generated from a random sample. However, unless our sample is very large, we don't expect the mean, standard deviation, range, median, correlation or r^2 in the population to be exactly the same as our sample, just very close. As explained in our discussion of sampling (Chapter 6), the reason we expect to be off a little is sampling error. Stated simply, sampling error is the tendency for random samples to differ slightly from the populations from which they are drawn.

When we use a random sample, probability theory lets us estimate just how far off we could be from the "real" population values (the population parameters) by calculating *confidence intervals* around our sample statistics. A confidence interval is the range of values within which we expect the real population value to fall. A related concept is the *confidence level*. The confidence level refers to the degree of certainty we possess that the true value is bracketed by the confidence interval. For example, a pollster might say, "I am 95% sure (confidence level) that the number of persons who will vote for the candidate is no less than 40% or more than 50% (the confidence interval). The midpoint of this interval, 45%, is the frequency actually observed in a sample of 400 persons. The confidence interval of 40%–50% is based on the mathematics of probability theory, indicating that samples of 400 persons who are nearly divided 50–50 have sampling errors of no greater than ±5%, 95% of the time. As we discussed briefly in Chapter 6 (on sampling), estimates of sampling errors are related to the sample size and variability within the sample.

The important idea here is that any descriptive statistic calculated on a random sample can serve as a best guess concerning the characteristics of the entire population from which the sample is drawn. However, because all such estimates are subject to sampling error, it is conventional and wise to think of the sample statistics as being one member of a range of possible answers and compute confidence intervals to determine the reasonable range that answers could take. This becomes important in situations in which precise estimates are important. In the preceding example, knowing that the confidence interval for the candidate was mostly below 50% was cause for alarm.

In order to calculate confidence intervals based on probability theory, it is necessary to calculate a statistic called a *standard error*. A standard error is simply a standard deviation of a collection of statistics (rather than raw scores). Like a standard deviation, a standard error reflects the variability in a group of scores expressed in terms of units of measurement of the variable in question. For example, were we to draw a small random sample from a population; calculate descriptive statistics of that sample, say, a mean; return the units to the population; draw another sample and calculate its mean; and continue this process until thousands of means were obtained, it would be possible to calculate descriptive statistics on this collection of means. One statistic could be the mean of the means and another could be the standard deviation of that collection of means. In this case, the standard deviation would actually be called a standard error. Thankfully, enterprising mathematicians have determined that rather than extracting thousands of samples, it is possible to come up with a good approximation of the standard error of a hypothetical distribution of statistics by using characteristics of the sample.

The reason that standard errors are important is that random sampling error distributes itself in Gaussian (bell-shaped) curves. Because we know a lot about the mathematical properties of bell curves, including the fact that their shape is partially determined by the standard deviation, it is possible to use knowledge of standard errors to calculate the range of values that the statistic might take in the larger population. In general, we expect that in 95% of random samples, the true population mean is no higher than +1.96 standard errors above the sample mean or 1.96 standard errors below the sample mean (confidence interval). This confidence interval is useful whenever we need to be only 95% sure (confidence level) that the population mean falls within the confidence interval. You might round this off to 2 standard errors to give you a rough practical rule that you can be 95% confident that the true population mean falls within ±2 standard errors of the sample mean. Thus, rounded, a mean stress score of 24 with a standard error of 3 would have a 95 confidence interval of approximately 18 to 30 [24 ± (3 × 2)]. That means that although 24 is our best guess for the average stress score, we can be 95% confident that the real value in the population is not smaller than 18 or larger than 30.

Whereas dedicated statistical packages and statistical calculators calculate standard errors automatically, spreadsheet programs do not. The only alternative is for you to enter the formula directly, which is really not that complicated. For the mean of continuously measured variables, the standard error of the mean is equal to the standard deviation of the sample divided by the square root of the sample size. This formula indicates that the larger the sample, the less error is contained in the mean as an estimate of the sample mean.

Standard errors for frequency counts are conceptually the same as standard errors for descriptive statistics, but use different mathematics. Remember why we are calculating standard errors. Faced with a number such as an approval rating of 60% based on a sample, we want to estimate the worst and best cases concerning what the population looks like. To do this, we first multiply the proportion approving (60%) by the number not approving (40%) and then divide by the number of cases in the survey. Finally, we take the square root of this number. The answer is the standard error. As before, an approximate 95% confidence interval is established by the range that stretches from two standard errors below your sample statistic to two standard errors above your sample statistic. Although the skillful computer users among you see immediately how to automate this task using Excel or Lotus 1-2-3, the majority simply want to calculate standard errors by entering the formula into a cell and then provide the necessary sample statistics. Because social work research is often expected to apply to a larger population, it is good practice to calculate standard errors and confidence intervals for all variables at the stage of descriptive statistics.

Although we tend to report scores as if they are fixed measures, it is important to remember that all descriptive statistics obtained from samples are just approximations of the population values and that small differences between descriptive statistics may reflect only sampling error. This insight is the basis for our next discussion, null hypothesis testing.

Null Hypothesis Testing.   **Null hypothesis testing** can be thought of as extending the idea of confidence intervals to estimating the likelihood that some statistic (e.g., a correlation) could really be zero in a population. That is, does the confidence interval for the statistic contain a zero (null)? If the confidence interval does contain a zero, we interpret the nonzero value we find in a sample as just a result of sampling error. This logic can be applied to virtually any descriptive statistic. For example, in a program evaluation that takes the form of an experiment, research hypothesis might be that the mean outcome for participants in the experimental program is higher than that of participants in the control program. However, if we obtain a small difference, how do we know that the difference isn't just an illusion generated by sampling error, the same force that gives each group's mean a confidence interval? It could be that if we drew repeated samples, most of them would produce no mean differences, a situation that would disconfirm our research hypothesis. Wouldn't it be convenient if we knew in advance what range of differences could be expected to occur in samples drawn from populations where the real difference is zero? Then all we would need to do is ask if the difference we found lies within that range. This is what the application of probability theory in null hypothesis testing does for us. Significance tests allow us to estimate how likely it is that the confidence interval for the statistic of interest to us (a correlation, a mean difference, or some other descriptive statistic) contains some value (usually zero).

In fact, null hypothesis testing has many variations. Although it is common to examine confidence intervals of statistics to see if a zero is plausible, in some cases, the value of interest is some other value. Perhaps you have two groups that seem to have different mean incomes and you want to find out if the confidence intervals for the groups contain both means (i.e., groups are equivalent). In cases like these, the value of interest will not be zero, but the mean of one of the groups.

You will recall from our discussion of research design that testing propositions and hypotheses is a logical process that involves rendering implausible a group of threats to internal validity, one of which includes sampling error. In significance testing, when zero falls outside of the 95% confidence interval (i.e., 1.96 standard errors distant from the obtained value) of a statistic being examined, we tend by convention to conclude that zero cannot be reasonably considered as belonging to that distribution of scores. This renders as implausible the explanation that the real statistic in the population could be zero and the observed value arose from sampling error (chance). This kind of backward logic is typical of hypothesis testing statistics. We don't "prove" that the effect is real, but examine the plausibility of chance as an alternative explanation by asking if the statistic we find fits with what we would expect if sampling error is the only force operating on the data.

The proposition that some effect arises due to sampling error is the definition of the **null hypothesis.** Generally, the null hypothesis is a statistical hypothesis stating that the value we find for some statistic fits within a sampling distribution of values that arise by chance when the real population value is zero. In practice, the statistic asks how far the score we obtained is from zero, in standard error units. Once that distance is estimated, normal curve statistics are used to estimate the number of samples out of a hundred that would be expected to have a value equal to or larger than the one we find assuming the true value is zero. That estimate is the familiar p value reported in the statistical portion of a research report. The p value is taken as the best estimate of the probability that the statistic we are examining could have arisen by chance from a population in which the real value is zero.

Historically, significance testing has involved deriving ratios that have known probability distributions so that it is easy to look up p values. The t-ratio, F-ratio, and chi-square all have known distributions. By expressing sample statistics in terms of these ratios, it becomes possible to estimate the standard errors of the chance distributions and calculate the potential for the sample statistics to have arisen by chance (sampling error). Once a t or F value is found, this ratio is looked up in a table and the approximate probability read. Mean differences use a t-test to get at the probability and multiple regression uses a combination of t-tests and F-tests. As we mentioned previously, the distribution of scores in a contingency table are generally tested for significant departure from equal proportionality by calculating a chi-square value, which is based on the ratio of discrepancies between expected and observed frequencies to expected frequencies. The significance associated with a chi-square test is also used as an approximation for the significance of lambda (Bohrnsted & Knoke, 1988).

With the advent of computer statistical programs, probabilities related to functions such as $t, f,$ and χ^2 are computed directly. The process is so automatic that it is reasonable to think of the values, $t, f,$ and χ^2, as merely steps in the process of obtaining p values, which are the probabilities that the statistics we find (e.g., correlations, mean differences, departures from equal proportionality) arise due to chance.

When reporting descriptive statistics that reflect patterns across two or more variables, including measures of mean differences, correlation coefficients, multiple regression R-squares, and partial regression weights, it is customary to also report their p value, unfortunately labeled "statistical significance." Much confusion could be avoided if we referred to the p value as "chance potential," but tradition persists. For a correlation, the chance potential is largely a function of the size of r (effect size) and n (sample size) and is calculated through a t-test. Statistical packages generally calculate precise probability values. If you use a spreadsheet to calculate correlations, you might want to have a significance table handy that tells you how large a correlation needs to be for a given sample size to possess a chance potential, p, that is less than or equal to .05, which is a traditional, albeit arbitrary, cutoff point (e.g., see Cohen & Cohen, 1983).

Another common use of the **t-test** is a comparison of the differences between two means. The t-test is used to evaluate the probability that the difference between the two groups arose by sampling error from a population in which the real difference is zero. The computation of t-tests differs, depending on how the means being compared are generated. The t-test for independent samples is used when the means come from separate groups. If you choose the t-test for independent samples, it is also necessary to determine if the variances in the two groups are significantly different and then choose a formula for equal variances or the formula for unequal variances. The *t*-test for paired samples is used when the data consist of repeated measures of the same individuals or when the observations have been linked through some matching strategy. A one-sample (student's) *t* is used when the data consist of a column of scores and the task is to see if the sample mean differs from a value selected by the researcher. Whatever formula is used to compute *t*, the resulting *p* value is an estimate of the potential that chance accounts for any apparent differences between the two sets of measures.

Here is an example concerning the efficacy of two different weight-loss programs. Assume that the participants are randomly selected and randomly assigned to one group designated as experimental or another group designated as control. The research question asks whether the average weight loss between the two groups is different. Once the mean weight loss for each group is found and compared, the logical question is whether the difference is large enough to reflect anything other than chance fluctuations. The logical choice for a significance test is a *t*-test for independent samples. If the variance of the weight loss in the two groups is equivalent, the value for equal variances is used. If the variances are significantly different, the value for unequal variances is used. If the design does not employ a control group, but simply a one-group pretest/posttest design, the matched or repeated measures *t* would be used. In all cases, the statistic of interest would be the mean difference, and the *p* value would only be the estimate of the likelihood that the mean difference arises due to chance.

The most common approach to testing for statistical significance in nominal variables involves the use of the *chi-square* test. Earlier, we discussed how to calculate expected frequencies from the marginals in a cross-tabulation table. The chi-square statistic compares the observed frequencies to frequencies expected if the data are proportioned equally among rows and columns. Chi-square is computed by taking each cell, subtracting the expected frequency from the observed frequency, squaring the difference, and dividing by the expected frequency. The process is repeated for each cell and the results summed. This process is expressed mathematically as

$$x^2 = \sum_{i=1}^{k} \left[\frac{(f_o - f_e)^2}{f_e} \right] \tag{8.3}$$

where

k = number of cells

f_o = observed frequencies

f_e = expected frequencies

The equation is simply a mathematical shorthand for what we described in words.

The reason that we convert the differences between expected and observed frequencies to a chi-square value is that the probability of obtaining a given value of chi-square in populations in which the real difference between observed and expected frequencies is zero has already been worked out by mathematicians. Thus, for any χ^2 value obtained, it is possible to estimate the likelihood that the discrepancies between expected and observed frequencies arise from sampling error. The odds that the differences between expected and observed frequencies arise due to chance can be estimated by looking up the obtained χ^2 value on a statistical table or in the case of dedicated statistical packages it is computed precisely. Often, the probability of χ^2 is used as a proxy to determine the significance of λ (Bohrnstedt & Knoke, 1988). In this case, the null hypothesis is that the proportion of error reduction reflected by a λ value arises due to sampling error in a population in which the real error reduction related to making predictions based on subpopulation modes is zero.

Issues in Hypothesis Testing

It is worth noting at this point that evaluating sampling error as a plausible explanation for some statistic is the sole contribution of significance tests. From our earlier discussion of inference, the hallmark of scientific argument is ruling out plausible alternatives, usually the threats to internal validity detailed in Chapter 5. Establishing statistical significance by evaluating the plausibility of sampling error or chance as an additional threat to internal validity is just one piece of the process of drawing credible inference.

When using significance tests to explore chance as a rival hypothesis in your own work, there are several other concepts that need to be considered. First, let's reexamine the p value and our choice of the cutoff point. The cutoff value we choose for p, also called the alpha level, reflects our willingness to take the chance of rejecting the null hypothesis when it is true. (So far, we have used an alpha value of .05 without justification.) The general null hypothesis we have proposed is that the statistic we found arose due to chance in a population in which the true statistic is zero. Therefore, rejecting a true null hypothesis means thinking you have found some effect, such as a nonzero correlation, mean difference, or discrepancy between expected and observed frequencies, when there really is no such effect in the population. Treating such a false effect as real is a logical mistake called a Type I, or alpha, error. Because scientists tend to be a conservative lot and by general agreement don't want the journals filled with "findings" that really reflect Type I errors, the criterion for rejecting the null hypothesis tends to be fairly stringent, such as .05 or sometimes .01. It is important to consider that these levels reflect social conventions and value judgments (that is, they are cultural) concerning how much risk of being fooled by sampling error we are willing to tolerate. You will recall that setting alpha at .05 means that we accept only those effects that are strong enough that we could expect to find such an effect due to chance in only 5 samples out of 100.

There is another side to inference, commonly called Type II, or beta, error. What happens if our research design is so insensitive that we accept the null hypothesis (conclude that the statistic in question arose due to chance sampling error) when the null hypothesis is in fact false (there really is an effect in the population)? By definition here we have made a Type II, or beta, error. The risk of beta errors is determined by how stringent the alpha level is set, how large the sample is, and how large the statistic is (effect size). In general, the larger the sample, the larger the effect we are examining, and the less stringent our alpha cutoffs are, the lower is the possibility of making a Type II error. Estimation of the probability of making a Type II error is sometimes called *power analysis.* **Power analysis** suggests that minimizing the risk of a Type II error to acceptable levels involves consideration of what is known about the phenomenon under study and adjusting sample sizes and alpha to balance the needs to keep Type II errors at bay. For example, if you are looking for statistical evidence of very small, subtle effects and as a practical matter Type II errors are of concern, you will need large samples and possibly less stringent alpha cutoffs. This is very important to social work researchers, since we tend to study variables that are the products of complex patterns of causes, each contributing only a small portion to outcomes and therefore having small effect sizes. Power analysis was discussed earlier (see Chapter 6).

A related phenomenon is that with very large samples, even effects that are so small as to have no practical value are likely to meet the tests for statistical significance. As discussed in Chapter 6, the random measurement errors in any sample tend to cancel each other as the sample size increases. For example, with sample sizes of 800, correlations as small as .10 have an 80% chance of being detected and found significant at the .05 level. An r value of .10 translates into an r^2 of only .01, indicating an overlap between two variables of only 1%. Effects of this size are not likely to have any practical value and therefore mounting such a sensitive study seems unproductive. Although excessively large sample sizes are not usually a problem in social work research, it is important to understand that they represent a research resource waste, just as samples that are too small to provide adequate statistical power are wasteful.

What the sensible social work researcher who is conducting a numerical analysis needs to do is consider the effect sizes that are likely to be important in treatment, or planning, or some decision-making context, and then when designing a study, select a sample size that is able to detect that size effect with reasonable sensitivity. Consulting an appropriate text on statistical power (such as Cohen, 1969) is the ideal approach.

However, here is a practical guideline for judging the adequacy of sample size. Effect sizes indicated by correlations in the .30 range are very common in studies of human behavior. Since the r^2 for a correlation of this size is only .09, such a relationship indicates a potential to account for only 9% of the variability in a variable. This is probably close to the lower boundary of what should be considered practical. Power analysis shows that sample sizes of 84 have a power of .80 and are probably adequate for a wide range of studies where the effect sizes are modest. Of course, this final decision of sample size must be considered in the overall context in which the research is taking place.

Summary

Analysis of numerical data is generally undertaken to reduce information overload, look for patterns, and estimate the generalizability of the findings to larger populations. Descriptive statistics reduce large numbers of observations to a more manageable set of numbers. Measures of central tendency provide estimates of typicalness, whereas measures of dispersion estimate variability. The different measures of central tendency and dispersion reflect subtly different definitions of the concepts of typicalness and variability. Means, modes, medians, standard deviations, and variances are examples of univariate descriptive statistics designed to represent the information in a collection of scores reflecting single variables.

Bivariate and multivariate descriptive statistics are used to explore patterns involving two or more variables. Correlation is the pattern between two variables that is most commonly studied. Correlation may be defined as Pearson's product/moment correlation coefficient when the variables of interest are either dichotomous, discrete, or continuous. When the variables of interest are categorical, statistics such as lambda can be used to determine if a correlation is present. Chi-square can be used to determine if correlation, defined as the departure from equal proportionality, is present and is often used to estimate the statistical significance of lambda. Cross-tabulation tables with column and row percentages are useful in determining the nature of significant departure from equal proportionality.

Extrapolation from samples to populations is largely about *confidence levels* and *confidence intervals*. A confidence interval is a range of scores between which we expect the true population value to lie. Confidence intervals are formed by estimating the properties of a sampling distribution, the frequency distribution we would expect if we took repeated samples of a given size. Standard deviations of sampling distributions of statistics are called *standard errors*. Confidence levels reflect the certainty we wish to have that the "true" value for a statistic in the population falls within the confidence interval we specify. The more confident we want to be that a given range contains the real population value, the wider that range needs to be. A confidence level of .95 is formed by calculating the standard error of the statistic in question and setting the lower boundary of the confidence interval at −1.96 standard errors below the value found in a sample and setting the upper boundary at +1.96 standard errors above the sample value. A confidence level of .95 indicates that we wish to set our prediction in such a way that in no more than 5 samples out of 100 would we expect that the real value would fall outside the confidence interval.

Significance tests extend the idea of confidence levels and confidence intervals to null hypothesis testing. Significance tests ask if some observed value for a statistic could have arisen by sampling error from a population in which the real value of the statistic is zero. The null hypothesis can be thought of as the proposition that the confidence interval of a statistic includes a zero value. The p value can be interpreted as an estimate of the "chance potential" or the probability that random sampling error caused the sample statistic to take a nonzero value. These statistics were designed to help researchers estimate the plausibility of sampling error as an explanation for observed patterns in data.

Generally, *t*-tests are used to examine sampling error in the comparison of mean differences between two groups. The two groups can be two independent groups or can be "paired," as in considering "before" and "after" treatment scores in a single group. This use of a *t*-test requires a dichotomous discrete independent variable that can be used to partition the data set into two groups and one continuous dependent variable for which comparisons are desired. Significance tests are also used to test the likelihood that correlation coefficients arise due to chance from populations in which the true correlation is zero. A *t*-test is used to determine the significance of a Pearson correlation coefficient. The probability value associated with χ^2 is used to test the statistical significance of the differences between expected and observed frequencies in a cross-tabulation table or the statistical significance of a λ test.

Setting the alpha level at levels such as .05 or .01 is a social convention intended to control the number of times that we reject null hypotheses when it is really true (Type I errors). Setting the power to .80 is intended to assure that studies are sufficiently sensitive to detect expected effect sizes (and thus reduce the likelihood of Type II errors). Statistical power analysis allows the social work researcher to estimate sample sizes needed to detect effects of various sizes. A practical rule to consider is that anything smaller than a medium-sized effect (e.g., $r = .30$) is probably too small to matter and sample sizes of 84 are needed to reliably detect relationships between variables at our arbitrarily defined medium size of $r = .30$ and a Type I error of .05.

CHAPTER

9

Analysis of Nonnumerical Data

Data Reduction, Patterns, and Generalizations

Relationship of This Chapter to the Whole

In this chapter, we examine techniques that are useful in abstracting meaning from collections of **nonnumerical data.** The approaches described here were designed to achieve tasks that are similar to those discussed in the context of numerical analysis: data reduction, pattern recognition, and testing generalizability. Despite the very different feel of nonnumerical and numerical data analysis, the goals are largely the same. In fact, many of the differences between numerical and nonnumerical data arise not from the different symbol systems employed (numbers as opposed to words, visual images, or others) as much as from the different purposes to which they are applied. For example, the common coupling of exploratory, meaning-generating activities with nonnumerical data, compared to the common coupling of hypothesis testing activities with numerical data, tends to mask the similarities in the data analysis tasks that lurk behind all forms of data.

Many of the characteristics associated with nonnumerical data analysis, for example, repeated cycles of observation, analysis, refined observation, and refined analysis, don't have as much to do with using words rather than numbers as much as using exploratory instead of confirmatory methods. However, behind all the differences in intent and data collection method, data analysis techniques are still designed to compensate for the same set of human limitations and address our needs to extract more general insights from collections of observations.

The main focus of this chapter is analysis of text data, specifically, narratives such as transcripts of interviews, speech, verbatim accounts of behavior observations, journals, and logs. Nonnumerical data may also consist of other forms, such as artifacts (material culture), physical traces resulting from human acts, and representations of behavior, such as electronic audio and video recording. We emphasize text data because these are the most common forms of nonnumerical data, and often narrative descriptions are also used to describe other forms of data

As we noted in the discussion of numerical data analysis, the operations we perform on data as we analyze them are intended to reduce the likelihood of introducing distortions reflecting characteristic human errors. There are undoubted many different ways to achieve the goal of error reduction. The data analysis procedures included here do not exhaust the range of possibilities, but were chosen because they illustrate how concerns about rigor in analysis of nonnumerical data may be addressed. The particular techniques we discuss here have the advantage of being relatively easy for the beginning social work researcher to use. This approach is consistent with our goal of providing the reader with practical skills through which to integrate scientific thinking and method into practice needs. The techniques we discuss should be taken as examples of a much larger class of techniques, some documented and others yet to be devised. Summaries of additional techniques are contained in sources cited in this chapter. Sherman and Reid (1994) provide an excellent and readable collection of papers on this topic.

Application of This Chapter to the Roles of Social Workers

Sherman and Reid (1994) note that social work practice has a natural affinity for scientific methods that involve describing in words. Words and the mental systems that lend words meaning are the cornerstone of social work as a profession and all of science as a way of knowing. Techniques discussed in this chapter are drawn largely from ethnographic methods with strong relevance to many social work tasks that involve discovery of meaning systems of others. We highlight one approach to ethnography that illustrates appropriate safeguards to systematic distortion and also provide techniques that can be applied usefully to exploration of meaning in systems of all sizes. The methods of James Spradley's (1980) **Developmental Research Sequence** (DRS) system work equally well in mapping meaning systems of individuals or collectives of all sizes. Christina Gladwin's (1989) ethnographic decision-tree modeling techniques are a logical extension of this rigorous approach to analysis of nonnumerical data collected in the context of exploratory, meaning-generating activities and provide an excellent approach to identification of patterns and testing the generalizability of meanings abstracted from non-numerical data. Both the DRS system and ethnographic decision-tree modeling approaches work equally well with individuals and complex systems.

Learning Objectives

After reading this chapter, you will be able to:

1. accomplish data reduction using domain analysis
2. accomplish pattern identification using taxonomic analysis
3. test for the generalizability of patterns using aspects of ethnographic decision-tree modeling.

Key Terms and Concepts

Relationship between Numerical and Nonnumerical Data Analysis

Although conducting analysis of text data feels different from numerical operations, such as calculating an average or a correlation, the techniques of numerical and nonnumerical analysis have more in common than is readily apparent. Analysis of nonnumerical data must accomplish many of the same tasks as numerical data analysis. For example, any reasonably long period of observation is likely to result in far more information than can be easily understood as a raw collection, necessitating some form of data reduction. Like numerical data reduction, nonnumerical data reduction is partially about alleviating information overload and partially about generating abstractions. In this chapter, we explore simple techniques used to organize text data into meaning units using domain analysis. These techniques result in identification of meaning units that make it easier to think and talk about the contents of a text, but also may provide fresh insights into the ways that experience is organized among the persons from whom the data are obtained. As we show, application of systematic techniques of data reduction can produce the strong logical trail from the abstractions of the analysis to the raw data that is also our goal regarding numerical data reduction.

Likewise, both numerical and nonnumerical analyses are concerned with detecting patterns of relationships between concepts. As we noted in the previous chapter, relationships between numerical variables tend to be expressed in terms of correlations and similar mathematically defined attributes. As illustrated in what follows, relationships between classes of words are often expressed as logical structures called taxonomies. In both cases, logical operations are applied to the symbols representing observations to show how classes of observations tend to go together. In the case of numerical correlation, we define "go together" as a comparison of standard scores. In the case of taxonomic analysis, "go together" is defined by how terms are grouped into categories by persons from whom the text data arises.

Even the process of significance testing in numerical data has its counterpart in nonnumerical data. Numerical significance tests are largely concerned with estimating the contribution of sampling error to a particular statistic. Rigorous methods of nonnumerical data analysis also attend to issues of generalizability by mapping inconsistency in meaning systems and identifying limits of generalizability. Techniques associated with approaches such as ethnographic decision-tree modeling (Gladwin, 1989) are used to determine the range of behaviors, situations, and actors in which models of decision making yield meaningful results. Yin (1994) has called this form of external validity **analytic generalizability.** That is, a constructed meaning system has analytic generalizability if the meaning system generates behaviors, explanations, and values that appear sensible and familiar to those whose meaning systems are being examined.

Although analyzing collections of narratives by looking for meaning categories is to some extent arbitrary (with a little imagination we could probably come up with many different attributes of textual data that could be studied), the emphasis on meaning categories and relationships among these categories has strong parallels with the way people naturally extract meaning from natural events. As we have suggested earlier, a preference for describing experience in terms of generalizations probably reflects basic mental processes that are close to the biology of the brain. Therefore, data reduction by grouping words into common categories may be useful across a wide variety of cultural conditions.

Analysis of nonnumerical data can be conveniently grouped into the same tasks we use in the context of numerical analysis: data reduction, pattern identification, tests of generalizability. As is the case with our discussion of numerical data analysis, this method of organization is used to emphasize the intention of the analysis, rather than similarity in method or technique. In all cases, the goals of data analysis are to convert the data into more mind-friendly forms, while preserving the connections with the observations. Now let us turn our attention to specific techniques.

Nonnumerical Data Reduction: Spradley's DRS System

Data reduction is the process of developing shorthand descriptions of collections of observations that preserve important attributes. Imagine a set of transcriptions reflecting the ongoing interactions between a client and a social worker. These transcriptions may include thousands upon thousands of words spoken with respect to a range of specific topics. Now imagine that you must meaningfully summarize all these words. This task shouldn't be that difficult to imagine, for indeed, variations on this basic demand are common in social work practice. However, extraction of meaning is fraught with difficulty. The greatest risk is that words relating to the preoccupation of the social worker and not necessarily those most important to the client are noted. Also, the social worker is likely to influence what is said by the nature of her questions or other aspects of her personal style. In research, as in professional practice, these problems are not likely to be totally eradicated, but can be minimized through careful use of self during the data collection process and the use of systematic methods of data reduction.

It may be useful to think about data reduction as answers to questions such as "What did she say about _____?" Generally, the questioner does not want you to repeat everything the speaker said about the topic in question, but to deliver a summary. The content of your summary is likely to be determined by concerns such as the kinds of information that the questioner and the speaker find important and understandable, plus some unique emphasis related to what you, the translator, find interesting and important. The translation rules you use to accomplish this everyday data reduction tend to be implicit and may vary from person to person. In scientific studies where we need to communicate such summary information in ways that are as consistent as possible, we tend to rely on explicit procedures that keep the summaries as grounded in the actual words of the speaker as possible and less in the idiosyncrasies of the person doing the summary.

Spradley (1980) provides useful techniques for summarizing nonnumerical data. For Spradley, data reduction typically consists of organizing words into clusters that reflect meaning categories. The data reduction process is directed toward identifying families or categories of syntactically related terms and the concepts behind categories. Representing the data in this way accomplishes a goal similar to that accomplished by descriptive statistics, reducing a great many observations to a much smaller number of content domains that reflect the essential meaning.

The DRS System.   Although many approaches to the analysis of nonnumerical data are possible, we highlight Spradley's (1980) Developmental Research Sequence (DRS) to illustrate a rigorous approach to nonnumerical data analysis that is easy for the beginner to comprehend. By rigorous we mean that the analysis is constructed so that generalizations arise from simple, clear manipulations of the original data, preserving the meanings while facilitating thinking and communication.

The DRS approach involves reducing nonnumerical data through four levels each of which represents an increasing degree of abstraction. The levels include (1) domain analysis, (2) taxonomic analysis, (3) componential analysis, and (4) theme analysis. Here we discuss the first three of these. Domain and taxonomic analyses are conceptually similar to the kind of data reduction that is accomplished by descriptive statistics and frequencies of numeric analysis. Componential analysis and theme analysis are designed to detect patterns among domains. Although we will not describe the entire DRS system here, the data analysis methods that Spradley (1980) proposes are good illustrations of rigorous nonnumerical data analysis.

Domain Analysis.   **Domain analysis** consists of examining narratives for words that share a semantic relationship. A **domain** is a cluster of *folk terms*, bound to a *cover term* by a common *semantic relationship*. For example, "part time," "extended degree," and "full time" (folk terms) "are kinds of" (semantic relationship) "matriculation status" (cover term). **Folk terms** are the ordinary words that persons use to describe objects and experiences. **Cover terms** are labels for categories containing potentially many folk terms. Cover terms may be an explicit part of the language of the speaker or may be labels in the language of the observer. A **semantic relationship** is the attribute that binds the cover terms together. Spradley (1980) lists many examples of semantic relationships. Some examples include "is a kind of," "is a place in," "is a part of," "is a way to," and "is a characteristic of." Table 9.1 illustrates some of the folk terms related to the cover term "matriculation status" under the semantic relationship "is a kind of." The table can be thought of as a partial map of the domain "matriculation status."

Table 9.1 was drawn so that included terms are shown on the left, the semantic relationship listed in the middle, and the cover term to the right. In this case, the text that was analyzed was a school catalogue and the content implied by the cover term "matriculation status" was formally defined in the text to include the three terms on the left. Alternatively, the data could have been student self-introductions at the beginning of a class. In either case, the analysis includes obtaining samples of speech converted into text and analyzing for related terms. In less familiar contexts, the domains are not as obvious and may take a considerable amount of creativity and questioning of informants to complete.

Spradley (1980) suggests that the domains related to social behavior can be grouped into nine major classes: spaces, actors, activities, objects, acts, events, times, goals, and feelings. In an analysis that attempts to be comprehensive, a good place to start might be to identify the major domains in each of these areas. A common approach to data reduction might be to ask structural questions such as: "What are all the [spaces, actors, activities, objects, acts, events, times, goals, or feelings] described in the text?" However, in a more focused context, the social worker may be interested primarily in one or two domains and look for folk terms related primarily to those domains.

The next step in a domain analysis is to inquire what semantic relationships connecting the terms may be implied in the text. Spradley (1980) lists several common relationships that may describe how terms are related. These include "is a kind of" (strict inclusion), "is a place in/part of" (spatial), "is a result of" (cause/effect), "is a way to do" (means/ends), "is a step/stage in" (sequence), and "is a characteristic of" (attributes). Many others are possible. "Is a value of" might be used to connect terms regarding value domains. "Is a place for doing" might be used to develop a domain connecting places and acts. The point here is that you are looking within the data for instances of language that give clues to how the

TABLE 9.1   Sample Domain Chart

Included Terms	Semantic Relationship	Cover Term
Full time Part time Extended degree	are kinds of	matriculation status

speaker organizes her or his experience of the world in some matter of interest to the researcher.

It might be useful here to consider that the collection and analysis of nonnumerical data tend to occur in minicycles of data collection, analysis, more data collection, and additional analysis. Often, the social situations that gave rise to the text under study did not produce all possible terms and domains. Thus, the first round of domains often are incomplete, speculative, and require collecting more data. Frequently, the researcher goes back to the field to obtain more text or explanation, clarification, and expansion. Whereas this process is unlikely to occur in the controlled experiment, it is good practice in exploratory studies because it produces summaries that are more complete and grounded.

Lengthy narratives, interviews, and extended periods of observation could include hundreds of domains. The proportion of the possible domains that are coded is a function of the reason the data are collected. If your goal is to determine the worldview of an individual or cultural group, you are likely to examine the broadest possible range of domains. If you are studying a more specific concept, for example, how children know that they are loved, you might focus, as did Rohner & Chaki-Sircar (1988) on domains that reflect how children construe relationships with parents and other persons.

Taxonomic Analysis.   Domains do not exist in linguistic vacuums, but are semantically related to other domains. **Taxonomic analysis** is the specification of relationships between domains. Just as folk terms can be linked to cover terms through semantic relationships, so domains can be linked by semantic relationships. Table 9.2 presents a taxonomic analysis of narrative data collected in the context of an ethnography of a medium-size residential facility for youth adjudicated as delinquent (Cournoyer, 1994). The table represents a partial taxonomic analysis of text data related to places.

The data summarized in Table 9.2 arose as part of an ethnographic study of an 85-bed residential facility for boys adjudicated delinquent. The ethnographic study was part of a larger multimethod study that included longitudinal follow-up, psychological testing, behavior observation, and other methods of data collection. The ethnographic portion of the study was undertaken in part as a response to anomalous numeric data concerning attrition (Cournoyer, 1994).

Table 9.2 is organized around the semantic relationship "is a place in." Domain analysis of a transcript of a tour guide's description and several ethnographic interviews are the source of the included terms. After careful rereading of the text, several clusters of folk terms and cover terms are identified. "Roberts, Colgate, Litchfield East, Litchfield West, Hartford East, Hartford West" are names of cottages where boys live. Within each of these are several types of rooms ("are places within cottages"). Consulting maps, visiting the buildings, and examining more text suggested the relationships represented in Table 9.2. The terms for the smallest places are contained at the far right and moving right to left is moving to cover terms for larger (more general) place names. Some of the included terms for very small spaces or repetitive terms have been excluded from the extreme right

TABLE 9.2   Taxonomic Analysis of Place Data on a Residential Campus

North Campus	Cottages	Colgate Hartford W. Hartford E. Litchfield Mendenhall W. Mendenhall E. Roberts	All cottages have a rec room, kitchen, shower, activity room, laundry, bedrooms, visiting room, storage room, staff room. Lots of public areas and few private.
	School	Classrooms Trade Shops Auditorium Circular Stair Infirmary Courtyard Town Hall Library	One academic classroom per cottage, trade suites including classrooms, shop areas, offices, and storage. The auditorium complex contains back stage, stage, seating, and kitchen. The infirmary contains a waiting room, nurse office, hospital room, and supply room.
South Campus	Cafeteria	Dining Room Kitchen Storage Offices	Tables, salad bar, tray return, foyer service, cooking, and cleaning areas. Walk-in freezers, basement. Manager's office, chef's office.
	Administration 1	Clerical Floor Supervisor Offices Business Office Attic	Secretaries, coffee, and meeting rooms. Gary, Chuck, Bernie, Laurie, and Bob. Visiting psychiatrists' offices. Evaluation, copiers, petty cash.
	Administration 2	Executive Offices Director's Office Conference Room Maintainance	Personnel, public relations, executive director, receptionist, and board room. Maintainance in basement.
	Activities Area	Gym Athletic fields Tennis Courts Pond Ski Lift Family Service	Pool, basketball court, and offices. Soccer field, baseball field, and track. Offices, meeting rooms, and family room.
East Campus	Vocational Agriculture	Director's Residence Produce Stand Barn Outbuildings Fields	Unknown. Storage, service counter, and scale. Large animal areas. Tools, tractors, trucks, and plows. Flowers, corn, tomatoes, and pumpkins.
	Apartments	Worker Apartments	Unknown.

column. For example, within every cottage, there are five different kinds of rooms where very different activities are conducted. Likewise, the cafeteria kitchen contains four distinct areas: serving areas, cooking areas, food-storage areas, and dishwashing areas. These fine distinctions are not included in the branching format of the rest of the table because the emphasis of this particular table is on the large places. These data are used to structure studies of how boys experienced these spaces and the smaller spaces in their immediate environments. The decision concerning how finely to pursue terms with slightly different meanings (or small spaces within larger ones) involves considering the salience of the distinctions and the focus of the research. A study that focused on cottage life or the worldview of a single client might have included smaller spaces, right down to the foot of the bed, where one boy spent as much time as possible.

Some of the cover terms contained in the table are folk terms and others are expressed in the language of the researcher. For example, very different kinds of activities occurred in the places designated in Table 9.2 as "North Campus" and "East Campus," but the social workers had no fixed terms for these places. They would say "Up by the school" (North Campus) or "On the farm" (around the vocational/agricultural building). "North and East Campus" were chosen by the researcher to facilitate communication with an audience outside of the agency, but agency social workers immediately understood the designation and generally agreed to the folk terms included in each.

Terms made up by the researcher are sometimes called **analytic cover terms** as opposed to folk cover terms that are actually found in informants' text and speech. In the context of social work tasks where our goal may include empowering individuals and groups through better awareness of self, the imposition of analytic categories may be of intervention value by pointing out domain relationships that have not yet reached the level of folk terms. It is important to note that the absence of a folk cover term does not necessarily imply a lack of salience of the domains or the imposition of the worldview of the observer. For example, Rohner and Cournoyer (1994) demonstrated that despite the occasional absence of folk terms that correspond to the concept "parental acceptance/rejection," the domain was recognizable in eight distinct linguistic and cultural groups. Another reason for employing analytic cover terms when folk cover terms are not available is that the analytic cover terms may be useful to the audience for whom the report is intended. The key is to be clear concerning the terms that are folk and those that are analytic.

Tables such as 9.2 are only one possible way to present a taxonomic analysis. The data contained in the table may also be expressed as a map. Line and node organizational charts are also excellent ways of representing some taxonomies. Likewise, an outline, such as the table of contents in this book, expresses the relationships in a simple domain. The format that is chosen largely reflects the relationships that underlie the domains. Maps work well when the relationships between domains are defined in terms of space. Taxonomies involving status hierarchies and other forms of interpersonal influence can be expressed in various ways including the line and node charts mentioned earlier. Whatever the technique selected, the key is to show how each domain relates to others.

Taxonomies of steps in a process might be better expressed in a flowchart diagram, such as the client pathway illustrated in Figure 9.1 on page 216. The figure represents the logic of a transitional housing program for homeless teens. The program was housed in a large multiservice agency that primarily provided case management services. After extensive review of documents and interviews with social workers on staff, a model close to that in the figure was created and reviewed with the staff. Although the staff had seen nothing like the diagram before, they quickly identified the flow of their program, corrected some misunderstandings, and entered into an animated discussion of the gaps between how they wished the program to work (as shown in the final model) and how it actually worked. The diagram served not only as a useful tool for helping the evaluators (Porteous & Cournoyer, 1994) to understand the program, it also helped identify departures from the original program concept, showed how these were related to client needs, and provided a model around which a quantitative study of decision making and outcomes could be mounted. We return to the use of client flow diagrams when we discuss testing generalizability of abstractions.

If you are beginning to think that you could spend a lot of time developing domains and taxonomies, you are correct. Ongoing ethnography at the residential facility for boys adjudicated as delinquent has led to the discovery of hundreds of domains and created taxonomies in areas such as "ways boys get into trouble," "ways boys work the program," "how boys get on alert," "stages in completing a referral," and many more. Because the goal of that project is broadly focused ethnography, the study produces large amounts of nonnumerical data in order to stay as close to the subjects' actual experience as possible. Under such conditions, it makes little sense to quickly foreclose the disciplined intellectual process of data reduction by identifying only the superficial or otherwise obvious domains. However, the analyses of social workers concerned with problem specifications from client perspectives may find a more focused analysis useful and less overwhelming. Just how comprehensive you become is a function of need, time, and your judgment on how adequately you have summarized the text .

The point of taxonomic analyses such as these is that they are intended to help organize and reduce a large volume of observations into a symbol system that conveys the meaning system of the informant. Keep in mind that such tables generally do not exist prior to the researcher creating them. With the exception of formal organizations, the relationships described in taxonomies are embedded in the words of the text, not often literally described. It is also important to understand that the taxonomies are abstractions of the text and comprise an approximation of the implicit knowledge of some group or individual. The inclusion of both folk and analytic terms should make it clear that this form of data reduction is interpretative and analytic. To the extent that the domains and taxonomies arise from actual text data, they are likely to be meaningful and grounded, but are interpretations nonetheless.

The significance of taxonomies and domains as interpretations is that they, like means and standard deviations (and other descriptive statistics), represent abstractions of data sets, not the individuals studied in any direct sense. That is, a

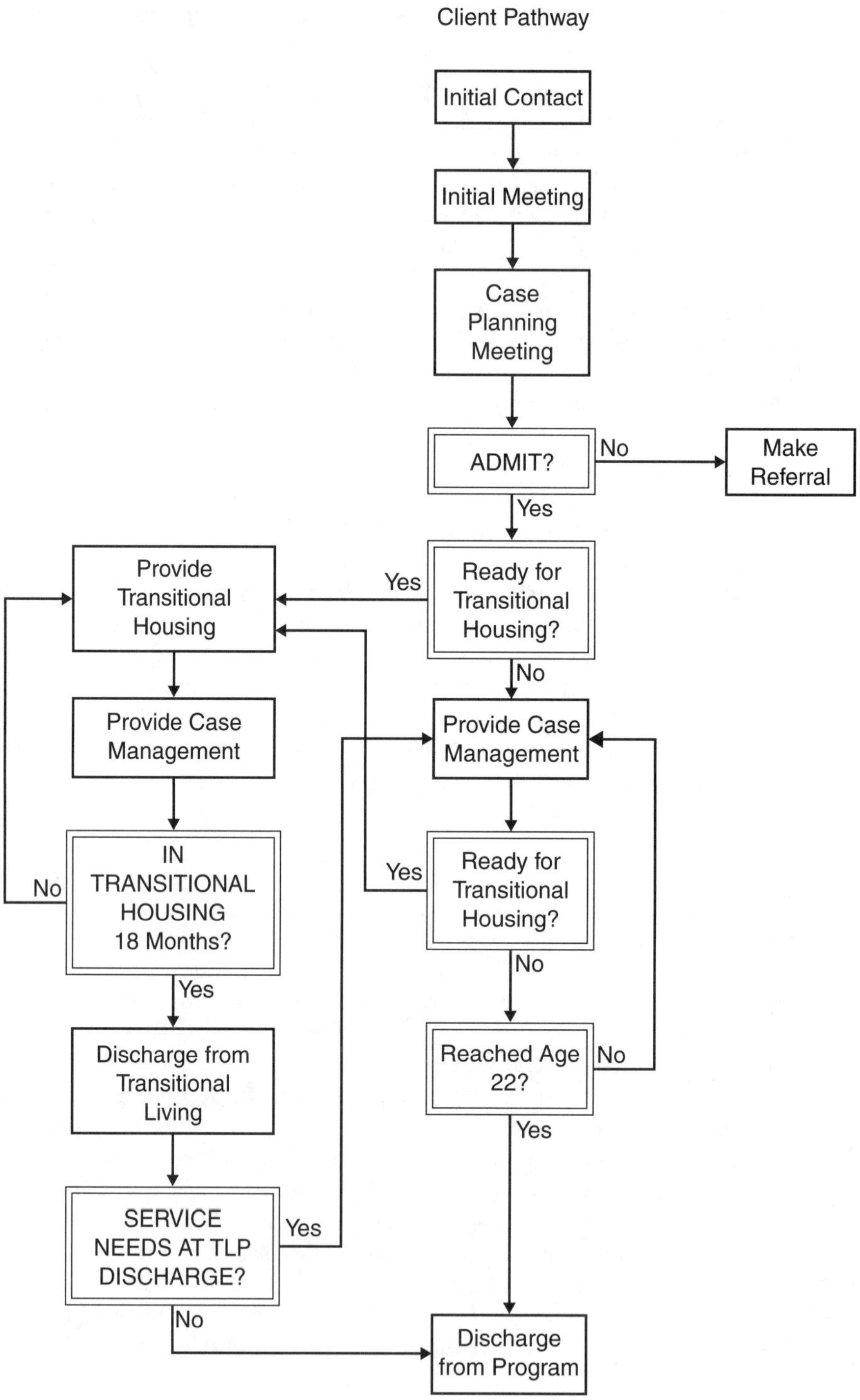

FIGURE 9.1   Client Pathway

Source: Adapted from Porteous, D. P., & Cournoyer, D. E. (1994). *Process evaluation report of the transitional living program.* Marlborough, CT: Global Associates.

cluster of buildings with a material existence does exist in a certain area. However, the existence of a place called North Campus is a matter of abstraction. The danger of reification of cover terms, the domains, and taxonomies is great, and no less troublesome than assuming that a test score represents a direct measurement of something "real." If we do a good job of taxonomic analysis, what we have is an approximation of the mental categories of our informants.

Reduction of text data tends to be accomplished in several stages. As the volume of data resulting from an exploratory study grows, some authors (Yin, 1994) suggest thinking about the data as including separate databases. Although Yin identifies two databases in case studies, we find it useful to think of three databases. First is the raw database, reflecting observations with little abstracting and generalizing. As much as possible, the language of this database is that of the people being observed. This would include documents, audio tapes, video tapes, transcripts, photographs, and verbatim quotes in logs and journals. The second database contains the products of data analysis, such as taxonomic tables and charts and perhaps narrative summaries. Although linked to the raw data by the use of systematic procedures, the analysis database consists of abstractions of the raw data and contains more of the language of the investigator. The third and final database consists of the formal report. The report is written in the language of the intended audience for the report. The point here is that the first two databases are intended to help the researcher to think and reason about the phenomenon under study and the last consists of translations that facilitate communication with the intended audience. Table 9.2 reduced a very large volume of place data contained in narratives and facilitated further analysis, but it is unlikely that it will be included, except by reference, in a final report. The logic behind thinking in terms of these three databases is to preserve the chain of evidence from the highest-order generalizations in the formal report through the analytic database and back to the raw narratives.

Taxonomic analysis is not greatly different from what goes on in the assessment phase of direct practice with individuals or stakeholder analyses associated with program planning and evaluation. In both cases, it is desirable to obtain an understanding of the worldview of an individual or group of individuals. Understanding how individuals or collectives organize their thinking about relevant domains (client goals, agency goals) is an essential element of practice. However, organizing text into domains and taxonomies is only the beginning of nonnumerical analysis. Whereas the domains and taxonomies tell us what goes together, other forms of analysis, such as componential analysis, help us to understand the values and basic concerns that lead to the taxonomies and a deeper understanding of the meaning systems of another. Let us turn our attention to this process.

Componential Analysis.   **Componential analysis** is the search for attributes on which domains are based, usually through the examination of contrasts. Componential analysis starts with domain and taxonomic analyses described before. Taxonomies reveal meaning categories and the clustering of terms within the category, but do not provide explanation or confirmation of the distinctiveness of the many domains. In componential analysis, the domains are reexamined for clues concerning the attributes that are used to sort experiences into separate domains in the taxonomy. These attributes provide the comparison sets through which people absorb information into existing categories or create new ones. The attributes that are detected are believed to reflect the values and concerns of the individual or group under study, what Spradley (1980) called cultural themes.

Componential analysis is conducted by starting with as many domains and taxonomies as are available and looking for the ways in which the domains differ. For example, in the ethnography of the residential facility, we noted that many of the domains in our list reflected differences between school programs and cottage life. Domains concerning activities, actors, time, and values all had separate groupings for cottage life or school life. At the root of many of these groupings was the distinction "PGI is easy to implement here." PGI stands for positive group interaction, the treatment modality of the facility. Informants also identified cottage life as a place where PGI takes place most easily and trade school as the place where PGI is most difficult to implement. This tendency to set up contrasts based on the ability to implement PGI helped identify an important cultural theme and identify a set of values concerning how youths and staff should act. Several informants noted an almost religious fervor concerning the PGI treatment model.

Componential analysis is a powerful technique in that while looking broadly and holistically at all the domains, it tends to reveal a few very simple, but powerful ideas through which the cultural scene is organized. This activity is consistent with several of our themes for nonnumerical data analysis, providing both data reduction and new insights concerning pattern identification.

In summary, domain analysis, taxonomic analysis, and componential analyses serve the tasks of both data reduction and pattern identification. Domain and taxonomic analyses primarily organize and reduce large amounts of text data, but also begin the process of identification of how concepts are the same and different. Componential analysis takes this process further, to a more general level by looking for patterns that account for the existence of the terms and relationships between them.

Testing for Generalization

In the context of nonnumeric data, particularly the kind of exploratory data described here, generalization refers to the extent to which the domains, taxonomies, and themes and values correctly reflect the way meaning is drawn from experience, either across time and situation or across individuals. Theoretically, once the domains and taxonomies are developed, it is possible to conduct a sampling survey and determine the extent to which cover terms, domains, taxonomies, patterns, and themes are shared across individuals. Such measures would be examples of what Yin (1994) called statistical generalizability. However, such an analysis would not answer questions concerning the completeness of the domains, taxonomies, and themes or the range of experiences to which they might apply. What then does generalization mean in the context of such a discovery process?

The products of a nonnumerical data analysis (domains, taxonomies, patterns, and themes) conducted on data collected for exploratory purposes have good generalization qualities when they present a worldview that is recognizable and reasonable to a competent member of the group being described. That is, the domains may not apply equally to all persons, situations, places, and so on, but every person should be able to identify the kind of persons to whom they should apply and verify that the rules make cultural sense. Likewise, generalization of inferred meaning categories outside of observed situations or with different populations requires that the meaning schemes be meaningful, not invariant. The measure is not how many individuals can correctly reproduce a taxonomic analysis, but in how many respects someone found the analysis to be complete or accurate. Obviously, errors in higher-order generalizations such as distinguishing attributes identified through componential analysis are more important than minor differences in the classification of terms.

This idea of generalization as "goodness of fit" of the structure is close to the meaning of the term "analytic generalizability" that Yin (1994) used to describe external validity in case studies. The key point is that in the context of exploratory nonnumerical data, we are not looking for statistical uniformity across some sample of individuals or events, or equal access to all the knowledge domains, but a recognition that the pattern of thought and implied action makes cultural sense (or individual sense in the context of single-system case studies).

Participant Observation and Analysis of Social Mistakes.   A useful approach to confirmation of analytic generalizability is a variant on the translation/back-translation method used in cross-cultural test validation. The translation/back-translation procedure for test validation involves two translations. First, a person translates from the original language to a new one. To verify that the translation was meaningful and accurate, the material is translated a second time, this time from the new language back to the original. Comparison of differences between the original version and the final translation is used to determine if the meanings have been retained and are likely to be correctly interpreted. In the context of nonnumerical data analysis, a process similar to back-translation occurs when the results of the analysis are subjected to verification by key informants or additional observation. This process is what precipitates the cyclical and feedback character of nonnumerical data analysis, particularly in exploratory contexts.

Participant observers have long used a "walking-around" version of the translation/back-translation process to test their culture learning. As the participant observer uncovers cultural patterns, the level of participation is likely to become more culturally competent, allowing the participant observer to move in more socially graceful ways and minimize social gaffs. Social workers pay careful note to their successes and failures as they apply their translated cultural knowledge, gaining perspective on the range of situations and individuals for whom the constructed principles work. Analysis of the nature of social blunders of the participant observer can provide insight into the analytic generalizability of inferred meaning and behavior categories. Thus, a narrative record, or journal, of the consequences of applying the acquired cultural knowledge in a variety of settings would be a good indication of the generalizability of abstractions made from the data.

Story Writing. A variant on the walking-around method is to attempt to create stories (text) involving lifelike persons in culturally relevant situations by using domains and taxonomies abstracted from data. Next, informants are asked if the stories are lifelike, and if not, where they are wrong. These data can be used to fine-tune the analysis. Remember, however, such schemes are intended to verify a goodness of fit between the inferred meaning systems and the implicit ways of knowing of the informants rather than obtaining perfect agreement on the accuracy of the inferred meaning systems. The level of correction offered by the informant is important. Revisions that only involve the most personal or minute corrections would be evidence of analytic generalizability in that the general theme or principle evidenced by the story is left intact and, presumably, correct.

As mentioned previously, the client path diagram contained in Figure 9.1 was used as part of an evaluation of a program for homeless youth. It arose in part out of the confusion of the evaluators concerning the boundaries of the particular program being evaluated (the Transitional Living Program) and other agency activities. The process of drafting this figure, reviewing it with staff, and ultimately with clients produced strong evidence of analytic generalizability, as well as substantial deviations in actual practice. As a complex, adapting system, it seemed unreasonable to assume that the agency would precisely match any particular model, so some degree of slippage was expected from this fact alone. However, statements like "Yes, this is basically what we are trying to do, but we have never seen it expressed like this" were common responses. Likewise, when interviewing clients, not all went through the steps of this flow model. For example, many clients self-discharged when they were able to arrange their own housing. These anomalies did not reflect failures of the program or the model, but the existence of the model helped place the exceptions in relief.

Ethnographic Decision-Tree Modeling. Another example of testing generality of principles inferred from nonnumeric data is presented by Gladwin (1989) in the context of her book on **ethnographic decision-tree modeling.** Gladwin shows that the "choice behavior" of individuals often can be represented in decision trees that demonstrate how values and beliefs are used to arrive at decisions. Figure 9.2 is an application of Gladwin's approach to the agency decisions to pursue or not pursue grants. The data were collected to facilitate a board level review of decision making at a private, nonprofit human service agency. The board had just undertaken a revision of its mission statement and service objectives and was concerned with the coherence of the document and its relationship to actual decision making. The model was drawn by reviewing documents and interviewing senior staff. The resulting model was first reviewed with the executive director, modified, tested against actual decisions, modified again, and then used to facilitate discussion of decision making by a subcommittee of the governing board.

The diagram suggests that the decision to apply or not apply for a particular grant is the consequence of applying a series of "if-then" rules and options. In this

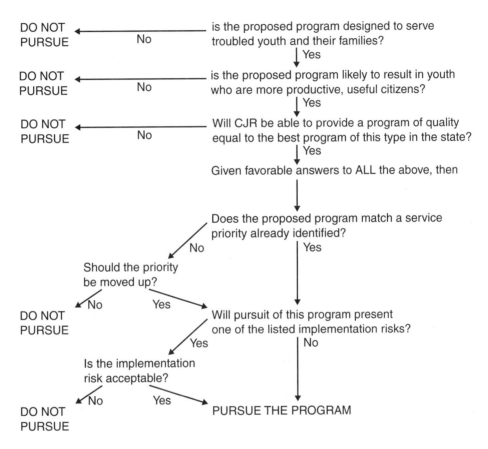

FIGURE 9.2   **Decision-Tree Model**

case, the agency seemed to use three exclusionary criteria, any of which would lead to a "do not pursue" decision related to a grant. However, proposals that passed these three criteria might still not be pursued if they failed to match a current service priority or presented unacceptable implementation risks. The details of the decision processes related to service priorities and implementation risks are complex decision trees in their own right that were not reproduced here.

Gladwin (1989) suggests that the generalizability of decision-tree models can be tested by applying the models to predict behavior that will occur in natural settings. In practice, one could interview a person after a decision was made to determine if the model produces the same conclusion as a real person or analyze new case data to see if the actual behavior agrees with the actions predicted by the decision tree. Alternatively, one could predict the action in advance when the knowledge base of the actors is clear and then observe the actual choice. Gladwin

suggests expressing the model in a computer program to protect against unconscious tendencies to "fudge" the results. Such tests could be very rigorous and
include data from different populations or different persons at different times to
test the generality of the models.

For example, the decision tree in Figure 9.2 was modified several times in
response to data supplied by informants. The ethnographer examined accounts of
actual decisions, interviewed teams who had just made the decisions, and asked
about outcomes and the facts related to the decision rules. When early versions of
the decision tree failed to reproduce actual decisions, a cycle of fact finding and
clarification was initiated. Interestingly, this cycle revealed both misunderstandings on the part of the investigator and inconsistencies between actual practice
and official policy. The decision-tree modeling approach and the approaches to
verifying the models are also relevant to micropractice settings such as child welfare decisions, residential placement, admission, discharge, and the like.

Testing Propositions and Theories.   The use of decision-tree modeling to test
compliance with policy clearly moves our discussion of data analysis into the
domain of testing propositions and theories. As we noted in Chapter 5 ("Research
Designs"), testing propositions is a holistic process that involves all aspects of the
inquiry, not just numerical significance tests. Such tests would be meaningless
unless certain properties of the measurement, sampling, data collection, and data
analysis process could be assumed. When those conditions are met, as they often
may be in the case of nonnumerical data, the results of the analysis can be applied
to the task of testing propositions. The test of a theory lies not in a statistical significance test, but the rigor of the whole process of inquiry. For example, the
decision-tree model in Figure 9.2 was intended to answer questions concerning
the consistency between official policy and action. Since the decision-tree model
was judged to represent agency policy reasonably well, it was possible to use the
decision tree to test the proposition that agency policy and agency action were
congruent. In another context, a client pathway diagram, contained in Figure 9.1,
which describes the expected path through which clients were to proceed from
admission to discharge, was used both as a descriptive tool and also to test the
proposition that a particular program was implemented in a way consistent with
contract specifications (Porteous & Cournoyer, 1994). In that case, an intervention
model implicit in the initial program funding application was compared to the
client pathway for consistency. This was a strong, grounded way to make generalizations concerning the congruence between the program promised and the program delivered from a service delivery perspective.

Summary

Analysis of nonnumeric data of an exploratory nature tends to proceed in minicycles of data collection, analysis, more collection, and more analysis. This refinement cycle is rooted in the exploratory process. Like numerical data analysis, the

success of data collection is based on the quality of the steps that have gone before, specifically the conditions under which the data were collected and the resulting validity and reliability of the observations. Domain, taxonomic, and componential analyses are rigorous methods of data reduction and pattern identification. By rigorous, we mean those techniques that are based on logical operations performed on data that maintain the critical link between abstractions and the observations on which they are based. The attributes of text data that are captured in this form of analysis include domains, taxonomies, and themes. It is useful to think of analysis of nonnumerical data containing three collections: raw text in the language of the persons under study; analytic text consisting of domain, taxonomic, and componential analyses, and process notes that reflect the language of the observer; and a final report that is written in the language of the stakeholders. Nonnumerical data are appropriate for testing various propositions, and it is possible to estimate the generalizability of abstractions from nonnumerical data. However, the products of the kinds of analyses discussed here are not appropriately subjected to tests of statistical generalizability, but rather analytic generalizability. Analytic generalizability refers to the extent to which the representations of meaning-systems constructed by the observer are congruent with the meaning assigning activities of the groups from which the text is obtained.

10 Practice Evaluation in Single and Multiple Systems

Balancing Rigor and Reality

Relationship of This Chapter to the Whole

This chapter explores application of the scientific method to practice evaluation. By evaluation, we mean the empirical study of social work intervention, including exploring the dimensions of **target problems,** monitoring service, delivery process, and examination of impact of interventions. In this chapter, you will see how the techniques presented in other chapters are applied in the context of the roles of social workers as evaluators of interventions with individuals and other single systems, and also conducting evaluations across multiple systems.

Practice evaluation requires a balance between the need for rigorous technique and limitations provided by the sociocultural situations in which the evaluation is conducted. Many of the approaches to evaluation based on laboratory research models run into serious implementation problems on either ethical or practical grounds. For example, experimental designs are desirable approaches to evaluation of the impact of programs because they provide the strongest inference. However, experiments require what is often an unrealistic degree of control over the lives of participants. Withholding treatment from a control group provides important protection against threats to internal validity, but in many cases, raises serious ethical and practical problems in the field. The best evaluations manage to overcome such obstacles, but the resulting designs may show the results of necessary compromises. We prefer to think of research design for evaluation as an exercise in damage control concerning sources of distortion and error rather than pursuing some ideal design. Strong designs are used to limit the impact of sources of error that are most likely to be operating, and thoughtful data collection and analysis are used to estimate the effects of other sources of error that could not be controlled. Doing this well requires a full complement of research skills and a degree of creativity in putting them all together.

Balancing **rigor** and practical limitations basically comes down to compromising on design in ways that introduce the least distortion into the evaluation. A randomized control group may not be feasible, but a matched control from a waiting list may work, if coupled with post hoc analyses of potentially important differences that could not be matched. Is the **matched control strategy** logically as strong as the randomly assigned control group? No. However, it provides some protection from some sources of error and is often ethically and practically more acceptable than random assignment. Sometimes the effects of potential sources of distortion and error can be estimated in the data analysis phase of a study. For example, in a study in which the characteristics of the interviewer have potential to bias responses, it would be possible to compare the pattern of responses across interviewers to estimate this effect. Likewise, if changes in the environment, such as public awareness campaigns, may interact with interventions, monitoring those campaigns and participants' awareness of them could allow any effects to be estimated, if not controlled, by the use of a randomly assigned control group. Evaluation occurs in a different social context than does academic knowledge building research, and it is frequently not possible or even desirable to set up rigidly controlled settings needed to set up some research designs. Conducting rigorous, ethical, and useful evaluation requires advanced planning, an eyes-open approach while the evaluation is in process, and flexibility. The key here is to have a large cache of tools so that you not only know what is optimal from a logical standpoint for any evaluation question, but also have enough alternatives so that you can navigate the maze of obstacles with a workable plan intact.

In applied settings such as evaluation, nearly every decision about research methods is tempered by sociocultural forces. For example, in evaluation research, changing roles and cultural preoccupations strongly influence our conceptualizations of target problems and interventions. The ability to negotiate with various stakeholders concerning events to measure that reflect shared goals is an important part of the conceptualization process that tends not to be taught in traditional social science research curriculums.

Conceptualization of real-world social problems involves choosing measures that not only meet scientific concerns of reliability and validity, but also are credible to the decision makers who use the results of the evaluation. Principles of sampling tell us that the times, events, and units that we examine need to be selected with care to assure that they are representative of the phenomena of interest. However, access to clients and clients' time is not controlled by social scientists, but clients' and service providers' own needs and concerns. Evaluators, whether time sampling the experience of an individual client or choosing multiple individuals for a multiclient evaluation, must find a balance between the desire for the most representative sample and ethical dilemmas, costs, intrusiveness, and timeliness.

The designs used are also subject to the demands of the social setting in which the evaluation is conducted. Many designs are excellent for discovering the unexpected consequences of service delivery, but lack the rigor necessary to conclusively establish the value of interventions. More rigorous designs may be better at assessing specific kinds of impact, but miss unexpected consequences. Likewise, the actual **social settings for data collection** also need to be chosen to match the demands of the questions being addressed. The choice of in-person interviews, questionnaires, assessment inventories, or other techniques depends on what is able to be done in a particular context, as on the desire to choose the most rigorous approach. Even data analysis looks different from the perspective of evaluation. Often, evaluators conduct detailed data analyses to assure themselves of what the data show, but then conduct simple, straightforward analyses that can be easily communicated to stakeholders. Ethical considerations dictate that we involve stakeholders in both the conceptualization of target problems and evaluation of the results of interventions. All of this needs to be conducted in a sociopolitical context that balances the needs for a rigorous scientific approach with the need to maximize relevance and minimize cost and intrusion.

In this chapter, we show how the scientific techniques discussed earlier in the book can be applied to questions related to practice evaluation. Although evaluations seldom address only one class of questions, for instructional purposes, we have divided this chapter into two main subsections. The first subsection discusses practice evaluations that focus on interventions in single systems, such as a single-client system or a program as a whole. The second subsection deals with practice evaluations that attempt to make generalizations across multiple systems. This type of evaluation would include the multiple-client comparison type of evaluation or evaluations that conduct comparisons over samples of complex systems such as communities, programs, and the like.

Application of This Chapter to the Roles of Social Workers

Social workers are trained to practice in systems of all sizes and may focus primarily on single systems in some contexts, across multiple-client systems in others, and are required by the NASW *Code of Ethics* to evaluate their practice in both contexts. Direct work with families and individuals are examples of practice focused on a single small system. Community organizing in a single community and monitoring the development of a single program are also examples of a single-system focus, but this time the system is a large complex entity. On the other hand, policy and planning contexts often involve addressing problems across two or more systems, such as developing estimates of the incidence of social problems or estimating the typical impact of various intervention types. Although we see much in common between single-system and multisystem evaluations, they differ in important ways. Evaluations in the context of single systems generally include a strong interest in an understanding of the uniqueness of the client system in question. Multiple-client system evaluations, conversely, tend to have as a primary interest generalizing across what is common in all the client systems observed. One result of this is that either type of focus produces a limited picture of the intervention of interest. Single-client system evaluations tend to be strongly grounded, sensitive, and holistic, but weak on generalizability and sometimes internal validity. Multiple-client system evaluations are potentially much stronger in some kinds of external and internal validity, but much less likely to be grounded and sensitive to the unique elements of individual systems. These differences arise in part from the nature of the questions asked, but also from differences in preferred research methods. The practicing social worker must recognize these differences and apply evaluative techniques that are appropriate to the task at hand. When conducting evaluations that ask if individual client's states have been favorably altered by an intervention (single-system impact studies), one of the most advanced approaches applied at the small-system level is the single-subject design (Bloom, Fischer, & Orme, 1999). These designs can also be applied to evaluations of single large systems, such as a single program or a community, if the questions are about system-level outcomes. In evaluations involving multiple systems, in which each system is an individual, the most advanced designs used in impact studies are the randomized experiments or quasi-experiments (Rossi & Freeman, 1993). From previous chapters, single-system designs don't have strong safeguards concerning sampling bias, but experimental designs tend to be less sensitive to client-specific differences and may introduce artificial contexts that undermine external validity. These two different classes of designs also require different skills of the social worker, place different levels of demand on client/participants, and require differing levels of resources.

The competent professional social worker needs to be able to conduct evaluations applicable to the systems' sizes and configurations (single or multiple) with which he or she regularly practices and also must be able to critically consume evaluations of systems of any size. This range of skill is necessary to meet the professional obligation to be able to both evaluate one's own practice and also critically appraise claims concerning interventions with various other systems that may influence client success. This chapter serves as an introduction to both.

Learning Objectives

After reading this chapter, you will be able to:

1. define three points of evaluations: problem identification, service monitoring, and impact evaluations

2. define and describe the importance of rigorous methods, stakeholder involvement, setting goals and standards for interventions, and tailoring evaluations to decision contexts
3. describe use of the single-system design in small single-system evaluation
4. describe the use of causal, intervention, and client pathway models in evaluation of large, complex single systems
5. describe the application of experiments and quasi-experiments in multisystem evaluations

Key Terms and Concepts

General Issues in Evaluation Research

Similarities between Single- and Multiple-System Evaluations.   Although it may be easier to learn about evaluation by treating single- and multiple-system evaluations separately, we see much in common in the evaluation of intervention with single-client systems and the evaluation of programs that involve comparison across multiple-client systems. In both cases, the focus of the evaluation tends to fall in one of three categories: (1) problem identification, (2) monitoring service delivery, or (3) impact evaluation. **Problem identification,** sometimes called needs assessment at the multiple-system level, or simply assessment at the single-system level, seeks to synthesize a view of the target problem, both conceptually and empirically. That is, needs assessment involves determining how to identify, describe, and prioritize problems within systems (conceptualization) and determining empirically the current state of the system with regard to one or more problems. The epidemiological study is an example of a problem identification type of evaluation at the multisystem level and the assessment phase of a single-system design is the parallel form in a single-system evaluation.

Monitoring service delivery is an evaluation focus intended to document delivery of the intervention. At a small single-system level, monitoring focuses on what was transferred from the helper to the client. Monitoring services or "effort" at the single-subject/small system level (Bloom, Fischer, & Orme, 1999) consists primarily of recording the range of activities that make up the intervention and perhaps time, money, or other appropriate indicators of the intervention. At a multisystem level, monitoring may focus on typical patterns of service across many individuals, including the appropriateness of the population served/not served, matches between policy and actual delivery patterns, and even similarities and differences in response to intervention.

Impact evaluation questions typically ask how persons bearing the target problem fared following the intervention. As mentioned earlier, the single-system design (Bloom, Fischer, & Orme, 1999) is a rigorous approach to conducting impact studies in single systems. Experimental and quasi-experimental designs provide very good inference in multisystem evaluation (Rossi & Freeman, 1993). The point of all this is that although the size of the system and the focus on individual system or multisystem comparisons all constrain the type of design used, evaluation activity can be generally conceptualized as composed of needs assessment, monitoring, and impact assessment. Not every practice evaluation focuses on all three. However, it should be possible to conceptualize a particular evaluation in terms of those activities that are of greatest interest.

Consensus has not been reached concerning a best way of approaching different evaluation questions. The size of the system, single-system versus multisystem focus, and interest in needs assessment, monitoring, or impact all influence the approach that is likely to yield the most useful results. Table 10.1 shows various combinations of evaluation interests and some common design approaches. For example, needs assessment in a small single system consisting of an individual or family is generally the purview of a clinically oriented professional and involves application of appropriate clinical diagnostic and assessment procedures that focus on both the individual and immediate environments. When the focus is on needs assessment in a single complex entity such as a formal organization, **systems analysis** provides useful approaches to conceptualizing needs and current states (Harrison, 1994) in terms of system characteristics. Such an analysis may focus on characteristics of systems believed to determine the capacity for systems to function and endure.

Needs assessment in multisystem contexts is about generating population estimates concerning the target problem. **Quantitative/descriptive studies** are often used to calculate population estimates of incidence and prevalence of target problems when the comparisons are across a large number of small systems (e.g., individuals). The **comparative-case study method** (Yin, 1994) may be useful in needs assessment across large multiple systems.

Monitoring involves other evaluative techniques. Case-study methods (Yin, 1994) are useful in monitoring service delivery, in both small and large single-system evaluations. In contrast, monitoring service delivery across a large number

TABLE 10.1 Addressing Various Evaluation Questions across and within Systems

Number and Size of System(s)	Focus of the Evaluation		
	Assessing Need	**Monitoring Delivery**	**Assessing Impact**
Single small-system (client)	Diagnostic assessment	Case study	Single-system designs (SSDs)
Single large-system (agency)	Systems analysis	Case study	Single-system designs
Small multisystem comparisons	Quantitative/ descriptive studies	Quantitative/ descriptive studies	Experiments or quasi-experiments
Large multisystem comparisons	Comparative case studies	Quantitative/ descriptive studies	quasi-experiments

of individual clients (i.e., small multiple systems) tends to take advantage of existing billing and recording systems within agencies or pooled across many agencies. These tend to be quantitative descriptive studies.

Both **case studies** and single-system designs (Bloom, Fischer, & Orme, 1999) are useful in assessing intervention impacts within a single system regardless of system size. Finally, impact studies that seek to generalize to populations tend to use experiments if the focus is on individuals, quasi-experiments, or secondary data analysis such as meta-analyses when the systems of interest are large.

These three points for evaluations—problem identification, monitoring service delivery, and impact evaluation—tend to run the full scientific cycle, from induction to deduction, regardless of system size. The problem identification form of evaluation tends to be mostly inductive, attempting to define and capture both the expected and unexpected in a target problem. In small systems, this means developing a sense of client concerns and potentials for change within the context of a client's immediate social system. In multiple-system evaluation, problem identification tends to focus on similarities across individuals, such as characteristics common to persons who have a target program and uncommon in those who do not. Monitoring activities, particularly in large-system evaluations, require a combination of inductive and deductive processes. Monitoring is inductive when used to synthesize an intervention model or client pathway. Monitoring is deductive when seeking to confirm the conformity of an intervention with specifications. Impact evaluation tends to be largely deductive, focusing assessing the contribution of the intervention to changes in the states of targets. In single systems, the deduction involves generalization of outcomes seen over a short time or in a narrow context of the client's life to other time periods and perhaps other contexts. In multiple-system evaluation, the deduction involves testing principles believed to generalize across individuals despite individual differences.

Despite the existence of different technologies for studying single systems or conducting studies that compare the impact of interventions across systems, it is not uncommon for the objectives and methods of both single- and multiple-system evaluation to be combined in a single evaluation. For example, single-system designs, both small and large, tend to focus primarily on the uniqueness of a particular system. However, increasingly, practitioners are encouraged to collect and review the results of single-system evaluations to see what information of a more general nature can be gleaned from cross-case analyses (Bloom, Fischer, & Orme, 1999; Yin, 1994). Some experts in large single-system case studies (Yin, 1994) propose to improve generalizability of single-system designs by selecting illustrative cases in a way reminiscent of purposive sampling. Likewise, many evaluations that are multiple-system-focused, such as quantitative studies of program outcomes in populations of clients, may also examine macro characteristics of the agency as a single case or may also include a few single-system evaluations to help keep conclusions grounded in the experiences of real people. Thus, the report of a multisystem study may include a qualitative, single-case profile describing the agency as an entity, a single-system study of a particular client placing agency intervention into the context of an individual client served, and a mass of statistical data examining population trends in response to the program. Such a collection is far more likely to meet the needs of multiple stakeholders and also provide a more balanced perspective on the entity being evaluated.

In summary, in evaluation of practice, as in other forms of scientific inquiry, the focus must be on reducing the impact of threats to clear inference. Applied research in natural settings places constraints on how the impact of threats to inference can be reduced. Good evaluation design is based on determining the focus of the evaluation and consideration of threats that are pertinent to that focus. Single-system evaluations focus primarily within the system and are less likely to control for representativeness of the system studied. Cross-system evaluations tend to be less likely to focus on the uniqueness in the response of individuals. Some potential threats can be eliminated through good design; other potential sources of error can be estimated through careful data analysis. In general, problem identification evaluations tend to be exploratory and inductive, whereas impact studies tend to be deductive.

Stakeholders.   Conducting evaluations requires careful attention to the values of the various stakeholders who are involved in the intervention or its impact. By **stakeholders,** we mean the person or groups of persons who can expect to be influenced by the success or failure of the intervention under study. Even single-client system evaluations are of interest to multiple stakeholders. Typically, stakeholders include persons in the client system(s) served, the person providing the intervention, management of the organization providing the intervention, persons representing one or more organizations that fund the services in question or similar services, the social work profession, and persons from related professions who also have a stake in the evaluation. What is important to know about stakeholders is that they tend to have overlapping conceptualizations of the target problem and often have different interests concerning the findings. Clients tend to want the problems to go away (or become manageable), workers want validation concerning their effectiveness, managers and fund-source representatives may also want validation of their resource allocation decisions, and the profession needs a repository of credible information about what works with what clients under what situations as well as what does not. Compounding this diversity, various stakeholders have different prerogatives and thus use the results of an evaluation in different decision contexts. All these create a complex environment in which evaluation questions are formed and explored.

Contemporary ethical and professional standards require that the perspectives of various stakeholder groups be actively considered in all phases of the evaluation. Program evaluation standards (Sanders, 1994) explicitly include attention to the needs and perspectives of various stakeholders as a standard for multiple system evaluation. Bloom, Fischer, and Orme (1999) make similar observations related to evaluations involving single systems. What all this means is that unless you have reason to believe that you are a genuine representative of all the various stakeholder groups, you are going to need a process for determining how the various parties conceptualize the problem, interventions, outcomes, and expectations.

At the single-system level, this means actively negotiating with persons in the target system about the nature of the target problem, interventions, and desired outcomes. Agency management obviously has a large stake in practice evaluation. In single-system evaluations, management may be involved as part of the process of supervision or through communication of agency standards for evaluation. In the context of multiple-system evaluations, individual clients and management may constitute only two of a large number of stakeholders. Political leaders, fund sources, and other groups may all constitute stakeholders concerning programs. In such a context, it might be necessary to conduct an exploratory survey or a focus group to properly conceptualize variables, establish goals and standards of the evaluation, and identify decision contexts in which the results are applied. We discuss such groups a little later.

Goals and Standards for Interventions.   Expectations concerning the goals of the programs and standards for outcomes are important types of input that can be obtained through actively engaging stakeholders. It never ceases to amaze just how differently various stakeholders conceptualize what a particular intervention is about or what it is expected to produce. In addition to differences in the way a target problem is defined, clients, service providers, fund sources, and other stakeholder groups are likely to define a successful intervention differently. Likewise, the standards through which we determine if the outcomes are adequate are also likely to vary from one class of stakeholder to another. By standards, we refer to expectations concerning what outcomes, under what conditions, and in what form or what quantity would be considered adequate. On ethical (Sanders, 1994) and practical grounds (Bloom, Fischer, & Orme, 1999; Rossi & Freeman, 1993), these differences need to be included in the conceptualizations of evaluations from the start.

The different ideas about both goals and standards across stakeholder groups are generally not as troublesome as a lack of standards. Our overwhelming experience is that service providers seldom have clear conceptualizations concerning what level of reduction in a target problem or what level of positive functioning is indicative of a successful program. What stakeholder groups often do have are very narrowly focused process objectives. Agency staff tend to think about service delivery as outcomes, and foundations and fund sources tend to specify goals in terms of access to service communities. Somewhere in our deliberations with stakeholders, we always ask a question such as: "If all your service objectives were met, what should the target problem look like?" This is where the social work evaluator becomes a change agent as well as an evaluation technician. The process of negotiating for outcomes and standards is one way to help agencies become more conscious of outcomes.

An example of the interplay of stakeholder perspectives can be seen in some recent interactions concerning an after-school arts program. The goal of the school program from the viewpoint of the art staff was to advance interest in the arts among inner-city youth. A foundation supporting the program seemed interested in improving local appreciation of cultural diversity in a multiethnic urban neighborhood. Parents wanted a safe, drug- and violence-free place to leave their children, and the youth wanted some activity to break the boredom of an urban summer. Thus, the goals of the program included fostering good attitudes and knowledge about the arts, expanding cultural awareness and sensitivity, and providing adequate child care and entertainment, depending on who was asked. Additionally, each stakeholder group had different ideas concerning *how much* of their specific outcome of interest constituted an acceptable outcome for the program. The evaluation that was ultimately developed included questions reflecting goals of each group and procedures for allowing participants to assess the adequacy of outcomes from the perspective of their unique expectations. The increased understanding that flows from the active involvement of stakeholders in the conceptual work of designing an evaluation is too precious to squander. Get out, mix it up with the stakeholders! They will undoubtedly teach you a few important lessons that result in evaluations that are more meaningful.

Utility and Feasibility of Evaluations. Professional standards among evaluators require that evaluations be both useful and feasible (Sanders, 1994). The criterion "useful" has two dimensions: First, there must be a reasonable purpose for conducting the evaluation, and, second, the results of the evaluation should be fit for that purpose. The customary way of meeting both criteria is to focus on decision makers and contexts in which the data are used to support the decision-making process and then ensure that the evaluation plan is capable of producing information that meets the decision makers' needs in terms of timeliness, rigor, accuracy, and sensitivity. That is, every piece of data collected must map to a specific decision context and be of adequate quality to support the decision in question. In a single-system design, the decision context might simply be the client and helper deciding whether to continue with an intervention, or to switch, modify, or terminate altogether. At a large-system level, the decision options may be similar and may also include the decision to replicate the intervention elsewhere. The feasibility criterion requires that if the evaluation cannot be completed in a way that matches the needs of decision makers, including timeliness, resources used, and applicability of findings, the evaluation should not be done. Also the cost and intrusiveness of the evaluation should be commensurate with the purposes to which the data are applied. Thus, a single-system evaluation that is very elaborate and time-consuming might not be feasible given the nature of the therapeutic relationship between the helper and client. Likewise, conducting an impact study to influence decisions to fund or not fund a program may not be feasible because of short lead time or other factors.

Rigor of Methods. Although practical and ethical constraints often require considerable compromises in the selection of research techniques in order for an evaluation to meet the criterion of being useful, evaluations must be reasonably rigorous. By rigorous, we are referring to the use of those techniques designed to minimize the impact of errors related to fallacies of human perception and reasoning. It is not necessary for all evaluations to emulate the power to attribute cause in true experiments, but all evaluations require valid and reliable measurements and some reasonable level of external and internal validity.

Here are two practical rules related to rigor. If you are conducting an impact evaluation and you cannot operationalize your major outcome indicators with a high degree of reliability and validity, it is likely that your evaluation will lack sufficient rigor to be useful. Unreliability is notoriously conservative in this context. It tends to mask changes in outcome variables and create the sometimes false impression that the intervention did not work. Variables with a very restricted range of variability and very small samples also tend to be very conservative, loading against detecting small effects. Lack of validity may also bias the evaluation against finding significant gains, but is equally likely to create a false impression of success by mislabeling what is found. In conducting exploratory meaning-generating activities, errors related to insufficient time in the field, poor communication skills, poor record keeping, and careless analysis tend to produce results that match the meaning systems of the investigator rather that the systems studied. Less rigorous field research methods also tend to produce a stronger sense of agreement between informants than really exists and may also introduce outright errors. These problems are worsened if the topics of interest involve attitudes and behaviors that are considered socially undesirable by either the dominant or host culture.

A practical rule related to sampling is that findings cannot be extrapolated to persons or situations that were not represented in the sample. If you hope to apply what you find in a practice evaluation to some other situation, the individuals or situations you sample must be representative of the populations and situations to which decision makers (including yourself) wish to apply your results. If you can't draw a sample that is representative of the populations of interest to the stakeholders, then it may not be feasible to conduct an evaluation that generalizes beyond the persons or situations actually observed.

Practice Evaluation in Single Systems

General Issues in Conducting Evaluations in Single Systems.   Single-system evaluations focus on a single unique system. The system involved can be a small single system, such as an individual client, or a large single system, such as an entire program, community, or some other large complex entity. Single-system focused evaluations have as their primary goal determining the needs, documenting interventions, and detecting impact in the particular system of interest. The techniques associated with single-system designs cover the full gamut of evaluation interests related to single systems, from problem identification, through monitoring the intervention delivery, and, ultimately, assessing changes in the target problem. Typically, the decision contexts for such evaluations involve negotiations with clients about future treatment and perhaps supervision of the helper.

Single-system evaluations often employ quasi-experimental designs when the evaluation question concerns impact of an intervention on a client problem. An adaptation of the time-series quasi-experimental design called the single-system design, or SSD for short, has become very popular with empirically oriented social work practitioners working with individual clients. An excellent description of these designs is presented by Bloom, Fisher, and Orme (1999). In their view, SSDs constitute a whole practice evaluation system that integrates scientific techniques into the helping process from problem assessment through measuring changes in a target problem.

Single-system designs can also be used when the single system is a complex entity such as a program or community as long as the evaluator is careful about the focus of the evaluation. Care concerning the focus is important because evaluations involving complex systems such as programs tend to alternate between treating the program as a whole and treating the program as a group of individual client systems. Single-system designs are useful in describing systems as wholes and less useful in examining group trends among a sample of clients in response to an intervention. In this section, we look at single-system evaluations as efforts to understand the dynamics of an intervention on a system taken as a whole (either a client system or program). In a subsequent section, we deal with studies that conduct cross-case comparisons of multiple systems.

An example might help clarify what we mean by a large group of individual cases being treated as a single system in an evaluation. Campbell's (1969) classic study of the effects of a statewide public policy, the 55-miles-per-hour maximum speed limit implemented in 1955, on traffic fatalities in the state of Connecticut is an example of a single-system evaluation of a large, complex single system. Campbell treated the state as a single complex system and recorded one characteristic of the state, the number of traffic fatalities statewide, over a period of nine years from 1951–1959. His analysis involved placing the nine data points on a graph and looking at the pattern over time in a manner typical of single-system evaluations. Contrast Campbell's approach with a multiple-system comparison approach such as that taken by the National Traffic Safety Board in which the data concerning speed and injuries from a large number of individual traffic accidents (conceptualized as individual "systems") are collected, pooled, and analyzed. Such a multisystem analysis would provide estimates of the relationship between speed and fatalities in the population, but not the direct test of a policy change *on a system* as Campbell's study did. The choice of a single-system or cross-system evaluation is largely a matter of the question being examined.

Single-system designs are highly recommended as ways to help practitioners evaluate the effectiveness of their interventions (Bloom, Fischer, & Orme, 1999). As in all scientific techniques, these designs are intended to provide protection from logical errors, thereby improving inferences related to the causal efficacy of interventions. However, single-system designs also tend to support a particular view of practice sometimes called "empirical social work practice" (Reid & Smith, 1989). SSDs provide a very respectful approach to practice (as well as evaluation) by actively involving clients and other stakeholders in dialogue concerning conceptualizations of target problems, expectations concerning outcomes of intervention, and processes for monitoring the impact of the intervention on target problems. We think that the active, open process of conducting practice evaluations using SSDs improves the power balance in professional-to-client relationships by empowering the clients to specify needs, outcomes, and monitoring processes, and by expressing the willingness of practitioners to be accountable.

Essentially, single-subject designs are time-series quasi-experiments with a sample size of one. Although time-series designs have few features that help make a case for generalizability, single-system designs do correct for many sources of error, particularly those related to internal validity. In spite of the limitations on the generalizability of findings from SSDs, Bloom, Fischer, and Orme (1999) suggest that with proper selection of single systems, these evaluations may be used to explore general principles related to the probable success of interventions in larger populations. Let us now look at how a single-system evaluation is conducted.

Problem Assessment and Diagnosis.   In small single-system evaluations, the phase of activity in which the change-worthy situation is identified is generally referred to as problem assessment or diagnosis. The problem assessment phase of the SSD consists of negotiating with clients around target problems, starting with client statements of concerns and ending in operational definitions that list specific events in specific contexts to be used as indicators of the status of the clients' concerns. The process also includes negotiating on the type or amount of change in the indicator needed before the participants consider the intervention successful. The end result reflects the conceptualizations of both the client and the helper.

Consider, for example, a client system composed of a couple seeking counseling. The couple expresses vague concerns about relationship difficulties. In discussion, the vague concern about relationships is expanded to include several classes of behaviors. As clarification continues, avoiding angry confrontations that sometimes end in violence is identified as a priority. Once a clear definition of the kind of confrontation of interest is established, a procedure for keeping track of specific occurrences of the problem is devised. This may involve having the partners keep a critical incident log recording a few particulars of the target behaviors whenever they occur or other measurement strategies. The final negotiation concerns setting expectations concerning the level at which certain aspects of the target behavior (e.g., shouting and hitting) should drop (e.g., a level of "no occurrences") if the intervention was to be successful. Perhaps, the clients decide that the standard of success includes zero loud arguments lasting more than three minutes of shouting or involving violence. The specific intervention is then negotiated and other concerns prioritized and addressed. Bloom, Fischer, and Orme (1999) list many steps and techniques in this process. The end product of this phase of the evaluation is a clear statement of the target problem to be addressed, a description of the intervention, and success criteria.

Problem assessment in large single systems such as communities follows a similar process of identification and clarification. Information about problems and needs is supplied by persons representing various stakeholder groups. A focus group (see what follows) facilitated by an evaluator is a productive approach to conducting needs assessment in large complex systems taken as wholes. Typically, the report of a problem assessment focuses on system characteristics that are likely to interfere with the ability of the complex system to maintain integration and function. Harrison (1994) provides some interesting guidelines for diagnosing organizations from a systems perspective.

Monitoring Service Provider Activities.   **Monitoring** is an evaluation activity that focuses on documenting the intervention. Monitoring typically involves documenting: what was done, the quality and quantity of what was done, and the rationale for doing what was done. In the case of small single systems, monitoring is largely about recording activities of the helper. Monitoring can also consist of comparing these actions to some standards (e.g., agency policy or standards from an accrediting organization or client expectations) concerning how interventions should be delivered. Finally, identification of some rationale linking the intervention to a desired outcome is also a part of the monitoring process.

Monitoring seems to be one of the least well-developed aspects of single-system design technology. Perhaps, this is a holdover from experimental design literature in which it was taken as a given that the experimental manipulation was given exactly as planned. This hardly seems to be a valid assumption in practice settings. It seems much more useful to assume that in our efforts to meet the needs of clients, interventions are likely to be modified to produce maximum effect. Therefore, it is important to have some sense of what was intended (an intervention plan or model) and what was actually done, in terms of relevant qualities and quantities of interventions.

The **intervention model** describes the assumptions behind the belief that the intervention should be realistically expected to result in improvements in the target problem in this particular client. There are no agreed upon standards concerning how these descriptions should be reported. We recommend that at a minimum, a monitoring report of a small single-system evaluation should include (1) a description of the intervention, (2) specification of the rationale for the intervention (an intervention model), (3) specification of standards for how the intervention is to be delivered, and (4) documentation of the intervention as actually delivered.

Monitoring interventions in the context of large complex single systems is similar to monitoring interventions in small single systems. Here, also, part of the monitoring process includes a specification of what should be and a description of what is. A monitoring report that focuses on a complex single system (such as a program taken as a whole) should describe (1) the intervention model, (2) the program model intended, (3) the degree of model implementation, and (4) the system functioning. The intervention model is a representation of how the program is expected to fit into the pattern of causes that perpetuate the target problem. That is, given the pattern of risk and protective factors that either maintain or alleviate the target program, where does this intervention fit in and how does it work? Does the program attack the major causes of the problem or address only a few or minor causes? Rossi and Freeman (1993) label the assumptions in this area as intervention hypotheses. The program model is the specification for how resources are used to address the target problem. The program model largely describes agency action (in which the intervention model describes the logic of how that action is likely to affect clients). Generally, the program model is described in a grant application, a proposal to a board, or in a procedure manual. Model implementation is largely a comparison of the current patterns of resource use to those contained in the program model. System functioning refers to the ability of the organization to maintain integration. Are sufficient inputs being obtained? Are communication networks intact? Are adequate roles and norms in evidence?

Here is an example of monitoring in a complex single-system perspective. Some time ago, we were asked to conduct an evaluation in a program for homeless teenagers. The first task involved describing the program as a complex system. From interviews and agency records, we determined that although being homeless was a requirement for participation in the program, the target problem that was addressed by the program was long-term economic dependency of the youth. We worked with the staff to identify an explicit causal model of the target problem. The staff felt (and the literature confirmed somewhat) that homeless youth were at risk of long-term economic dependency due to factors that were both antecedents and consequences of their homelessness. Specifically, personal and behavioral characteristics of the youth, family support systems, and lack of skills or work experience often precipitated the homelessness of the youth. However, the same group of factors was believed to be an important contributor to the long-term economic dependency of the youth, as was the additional risk provided by being homeless. The intervention model was fairly clearly specified in a grant application that led to funding of the program. The program promised to arrange various housing options, hire social workers to do case management, and form linkages with programs that could provide services to address social, behavioral, and occupational skills of their clients, thereby keeping clients safe and surrounded by services that addressed their specific risk profiles. The grant proposal also contained a plan for implementation of the program, including developmental milestones such as hiring staff, recruiting host families, and the like. The monitoring portion of the evaluation consisted of making the causal and intervention models explicit, describing the program in terms of a client pathway diagram, and placing the developmental milestones for the program on a timeline with completion status noted. We also noted the organizational structure of the program's host agency and described its operation. It is important to keep in mind that in this activity, we were merely documenting the development of a complex entity, its rationale, and its goals and capacities. This is quite different from monitoring the progress of individual clients and making cross-client generalizations. These generalizations were made also, but employed a different methodology (see multisystem evaluations later).

Measuring Client-Level Outcomes. A major contribution of SSD technology is to provide a means of empirical verification of the impact of the intervention on the target problem. As a modified time-series quasi-experiment, the client system is used as its own control. That is, SSDs consist of a collection of measures of the target problem as it exists before intervention that is compared to measures of the target problem as it exists after the intervention. Data analysis in SSDs involves comparison of measures taken in the two time periods, a *baseline period* and an **intervention period.** By comparing, usually visually, the pattern of the problem before intervention to the pattern following intervention, conclusions concerning the effectiveness of the intervention are drawn.

The simplest SSD is the **AB design,** which consists of a baseline **(A)** period during which states of the target problem are assessed, but intervention has not yet begun, and an intervention period **(B)** in which the intervention is applied. Note that the graph in Figure 10.1 is scaled so that instances of the target behavior are labeled on the vertical axis and time on the horizontal axis. As we discuss, comparison of the shape and slope of the line over time is used to determine the success of the intervention.

The baseline period is the pretreatment state of the target problem. The length of this period and the number of observations needed are not fixed quantities, but determined by the volatility of the target behavior. The reason that baseline data are collected is to determine trends in the target behavior without intervention. Is the behavior already increasing, decreasing, staying the same, or fluctuating widely before intervention? The pattern found has serious consequences for interpretation of postintervention states. For example, in Campbell's (1969) large single-system evaluation of the Connecticut speed limit, traffic fatalities were found to vary widely from year to year, but clearly decreasing over time before the intervention. The large drop in fatalities following the adoption of a lower speed limit was found consistent with the natural variability in traffic fatalities and not evidence of an effective public policy. In general, the pattern in the target behavior prior to intervention is used to help interpret the meaning of the pattern after intervention.

A variant on the AB design, the **ABAB design,** is useful when the intervention being tested is expected to be needed long-term. An example provided by a

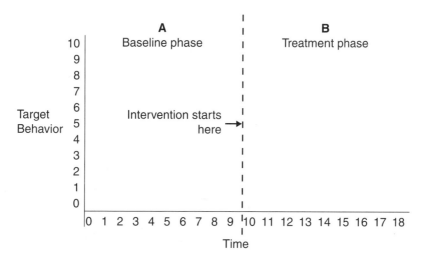

FIGURE 10.1   AB Single-System Design

former student can illustrate the ABAB design. The target problem was forgetting to take medications. In the A phase, the frequency of missed medications was assessed (by asking a family member to count what was left in the medicine bottle at the end of each day). At the conclusion of the baseline period (A), a pillbox labeled with days and hours was introduced to the client. During the treatment phase, the client continued to use the device and the family member recorded missed medications (the B phase). At the conclusion of the treatment phase, the pill container was removed and the number of missed medications observed for a few days (the second A phase). Finally, the pill container was reintroduced (the second B phase) and the target behavior recorded for another several days. Hypothetical data from this ABAB design are illustrated in Figure 10.2.

Can you see the advantage of the ABAB design in strengthening inference about the (continuing) importance of the intervention? By noting a degradation of performance after removal of the intervention, the status of the intervention as the cause of the improved performance is strongly supported. Of course, this type of design is suitable only for interventions that are likely to be part of a long-term maintenance strategy. Likewise, it would be important that removal of the intervention was unlikely to result in serious harm. The ABAB design is less useful in evaluating the effectiveness of a one-shot intervention. However, when appropriate, the ABAB design strengthens inference about the intervention as a cause of improvement in the target problem.

Many different combinations of baseline and intervention designs are possible. For example, ABC designs and ABAC designs involve multiple interventions (B and C are different interventions). The **ABC design** uses a single baseline (A), followed by the first intervention (B). The second intervention **(C)** immediately follows the B intervention. During each phase, the status of the target problem is mea-

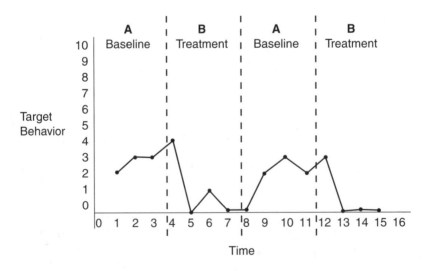

FIGURE 10.2   ABAB Single-System Design

sured and placed on a graph. A variant, the **ABAC design,** includes new baselines or nonintervention periods (the second A) between interventions. Other designs test the same intervention, under increasing intensities (the $AB^1B^2B^3...$). For a complete discussion of SSDs the reader is directed to Bloom, Fischer, and Orme (1999).

Practice Evaluation across Multiple Clients or Systems

General Issues in Evaluation across Multiple-Client Systems. Sometimes the evaluation question is more general than the impact of an intervention on a single system—be it an individual or a complex entity. When the research question involves the characteristics of a population—the incidence and prevalence of a target problem, how well individuals in a population respond to a particular type of treatment, or correlations between various risk factors and the problem—the logical approach is a multiple-system comparison. These types of evaluation are often simply called program evaluations. The methods used in this type of evaluation are designed to produce valid inference about the characteristics of populations. Therefore, multiclient system evaluations tend (1) to employ strong sampling strategies such as random sampling; (2) to be quantitative, emphasizing numerical data and analyses; (3) to begin with fixed conceptualizations of target problems and populations; and (4) to be more confirming than exploratory (although multiclient needs assessment is sometimes exploratory).

The large-scale population survey associated with an epidemiological study is a prime example of needs assessment. These studies generally involve searching for patterns in large quantities of quantitative data on persons with or without a target problem. Service monitoring activities tend to focus on counting clients and services and quantifiable states, looking for similarities and differences across individuals in the consumption of services. Impact studies tend to employ (wherever possible) group designs such as experiments and quasi-experiments. When appropriate, the completely randomized, double-blind, placebo control designs used in some forms of medical research are a model for this type of evaluation.

Ideally, evaluation involving generalizations across multiple systems would be built on a solid foundation of single-system evaluations that provide a grounded perspective on the target problem and efficacy of interventions. This would be helpful since the designs required to establish generalizability across individuals also tend to introduce a degree of artificiality in the intervention process that may diminish the external validity of the findings. That is, multiclient system evaluations sometimes sacrifice a more natural setting for a more controlled one to improve internal validity. However, it may be that the results in a controlled setting are different than what would be found in an applied setting. Social workers who are interested in multiclient system evaluations need to balance the need for rigorous methods that control for threats to internal and external validity, without adding new threats in the form of an artificial service delivery setting. Let us now look at some common approaches to multisystem needs assessment, monitoring, and impact studies.

Needs Assessment. In large-system evaluations, the problem identification phase is generally labeled as **needs assessment.** Needs assessments are sometimes considered "diagnostic procedures" (Rossi & Freeman, 1993) at a group level. Needs assessment tends to be an exploratory activity through which the dimensions of a target problem emerge with increasing clarity. We see four potential goals that pertain to needs assessment. These include (1) generating definitions of the target problem as a multiple-client system phenomenon; (2) estimating the prevalence, incidence, and severity of the problem in some population; (3) developing a causal model of the problem; and (4) developing intervention models that explain how one or more interventions are likely to influence the target problem.

Needs assessment has two interrelated aspects: achieving conceptual clarity concerning some target problem and documentation of the empirical dimensions of the target problem in a particular population. The conceptual aspect is typically explored by attempting to refine and integrate the conceptualizations of the target problem of stakeholders through reading, interviewing, or perhaps conducting focus groups associated with exploratory research. The empirical aspect of needs assessment is accomplished by either direct observation or obtaining reports of other's observations. A good deal of this work is done in libraries, reviewing documents, and key informant interviewing.

The first task of any multiple-system evaluation is reaching consensus about what the target problem is. Specifically, a definition of the dimensions of the problem needs to be expressed clearly and in terms that the stakeholders can agree on. Although persons within a particular stakeholder group share vague working definitions of problems, these are likely to be imprecise and differ from the conceptualizations of other stakeholder groups. The objective of efforts at achieving conceptual clarity is what we called a nominal definition earlier in this book.

The evaluator has an important role to fill in helping to achieve consensus and conceptual clarity concerning target problems and related interventions. Defining the target problem and alternative states that are more desirable is a political process. In evaluations across multiple individuals, it is often desirable to explore those conceptualizations and their implications for evaluation by conducting a focus group composed of representatives of the various stakeholder groups. In our evaluation work, we frequently use focus groups and invite participants to explore different perspectives on a target problem, its causal structure, the nature of interventions, and information needed to support decision making concerning the target problem. A typical group contains representatives of all major stakeholder groups and meets three times. The agenda tends to vary with the context, but in general, the tasks include clarifying the dimensions of the target problem and intervention, establishing expectations and standards for outcomes, negotiating roles of stakeholders concerning participation in the design and implementation of the evaluation, and reviewing the decision contexts in which each stakeholder group needs data to facilitate decision making. The agenda proposed by the evaluator is amended as negotiated by the group members.

We tend to favor a structure in which the evaluator serves as a facilitator and expert, bringing in knowledge gleaned from professional experience or the library to assist the participants. This tends to be achieved by asking questions, listening and spending a good deal of time in the library, or connected to a library electronically, to discover what consensus exists concerning ways of thinking about the target problem. The results of these explorations are generally prepared by the evaluator and reviewed at successive meetings. The goal of the focus group is a clear conceptualization of the target problem and target population that fairly represents the diversity of opinion among the stakeholders. Although stakeholders typically do retain their unique conceptualizations of target problems, we have seen repeatedly how useful such a process can be in helping stakeholders to clarify their own thoughts and develop a conceptual base that allows meaningful communication with other stakeholders.

The aspect of needs assessment that includes understanding the empirical dimensions of the target problem in a population is intended to produce estimates of the **incidence** (rate at which new cases of the problem emerge), **prevalence** (proportion of the population afflicted with the target problem), **severity** (degree of harm created by the problem), responsiveness of the problem to current treatments, and verification of forces influencing the problem. Studies of the empirical dimensions of the target problem are often a mix of numerical and nonnumerical data. Rates of incidence, prevalence, and cure tend to be numerical. Models of the causal structure of the problem and models of effective interventions, although often based on quantitative studies, tend to be pictorial syntheses of the numerical data expressed in words and charts.

Once a target problem has been sufficiently defined, it may be possible to draw a causal model of the target problem. A **causal model** is a visual representation of the forces operating on an individual that potentially cause the problem or worsen it (risk factors) and factors that have the potential to prevent the problem or ameliorate it (protective factors). We prefer an approach to writing causal models that is a modification of procedure described by Cohen and Cohen (1983) in their discussion of path analysis. Basically, a path diagram is a picture describing the observed or proposed relationships between an outcome (or outcomes) of interest and a set of variables believed to be causes. The models are drawn by connecting nodes representing variables with arrows pointing from causes to their effects. That is, the presence of an arrow implies causal influence (in path analysis, these arrows also imply the existence of a statistical relationship between cause and effect, such as a partial correlation). At least one node is an outcome representing the target problem. Other nodes are the risk and protective factors and connected to each other and the outcome by lines that represent what is known or speculated about the relationship between the nodes. It is customary to draw causal diagrams so that causes are on the left and the target problem on the right. Figure 10.3 (see page 244) is an example of a simple causal model that arose from stakeholder discussion concerning factors that influenced the ability of homeless youth to obtain and retain jobs.

Drawing causal models is a combination of empirical science, art, and communication. In the context of a program evaluation, the causal model is intended primarily to help stakeholders and consumers of the evaluation clarify

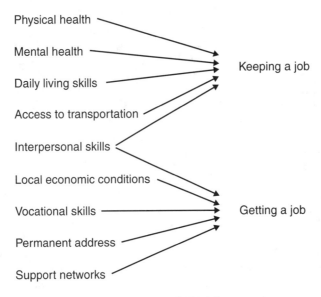

FIGURE 10.3   A Simple Causal Model

their thinking about what drives a particular target problem. Therefore, simple models with nodes representing complex processes tend to be preferred in this context. Also, the labeling of the models needs to reflect the language of the consumers of the evaluation to the extent possible. Artistically pleasing arrangements including the use of color and form tend to maintain interest and therefore usefulness. The degree of empirical rigor that goes into forming a causal model should be a function of the state of social science research on the problem of interest. When the problem of interest has received much research attention, fairly complete models that identify all major classes of risk and protective factors may be specified, and the degree of confidence for proposed causal relationships may be quite high. For problems in which no models or very limited models exist in the literature, many paths may be speculative and whole classes of causes left out. We are not above including hunches, our own and those of stakeholders, in the model to clarify group perspectives on the target problem. However, the part of us that makes us professional evaluators requires that we attempt to verify the relative level of confirmation for proposed relationships contained in the professional literature and include some indication of this as part of our models.

We consistently use causal models in our program evaluation work to help stakeholders clarify and sharpen their thinking about the problem and intervention. Besides providing a common frame of reference for considering risk and protective factors, causal models can help place interventions in the larger context of factors that have a known or suspected influence on the problem. Recognizing that a treatment influences only one of several classes of risk factors can provide a more realistic understanding of what can be accomplished by the program. Causal models are also useful to program staff as they attempt to fine-tune programs by calling attention to protective factors and risk factors that may have been over-looked in the initial specification of a target problem. Well-thought-out causal models can also facilitate thinking about the logic behind an intervention. A model can help staff focus on why it is that the program seems to produce the impact that it does and preserve the effective elements of the process. Pictorial representations of these intervention assumptions are sometimes called intervention models. Intervention models are discussed in the context of monitoring of services since they usually originate in the program logic contained in grant applications, contracts, or program descriptions that are encountered in the context of program monitoring.

Here are some basic points that should be included in the problem statement portion of a program evaluation: (1) clear definitions of the target problem, including an appreciation of different perspectives on the target problem among various stakeholders; (2) estimation of the incidence and prevalence of the target problem in a clearly defined population; (3) a causal model specifying likely risk and protective factors; and (4) what is known about responsiveness of the problem to intervention. Although a major research activity designed to produce all of this information is often impractical, these can be estimated from a combination of examination of the professional literature and application of "practice wisdom."

Program Monitoring in Multiclient System Evaluations. Earlier, we discussed monitoring the service output of an entire complex organization as a single system. There we discussed developing an intervention model, tracking program deployment, and diagramming client pathways. This process typically focuses on the initial program plan, developmental milestones, obstacles, changes in design and approach, and assessment of deployment. This is clearly a single- (large-) system-level analysis, but is essential if other aspects of the monitoring involving multiple clients are to make any sense. In this section, we deal with a multisystem program monitoring activity that consists of a description of the services delivered to individual clients and comparisons across clients. This activity results in profiles of services provided and other agency actions such as referrals and discharges, in addition to client characteristics. In some cases, the monitoring may also contain information concerning outcomes if these are recorded during the course of treatment.

Monitoring across individuals usually includes compiling a client database file. Such a file may facilitate analysis of policy implementation. One project in which we were involved examined the payments made to foster parents to see if policies concerning rates of compensation were being correctly implemented. Another monitored the frequency of case reviews to determine if a statutory requirement for six-month reviews was being met. Still another examined discharge status to determine the proportion of clients who successfully completed the program. Some studies of this type may examine program efficiency in terms of costs per unit.

Program monitoring may also focus on the match between the population served by the program and the population specified as having the target problem. Are all the clients served by the program in the population defined as "in need" (or at risk for prevention programs) or do some not meet the criterion? One of our students conducted an evaluation of a program designed to provide free meals to poor inner-city children during the summer and found that a large proportion of the participants did not meet poverty guidelines! Some writers (Rossi & Freeman, 1993) describe this problem as poor *selectivity* in client recruitment. **Selectivity** is about criteria for excluding clients. **Sensitivity** is about criteria for including clients in a program.

Sensitivity is about assuring that all persons who meet criteria are served. Problems with selectivity are typically identified by looking at the characteristics of the population actually served by a program. Basically, the population should be homogeneous with regard to all having the target problem or meeting the same risk criteria. However, sensitivity problems can be determined only by comparing the characteristics of the population served with estimates of the characteristic of the population at need or risk. For a full coverage program (one intended to serve all persons at need in a specified population) comparison of the number of persons served to estimates of persons at need or risk would provide a reasonable test of appropriate sensitivity. However, for a partial-coverage program (perhaps one of several agencies serving persons with a particular problem), the issue of sensitivity is less clear. If the concern is that certain economic or ethnic groups may be disproportionately served, it is possible to look at the composition of the client population and compare the proportions in various social classes or ethnic groups and compare these to estimates of the same characteristics of the population at large. For example, a group of colleagues interested in the effects of managed care and funding for hospitals on service to poor urban minorities compared the proportion of poor minorities in the service area of acute care hospitals to the proportion of these groups who actually received services at the hospitals as a way to examine potential selectivity problems.

Some forms of **efficiency analyses** are also properly forms of program monitoring. Asking the number of units of direct service that an agency provides, determining the cost of delivering a unit of service, or perhaps comparing the proportion of funds that go to management and fund raising with those spent on direct service delivery are examples of efficiency questions. Efficiency analyses are complicated by conceptual problems related to (1) how one defines a unit of service and service delivery as opposed to system maintenance and (2) the accounting models used to estimate costs. Agreement on specifications of units of service for human services has been actively pursued for decades with little strong agreement. Ad hoc definitions allow this form of monitoring to be conducted, but complicate comparison to alternative interventions. It is difficult to compute a cost per unit of direct service if a unit cannot be defined and distinguished from other kinds of agency activity. Likewise, computing costs is strongly influenced by assumptions about the accounting models used to establish costs. The cost basis is also complicated. For example, how (if at all) do volunteer or in-kind contributions become factored into costs per unit of service? In evaluation, we have encountered organizations that provided large portions of their services through the use of volunteers and used the agency budget to supervise volunteers and raise more money. In cases like these, the inclusion of volunteers in the cost basis would provide a less favorable view of the agency's cost per unit, but provide a much more favorable ratio of resources dedicated to service delivery as opposed to system maintenance

Some program monitoring also involves documenting outcomes for clients. These studies sit right at the border between program monitoring and impact studies (our next topic). Some programs supplement service monitoring activities with surveys or assessments on clients just prior to or following discharge to determine the status of the target problems that led them to seek intervention. Sometimes these evaluations involve client self-reports such as client satisfaction surveys and may involve a mixture of process and outcome-oriented questions. In other cases, the agency regularly tabulates the number of cases closed as successful, the number of planned discharges, the number graduated, or some similar agency action that implies a successful transaction. One agency we know contacts former clients one year after discharge to determine if the target problem has returned. Compilation of such data is an important aspect of program monitoring and can give useful perspectives on effectiveness. If few clients at or following discharge show evidence of improvement in the target problem, the obvious conclusion is that at a group level, the intervention is not working. Unfortunately, inference is less simple if monitoring reveals that large numbers of clients have experienced positive changes in the target problem. It may be true that the intervention produced those positive outcomes, but the unstructured observation of a positive change does not rule out a host of alternative explanations. Perhaps the problem ran its course. Or maybe something in the client's life unrelated to the intervention has changed. Or maybe maturation can account for the change. If this list is beginning to look like the familiar list of threats to internal validity, it should. The threats to internal validity discussed earlier are the problem.

Lest you think that the operation of threats to internal validity are unimportant, consider the following. An enterprising social work student undertook the evaluation of a "personal safety curriculum" designed to help young children avoid exploitation. The intervention was designed to be delivered in classrooms over several months and focused on safe ways to interact with strangers. The evaluator conducted a quasi-experiment in which one classroom received the intervention and another classroom in the same school did not. An instrument that measured knowledge and attitudes was devised and administered preintervention and postintervention to both groups. Interestingly, both the experimental and control groups made significant gains over the course of the program. It seemed possible that some diffusion of treatment occurred if the students in the experimental group talked about their experiences. However, a multimillion dollar advertisement campaign on personal safety for children broadcast over radio and television during the same period (an effect of history) likely had strong effects on both the experimental and control groups. Had the control group not been assessed, the evaluator would have concluded (falsely) that the program had been a success. Since new programs (the ones most often evaluated) tend to be funded around human service fads, it is likely that interventions at many levels are likely to be going on at the time of the evaluation. A simple descriptive study of outcomes is not sufficiently rigorous to isolate the program from other potential explanations. Without adequate methods to minimize the impact of these threats, our conclusions about the effectiveness of the intervention may be erroneous. As discussed in the next section, stronger designs are preferred for rendering these threats implausible in the context of impact studies.

What should a monitoring report contain? This depends more on the particular reasons for doing the evaluation than does the problem description (needs assessment) portion of the evaluation. However, it should almost always include descriptions of (1) the population served, including empirical evidence of selectivity and sensitivity if these are of concern; (2) description and counts of the units of service provided; (3) costs of providing services; and (4) outcomes or disposition of clients. All of these may be grouped by client characteristics or some other dimension (e.g., an agency designation, such as type of service provided) as the questions at hand require.

A final note concerns the quality of agency client-level information. Our experience with this form of data is that from the standpoint of evaluation research, the quality runs from fair to poor. Agency files that are incomplete, inaccurate, or missing are very common. If your evaluation concerns the kind of cross-client service monitoring mentioned here, be prepared to do a lot of data quality control checking. Consider drawing a random sample and then verifying everything in the sample from an independent source. Absent such care, you run the risk of analyzing what we referred to in the data analysis chapter as "a pile of numbers" with little connection to actual profiles.

Impact Evaluations.   Impact evaluations focus on the status of the intervention as a cause of changes in the target problem. As mentioned earlier, some monitoring studies involve documentation of client states following an intervention. However, impact evaluations go further in that they are designed to estimate the likelihood that the intervention produces those client states. Impact studies tend to be deductive. They test propositions like "Reductions in the target problem in persons who receive the intervention can be attributed to that intervention."

The prototype impact study is an experiment. Think back to the chapter on research design. The true experiments are best at providing strong tests of causal hypotheses that underlie impact studies. It is often feasible to conduct experiments as impact studies when the services being provided are not of an emergency nature and whenever some clients are served sooner and others later. For example, we were once asked to design a study to test the effectiveness of a cultural sensitivity training for welfare workers. A true experimental design, the pretest/posttest control group design was easily employed. Three hundred persons were to receive the training. Management agreed to select a random sample of 60 persons from the population of 300, and through random assignment, 30 were assigned to the first training (experimental group) and 30 were designated as the control group and assigned to the second training to be held later. Both groups took a knowledge and attitude test at the same time, and after the training of the experimental group was completed, the two groups took the posttest at the same time. Because of the rigor of the experimental design, the gains found in the experimental group could be attributed only to the influence of the training. This approach works well whenever persons can be randomly assigned to either the first offering of the program or a later offering, with persons in the later group serving as a control group for the experiment. This logic could be applied to evaluation of programs with waiting lists, in which a lottery-type activity was used to decide who to serve and who to assign to the waiting list.

When true experiments are not feasible, it is still possible to conduct impact studies that provide some protection from error. One way to tighten up nonexperimental studies of impact is the use of *generic controls.* **Generic controls** are estimates of the target problem in a known (untreated) population. For example, one study in which we were involved asked whether a program designed to encourage girls to participate in advanced math and science in high school was working. Because the program was full coverage (statewide), it was not possible to construct a suitable control group. However, data concerning the proportion of female students in the state who participated in such courses in the year before the new program as well as regional proportions were available. Our suggestion was to compare the proportion of females in a random sample of advanced math classes following the program to the two generic estimates of what the population would look like without the intervention.

Advanced mathematical techniques also allow "statistical control" to be used in some situations to isolate facts related to outcomes. A common example of the statistical control approach is to obtain client-level records of a diverse population, some of whom have received the intervention in question and some of whom have not. In addition to recording the level of the target problem and presence or absence of an intervention, this kind of approach also requires measuring characteristics of the client or environment that are likely to provide alternatives to the assumption that differences between treated and untreated clients were due to the intervention. Statistical techniques related to partial correlation allow the contribution of levels of service to be isolated from other measured factors. Multiple regression represents the most common family of such techniques and is standard fare in social science statistics courses.

In our experience, true experiments as impact studies are infrequent. In fact, this kind of study is what decision makers intend to avoid when they tell us that they don't want the evaluation to be "too scientific." Often, just documenting outcomes and the proportion of clients with successful outcomes is sufficient for the purposes of most stakeholders. If there are compelling reasons to conclude that the program is the probable cause of any change in outcome without the advantage of strong designs, there is little reason to go to the time, expense, and intrusiveness of an experiment. However, as Royse and Thyer (1996) note, the evaluator must preserve a degree of independence and not allow the needs and wishes of any stakeholder to defeat the goal of obtaining verifiable information about interventions. This means mounting the most rigorous evaluation possible and sometimes not conducting evaluations if they cannot be conducted at some minimum level of objectivity. The stronger the claims, the stronger the evidence needs to be. When strong evidence is needed, experimental designs and strong quasi-experiments using sound statistical analysis are still the best approaches.

Summary

This chapter has described the business of evaluating the client systems with which social workers are involved. Many times, these client systems are composed of only one person or a family. Other times, these single social systems are composed of many people or even groups of people connected to form a complex social entity like a human service delivery organization. Practicing social workers are sometimes interested in evaluating their efforts with only one client system—regardless of size—whereas at other times, understanding the impact of a planned intervention may require us to look across two or more of these systems. Although the specific techniques that we employ may vary, these are all common situations for the application of practice evaluation.

All evaluation is focused on at least one of three general areas: needs assessment, monitoring, or impact assessment. Like the variation in system size, these different points call forth different evaluative techniques, but they all contribute valuable information in understanding the helping process. They are in some ways cumulative in that need assessment seeks to specify a problem state, monitoring follows the process on intervening with that problem state and impact studies determine the degree to which the intervention caused an improvement in the problem.

Beyond being something that every social worker is required to do by the NASW *Code of Ethics,* evaluation provides the practitioner with important feedback. It is through these activities that we gain confidence that we are a part of a change system that is working positively on the client's behalf. By involving all of the relevant stakeholders in an evaluation, we are better able to reflect the multiple meanings that may be drawn from problematic social contexts, as well as the multiple form that solutions to problem states may take. In the process of meeting these diverse needs and interests, the evaluator plays a political role of negotiating compromises as well as refined understandings—all the while seeking to incorporate the strongest techniques into the evaluation in order to provide the highest-quality information for future decision making.

APPENDIX

Table of Random Numbers

03418073	80068362	19867550	88912626	27066866	85622730
16513566	50630207	76223029	75774407	42298651	73702200
36573382	74791711	69023713	94936981	45417646	21662038
73424482	05493280	95300150	37171545	90472121	97756890
81743672	47596667	70561846	21021149	17282632	78701132
64857936	41059603	46329844	99359111	69814142	98825037
36252937	35953856	62508011	19653920	29010895	12817774
08310190	41807306	01004059	48950267	03952147	00598163
37748344	38752403	47917112	77547533	44285409	35782952
93997009	07199316	87267678	90408033	68852809	06515702
86242256	98931852	62230293	61589404	00170904	36782463
96240120	83678701	23285623	12775048	75183059	09378338
54368725	83123264	96624653	21726127	69985046	03332621
09613331	54646443	73274941	42683198	60743886	74855800
48921171	47062594	89831233	59025854	23734245	16342662
28476821	19568468	30079043	43537706	25357830	25122837
98419141	38859218	86541337	44392224	79897458	96731468
87395856	58715405	24289682	62768915	31873533	30207221
81627857	21854305	71480453	61760308	30954927	71309549
70497757	68938261	23456526	16171874	80730613	32642598
51805170	69151891	97479171	44923298	73873104	94808802
63405255	15018159	96432386	18671224	07412946	71459090
29053621	19696646	43480944	72569961	73744926	60115360
27814570	35334330	34543901	56718650	30185862	23456526
29181799	90920743	16428114	46079898	14590899	73424482
72228156	47596667	00542711	01559496	89468062	66032899
38795129	79299295	69066439	99188208	36808374	45439009
46122623	79577014	91305277	56181576	53621021	79427473
11429182	88955351	86605426	44456313	52381970	56910917
59987182	31788080	46037172	02905362	85045930	77526170

89510788	17047639	32001709	97885074	31723991	43388165
36466567	45716727	30506302	96325572	65050203	51911985
55714591	94146550	71917712	59880367	46955779	86562700
08352916	58128605	13138218	93420209	81157872	56996368
04550310	38478744	07263405	75005341	45396283	29715873
99743645	77697073	93911557	50651570	41636403	28775903
00256356	41230506	31809442	07712027	19376202	84981842
40974151	83635975	16983551	70668661	96774190	97756890
25614185	19632557	16983551	70668661	96774190	97756890
52424696	48301645	65242470	60093997	99487289	35056612
76522111	93697928	10937834	61033967	03012177	85900449
59773553	70519120	29694510	55244606	73232221	35312967
78551592	22025208	07434309	84170049	19953002	01538133
61076693	60499893	91540269	12112796	07049776	11578723
06109806	29010895	27280496	96698846	04635762	60029908
19376202	25486007	08077709	91219825	19995727	33279398
91177099	00064089	91946165	56056398	97116001	52681051
17239906	57551805	97415082	75603504	21918394	32087161
13629566	05041658	89233070	61674856	77654347	14056826
16791284	54518265	28583636	91988891	22324290	60649434
69130528	76628925	01431318	50779748	43858150	11941893
86114078	87310404	76479385	58342239	70561846	40162359
92181158	97286905	66096988	19568474	44627216	04422132
49177526	90643025	94125187	02755821	10788293	03311258
97158727	83379620	34757530	91988891	37128819	14441359
16257210	16214484	35184790	48258919	67699210	37022004
45139927	09186071	12668233	89062166	85836360	57786798
79641102	61525315	78936125	98846400	79085672	25550096
23691519	84405042	36381115	24973296	18884854	39756462
28861354	12540056	21512497	96090579	51890622	86477249
70625935	45097202	83614612	54966887	60734886	62102115
08352916	61803034	88015381	56932279	51719718	60521256
81200598	15317240	00875881	72078616	45460372	21469771
33048494	72121342	09933775	02328562	90707116	68254646
12369152	66844691	90130314	14313181	53065584	60841701

59367657	15359966	30207221	01025422	68254646	35334330
96624653	18948943	42960906	11749626	61375774	40717795
45097202	61760308	19653920	63405255	18201239	97799616
87694937	26981414	64238411	80602435	43537706	51484726
21192053	48216193	83187353	32279428	24396497	57679983
33155309	45823542	73317667	98974578	1610767	57573168
39457381	16470840	11578723	52104251	8269601	65947447
01559496	51634266	83123264	61204871	49006623	02114933
77248451	90493484	04123051	42127751	25571459	99636830
69515061	37513352	78145695	53984191	93377483	80346080
98376415	80452895	55800043	40717795	14505448	05490280
05618458	88250374	44947661	82845546	46827601	17004914
71886349	76180303	30655843	96432398	12048708	60820338
65520188	01922666	16769921	03717155	9570605	00769066
47233497	61525315	85473190	40140996	88912626	75090793
22238838	91113010	03973510	24716941	53001495	42768639
36893826	85238197	92565691	58192694	13864559	98419141
23648793	87417219	24054689	51057466	39713736	83956420
68382824	18372143	43665883	92608417	27878658	89745781
03524888	52552873	78615680	79683828	76479385	71822260
09271523	85580004	82461013	94552446	0965606	50630207
65840632	42555010	17368084	45161290	42426832	70775475
69408246	83593249	05682547	57466353	5981628	69771416
71352275	52723777	40461440	17795343	40418714	57124546
95001068	78701132	43024995	63277078	19888913	55928221
83400983	31488998	24204230	79833369	42298654	55650502
72719504	60713523	35398419	09100620	15060884	11535997
60222175	50651570	93975646	31809442	70583209	50267037
65007477	84319590	93078402	84597308	17923521	20657979
05105747	80495621	63682974	19141209	70732749	60264901
76522111	75646229	17239906	90215766	31040376	22345653
23712882	15402692	36445204	76009400	82439650	51121555
64024781	60414441	64879299	57765435	63789789	00213630
34095279	81350139	83251442	40162359	02563555	58897671
24311045	35654775	37235633	20999786	26810511	78252510

37534715	90408033	56141850	26169622	11493271	32963042
29651784	90215766	49049348	89980773	31104465	53791925
83657338	27002777	91091647	44007691	26490066	35099338
81179235	72719504	47383038	44434950	20615253	24909207
15509507	89788507	21085238	45973083	14825892	83016450
31980346	69707328	74983978	44520402	37256996	30591754
95968401	71907712	70882290	76757103	89275796	17944884
43003632	50117496	64473403	60136723	36509293	54368725
97350993	30912198	86819056	06323435	14249092	74300363
08801538	78936125	45417646	48728904	18094424	47340312
25699637	85067293	85943175	48515275	99914548	33219398
32236702	64772485	22837001	38068789	4157231	85345012
57936338	27793207	68190558	76116215	75667592	30890835
95684683	52211066	90066225	75154881	8431959	00341807
76265755	28904080	07669301	07113865	55992309	58534501
47233497	27878658	43238624	42341380	17261269	13202307
82161931	27494125	77568896	4714805	13650929	32151250
00064089	56462294	19953002	65242470	26938688	05191199
07626576	43110447	27130955	54560991	04315317	65776544
03952147	30378124	37491989	89703055	07776116	45994446
99423200	88164922	07861568	83828242	19504379	95770135
74065371	92736595	02883999	18927580	03567614	77675710
96005127	29523606	21704764	29502243	8688314	76949370
48045290	35142064	51570177	24887845	75090793	52168340
10831019	51207007	03524888	12839137	86947234	25913266
27921384	41294595	56462294	25785096	95471053	74983978
94189276	65434736	72676779	58577227	06366161	57679983
61503952	91241188	92864773	26233711	00598163	17667165
47553942	80324717	79342021	98974578	85644093	47853023
27515488	65285196	19974365	19397652	61418500	73787652
68916898	59752190	20572527	40696432	22260201	63148900
82418287	52916044	59154027	27430036	38132878	12176885
48942534	79192480	59837642	33326212	38111515	41251869
51271096	74877163	56975005	06985687	46635334	33774834
01089511	49861141	39265114	33753472	3076266	64516129

91796625	72762230	48194830	39243751	82332835	21491134
54475539	08651997	84319590	09762871	46549883	23136082
98077334	92800684	60991241	13415937	69493698	34394360
17987610	64793848	19312113	30079043	13180944	85494552
04486221	88698996	06366161	71864986	35184790	79000214
94381542	81798761	24439222	38068789	54795984	51976704
43644520	56547746	42255928	95577868	36103397	33497116
76500748	19077120	78637043	12326426	75133519	21384320
47703482	00213630	65498825	34330271	67592395	27515488
80474258	13522752	18500320	33133946	73360393	63148900
37086093	94381542	93655202	79662472	58256783	94659261
88720359	33304849	16983551	16385395	92117069	77825251
34650716	97906430	30121769	44926298	78402051	59111301
81949302	13843196	32450331	56419569	78722495	40568255
94253365	25293741	91625721	78701132	11535997	87630848
97927793	23627430	87694937	22067934	72270882	45930357
87160863	89873959	45780816	80986969	84789575	71587268
61803034	53556932	66566973	76308481	18543046	38453322
12988678	27451399	33988464	99252297	38709677	82717368
03610340	93163854	07049776	63426618	43024995	58449049
03546251	66887417	29032258	23136081	76116215	63439344
10596027	95236061	58427686	04977569	48750267	13565478
18778039	32663961	03610340	95797198	57402265	80495621
73210852	04593036	33945738	54689169	63811152	62208930
44285409	42405469	97265542	88805811	53962829	35612049

GLOSSARY

A Symbol used to represent the baseline period in a single-system design

AB design Single-system design composed of a single baseline period and a single intervention period

ABAB design Single-system design composed of a baseline period, an intervention, withdrawal of treatment, and a repeat of the initial intervention

ABAC design Single-system design composed of a baseline period, an intervention, withdrawal of treatment, and a different intervention

ABC design Single-system design composed of a baseline period, an intervention, and then a second intervention

alpha *See* Cronbach's alpha

analytic cover term Label for a domain in the language of the investigator

analytic generalizability Form of external validity in exploratory research that focuses on the congruence between constructed meaning systems and actual meaning systems of the population being studied

anecdotal information Information describing some incident, often obtained out of context and containing some invention and speculation

anomalies Observations that don't fit prevailing ideas, theories, or paradigms

anonymity Being unidentified. This condition is preserved by collecting data in such a way that identifying information is never recorded

attributes States or levels that a variable may take. "Orange" is an attribute that the variable "color" may take

authority Reliance exclusively on the opinions of those persons socially designated as producers of knowledge as a mode testing truth of propositions

B Symbol used to represent the intervention period in a single-system design

baseline period Within single-system designs, the period prior to the commencement of the intervention

behavior checklist Fixed strategy for coding direct observations involving a preestablished list of behaviors to be observed

biased language Language that reflects a strong value orientation. Biased language tends to produce systematic error in responses

binomial sampling distribution Theoretical distribution in the shape of the bell curve. The height of the curve represents the probability of sets of events occurring by chance

bivariate correlation Statistic used to estimate the extent to which pairs of variables seem to "go together." Pearson's *r* is one example

bivariate descriptive statistics Class of statistics that allow us to abstract information about relationships between variables in pairs

C Symbol used to represent a second, different intervention in a single-system design

case study Research design involving a single system or small group of systems and employing nonexperimental methods

category partition scales Response format in which the response category is partitioned into levels such as Likert and Osgood scales

causal model Representation of the system of factors that drive a target problem

central tendency Score representing what is typical or representative in a group of scores

change target Object of an intervention, which will be changed or altered as a result of the intervention

chi-square test Statistic used to determine if the frequencies in a contingency table are equally proportional. It is the squared differences between the observed and expected frequencies, divided by the expected frequency for each cell, summed across all cells

cluster sampling Sampling procedure in which the sampling unit is actually a group of elements

Code of Federal Regulations 45 CFR 46 Federal regulations applicable to any biomedical or behavioral research that involves human subjects

coding rules Specifications describing how an arbitrary symbol system is to be matched to each attribute that a variable might take

coefficient of determination Proportion of the variance in some outcome variable that can be accounted for by predictor variables. Another name for *r* squared

comparative case-study method Form of multiple case study in which cases are selected to facilitate contrasts

compensatory adjustment Uncontrolled adjustments made to equalize the treatments between control and treatment group members or extreme behaviors (positive or negative) made by control group members because of their control group membership

componential analysis Analytic technique involving examination of the distinctiveness of domains in order to identify cultural themes (values and concerns of a group under study)

conceptualization Thinking through the terms and relationships in a research question and specifying them in ways that are meaningful to relevant others

conceptualization process Steps through which personal ideas are transformed into forms that can be shared with others

concurrent validity Type of criterion-related validity in which the construct in question and the criterion are measured at the same time

confidence interval Range within which the "true" population value has a known probability of occurring

confidence level Degree of certainty that the true value is included in the confidence interval

confidentiality Restriction of access to information usually provided in research by not discussing individual subjects and keeping records locked or otherwise secured

construct validity Extent to which scores on an instrument compare to expectations provided by relevant theory about how it should perform relative to other measures

content validity Degree to which a measurement instrument includes the full range of meaning included in the nominal definition of the construct being measured

contingency question Question that is branched to or from another question and that involves skipping questions

continuous variable Variable defined in terms of interval, ratio, or sometimes ordinal measurement

contrast questions Used to explore meaning systems by discovering the basis for classification of objects into different groups

control group Group of research subjects from whom the intervention being tested is withheld in order to draw comparisons to another group of subjects who receive the intervention

control variable Variable other than the independent variable that is believed to exert an influence on a dependent variable. Control variables are assessed in order to improve the internal validity of a study

convenience sampling Sampling procedure that selects units on the basis of accessibility

convergent validity Type of construct validity indicated when alternative ways of measuring a variable produce similar scores

correlation Tendency for scores on one variable to be useful in predicting the scores on another variable with which it is correlated. Correlation is often operationalized as Pearson's *r* statistic

correlation coefficient Number representing the strength of a correlation between two variables

cover term Label for a domain (collection of syntactically related folk terms) in the language of the persons being studied. *See also* analytic cover term

criterion-related validity Reflects how well scores on a measurement instrument correspond to some meaningful outcome or criterion

critical thinking Process of generating and applying knowledge while seeking to avoid the pitfalls and fallacies of human reasoning through careful reflection on the validity of statements

Cronbach's alpha Index of the extent to which test items are all pulling the direction of the construct being measured; the average of the inter-item correlations for all of the items in a scale

data analysis Systematic procedures for extracting generalizations from observations

data monitoring Assessing the data for preliminary findings as the study progresses to discharge ethical responsibility to terminate a study if harm or conclusive evidence of effectiveness is obtained

data reduction Process of describing the characteristics of a collection of numbers

debriefing Complete explanation of the research following participation including any deception

deception Withholding relevant information from research participants at any stage in the research process

deduction Form of logic that involves moving from general principles to specific events

deontological ethics   Ethics that assume the existence of immutable principles; the rightness or wrongness is in the doing, not consequences. *See also* teleological ethics

dependent variable   Variable taken as the outcome or result of an intervention, especially in the context of a true experiment

descriptive inference   Inference that allows us to describe a larger class of phenomena when only a subset has actually been observed and studied

descriptive questions   In ethnographic research, questions that ask the interviewee to describe some phenomenon in his or her own language

descriptive statistics   Numbers that reflect attributes of an entire set of numbers

Developmental Research Sequence   Approach to exploring meaning systems characterized by the use of ethnographic methods to elicit data, grouping of words into syntactically related clusters, and inferring values from properties of clusters

dialogue   Two-way communication between the social work researcher and a participant for the purpose of finding answers to the researcher's questions

diffusion   Unintended extension of the independent variable into the control group. A threat to internal validity

direct observation   Form of data collection characterized by clearly delineated roles of "observer" and "subject"

discrete variable   Variable defined in terms of nominal measurement

discriminant validity   Type of construct validity indicated when scores on a measure are distinct from measures of different, unrelated constructs

dispersion   Scatter or variability in a collection of scores

disproportionate stratified sampling   Sampling procedure that involves selecting a number of elements in some stratum that is different (disproportionate) than the proportion of the sampling frame that is in that stratum

domain   Cluster of folk terms bound to a cover term by a common semantic relationship

domain analysis   Approach to analysis of meaning systems that consists of grouping folk terms into categories of syntactically similar terms

double-barreled question   Form of question in which two distinct questions are combined

ecological fallacy   Error that is made when characteristics of units at one level of aggregation (often the unit of analysis) are ascribed to units at a different level of aggregation

effect size   Magnitude of the phenomenon that we wish to observe

efficiency analysis   Evaluations that examine both costs and impacts of interventions

element   Individual entity that has been selected as a member of a sample

empirical generalizations   Abstractions drawn from collections of observations

empirical observation   Specific, unique piece of information originating in a sensory experience

empirical referents   Observables through which operational definitions are specified

empiricism   Way of generating knowledge that assumes that knowledge is located in the empirical world and can be derived directly from experience without deductive processes

epistemology   Study of the basis of knowing or nature of knowledge

equitable selection of subjects   Ethical principle requiring that all relevant subjects (at least in theory) have an equal chance of being included in our research

ethical analysis   Process by which social workers can identify and reason about ethical dilemmas encountered in practice

ethical dilemma   Circumstance that arises when two different ethical principles can be applied to the same situation to produce conflicting results

ethics   Principles of conduct that arise from values

ethnographic decision-tree modeling   Approach to the analysis of decision making characterized by the use of ethnographic eliciting techniques to determine a set of rules used to represent decision criteria in some domain

ethnographic interview   Technique for developing a description of the beliefs and customs of another

exhaustive   Property of an attribute list indicating that the list covers the full range of variation of a variable

expected frequency   Count expected in a cell in a cross-tabulation if the rows and columns are uncorrelated. Product of the row and column marginals divided by the total frequency

external validity   Ability to generalize the findings of a study beyond the actual sample and setting with which the study was conducted

face validity   Superficial appearance that the items on an instrument appear to be logically related to the construct that the instrument is intended to measure

factor analysis   Multivariate statistical technique that is conceptually similar to correlation and is used to identify tendencies for groups of observations to cluster together

fallacies of reason   Regularized ways of mishandling information

Fixed-response strategy   Data collection strategy in which data must be fit into preexisting categories

flexible-response strategy   Data collection strategy in which data are unconstrained by categories supplied by the investigator

folk terms   Ordinary words that persons use to describe objects and experiences

generic control   Estimates of the target problem in a known untreated population that are used in lieu of a control group

grounded theory   Theory that arose from inductive field work

grounding   Checking or confirming insights drawn from the research process with people from within the social environment studied

Guttman scale   Approach to instrument design that arranges questions in a decreasing order of intensity or complexity

haphazard sampling   Sampling procedure that selects units unsystematically but without using random sampling procedures

history   Cover term for all factors external to the study participant and the study itself that may influence research subjects

hypothesis   Statement about the predicted relationship between two or more variables according to a theory

impact evaluation   Form of evaluation that focuses on changes in the target problem following intervention

incentives   Items used to encourage participation in a research activity

incidence   Rate at which new cases of a target problem emerge

independent variable   Variable taken as the cause in an experiment. In a true experiment, the independent variable is the factor manipulated

by the experimenter. In an evaluation, the independent variable is generally the intervention or treatment

indicator variables   Proxy variables used to measure abstract concepts

induction   Form of logic that involves moving from specific observables to general principles

inference   Drawing meanings from experience through reasoning

informed consent   Securing research subjects' consent to participate in the research after they have been informed with respect to the nature of the participation

institutional review board   Body charged with examining research proposals for compliance with 45 CFR 46

instrumentation   Unintended change in the measurement instrument itself. A threat to internal validity

interaction effects   Unintended influences resulting from the mutual influence of selection, history, testing, and so on

interchangeability of indicators   Proposition that a complex construct often can be measured equally well by any one of a large number of possible indicators

internal consistency reliability   Form of reliability reflecting the extent to which individual items on a scale are responded to in a similar way by respondents; often assessed using Cronbach's alpha

internal validity   Ability to infer causality in a study

interrater reliability   Form of reliability measured by the stability of scores across observers

interrupted time-series design   Use of a series of measurements over time that is "interrupted" by the occurrence of the independent variable in such a way that the causal influence of the independent variable may be inferred

intersubjective   Another word for objective; true because multiple observers agree

interval measurement   Measurement in which the quantity that separates adjacent attributes is the same across the whole range of the variable

intervention model   Representation of the rationale for a program that shows how program activity will bring about change in a target problem

intervention period   Within single-system designs, period during which the intervention is being applied and presumed active

key informant sampling   Sampling procedure that selects subjects based on their status as "expert" or having a valued perspective on the research topic

lambda   Statistic that reflects the degree to which classification on one nominal variable can be used to predict classification on another nominal variable

latent construct   Theoretical construct that cannot be observed directly

levels of measurement   Characteristics that underlie the differences between the attributes of a variable (i.e., nominal, ordinal, interval, and ratio)

Likert-type scale   Response format provided by the questioner that asks respondents to rate statements using a fixed, ordinal response set balanced around an implied neutral point

log   Written self-report of events usually completed by participants in natural settings

logical positivism   Belief that there is a reality that exists outside of people and knowledge about this reality can be verified empirically

margin of error   Width of a confidence interval around an estimate

matched control strategy   Alternative to construction of a control group that involves matching each experimental group member with someone with similar characteristics who has not received the experimental intervention

maturation   Changes that take place internal to the research participant. A potential threat to internal validity

maxmincon principle   Approach to question writing characterized by maximizing individual variance along the dimension of interest, minimizing sources of error, and controlling extraneous sources of variation

mean   Arithmetic average, that is, the sum of all the scores divided by the number of scores. A descriptive statistic that reflects central tendency

meaning systems   Rules that determine the mental categories by which experience will be organized

measurement   Process of representing observations in terms of organized symbol systems

measurement error   Proportion of observed scores that reflect something other than the variable being measured

measures of central tendency   Class of statistics used to represent that which is typical or representative of a group of scores

measures of dispersion   Class of statistics used to represent the diversity in the group of scores, often in terms of the extent to which the actual scores differ from what has been identified as typical

median   Score that divides a distribution of scores in half; 50% of the scores fall below the median and 50% of the scores fall above the median. A measure of central tendency

mode   Number that appears most often in the data set. A measure of central tendency

monitoring   Form of evaluation intended to document delivery of the intervention

mortality   Tendency for subjects to drop out of the study for any reason. Uneven mortality between treatment and control groups is a threat to internal validity

multiple *R*-square   Squared correlation coefficient representing the extent to which a group of predictor variables is correlated with a single quantitative outcome variable

multiple regression analysis   Multivariate statistical technique used to examine patterns of relationship between a single-outcome variable and a group of predictor variables

multistage sampling   Sampling procedure that involves more than one round of sampling

multivariate statistics   Statistics that provide information about patterns involving two or more variables

mutually exclusive   Property of fixed-response categories in which a response may logically be placed in one and only one response option

mysticism   Way of understanding reality that relies on neither logic nor data

needs assessment   Form of evaluation that involves conceptualization, estimation of the prevalence and incidence, and description of the causal structure of target problems

nominal definition   Definition that is expressed in terms that are meaningful to others

nominal measurement   Level of measurement in which each attribute defines a different status that is separated from other statuses in *only* an "is not equal to" relationship

nonnumerical data   Any form of data not coded into numerals, including speech, texts, pictures, sound recordings, physical artifacts, and physical traces resulting from human acts

nonprobability sampling Sampling procedure that does not utilize random selection processes

null hypothesis Proposition that some effect arose due to sampling error; proposition that the value found for some statistic fits within a sampling distribution of values that arose by chance when the real population value is zero

null hypothesis testing Extension of the idea of confidence intervals to estimating the likelihood that some statistic (e.g., a correlation) could really be zero in a population

objectivity Tendency for different observers using the same methods to all report the same experience. *See also* intersubjective

observed score Score as recorded; a score that represents $score_{true}$ plus error

operational definition Term for specification of (1) the classes of empirical events that map to a construct, (2) social situations in which such events can be unambiguously observed, and (3) precise coding rules for converting observations into symbols

ordinal measurement Measurement in which the response options reflect ranking (is more/less than)

Osgood Semantic Differential Scale Response format in which respondents are asked to choose a position between polar opposites

overgeneralization Error of inference resulting from extension of principles derived from specific experiences to other contexts or experiences to which they do not logically apply

p Symbol attached to the probability that the statistic we are examining could have arisen by chance from a population in which the real value is zero. Probability that the null hypothesis is true

paradigm System of beliefs about reality

paradigm shift Transition from one system of beliefs about reality to another

partial regression weight Correlation coefficient between two variables adjusted for correlations between those variables and one or more other variables

Pearson's r Statistic that reflects the degree of correlation between two variables. An index of the tendency for scores on two variables to "go together" in the sense that for most people, the two scores are equally distant from their respective means

personal conceptions Subjective definitions, beliefs, and feelings individuals associate with experiences

population Theoretical aggregate that includes all possible members of some group

posttest Research measurement taken after the introduction of the independent variable

power analysis Estimation of the probability of detecting an effect size of interest given a sample size and Type I and Type II error limits

practice evaluation Empirical study of intervention including exploration of the dimensions of a target problem, monitoring service delivery, and examination of impacts

precision Fineness of a measurement characterized by the distance between adjacent points on the scale

predictive validity Type of criterion-related validity in which the measure in question is compared to a criterion measurement taken at some time in the future

premature closure Stopping a logical process before completion. In logic, failure to consider all alternatives. In sampling procedure, stopping short of the number of observations necessary to draw clear inference

pretest Measurement taken before the independent variable is introduced

prevalence Proportion of a population afflicted with a target problem

probability sampling Sampling procedure that utilizes a random selection process

probability theory Body of mathematics that predicts the likelihood of an event occurring

problem identification Identification of change-worthy states of clients—diagnosis

proper credit Giving credit for another's work, or acknowledging substantial contributions of others

proportionate stratified sampling Sampling procedure that involves selecting a number of elements in some stratum that is the same as the proportion of the sampling frame in that stratum

public constructs Meaning units that reflect agreements of individuals concerning rules for assigning a label to experiences. *See also* nominal definition

purposive sampling Sampling procedure that utilizes intentional but not random processes

qualitative methods Label that has been attached to scientific activity that couples the use of nonnumerical data, induction, and exploratory methods

quantitative/descriptive study Research design characterized by use of numbers and description rather than experimentation

quantitative methods Label that has been attached to scientific activity that couples use of numbers, deduction, and hypothesis testing

quantitative variable Variable measured on a ratio, interval, or sometimes ordinal scale

quasi-experimental designs Designs that rely on alternatives to random assignment and experimental manipulation to rule out threats to internal validity

quota sampling Form of purposive sampling in which clients are selected by some nonprobability strategy until some prespecified number of subjects has been selected in each preselected category

random assignment Any procedure of assigning subjects to groups that ensures that each subject has an equal chance of being assigned to any particular group

random error Distortion of a measure that occurs in no discernible pattern

randomized posttest-only design Design involving randomly assigned treatment and control groups, each of which receives only a posttest. A true experimental design

randomized pretest–posttest design Design involving randomly assigned treatment and control groups, each of which receives a pretest and a posttest. A true experimental design

random sampling Method of selecting samples that ensures that each unit in a population has an equal chance of selection. Selection by lottery is an example of simple random sampling

random selection Process by which each element in a sampling frame has an equal chance of selection

range Descriptive statistic reflecting the number of units between the highest and lowest scores. A measure of dispersion

ratio measurement Measurement in which each attribute is defined as a specific distance from a zero point that reflects a true absence of the quality being measured

rationalism Way of knowing based on a compelling logical argument without recourse to an empirical test

reactivity Tendency for a measure to provoke a reaction that is unrelated to the constructs being measured

reason Drawing of conclusions and making inferences

referents Real-world things that allow us to accurately infer that the quality indicated by a mental construct is present

reification Confusing mental representations with the events they symbolize

reliability Consistency or stability of a measure

replication Characteristic of an observation that it can be elicited repeatedly under the same or similar conditions

representativeness Adequacy with which a collection of observations reflects the variability in some population of interest

researchable Requirement that it is possible to envision conditions under which a credible answer to the question can be obtained

research design Organization of specific acts that scientists perform into patterns that support the strongest inference possible given the question being posed

respect for privacy Ethical responsibility of the social work researcher to seek only that information that is relevant to the investigation

response set Tendency to respond habitually and automatically to test items without careful reflection on individual items

rigor Extent to which research or an evaluation is likely to have avoided errors and provided protection from the fallacies of human reasoning

risk of harm Ethical principle requiring that a research study not present harm or unreasonably harm participants

r-square Correlation coefficient r multiplied by itself—the proportion of the variance that two variables have in common. Also known as the coefficient of determination

sampling Taking a small portion of a population with the intention of using that portion to reflect the whole

sampling bias Error that systematically distorts the characteristics of a sample with respect to the population it is intended to represent

sampling error Discrepancy between the characteristics of a sample and the characteristics of the population from which they were drawn. Sampling error generally refers to random (not systematic) sources of error

sampling frame List of the units in a population

sampling interval In the context of systematic sampling, the span or range between each selected element

sampling techniques Procedures designed to ensure that a collection of units is representative of the population from which it was drawn

sampling unit Part of a population that is selected at some stage in a sampling procedure

science Way of knowing that relies on both empirical data and the application of logic. *Science* refers to both the logical and cultural aspects of this way of knowing

scientific method Techniques designed to limit the influence of human error through clear definitions of concepts, precise coding rules, and selection of conditions of observation that are less vulnerable to errors and deceptions

selection bias Process that results in experimental and control groups that differ from each other at the start of the experiment. A threat to internal validity

selectivity Ability of a program to exclude persons not in the target population

semantic differential Response format that asks respondents to respond to a scale marked by polar opposites

semantic relationship Attribute that binds folk terms together. "Is a place in" is a semantic relationship that binds folk terms for places together

sensitivity Ability of a program to include all persons in the target population

significance testing Estimation of the likelihood that the discrepency between some statistic and an expected value, usually zero, is the result of sampling error

simple random sampling Sampling procedure in which each element has an equal chance of selection—a lottery

single-system design Approach to evaluation in single systems that tends to focus on both monitoring and impact. Single-system designs are similar to time-series group designs

snowball sampling Sampling procedure that selects elements by referral from previously selected elements

social settings for data collection Social contexts in which data collection is conducted including dialogue, written questioning, and direct observation

Solomon four-group design Design involving four groups and incorporating the structure of both the randomized pretest–posttest and randomized posttest-only designs; a true experimental design

stakeholder Person or persons likely to be affected by an evaluation

standard deviation Square root of the variance; a descriptive statistic reflecting dispersion in a group of scores

standard error Standard deviation of the sampling distribution of a statistic

standard score Transformation of a raw score into a number that reflects how far a particular score is from the mean in standard deviation units; the raw score minus the mean, divided by the standard deviation

statistical control Use of statistical procedures to separate the influences of identifiable alternative explanatory variables

statistical power Ability to detect characteristics or effects in samples when they are actually present

statistical regression Tendency for scores of extreme groups to moderate (move closer to the mean) in subsequent testing; a threat to internal validity when extreme groups are used

statistical significance Potential for sampling error to explain the value of some statistic; generally reflected in a *p* value that is compared to some standard called the alpha value

stratified sampling Sampling procedure that employs a random selection process within homogeneous subsets of the sampling frame

structural equation modeling Multivariate statistical technique used to analyze causal relationships in nonexperimental data

structural questions In ethnographic research, questions intended to discover the categories a person used to structure their experience

structured interview Fixed-response type of dialogue

summated-rating scale   Instrument scored by combining the responses to many questions to produce one score reflecting the variable of interest

systematic error   Distortion of a measurement in some regularized way—bias

systematic sampling   Sampling procedure that selects every *n*th element from a sampling frame after a random start

systems analysis   Approach to evaluation of complex systems that treats them as whole entities composed of interrelated parts, with a boundary, existing in a larger social context

target problem   Condition determined to be in need of change

taxonomic analysis   Analytic technique designed to specify the relationships between groups of folk terms (domains)

teleological ethics   Ethics that hold that "right" and "wrong" are judged in the outcome or consequences of some action—"ethics of ends." *See also* deontological ethics

testing   Threat to internal validity provided by the sensitization that can occur with subjects as a result of their exposure to the constructs that are involved in the study, especially in a pretest

test-retest reliability   Form of reliability measuring stability of scores over time

theory   Network of propositions that seeks to explain the relationships among a related set of variables

threats to external validity   Factors that limit the ability of findings to be generalized beyond the study

threats to internal validity   Factors that operate to potentially produce changes in subjects that are mistakenly taken to be caused by the independent variable(s)

Thurstone scale   Approach to scoring an instrument that uses weights attached to each item

time ordering   Requirement that "causes" must precede "effects"

time sampling   Specification of the time period during which observations are to be conducted

triangulation   Using multiple assessment strategies or indicators

true experiments   Research designs that involve random assignment, manipulation of the independent variable, and intentional timing of measurement

t-test   Statistic designed to test the likelihood that the differences between two means reflect sampling error. The t-test is the mean difference divided by the standard error of the mean difference

Type I or alpha error   Mistakenly rejecting the null hypothesis when in fact the null hypothesis is true

Type II or beta error   Mistakenly accepting the null hypothesis when in fact the null hypothesis is false

unit of analysis   Element or group of elements about which inference is made

unit of observation   Element that is observed in order to gather data

univariate descriptive statistics   Numbers used to create short descriptions of a single variable

validity   Extent to which a test reflects the construct that it proposes to measure

values   Ideals we hold for personal conduct

variables   Characteristics, aspects, or traits of units that we study; a cover term for a set of attributes

variance   Average of the squared deviations from the mean

voluntary participation   Ethical principle that participation be based on choice free of deception or coercion

volunteer sampling   Sampling procedure utilizing individuals who self-select participation

vulnerable populations   Group of individuals generally at risk of being overwhelmed due to insufficient supports or noxious elements in the environment

withdrawal designs   Single-system designs that include suspension of an intervention at points to assess impact. ABAB and ABAC designs are examples of withdrawal designs

REFERENCES

Achenbach, T. M., & Edelbrock, E. (1983). *Manual for the child behavior checklist and revised child behavior profile*. Burlington, VT: University of Vermont, Department of Psychiatry.

American Psychological Association. (1974). *Standards for educational and psychological tests*. Washington, DC: Author.

Anastasi, A. (1954). *Psychological testing*. New York: Macmillan.

Anastasi, A., & Urbina, S. (1997). *Psychological testing* (7th ed.). Upper Saddle River, NJ: Prentice-Hall.

Berger, F., & Luckmann, T. (1966). *The social construction of reality*. Garden City, NY: Doubleday.

Bloom, M., Fischer, J., & Orme, J. G. (1999). *Evaluating practice: Guidelines for the accountable professional* (3rd ed.). Boston: Allyn & Bacon.

Bloom, M., & Orme, J. (1993). Ethics and the single-system design. *Journal of Social Service Research, 18*(1/2), 161–180.

Bohrnstedt, G., & Knoke, D. (1988). *Statistics for social data analysis* (2nd ed.). Itasca, IL: Peacock.

Campbell, D. T. (1969). Reforms as experiments. *American Psychologist, 24*, 409–429.

Campbell, D. T., & Fiske, D. W. (1959). Convergent and discriminant validation by the multitrait multimethod matrix. *Psychological Bulletin, 56*(2), 81–105.

Campbell, D., & Stanley, J. (1963). *Experimental and quasi-experimental designs for research*. Boston: Houghton Mifflin.

Carlson, R. W. (1985). Connecting clinical information processing with computer support. *Computers in Human Services, 1*(1), 51–66.

Cochran, W. G. (1977). *Sampling techniques* (3rd ed.). New York: Wiley.

Code of Federal Regulations. (1997). Protection of human subjects. *Code of Federal Regulations, 45*(46).

Cohen, J. (1969). *Statistical power analysis for the behavioral sciences*. New York: Academic Press.

Cohen, J., & Cohen, P. (1983). *Applied multiple regression/correlation analysis for the behavioral sciences* (2nd ed.). Hillsdale, NJ: Erlbaum.

Cook, T., & Campbell, D. (1979). *Quasi-experimentation: Design and analysis issues for field settings*. Boston: Houghton Mifflin.

Costantino, G., Malgady, R. G., & Rogler, L. H. (1988). *TEMAS (tell-me-a-story) manual*. Los Angeles: Western Psychological Services.

Cournoyer, D. E. (1994). *Predicting attrition of youth in residential care for delinquency and conduct disorder*. Unpublished manuscript. West Hartford: University of Connecticut.

Cournoyer, D. E. (1996). *Predicting attrition of youth in residential care for delinquency*, unpublished agency report.

Crossen, C. (1994). *Tainted truth: The manipulation of fact in America*. New York: Simon & Schuster.

Denova, C. C. (1979). *Test construction for training evaluation* (American Society for Training and Development). New York: Van Nostrand Reinhold.

Erdos, P. (1983). *Professional mail surveys*. Malabar, FL: Krieger.

Gilligan, C. (1982). *In a different voice: Psychological theory and women's development*. Cambridge, MA: Harvard University Press.

Gillovich, T. (1991). *How we know what isn't so: The fallibility of human reason in everyday life*. New York: The Free Press.

Gladwin, C. H. (1989). *Ethnographic decision tree modeling*. Sage University Paper Series on Qualitative Research Methods, Vol. 19. Beverly Hills, CA: Sage.

Glaser, B. (1978). *Theoretical sensitivity*. Mill Valley, CA: Sociology Press.

Glaser, B., & Strauss, A. (1964). The social loss of dying patients. *American Journal of Nursing, 64*, 119–122.

Glaser, B., & Strauss, A. (1967). *The discovery of grounded theory*. Chicago: Aldine.

Grigsby, K., & Roof, H. (1993). Federal policy for the protection of human subjects: Applications to research on social work practice. *Research on Social Work Practice, 3*(4), 448–461.

Harrison, M. I. (1994). *Diagnosing organizations: Methods, models, and processes* (2nd ed.). Thousand Oaks, CA: Sage.

Heineman, M. (1981). The obsolete scientific imperative in social work research. *Social Service Review, 55*, 371–379.

Hudson, W. (1982). *The clinical measurement package: A field manual*. Homewood, IL: Dorsey.

Hudson, W. (1985). Indexes and scales. In R. Grinnell, Jr. (Ed.), *Social Work Research and Evaluation* (2nd ed., pp. 185–205). Itasca, IL: Peacock.

Humphreys, L. (1979). *Tearoom trade: Impersonal sex in public places*. New York: Aldine.

Jensen, D. (1989). Pathologies of science, precognition, and modern psychophysics. *The Skeptical Inquirer, 13*(2), 147–160.

Jones, J. H. (1981). *Bad blood.* New York: Aldine.

Jones, R. (1990). Inconsistency of research results and researchers' responsibility. *Psychological Reports, 66,* 689–690.

Jöreskog, K., & Sörbom, D. (1993). *LISREL8: Structural equation modeling with the SIMPLIS command language.* Hillsdale, NJ: Erlbaum.

Kerlinger, F. (1973). *Foundations of behavioral research* (2nd ed.). New York: Holt, Rinehart & Winston.

Klein, W., & Bloom, M. (1994). Is there an ethical responsibility to use practice methods with the best empirical evidence of effectiveness? Yes. In W. Hudson & P. Nurius (Eds.), *Controversial issues in social work research.* Boston: Allyn & Bacon.

Klein, W., & Bloom, M. (1995). Practice wisdom. *Social Work, 40,* 799–807.

Klein, W., & Botticello, P. (1997). Residents with AIDS: A comparison of facilities with experience and those without. *AIDS Patient Care and STDs, 11*(4), 279–286.

Klein, W., Weisman, D., & Smith, T. (1996). The use of adjunct professors: An exploratory study of eight social work programs. *Journal of Social Work Education, 32*(2), 253–264.

Kuhn, T. (1970). *The structure of scientific revolutions* (2nd ed.). Chicago: University of Chicago Press.

Lazarsfeld, P. (1959). Problems in methodology. In R. K. Merton, L. Broom, and L. S. Cottrell, Jr. (Eds.), *Sociology today* (Vol. 1, pp. 39–78). New York: Harper & Row.

Lennon, T. (1996). *Statistics on social work education in the United States: 1996.* Alexandria, VA: Council on Social Work Education.

Levy, C. (1993). *Social work ethics on the line.* New York: Haworth Press.

Levy, D. A. (1997). *Tools of critical thinking: Metathoughts for psychology.* Boston: Allyn & Bacon.

Lewis-Beck, M. S. (1980). *Applied regression: An introduction.* Sage University Paper Series on Quantitative Applications in the Social Sciences, No. 22. Beverly Hills, CA: Sage.

Lin, N. (1986). Modeling the effects of social support. In Nan Lin, Alfred Dean, & Walter Ensel (Eds.), *Social support, life events and depression* (pp. 173–209). New York: Academic Press.

Macklin, R. (1989). The paradoxical case of payment as benefit to research subjects. *IRB, 11*(6), 1–3.

Matsumoto, D. (1994). *People: Psychology from a cultural perspective.* Pacific Grove, CA: Brooks/Cole.

McClendon, M. (1994). *Multiple regression and causal analysis.* Itasca, IL: Peacock.

Milgram, S. (1963). Behavioral study of obedience. *Journal of Abnormal and Social Psychology, 67*(4), 371–378.

Miller, G. A. (1956). The magical number seven, plus or minus two: Some limits on our capacity for processing information. *Psychological Review, 63,* 81–97.

Millstein, K., Dare-Winters, K., & Sullivan, S. (1994). The power of silence: Ethical dilemmas on informed consent in practice evaluation. *Clinical Social Work Journal, 22*(3), 317–329.

Murray, H. A., et al. (1943). *Thematic apperception test manual.* Cambridge, MA: Harvard University Press.

National Association of Social Workers. (1997). *Code of ethics.* Washington, DC: Author.

Nelson, J. (1994). Ethics, gender, and ethnicity in single-case research and evaluation. *Journal of Social Service Research, 18*(3/4), 139–152.

Nunnally, J. (1978). *Psychometric theory.* New York: McGraw-Hill.

Nurius, P., & Hudson, W. (1993). *Human services: Practice, evaluation and computers.* Pacific Grove, CA: Brooks/Cole.

Orme, J., & Combs-Orme, T. (1986). Statistical power and Type II errors in social work research. *Social Work, 22*(3), 3–10.

Porteous, D. P., & Cournoyer, D. E. (1994). *Transitional living program process evaluation.* Unpublished manuscript. Marlborough, CT: Global Associates.

Reamer, F. (1990). *Ethical dilemmas in social service* (2nd ed.). New York: Columbia University Press.

Reid, P. N., & Gundlach, J. P. (1983). Reid-Gundlach social service satisfaction scale (R-GSSSS). In K. Corcoran & J. Fischer (Eds.), *Measures for clinical practice: A sourcebook.* New York: The Free Press.

Reid, W. J., & Smith, A. D. (1989). *Research in social work* (2nd ed.). New York: Columbia University Press.

Rohner, R. P. (1986). *The warmth dimension: Foundations of parental acceptance/rejection theory.* Beverly Hills, CA: Sage.

Rohner, R. P., & Chaki-Sircar, M. (1988). *Women and children in a Bengali village.* Hanover, NH: University Press of New England.

Rohner, R. P., & Cournoyer, D. E. (1994). Universals in youths' perceptions of parental acceptance and rejection. *Cross-Cultural Research, 28*(4), 371–383.

Rohner, R. P., Kean, K., & Cournoyer, D. E. (1991). Effects of corporal punishment, perceived caretaker warmth, and cultural beliefs on the psychological adjustment of children in St. Kitts, West Indies. *Journal of Marriage and the Family, 53,* 681–693.

Rohner, R., & Rohner, E. (1982). Encultrative continuity and importance of caretakers: Cross-cultural codes. *Behavior Science Research, 17,* 91–114.

Rorschach, H. (1942). *Psychodiagnostics: A diagnostic test based on perception* (P. Lemkau & B. Kronenberg, Trans.). Berne: Huber.

Rosencranz, H., & McNevin, T. (1969). A factor analysis of attitudes toward the aged. *The Gerontologist, 9*(1), 55–59.

Rossi, P., & Freeman, H. (1993). *Evaluation: A systematic approach* (5th ed.). Newbury Park, CA: Sage.

Royse, D., & Thyer, B. A. (1996). *Program evaluation: An introduction* (2nd ed.). Chicago: Nelson-Hall.

Rummel, R. J. (1970). *Applied factor analysis.* Evanston, IL: Northwestern University Press.

Sanders, J. R. (Ed.). (1994). *The program evaluation standards* (2nd ed.). (The Joint Committee on Standards for Educational Evaluation.) Thousand Oaks, CA: Sage.

Sherman, E., & Reid, W. J. (1994). *Qualitative research in social work.* New York: Columbia University Press.

Spradley, J. (1979). *The ethnographic interview.* New York: Holt, Rinehart & Winston.

Spradley, J. (1980). *Participant observation.* New York: Harcourt Brace Jovanovich.

Straus, M. (1991). *Beating the devil out of them: Corporal punishment in American families.* New York: Macmillan.

Sudman, S., & Bradburn, N. M. (1982). *Asking questions.* San Francisco: Jossey-Bass.

Tyson, K. (1995). *New foundations for scientific social and behavioral research: The heuristic paradigm.* Boston: Allyn & Bacon.

Wallace, W. (1971). *The logic of science in sociology.* Chicago: Aldine de Gruyter.

Williams, E. B. (Ed.). (1977). *The Scribner Bantam English Dictionary* (rev. ed.). New York: Charles Scribner's and Bantam Books.

Witkin, S. (1991). Empirical clinical practice: A critical analysis. *Social Work, 36,* 158–163.

Yin, R. K. (1994). *Case study research: Design and methods* (2nd ed.), Applied Social Research Methods Series, Vol. 5. Thousand Oaks, CA: Sage.

INDEX